Adaptive Code: Agile coding with design patterns and SOLID principles

Second Edition

Gary McLean Hall

PUBLISHED BY
Microsoft Press
A division of Microsoft Corporation
One Microsoft Way
Redmond, Washington 98052-6399

Library of Congress Control Number: 2016936931
ISBN: 978-1-5093-0258-1

Printed and bound in the United States of America.

1 17

Microsoft Press books are available through booksellers and distributors worldwide. If you need support related to this book, email Microsoft Press Book Support at mspinput@microsoft.com. Please tell us what you think of this book at https://aka.ms/tellpress.

Acquisitions and Development Editor: Devon Musgrave
Editorial Production: Online Training Solutions, Inc. (OTSI)
Technical Reviewer: Bruce Johnson
Copyeditor: Kathy Krause (OTSI)
Indexer: Susie Carr (OTSI)
Cover: Twist • Seattle

For Alexander George

—G<small>ARY</small> M<small>c</small>L<small>EAN</small> H<small>ALL</small>

Contents at a glance

Contents

What do you think of this book? We want to hear from you!

Microsoft is interested in hearing your feedback so we can continually improve our books and learning resources for you. To participate in a brief online survey, please visit:

microsoft.com/learning/booksurvey

Chapter 4   Interfaces and design patterns   115

Chapter 5   Testing   147

Chapter 8   The open/closed principle   249

What do you think of this book? We want to hear from you!

Microsoft is interested in hearing your feedback so we can continually improve our
books and learning resources for you. To participate in a brief online survey, please visit:

microsoft.com/learning/booksurvey

Introduction

The title of this book, *Adaptive Code*, is a good description of the outcome of applying the principles in the book: the ability of code to adapt to any new requirement or unforeseen scenario while avoiding significant rework. The aim of this book is to aggregate into one volume many of the current best practices in the world of C# programming with the Microsoft .NET Framework. Although some of the content is covered in other books, those books either focus heavily on theory or are not specific to .NET development.

Programming can be a slow process. If your code is adaptive, you will be able to make changes to it more quickly, more easily, and with fewer errors than you would if you were working with a codebase that impedes changes. Requirements, as every developer knows, are subject to change. How change is managed is a key differentiating factor between successful software projects and those that fail. Developers can react in many ways to requirement changes, with two opposing viewpoints highlighting the continuum that lies between.

First, developers can be *rigid*. In this approach, from the development process down to class design, the project is as inflexible as if it were implemented 50 years ago by using punch cards. Waterfall methodologies are conspicuous culprits in ensuring that software cannot change freely. Their determination that the phases of analysis, design, implementation, and testing are distinct and one-way make it difficult—or at least expensive—for customers to change requirements after implementation has begun. The code, then, does not *need* to be built for change: the process all but forbids alterations.

Second, developers can be *adaptive*. Agile processes are not just an alternative to such rigid methodologies, but a *reaction* to them. Their aim is to embrace change as a necessary part of the contract between client and developer. If customers want to change something in the product that they are paying for, the temporal and financial cost should be correlated to the size of the change, not the phase of the process that is currently in progress. Unlike physical engineering, software engineering works with a malleable tool: source code. The bricks and mortar that form a house are literally fused together as construction progresses. The expense involved in changing the design of a house is necessarily linked to the completion of the building phase. If the project has not been started —if it is still just in blueprints— change is relatively cheap. If the windows are in, the electricity wired up, and plumbing fitted, moving the upstairs bathroom down next to the kitchen could be prohibitively expensive. With code, moving features around and reworking the navigation of a user interface should not be so significant. Unfortunately, this is not always the case. The temporal cost alone often prohibits such changes. This is largely a result of a lack of adaptability in code.

Who should read this book

This book is intended to bridge a gap between theory and practice. The reader I had in mind while writing this book is a programmer who seeks more practical examples for design patterns, SOLID principles, unit testing and refactoring, and more.

Capable intermediate programmers who want to plug the gaps in their knowledge or have doubts and questions about how some of the industry's best practices fit together will benefit most from this book, especially because the day-to-day reality of programming rarely matches simple examples or theory. Much of SOLID is now understood, but the intricacies of the open/closed principle (covered in Chapter 8) and Liskov substitution (covered in Chapter 9) are not fully comprehended. Even experienced programmers sometimes do not fully realize the benefits provided by dependency injection (covered in Chapter 12). Similarly, the flexibility—adaptability—that is lent to code by interfaces (covered in Chapter 4) is often overlooked.

There is also plenty of content in this book for the more junior developer to learn, from the ground up, which aspects of common patterns and practices are benevolent and which are, in the long term, problematic. The different codebases that I see while consulting have a lot of problems in common. The general theme is that the code is *almost there* with respect to adaptability, but it just needs a slight push in the right direction to make it significantly more adaptive to change. Specifically, the Entourage anti-pattern (covered in Chapter 11) and the Service Locator anti-pattern (covered in Chapter 12) are prevalent in the code of stalled projects. Practical alternatives, and their rationales, are provided in this book.

Assumptions

Ideally, you should have some practical experience of programming in a language that is syntactically similar to C# such as Java or C++. You should also have a strong foundation in core procedural programming concepts such as conditional branching, loops, and expressions. You should also have some experience of object-oriented programming concepts using classes. and at least a passing familiarity with interfaces.

This book might not be for you if...

This book might not be for you if you are just starting out on a journey to learn how to program. This book covers advanced topics that assume a thorough understanding of fundamental object-oriented programming concepts, such as classes and interfaces, in addition to control structures such as if-statements and loops.

Organization of this book

This book is made up of four parts, each of which builds on the last. That said, the chapters can also be read out of order. Each chapter covers a self-contained subject in detail, with cross references included where appropriate.

Changes in the second edition

For readers of the first edition, there are compelling reasons to invest in this updated version:

- A new chapter on Kanban has been added to complement the chapter on Scrum.

- Testing and refactoring now each have their own full chapters so that more content can be covered.

- The dependency inversion chapter has been rewritten to include a section on abstraction design.

- A new chapter on coupling and cohesion has been added.

- The sample code has been updated to C# 7.0 and .NET 4.6.2 in Microsoft Visual Studio 2017.

- All other chapters have had edits and tweaks.

Part I: Agile development frameworks

This part introduces the context that makes it so important to write code to be adaptive. It covers two Agile frameworks, Scrum and Kanban, to show that change is inevitable and must be accommodated both in your delivery process and in your code.

Chapter 1: Introduction to Scrum

This chapter sets the scene for the book by introducing Scrum, which is an Agile framework for software delivery. It includes an in-depth overview of the artifacts, roles, metrics, and phases of a Scrum project. Also covered in this chapter are the problems that teams using Scrum often encounter, and how to identify those problems and fix them.

Chapter 2: Introduction to Kanban [NEW]

To complement the chapter on Scrum, the second edition introduces Kanban as an alternative Agile framework; Kanban focuses more on the continuous flow of deliverable features. This chapter covers the artifacts of Kanban and provides examples for spotting problems in the flow of delivery.

Part II: Foundations of adaptive code

This part lays the foundations for building software in an adaptive way. It covers adaptability at all levels of the code and focuses on details around interfaces, design patterns, refactoring, and unit testing.

Chapter 3: Dependencies and layering

This chapter explores dependencies and architectural layering. Code can only be adaptive if the solution's structure allows it to be. The different types of dependencies are described: first-party, third-party, and framework. The chapter describes how to manage and organize dependencies, from anti-patterns (which should be avoided) to patterns (which should be embraced). It also introduces advanced topics such as aspect-oriented programming and asymmetric layering, providing further depth.

Chapter 4: Interfaces and design patterns

Interfaces are, by now, ubiquitous in modern .NET development. However, they are often misapplied, misunderstood, and misappropriated. This chapter shows some of the more common and practically useful design patterns, exploring how versatile an interface can be. Leading the reader beyond the simple extraction of an interface, the chapter shows how interfaces can be elaborated in many different ways to solve a problem. Mixins, duck-typing, and interface fluency further underscore the versatility of this key weapon in the programmer's arsenal.

Chapter 5: Testing [NEW]

Unit testing is a non-negotiable prerequisite to any software project. Closely related to refactoring, the two practices work in unison to produce adaptive code. Without the safety net of unit tests, refactoring is prone to error; without refactoring, code becomes unwieldy, rigid, and hard to comprehend. This chapter takes an example of unit testing from humble beginnings and expands it to use more advanced—but practical—features such as fluent assertions, test-driven development, and mocking.

Chapter 6: Refactoring [NEW]

To refactor is to improve the design of code after it has been written. This chapter gives examples of real-world refactors that improve the readability and maintainability of source code. Code must have tests so that it can be safely refactored, but this chapter also covers how to add tests to existing code so that it can be safely refactored.

Part III: SOLID code

This chapter builds on the foundations laid in Part II. Each chapter is devoted to examining one principle of SOLID. The emphasis in these chapters is on practical examples for implementing the principles, rather than solely on the theory of why they are important. By placing each example in a real-world context, the chapters in this part of the book clearly demonstrate the utility of SOLID.

Chapter 7: The single responsibility principle

This chapter shows how to implement the single responsibility principle in practice by using the Decorator and Adapter patterns. The outcome of applying the principle is an increase in the number of classes and a decrease in the size of those classes. The chapter shows that, in contrast with monolithic classes that provide extensive features, these smaller classes are more directed and focused on solving only a small part of a larger problem. It is in their aggregation that these classes then become more than the sum of their parts.

Chapter 8: The open/closed principle

The open/closed principle (OCP) is simply stated, but it can have a significant impact on code. It is responsible for ensuring that code that follows the SOLID principles is only appended to and never edited. This chapter also discusses the concept of predicted variation in relation to OCP and explores how it can help developers identify extension points for further adaptability.

Chapter 9: The Liskov substitution principle

This chapter shows the positive effects that result from applying the Liskov substitution principle has to code, particularly the fact that the guidelines help enforce the open/closed principle and prevent the unintended consequences of change. Contracts—through preconditions, postconditions, and data invariants—are covered by using the Microsoft Code Contracts tooling. The chapter also describes subtyping guidelines such as covariance, contravariance, and invariance, along with the negative impact of breaking these rules.

Chapter 10: Interface segregation

Not only should classes be smaller than they commonly are, this chapter shows that interfaces are, similarly, often too big. Interface segregation is a simple practice that is often overlooked; this chapter shows the benefits of limiting interfaces to the smallest size possible, along with the benefits of working with smaller interfaces. It also explores the different reasons that might motivate the segregation of interfaces, such as client need and architectural need.

Chapter 11: Dependency inversion [NEW]

This chapter shows the importance of managing dependencies and demonstrates how to achieve decoupled modules. A common anti-pattern is discussed, and its preferred alternative is detailed. This chapter also walks through an example abstraction that proves that interfaces are only part of the solution.

Part IV: Applying adaptive code

This part provides a logical follow-up to the SOLID chapters by introducing the theories and practices that hold everything together.

Chapter 12: Dependency injection

This chapter contains the cohesive glue that facilitates the rest of the features in the book. Without dependency injection (DI), there is a lot that would not be possible—it really is that important. This chapter contains an introduction to DI and a comparison of the different methods of implementing it. It includes discussions on object lifetime management, Inversion of Control containers, common anti-patterns relating to service location, and the identification of composition and resolution roots.

Chapter 13: Coupling, cohesion, and connascence [NEW]

All design patterns aid in keeping coupling low and cohesion high. This chapter defines both coupling and cohesion and introduces the measurement of coupling strength via connascence.

Appendix

The appendix is a very brief introduction to Git source control that should, at the very least, allow you to download the code from GitHub and compile it in Visual Studio 2017. It is not intended as a thorough guide to Git—there are some excellent sources already out there, such as the official Git tutorial:

http://git-scm.com/docs/gittutorial

A quick web search will find other sources.

Conventions and features in this book

Throughout this book, there are a number of repeated conventions. These are mainly standard to Microsoft Press publications, but it won't hurt to explain them up front.

Code listings

Code listings are included where appropriate, and a callout is made to them where relevant, as shown in Listing I-1.

LISTING I-1 This is a code listing. There are plenty of these in the book.

```
public void MyService : IService
{

}
```

Whenever your attention should be drawn to a certain part of the code—for instance, when changes have been made to a previous example—the code will be highlighted in bold.

Readeraids and sidebars

Readeraids are used for small asides, such as notes or warnings, whereas sidebars are reserved for larger digressions. Here are some examples:

> **Note** This is a reader-aid. Elements such as these contain small information nuggets that are related to the main content but have some kind of added importance.

> ### This is a sidebar
>
> Although this one is necessarily short, sidebars are usually reserved for longer discussions on topics that are somewhat tangential to the main topic.

Images

Sometimes, an explanation—no matter how florid—is not enough. In these cases, an image is provided. All diagrams were created in Microsoft Visio with no theming, to create a high-contrast and to focus solely on exposition. Screenshots were taken with a high-contrast theme applied.

System requirements

You will need the following to use the code samples referred to in this book:

- Visual Studio 2015 or later, any edition
- Microsoft SQL Server 2008 Express Edition or later (2008 or R2 release), with SQL Server Management Studio 2008 Express or later
- An Internet connection for downloading code samples

Depending on your Windows configuration, you might require Local Administrator rights to install or configure Visual Studio and SQL Server products.

Downloads: Code samples

As far as possible, I ensured that the code listings were part of a larger example that could be run either as a standalone application or a unit test. I wrote many of the simpler unit tests by using MSTest so that no external test runner was needed, but I wrote the more complex unit tests by using NUnit. I used Visual Studio 2017 Professional to write all of the code. Although I wrote some of it by using the Community version, it has all been compiled and tested on the full version. As far as possible, I didn't use features that were unavailable to the Community versions of Visual Studio 2017, but for some topics, this was not possible. Readers wanting to run this code will need to install a paid-for version.

The code itself is available from GitHub, at the following address:

https://github.com/AdaptiveCode/AdaptiveCode

The Appendix contains explanations for using Git and how the code in the Adaptive Code repository is organized.

To make a comment where I am likely to see it, see the GitHub repository. You can also follow me on Twitter:

@garymcleanhall

Acknowledgments

The byline for this book is not really accurate. I couldn't have written any of this without the following people, all of whom have helped me in different ways.

Victoria, my wife, for enabling me to write once again.

Amelia, the best daughter in the world.

Alexander, my son, for his squawks of encouragement.

My family, for their unerring support.

Kathy Krause at Online Training Solutions, Inc., for her excellent work making this book readable.

Devon Musgrave, for all of his hard work in making the first edition a success.

Errata, updates, & book support

We've made every effort to ensure the accuracy of this book and its companion content. You can access updates to this book—in the form of a list of submitted errata and their related corrections—at:

https://aka.ms/AdaptiveCode2E/errata

If you discover an error that is not already listed, please submit it to us at the same page.

If you need additional support, email Microsoft Press Book Support at *mspinput@microsoft.com*.

Please note that product support for Microsoft software and hardware is not offered through the previous addresses. For help with Microsoft software or hardware, go to *https://support.microsoft.com*.

Free ebooks from Microsoft Press

From technical overviews to in-depth information on special topics, the free ebooks from Microsoft Press cover a wide range of topics. These ebooks are available in PDF, EPUB, and Mobi for Kindle formats, ready for you to download at:

https://aka.ms/mspressfree

Check back often to see what is new!

We want to hear from you

At Microsoft Press, your satisfaction is our top priority, and your feedback our most valuable asset. Please tell us what you think of this book at:

https://aka.ms/tellpress

We know you're busy, so we've kept it short with just a few questions. Your answers go directly to the editors at Microsoft Press. (No personal information will be requested.) Thanks in advance for your input!

Stay in touch

Let's keep the conversation going! We're on Twitter: *http://twitter.com/MicrosoftPress.*

Agile development frameworks

> **Note** If you are already familiar with Scrum, Kanban, or other Agile software development frameworks, feel free to skim this part of the book or skip it altogether. The aim of these chapters is to provide a foundation that explains why adaptive code is so imperative in Agile environments.

Software products are built collaboratively, not in isolation. They are the result of many people operating in different roles to achieve a common aim. The governing processes that guide the delivery of software products have a great influence on the products' quality, timeliness, and economic success. If the wrong process is used, the product is hampered before it has even begun. When a complementary process is used, the product is able to flourish and has a strong chance of thriving.

This part of the book introduces two software development *frameworks*—Scrum and Kanban. Note that neither Scrum nor Kanban is a process. Neither are to be slavishly adhered to. The term "framework" is preferable to "process" because it implies guidelines and boundaries but not rigid, sequential steps.

Agile frameworks put the inevitability of change at the fore-front and tackle it head on. Not only do they embrace change, they demand it. Your development framework might be Agile—that is, it might encourage innovation and iterative improvement—but your code might not. The chapters in this part of the book ground the rest of the content of the book, add context, and answer the following question:

> Given that Agile frameworks are now prevalent, how can you ensure that the code you write enables and complements your development framework?

Although this book is about code quality and not necessarily about software development processes, a solid understanding of Scrum and Kanban is imperative, because it illuminates the collaborative nature of writing code.

CHAPTER 1

Introduction to Scrum

After completing this chapter, you will be able to

- Assign roles to the major stakeholders in a project.

- Identify the documents and other artifacts that Scrum requires and generates.

- Measure the progress of a Scrum project on its development journey.

- Diagnose problems with Scrum projects and propose remedies.

- Host Scrum meetings in an effective manner for maximum benefit.

- Justify the use of Scrum over other methodologies, both Agile and rigid.

Scrum is a project management methodology. To be more precise, it is an *Agile* project management methodology. Scrum is based on the idea of adding value to a software product in an iterative manner. The software development process is repeated—iterated—multiple times until the software product is considered complete or the process is otherwise stopped. These iterations are called *sprints*, and they culminate in software that is *potentially* releasable. All work is prioritized on the *product backlog* and, at the start of each sprint, the development team commits to the work that they will complete during the new iteration by placing it on the *sprint backlog*. The unit of work within Scrum is the *story*. The product backlog is a prioritized queue of pending stories, and each sprint is defined by the stories that will be developed during an iteration.

Figure 1-1 shows an overview of the Scrum process.

Product backlog

The product backlog contains features and stories to be implemented.

Sprint backlog

Stories that have been committed to the sprint are moved to the sprint backlog. Each story is implemented in priority order.

Sprint

Each sprint lasts between one and four weeks. With each day of the sprint, the team works toward completing the committed stories.

Release

After each sprint, newly implemented features are released in a new version of the product.

FIGURE 1-1 Scrum works like a production line for small features of a software product.

Scrum is Agile

Agile is a family of lightweight software development methods that embrace the changing requirements of customers even as the project is in progress. Agile is a reaction to the failings of more rigidly structured practices. The Agile Manifesto exemplifies the contrast. It can be found on the web at *www.agilemanifesto.org*.

The Agile Manifesto was signed by 17 software developers. The Agile method has grown in influence in the intervening years to the extent that experience in an Agile environment is now a common prerequisite for software development roles. Scrum is one of the most common implementations of an Agile process.

Scrum involves a mixture of documentation artifacts, roles played by people inside and outside the development team, and ceremonies—meetings that are attended by appropriate parties. A single chapter is not enough to explore the entirety of what Scrum offers as a project management discipline. However, this chapter offers enough detail to provide both a springboard to further learning and an orientation for the day-to-day practices of Scrum.

The rest of this chapter covers the most important aspects of Scrum in more depth. Scrum's positive attributes are considered, along with an honest appraisal of its shortcomings. This chapter and Chapter 2, "Introduction to Kanban," form the first part of the book and set the scene for the rest of the content. Writing code in such a way that it remains adaptive to change is a high priority when working within an Agile software development process. There is little point in having a process in which you claim to be able to handle change gracefully when the reality is that change is incredibly difficult to *implement* down at a code level.

Cynefin

To further answer the question, "Why Agile?" the Cynefin framework comes to our aid.

Cynefin (pronounced *ki-neh-vin*) is a *sense-making* framework. Figure 1-2 shows the different types of management modes that types of work might fit into.

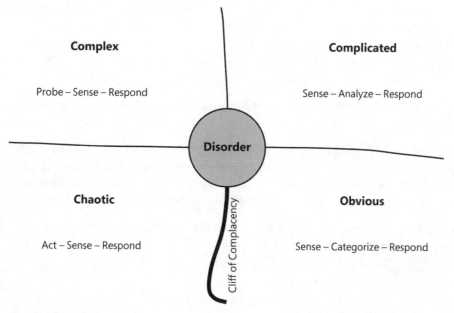

Complex

Probe – Sense – Respond

Complicated

Sense – Analyze – Respond

Disorder

Chaotic

Act – Sense – Respond

Cliff of Complacency

Obvious

Sense – Categorize – Respond

FIGURE 1-2 The Cynefin sense-making framework looks a little like a decision matrix, but don't be fooled.

Although this looks like a typical two-dimensional decision matrix or categorization matrix, it is different in an important way. With a 2 × 2 categorization matrix, the framework precedes the data. That is, new data coming in can be categorized if you have measurements for the two variables that are isolated by the framework. With Cynefin, the data precedes the framework, and therefore a more heuristic discovery is required to determine how best to proceed.

The vertical split differentiates the options by their relationship to cause and effect. The right side of the framework represents ordered problems that exhibit predictable cause and effect, whereas the left side represents unordered problems.

The "obvious" quadrant is where traditional management goes: a command-and-control model of best practices. When work fits this quadrant, you proceed to *sense* and *categorize*. This quadrant will be revisited later, because all is not quite as it seems.

Proceeding counterclockwise, the next quadrant is "complicated." Here, there are no well-defined "best practices," only a choice of *good practices*. You proceed to *sense* and *analyze* before responding. This is where the bulk of expert-domain work fits, such as software development.

Next, you cross over to the unordered realm of "complex" problems. Here, there are not even "good practices" to be found, just *emergent practices*. There is no understood causality; therefore, you proceed to *probe* and then *sense*. If probing reveals positive outcomes, you amplify this behavior. If probing reveals negative outcomes, you dampen that behavior.

The final quadrant is the realm of "chaotic" problems. Here, *novel practice* is your main tool, and you proceed to *act* and then *sense*. Rarely should you knowingly venture into chaos, and only for cutting-edge innovation. Try to stabilize back toward the "complex." Never should you unknowingly fall into chaos. This is represented by the "cliff of complacency" which, highlights the perils of being too comfortable in a "simple" problem domain. Limit the amount of work that fits into the "simple" domain, because it can easily descend into chaos.

Start your decision-making by acknowledging that you are in the center of the model: the disordered world.

Much of this book ushers software development into the complicated quadrant, rather than viewing delivery as a simple problem with process-like steps that can be followed to guarantee success. This is the problem of software delivery via a waterfall approach: it oversimplifies the complicated and mocks our efforts by waltzing us over the cliff of complacency into chaos.

Lean, or Agile, approaches to software acknowledge that the problem of software delivery is at least complicated and can even be complex.

Scrum versus waterfall

In my experience, the Agile approach works better than the waterfall method of software development, and I evangelize only in favor of Agile processes. The problem with the waterfall method is its rigidity. Figure 1-3 provides a representation of the process involved in a waterfall project.

Note that the output from one stage becomes the input to the next. Also note that each phase is completed before moving to the next phase. This assumes that no errors, issues, problems, or misunderstandings are discovered after a phase has completed. The arrows point only one way!

The waterfall process also assumes that no changes will be required after a phase has completed, something that is contrary to empirical and statistical evidence. Change is a natural part of life, not just of software engineering. Waterfall approaches assert that change is expensive, undesirable, and—most damningly—*avoidable*. Waterfall approaches presume that change can be circumnavigated by spending more time on requirements and design, so that changes *do not occur* during subsequent phases. This is preposterous, because change will *always* happen.

Agile processes respond to this fact by adopting a different approach that welcomes change and allows everyone to adapt to the changes that *will* occur. Although Agile—and therefore Scrum—allows for change at a process level, *coding for change* is one of the hardest, yet most important, tenets of modern software development.

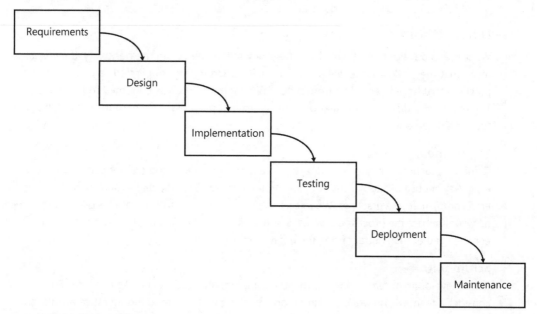

FIGURE 1-3 The waterfall development process.

This book shows you how to produce code that is adaptive enough to survive inevitable changes in requirements.

Waterfall methodologies are also document-centric, generating a lot of documentation that does not directly improve the software product. Agile, on the other hand, considers working software to be the most important document of a software product. The behavior of software is, after all, dictated by its source code—not by the documents that accompany that code. Furthermore, because documentation is a separate entity from the source code, it can easily fall out of sync with software.

> **Note** This is not to say that documentation is unimportant or that Agile processes never produce documentation. It is a matter of emphasis—Agile emphasizes working software, whereas waterfall methods emphasize documentation.

Scrum prescribes some metrics that provide feedback on the progress of a project and its overall health, but this is not documentation about the product. Agile, in general, favors just enough documentation to avoid being irresponsible, but it does not mandate such documentation. Some code can certainly benefit from supporting documentation, providing that it is not written once and never read again. For this reason, living documents that are easy to use, such as wikis, are common tools in Scrum teams.

The aim of Scrum as a process is not only to iteratively refine the software product, but also to iteratively refine the development process. This reminds teams to adopt process changes to ensure that the process is working for them, given their unique situations and context.

Different forms of Scrum

Whenever a development team claims that they follow the Scrum methodology, they usually mean that they follow some *variant* of Scrum. Pure Scrum does not include a lot of common practices that have been taken from other Agile methods, such as Extreme Programming (XP). There are three different subcategories of Scrum that progressively veer further away from the "purist" implementation.

Scrum and...

Common practices like writing unit tests first and pair-programming are not part of Scrum. However, they are useful and worthy additions to the process for many teams, and so they are considered complementary practices. When certain practices are added from other Agile methods such as XP or Kanban, the process becomes "Scrum and..."—that is: Scrum plus extra best practices that enhance, rather than detract from, the default Scrum process.

Scrum but...

Some development teams claim to be practicing Scrum, but they omit key aspects. For example, consider a team whose work is ordered on a backlog that is carried into iterative sprints, and that has retrospectives and daily stand-up meetings, but that doesn't estimate in story points and instead favors real-time estimates. This sort of diluted version of Scrum is termed "Scrum but...." Although the team is aligned with Scrum in a lot of areas, they are misaligned in one or two key areas.

Scrum not...

If a development team moves far enough away from the Scrum method, they end up doing "Scrum not...." This causes problems, particularly when team members expect an Agile methodology and the actual process in place is so different that it barely resembles Scrum at all. I find that the daily stand-up meeting is the easiest part of Scrum to adopt, but relative estimation and a positive attitude to change are much more difficult. When enough parts of the Scrum process are neglected, the process is no longer Scrum.

Roles and responsibilities

Scrum is just a process, and—I cannot stress this enough—it is only as effective as the people who follow the process. These people have roles and responsibilities that guide their actions.

Product owner

The role of product owner (sometimes called the *PO*) is vital. The product owner provides the link between the client or customer and the rest of the development team. A product owner's responsibilities include:

- Deciding which features are built.
- Setting the priority of the features in terms of business value.
- Accepting or rejecting "completed" work.

As a key stakeholder in the success of the project, the PO must be available to the team and be able to communicate the vision clearly. The long-term goal of the project should be clear to the development team, with changes in focus propagated throughout the team in a timely manner. In short-term sprint planning, the product owner sets out what will be developed and in what order. Product owners determine the features that will be needed along the road to making a release of the software, and they set the priorities for the product backlog.

Although the product owner's role is key, he or she does not have unlimited influence over the process. The product owner cannot influence how much the team commits to for a sprint, because this is determined by the team itself based on its velocity. Product owners also do not dictate *how* work is done—the development team has control over the details of how it implements a certain story at a technical level. When a sprint is underway, the product owner cannot change the sprint goals, alter acceptance criteria, or add or remove stories. After the goals are decided and the stories are committed to the sprint during sprint planning, the sprint in progress becomes immutable. Any changes must wait until the next sprint—unless the change is to cancel the sprint or project in its entirety and start again. This allows the development team to retain total focus on achieving the sprint goal without moving the goalposts.

Throughout the sprint, as stories progress and are completed, the product owner will be asked to verify how a feature works or comment on a task that is in progress. It is important that product owners be able to devote some time during the sprint to liaise with the development team, in case the unexpected occurs and confusion arises. In this way, by the end of the sprint, the product owner is not presented with "completed" stories that deviate from their initial vision. Product owners do, however, get to decide whether a story meets the acceptance criteria supplied and whether it is considered complete and can be demonstrated at the end of the sprint.

Scrum master

The Scrum master (SM) shields the team from any external distractions during the sprint and tackles any of the impediments that the team flags during the daily Scrum meeting. This keeps the team fully functional and productive for the duration of the sprint, allowing it to focus wholly on the sprint goals.

Just as the product owner owns the product—what is to be done—the Scrum master owns the process—the framework surrounding *how* it is to be done. Thus it is the Scrum master's responsibility to ensure that the process is being followed by the team. Although the Scrum master can make some suggestions for improving the process (such as switching from a four-week sprint duration to a two-week duration), the Scrum master's authority is limited. Scrum masters cannot, for instance, specify how the team should implement a story, beyond ensuring that it follows the Scrum process.

> **Tip** Scrum masters are *servant leaders*. This means that they do not embody an accumulation of power at the top of a pyramid of roles. Instead, they seek to devolve power into each team member. This empowerment of their team leads to better engagement and a stronger sense of purpose and place within the project.

As owners of the process, Scrum masters also own the daily Scrum meeting. The Scrum master ensures the team's attendance and takes notes throughout in case any actionable items are uncovered. The team is not *reporting* to the Scrum master during the Scrum meeting; they are informing *everyone* present of their progress and impediments.

Development team

Ideally, an Agile team consists of *generalizing specialists*. That is, each member of the team should be multidisciplinary—capable of operating effectively on several different technologies, but with an aptitude, preference, or specialization in a certain area. For example, a team could consist of four developers, each of whom is capable of working very competently on ASP.NET MVC, Windows Workflow, and Windows Communication Foundation (WCF). However, two of the developers specialize in Windows Forms, and the remaining pair prefer to work with Windows Presentation Foundation (WPF) and Microsoft SQL Server.

Having a cross-functional team prevents siloes where one person—the "web person," the "database person," or the "WPF person"—has sole knowledge of how that part of the application works. Siloes are bad for everyone involved, and there should be heavy emphasis placed on breaking down siloes wherever possible. Siloes are bad for the company because it makes them depend too heavily on a single resource to provide value in a certain area. This can become a bottleneck to the throughput of the team. And the individuals themselves suffer because they become entrenched in roles that "only they can do." In Scrum, the code is owned by the whole team.

Software testers are responsible for maintaining the quality of the software while it is being developed. Before a story is started, the testers might discuss automated test plans for verifying that the implementation of a story meets all of the acceptance criteria. They might work with the developers to implement those test plans, or they might write such tests themselves. After a story is implemented, the developer can submit it for testing, and the test analyst will verify that it is working as required.

Pigs and chickens

Each role of the Scrum process can be categorized as a pig or a chicken. These characterizations relate to the following story: A chicken approaches his friend, the pig, and says, "Hello pig, I've had an idea. I think we should open a restaurant!" At first, the pig is enthusiastic and enquires, "What should we call it?" The chicken replies, "We could call it Ham 'n' Eggs." The pig ponders this briefly before exclaiming in outrage, "No way! I'd be *committed*, but you'd only *contribute*!"

This fun allegory highlights the level of involvement that certain members need to have in a project. Pigs are entirely committed to a project and will be accountable for its outcome, whereas chickens merely contribute and are involved in a more peripheral manner. The product owner, the Scrum master, and the development team are all pigs inasmuch as they are committed to the delivery of the product. Most often, customers are contributing chickens. Similarly, executive management will contribute to the project, so they are also considered chickens rather than pigs.

Artifacts

Throughout the lifetime of any software project, many documents, graphs, diagrams, charts, and metrics are created, reviewed, analyzed, and dissected. In this respect, a Scrum project is no different from any other. However, Scrum documents are distinct from documents of other types of project management in their type and purpose. A key difference between all Agile processes and more rigid processes is the relative importance of documentation. Structured Systems Analysis and Design Methodology (SSADM), for example, places a heavy emphasis on writing lots of documentation. This is referred to pejoratively as Big Design Up Front (BDUF): the errant belief that all fear, uncertainty, and doubt can be eliminated from a project if sufficient attention is paid to documentation. Agile processes aim to reduce the amount of documentation produced to only that which is absolutely necessary for the project to succeed. Instead, Agile favors the idea that the code—which is the most authoritative documentation—can be deployed, run, and used at any time. It also prefers that all stakeholders communicate with each other directly rather than write documents that might never be read by their most important audience. Documentation is still important to an Agile project, but its importance does not supersede that of working software or communication.

The Scrum board

Central to the daily workings of a Scrum project is the Scrum board. There should be a generous amount of wall space reserved for the Scrum board—if the board is too small, the temptation is to omit important details. Wall space might well be at a premium in your office, but there are tricks that you can use. Perhaps that large, neglected whiteboard could be repurposed as a Scrum board. With the aid of magnets, metal filing cabinets can double as the Scrum board. If your office is rented or you otherwise cannot deface the walls, "magic" whiteboards—which are simply wipe-clean sheets of static paper—are ideal. Try to identify a suitable place that could perform this function in your office. Whatever you choose, however you designate it, if it doesn't feel right after a couple of iterations, feel free to change it. Physical Scrum boards are an absolute must. There is nothing that can replace the visceral experience of standing in front of a Scrum board. Though digital Scrum tools have their uses, I believe that they are complementary, rather than primary, to the Scrum process. If you can evaluate a digital Scrum board, note the number of times that something appears more difficult to accomplish than if the board were physical. In my experience, digital Scrum boards are a pain, not a pleasure. Figure 1-4 shows an example of a typical Scrum board.

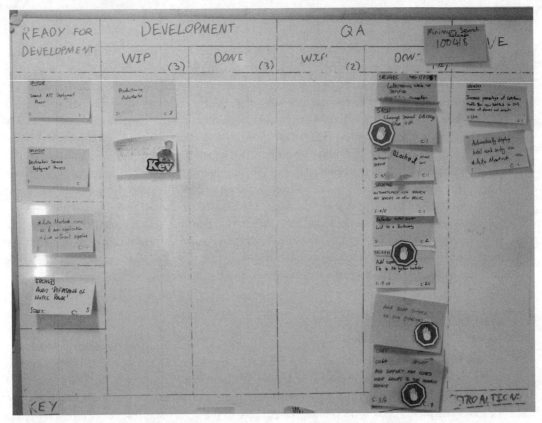

FIGURE 1-4 A Scrum board is a snapshot of the state of the work currently in development.

A Scrum board is a hive of information. It holds a lot of details, and discerning what is happening might be daunting. The rest of this section explains each aspect in detail.

Cards

The primary items on the Scrum board are the cards. The cards represent different elements of progress for a software product—from a physical release of the software down to the smallest distinct task. Each of these card types is typically represented by a different color, for clarity. Due to space constraints, the Scrum board usually shows only the stories, tasks, defects, and technical debt associated with the current sprint.

> **Tip** Colors alone might not be sufficient for the requirements of everyone on the team. For example, consider coupling colors with distinct shapes for team members who can't distinguish colors.

Hierarchy of composition Figure 1-5 shows how the cards on a Scrum board are related. Note that it is implied that a product is composed of many tasks. Even the most complex software can be distilled into a finite list of discrete tasks that must be performed, each paving the way to completion.

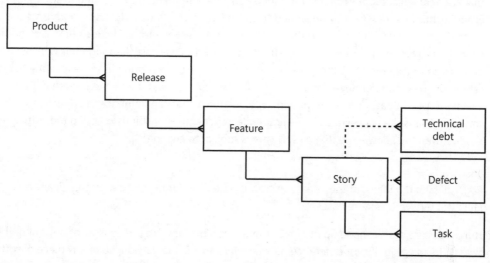

FIGURE 1-5 The cards on the Scrum board represent different parts of an aggregated product.

Product At the top of the Scrum food chain is the software product that is being built. Examples of products are bountiful: integrated development environments, web applications, accounting software, social media apps, and many more. This is the software that you are developing and the product you intend to deliver.

Teams usually work toward only one product at a time, but sometimes teams are responsible for delivering multiple products.

Release For every product that you develop, there will be multiple releases. A release is a version of the software that end users can purchase or use as a service. Sometimes a release is made only to address defects, but a release could also be intended to provide value-add features to key clients or to make a beta version of the software available as a sneak preview.

Web applications are often implicitly versioned with only a single deployment that supersedes all prior releases. In fact, the Google Chrome web browser is an interesting example. Although it is a desktop application, it is deployed as a stream of micro-releases that are seamlessly deployed to desktops without the usual fanfare that accompanies rival browsers. Internet Explorer 8, 9, and 10 each had their own advertisements on television, but Chrome does not follow this pattern—Google simply advertises the browser itself, irrespective of version. Iterative releases like this are becoming more common. Scrum can direct this release pattern by focusing on the potential to deliver working software after every sprint.

Minimum viable product

The first release can be aligned to a *minimum viable product (MVP)*—the basic set of features that are deemed sufficient to fulfill the fundamental requirements. For accounting software, for example, this feature set could be limited to the ability to create new clients, add transactions (both deposits and withdrawals) to their accounts, and present a total. The idea here is to bootstrap the project so that it becomes self-funding as soon as possible. Although this is unlikely to occur as a result of the MVP, the hope is that the MVP will at least bring in some revenue to offset the ongoing costs of development. Not only this, but that first deployment, even if it targets a restricted client base, is likely to provide vital feedback that can influence the direction of the software. This is the nature of Scrum—and Agile in general—constantly evolving the software product with the knowledge that all software is subject to change.

Regardless of the intent of the release or how it is deployed (or even how often), ideally a single product will survive several releases.

Feature   Each release is made up of one or more features that were previously not present in the software. The most significant difference between version 1.0 and version 2.0 of any piece of software is the addition of new features that the team believes will generate sufficient interest to persuade new users to make a purchase and existing users to upgrade.

The term *minimum marketable feature (MMF)* is useful to delineate features and compose a release. The following is a list of example features that are generic enough to be applied to many different projects, yet specific enough to be real-world features:

- Exporting application data to a portable XML-based format
- Rendering webpage requests quickly
- Archiving historical data for future reference
- Copying and pasting text
- Sharing files across a network with colleagues

Features are marketable if they have some value for the customer. When distilled down to the smallest amount of functionality possible while still retaining its value, the feature is also minimal.

Epics/features vs. MMFs vs. themes

You might be more used to the term *epic* rather than *feature* when talking about Scrum, but I have taken the liberty of switching this out for my preferred term. Epics and features are often considered "large stories": that is, stories that are much larger than MMFs and that cannot be delivered in a single sprint.

Features are also similar to Scrum *themes* in that they serve to group stories that fulfill a common goal.

Features can be broadly grouped into three categories for each release: required, preferred, and desired. These are mutually exclusive options that reflect the overall priority assigned to each feature. The development team is instructed to work on all *required* features before tackling the *preferred* features, with the *desired* features being addressed only if time allows. As you might have guessed, these categories—and, indeed, the features themselves—are always changeable. They can be canceled, re-prioritized, altered, and superseded at any time. The team is expected to switch focus gracefully (with the proviso that deadlines and funding might also change in kind). Everything in Scrum is a moveable feast, and this book is aimed to help you deal with that reality.

User story   The user story is probably the Scrum artifact that most people are familiar with, but ironically, it is not prescribed by Scrum. User stories are an artifact of Extreme Programming, but they have been co-opted by Scrum because they are so commonly used. User stories are specified by using the following template:

> *"As a [user role], I want to [verb-centric behavior], so that [user value added]."*

The square brackets denote parameterization that distinguishes one user story from another. A concrete example should illuminate further:

> *"As an unauthenticated but registered user, I want to reset my password, so that I can log on to the system if I forget my password."*

There are many things to note about this user story. First of all, *there is not nearly enough detail to actually implement the behavior required.* Note that the user story is written from the perspective of a *user*. Although this would seem to be obvious, this point is missed by many and, too often, stories are wrongly written from the perspective of developers. This is why the first part of the template—*As a [user role]*—is so important. Similarly, the *[user value added]* portion is just as important because, without this, it is easy to lose sight of the underlying reason that the user story exists. This is what ties the user story to its parent feature; the example just given could belong to a feature such as *"Forgotten user credentials are recoverable."* And the story would probably be grouped with the story in which the user has forgotten his or her logon name and the story in which the user has forgotten both logon name and password.

Given that this user story is not sufficient to begin development, what is its value? A user story represents a conversation that is yet to occur between the development team and the customer. When it comes time to implement the story, the developers assigned to it will start by taking the story to the customer and talking through the customer's requirements. This analysis phase will produce several acceptance criteria that determine whether a user story can be deemed complete.

After the requirements have been gathered, the developers convene and lay out some design ideas to meet these requirements. This phase might include user interface mockups that use Balsamiq, Microsoft Visio, or some other tool. Some technical design concepts will detail how the existing code base must be altered to meet these new requirements, often using Unified Modeling Language (UML) diagrams.

After the design is ratified, the team can start to break the user story down into tasks and then work toward implementing the story by performing these tasks. When they reach a point where they are satisfied that the story is working as required, they can hand it over to be acceptance tested. This final phase, also known as *quality assurance (QA)*, double-checks the working software against the acceptance criteria and either approves or rejects it. When it is approved, the user story is complete.

Let's recap for a minute. With a user story for guidance, developers gathered requirements in an analysis phase, generated a design, implemented a working solution, and then tested this against the acceptance criteria. This sounds a lot like waterfall development methodologies! Indeed, that's the whole point of user stories—to perform the entire software development life cycle, in miniature, for each story. This helps to prevent any wasted effort because it is not until the user story is ready to be taken from the Scrum board and implemented that the developers can be sure it is still relevant to the software product.

User stories are the main focus of work in Scrum; they hold the incentive that Scrum provides for team members: story points. The team assigns each user story its own story point score during sprint planning and, after the user story is complete, the story points are considered to be earned and are claimed from the sprint total. Story points are explained in further detail later in this chapter.

Task   There is a unit of work smaller than a user story—the task. Stories can be broken down into more manageable tasks, which can then be split between the developers assigned to the story. I prefer to wait until the story is taken off the board before I split it into tasks, but I have also seen this done as part of sprint planning.

Although user stories must incorporate a full vertical slice of functionality, tasks can be split at the layer level to take advantage of developer specializations within the team. For example, if a new field is required on an existing form, there will probably need to be changes to the user interface, business logic, and data access layers. You could divide this into three tasks that target these three layers and assign each to the relevant specialist: the WPF developer, the core C# expert, and the database guru, respectively. Of course, if you are lucky enough to have a team of generalizing specialists, anyone should really be able to *volunteer* for any task. This allows everyone to work on various parts of the code, which improves their understanding in addition to boosting their job satisfaction.

It is important to note that the user stories are the bearers of story points and that these do not transfer down to their constituent tasks. A five-point story that is broken into three distinct tasks is not composed of two one-point tasks and a three-point task. This is because there is neither incentive nor credit for partially completed work. Unless the story—as a whole—is proven complete by the QA process before the end of the sprint, the points that it contains are not claimed, even in part. The story remains in progress until the next sprint, when ideally it will be completed early in the iteration. If a story takes too long to complete and remains in progress for a long time—more than a full sprint's length— it was probably too big in the first place and should have been sliced into smaller, more manageable stories.

Technical debt   Technical debt is a very interesting concept, but it is easily misunderstood. Technical debt is a metaphor for the design and architectural compromises that have been made during a story's journey across the Scrum board. Technical debt has its own section later in this chapter.

The vertical slice

When I was growing up, every Christmas my father would make trifle. This is a traditional English dessert that is made from various layers. At the bottom there is sliced fruit; then there are layers of sponge cake, jelly, and custard; and on top is whipped cream. My brother used to dig his spoon all the way through the layers, whereas I would eat each layer in turn.

Well-designed software is layered just like a trifle. The bottom layer is dedicated to data access, with layers in between for object-relational mappers, domain models, services, and controllers—with the user interface on top. Much like eating trifle, there are two ways to slice any part of a layered application: vertically and horizontally.

By slicing horizontally, you take each layer and implement what is required of those layers as a whole. But with this approach, there is no guarantee that each slice will align with the others. The user interface might allow the user to interact with certain features that layers below have not yet implemented. The net effect is that the client cannot use the application until a significant proportion of each layer has been completed. This delays the important feedback loop that Agile methods give you and increases the likelihood that you will build more than is needed—or simply the wrong thing.

Slicing vertically is what you should aim for. Each user story should incorporate functionality at each layer and should be tethered at the top to the user interface. This way, you can demonstrate the functionality to the user and receive feedback quickly. This also avoids writing user stories that are developer-centric, such as, *"I want to be able to query the database for customers who have not paid this month."* This sounds too much like a task; the story could be about generating a report on the outstanding unpaid accounts.

Defect   A defect card is created whenever acceptance criteria are not met on a previously complete user story. This highlights the need for automated acceptance testing: each batch of tests written for a story forms a suite of regression tests to ensure that no future work is able to introduce a breaking change.

Defect cards, like technical debt, do not have story points assigned to them, thus removing the incentive to create defects and technical debt—something that developers want to avoid even if full eradication of defects and technical debt is unattainable.

All software has defects. That is just a fact of software development, and no amount of planning or diligence will ever account for the fallibility of humans. Defects can be broadly categorized as A, B, or C: *apocalyptic* defects, *behavioral* errors, and *cosmetic* issues.

Apocalyptic defects result in an outright crash of the application or otherwise prevent the continuation of the user's work. An uncaught exception is the classic example because the program must terminate and be restarted or—in a web scenario—the webpage must be reloaded. These defects should be assigned the highest priority and should be fixed before a release of the software.

Card sharp

A lot of options are available for customizing and personalizing the cards on the Scrum board.

Color scheme

Any color scheme will suffice for the cards, but there are a few that, in my experience, make the most sense. Index cards are ideal for features and user stories, whereas sticky notes make excellent task, defect, and technical debt cards because they can be stuck to a relevant story. Here are my recommendations:

- Features: green index cards

- User stories: white index cards

- Tasks: yellow sticky notes

- Defects: red/pink sticky notes

- Technical debt: purple/blue sticky notes

Note that user stories and tasks, being the most common kinds of cards you will create, use the most commonly available index cards and sticky notes. The last thing you need is to run out of index cards, so try to use the most commonly available colors.

Who creates cards?

The simple answer to the question, "Who can create the cards?" is: anyone. This does, of course, come with some conditions. Though anyone can create a card, its validity, priority, criticality, and other such states are not something that should be decided by one person alone. All feature and story cards should be verified by the product owner, but task, defect, and technical debt cards are entirely the domain of the development team.

Avatars

Much like the avatars found online in forums, on blogs, and on Twitter, these are miniature representations of the various members of the team. Feel free to allow your team members to express themselves through their avatars, because it certainly adds a sense of fun to the Scrum process. Of course, steer them away from anything likely to cause offense, but there should be a sense of distinct identity for each person's avatar.

Over the course of an iteration, these avatars will be moved around a lot and will be handled on a daily basis. Because you have index-card stories and sticky-note tasks already on the board, these avatars should be no bigger than 2-inch squares. Laminating them will also help to protect them from becoming dog-eared or torn, and reusable adhesive or a little piece of tape should hold them in place.

Behavioral errors might not be as serious but can infuriate users. These types of errors could be even more damaging than simply crashing the application. Imagine erroneous currency conversion logic that rounds pennies wrong. Whether the algorithm favors the customer or the business, someone is going to lose money. Of course, not all logic errors are quite this serious, but it is easy to understand why they should be given a high priority.

Cosmetic issues are typically problems with the user interface—badly aligned images, a window that doesn't expand to full screen gracefully, or an image on the web that never loads. These issues do not affect the use of the software, just its appearance. Although these issues are often given a lower priority, it is still important to remember that appearances count toward the user's expectations of the software. If the user interface is badly designed with buttons that don't work and images that don't load, users are less inclined to trust the internal workings of that software. Conversely, a shiny user interface with plenty of bells and whistles might convince users that your software is just as well designed internally. A common trick for projects that have developed a poor reputation is to redesign the user interface—perhaps even rebranding the entire product—to improve perceptions and reset expectations.

Swimlanes

Scrum boards have vertical lines drawn on them to demarcate the swimlanes. Each swimlane can contain multiple user story cards to denote the progress of that story throughout its development life cycle. From left to right, the basic swimlanes are Backlog, In Progress, QA, and Done.

A story in the backlog has been "committed to" for the sprint and should—unless canceled—be taken from the board and work on it should begin. This column can be ordered by priority so that the top item is always the next one that should be implemented.

After the story is taken from the backlog and a conversation has taken place with the product owner about the scope and requirements, the card is returned—with newly derived tasks—to the In Progress swimlane. At this point, the avatars of all team members involved in the story should also be attached. The story now counts toward any swimlane limits that might be associated with the in-progress phase. For example, you might require that only three user stories be in progress at a time, thus coercing the team to complete already-started stories in preference to those that have not yet been started. Remember: there is no incentive for partially completed work.

After analysis, design, and implementation have been carried out for a story, it is considered "developer complete" and can be moved to the Quality Assurance (QA) swimlane. Ideally, the QA environment should mirror the production environment as closely as possible, to avoid any environmental errors that can occur from even minor differences in deployment. The test analysts will assess the story in conjunction with the acceptance criteria. In essence, they try to break the story and prove that the code does not behave in the manner in which it ought. Typically, they attempt to provide unusual and erroneous input to certain operations, ensuring that validation works correctly. They might even look for security loopholes to ensure that malicious end users cannot gain access above their specified privilege level. When the QA is fully complete, the user story is moved across to the Done swimlane. Any story points associated with the story are then claimed, and the sprint burndown chart (which shows the progress of the sprint) can be amended. These artifacts are covered in more detail later.

The Scrum board can be further split by using *horizontal swimlanes*. These swimlanes can be used to group the stories by feature, so that everyone can see at a glance where effort is being concentrated, and thus where bottlenecks need to be alleviated.

One special swimlane at the top of the board is the Fast-Track lane, into which any very high–priority tasks can be placed. Team members can be instructed to "swarm" on a fast-track item so that it is completed as quickly as possible, often to the detriment of any other outstanding work. Swarming ensures that the team stops what they are doing to collaborate on a problem or task that has overriding priority. It is a useful tool and should be used sparingly, when such a priority occurs. Apocalyptic defects found in production are the most common fast-track items.

Technical debt

The term *technical debt* deserves further explanation. Throughout the course of implementing a user story, it is likely that certain compromises will need to be made between the "ideal code" and code that is good enough to meet the deadline. This is not to say that poor design should be tolerated or encouraged in order to hit a deadline, but that there is value in doing something simpler now, with a view to improving it later.

Good and bad technical debt   Debt is likely to accrue gradually over the lifetime of a project. It is termed *debt* because that is a great metaphor for how it should be viewed. There is nothing wrong with certain types of financial debt. If, for example, you have the option of spreading the payments for a car over 12 months with low-interest repayments, you are in debt. But this could be a good decision if you need the car for commuting and cannot afford the payment in full. The car will allow you to generate the revenue necessary to pay the repayments, because you can now get to work on time.

Of course, some debt is bad. If you take out a credit card and pay for something extravagant without first calculating how you will repay the debt, you can end up in a cycle of balance transfers, trying to keep interest payments at a minimum. This will, in hindsight, look like a bad financial decision based around bad debt. The key is to look carefully at the options and decide whether the debt is worth taking on or whether you should just pay up front.

The tradeoff is the same in software. You could implement a suboptimal solution now and meet a deadline or spend the extra time now to improve the design, perhaps missing the deadline. There is no right answer that fits all situations, just guidelines for detecting good and bad technical debt.

The technical debt quadrant   Martin Fowler, a prominent Agile evangelist, defined a technical debt quadrant for categorizing the concessions and compromises that might be needed to mark a story as done. The two axes that divide a plane into quadrants, x and y, correspond to the questions, "Are we accruing this technical debt for the correct reasons?" and "Are we aware of alternatives to avoid this technical debt?", respectively.

If you answer "Yes" to the former question, you are adding prudent technical debt: you can point to valid reasons for adding it, and your conscience is clear. If you answer "No," this debt is reckless and you would be better advised to deal with this debt now, rather than allow it to accumulate.

For the latter question, an affirmative answer means that you have considered the alternatives and decided to take on the debt. A negative answer indicates that you cannot think of other alternatives.

The results of these questions generate four possible scenarios, as shown in Figure 1-6:

- **Reckless, deliberate**   This type of debt is the most poisonous. It is equivalent to saying something like, "We don't have time for design," which indicates a very unhealthy working environment. A decision such as this should alert everyone that the team is not adaptive and is marching steadily toward inevitable failure.

- **Reckless, inadvertent**   This type of debt is most likely created by a lack of experience. It is the result of not knowing best practices in modern software engineering. It is likely that the code is a mess, much like in the previous case, but the developer did not know any better and therefore could not find any other options. Education is the answer here: as long as developers are willing to learn, they can stop introducing this kind of technical debt.

- **Prudent, inadvertent**   This occurs when you follow best practices but it turns out that there was a better way of doing something, and "now you know how you should have done it." This is similar to the previous case, but all of the developers were in agreement at the time that there was no better way of solving the problem.

- **Prudent, deliberate**   This is the most acceptable type of debt. All of the choices have been considered, and you know exactly what you are doing—and why—by allowing this debt to remain. It is most commonly associated with a late decision to "ship now and deal with the consequences."

	Reckless	Prudent
Deliberate	"We don't have time for design."	"We must ship now and deal with consequences."
Inadvertent	"What's layering?"	"Now we know how we should have done it."

FIGURE 1-6 The technical debt quadrant, as explained by Martin Fowler, helps developers visualize the four different categories of debt.

Repaying debt   Technical debt is not directly associated with any story points, yet the debt must be repaid despite the lack of direct incentive. It is best to try to attach a technical debt card to a story and refactor the code so that the new design is implemented along with associated new behavior. The next time that a story is taken from the board, check whether any of the code that will be edited has a technical debt attached, and try to tackle the two together.

Digital Scrum boards

A digital Scrum board, unless constantly projected on a wall, hides some of the most important information about a project. By being open with this information and displaying it for the whole company to see, you invite questions about process that otherwise would not be asked. Being transparent with process is a huge benefit, especially when you are implementing Scrum for the first time in a company. It encourages buy-in from important stakeholders that you would do well to involve in the process.

It is a cliché, but people really do fear change. Fear is just a natural reaction to the unknown. By educating people on what you are doing and what certain charts mean (and why their wall is now covered in dozens of index cards), you foster a spirit of collaboration and communication that really is priceless. Being required to explain these things to non-technical people can also be helpful to you, because in doing so you might come to understand the process better yourself.

As with all tools, the best ones are high-touch and low-resistance. They will be used very often, and there will be no barriers to their use. When a tool becomes even mildly inconvenient to use, it will gradually be more and more neglected. What was initially used often and diligently kept up to date will no longer be tended, and it will rapidly fall behind reality.

The definition of done

Every project needs a *definition of done (DoD)*. This is the standard that every user story must adhere to in order to be considered done. How many times have you heard these lines from a developer?

> *"It's done, I just have to test it...."*

> *"It's done, but I found a defect that I need to fix...."*

> *"It's done, but I'm not 100-percent happy with the design, so I'm going to change the interface...."*

I have used these myself in the past. If the story truly was done, there would be no caveats, conditions, or clauses required. These examples are what developers say when they need to buy themselves a little more time due to a bad estimate or an unforeseen problem. Everyone must agree on a definition of "done" and stick to it. If a user story doesn't meet the criteria, it can't possibly be done. Story points are never claimed until the story meets the definition of done.

What goes into a definition of done? That is entirely up to you, your team, and how stringent you want your quality assurance process to be. However, the following demonstrates a standard DoD as a starting point.

In order to claim that a user story is done, you must:

- Unit-test all code to cover its success and failure paths, with all tests passing.

- Ensure that all code is submitted to the Continuous Integration builds and compiles—without errors—with all tests passing.

- Verify behavior against the acceptance criteria with the product owner.

- Have a developer who did not work on the story peer-review code.

- Document just enough to communicate intent.

- Reject reckless technical debt.

Feel free to remove, amend, or append any rules, but be strict with this definition. If a story does not meet all criteria, it either needs more work—it is not *done*—or the prohibitive criteria from the definition of done should be dropped. For example, if you feel that code reviews are arcane or pedantic, feel free to omit that rule from your DoD.

Charts and metrics

There are several charts that can be used to monitor the progress of a Scrum project. Scrum charts can indicate the health and historical progress of a Scrum project, in addition to predicting probable future achievement. All of these charts should be displayed prominently by the Scrum board in a size sufficient to be read from a few feet away. This shows the team that these metrics are not being used behind their back, that they are not a way of measuring their progress for the consumption of management. Instead, be very up front about how progress is measured, and make it clear that these charts are not being made for performance reasons, but to diagnose problems with the project as a whole.

On a related note, try to avoid measuring anything on a personal level—such as story points achieved per developer. This conveys a poor message to the team: that they can sacrifice team progress for personal progress. Developers will readily attach themselves to such measurements and try to save face by monopolizing larger stories, trying to achieve points all by themselves. Be careful what you incentivize.

Caution Be wary of what you measure—there is an "observer effect." For instance, for some metrics, the act of measuring is not possible without first altering that which is measured. Take, for example, measuring tire pressure on a car. It is very difficult to measure the pressure without first letting a little air out of the tire, thus altering the pressure. This same principle applies to human nature, too. When the team knows that they are going to be measured by some criteria, they will do whatever they can to improve their statistics to look good. This is not to say that you are managing a group of Machiavellian troublemakers, but when the team realizes that story points will be used to measure their progress, they might be inclined to assign higher points for the same effort. Use triangulation (which is covered in the "Sprint retrospective" section later in this chapter) to reconcile estimated effort with actual effort.

Story points

Story points are intended to incentivize the team to add business value with every sprint. Story points are assigned to user stories by the whole development team during the sprint planning meeting (see the "Sprint planning" section later in this chapter). A story point is a measure of relative effort required to implement the behavior that the user story represents. This is the inclusive effort required to fulfill the entire software lifecycle—requirements analysis, technical design, and code implementation with unit testing, plus quality assurance against acceptance criteria and deployment to a staging environment. Although every story should already be small enough to fit comfortably inside a sprint, stories might still vary significantly in size.

At one end of the scale is a "one-point story," which requires minimal effort to implement. An interesting and important fact about story points is that they are meaningless outside of the team that assigned them. A one-point story for one team might be a three-point story for another team. What occurs over multiple sprints is a consensus on the approximate effort required for a story.

One thing that a story point definitely does not represent is effort measured in absolute terms—days, hours, or any other temporal measurement. Story points do, very roughly, correspond to a historical range of times, as shown in Figure 1-7. In this chart, the vertical bars represent the minimum, maximum, and average actual time taken for stories of a corresponding size.

FIGURE 1-7 Min/max/average chart showing correlation between estimated effort and actual effort.

The main takeaway from this chart is that larger stories have correspondingly larger ranges—the larger a story is assumed to be, the harder it is to accurately predict how long it will take to complete.

Velocity

Over multiple sprints, it is possible to calculate a running average of the achieved story points. Let's say that a team has completed three sprints, meeting the definition of done on stories totaling 8, 12, and 11 story points. This is a running total of 31 and a running average of 10 points. This is the team's *velocity*, and it can be used in two ways.

First, a team's velocity can form a ceiling for how many points a team should commit to for the next sprint. If the team is averaging 10 points per sprint, committing to more than that amount for a single iteration would be more than just optimistic—it would be setting them up for a morale-sapping failure. It is better to set an achievable goal and meet or exceed it than to set an unrealistic goal and fall short. If the team took these 10 points and actually implemented 11, it would feed into a new velocity of 11: (12 + 11 + 11) / 3. This is the Scrum feedback loop in action.

A second use for the velocity is to analyze problems with delivery. If the velocity of a team drops by a significant percentage for one sprint, this probably indicates that something bad happened during that sprint that needs to be rectified. Perhaps the stories were too large and their true scale was underestimated, thus keeping them in progress for a long time and requiring them to survive for more than one sprint. Alternatively, a simpler explanation could be possible—that too many key staff members were on vacation (or ill) all at the same time and progress naturally slowed. On the other hand, perhaps too much time was spent refactoring existing, working code, with not enough emphasis on introducing new features to the system. Whatever the reason, a 25-percent drop in velocity is not *always* disastrous, but it *could* be indicative of further problems to come that you should address as soon as possible. Week-after-week reductions in velocity—protracted deceleration—is a definite problem and probably points to code that is not adaptive to change; something that this book will help you address.

Sprint burndown chart

At the start of each sprint, a two-dimensional Cartesian graph is created and placed by the Scrum board. The total number of story points is charted along the y-axis, and the number of working days is plotted along the x-axis. A straight diagonal line (also known as the *line of best fit*) is then drawn to show the ideal progression of the sprint, as shown in Figure 1-8.

FIGURE 1-8 A sprint burndown chart at the beginning of a sprint. The straight line shows the "line of best fit" to the sprint goal (23 story points, in this example).

At each morning's stand-up Scrum meeting, the points associated with any completed user stories are claimed and deducted from the current remaining total. As illustrated in Figure 1-9, this shows the actual progress of the sprint against the necessary progress in order to achieve the sprint goal.

FIGURE 1-9 A sprint burndown chart partway through a sprint. In this instance, the team is sticking closely to the "path of perfection," although no progress was made between Friday and Monday of the first week.

Drawing the actual-progress line and required line in different colors helps differentiate the two. If at any time during the sprint the actual line is above the required line, the chart is indicating that there is a problem and that the amount of work that will be delivered is less than planned. Conversely, if the actual line is below the required line, the project is ahead of schedule. It is likely that during the course of a sprint, the actual line will oscillate above and below the line a little, without indicating any real problems. It is the larger divergences that need to be explained.

Burndown charts are useful when there is a fixed amount of work required in a fixed amount of time. Under these conditions, it is not possible to dip below the x-axis. (When y=0, you have completed all work assigned.)

Feature burnup chart

Just as the sprint burndown chart tracks progress at story level throughout a sprint, the feature burnup chart shows the progress of completed features as they are implemented. At the end of each sprint, it is possible that a new feature might have been implemented in its entirety. The best thing about this graph is that it is very difficult to fake the delivery of completed features without having symptoms manifest quickly. The idea is to watch this graph increase linearly over time, without significant plateaus. Figure 1-10 shows an example of a good feature burnup chart.

Although the gradient might be shallow, this graph implies that the team has found a good rhythm to their development and is consistently delivering features at a fairly predictable rate. Though there are slight deviations from a perfectly straight line, these are nothing to worry about.

FIGURE 1-10 The feature burnup chart covering an adjusted calendar year for a healthy project making consistent progress.

On the other hand, the burnup chart shown in Figure 1-11 shows that a definite issue has occurred during development. The team started very strongly, delivering lots of features extremely quickly, but they have since stalled and only delivered two completed features over the past eight months.

FIGURE 1-11 The feature burnup chart covering an adjusted calendar year for a project that has stalled.

The problem here is quite clear: the code was not adaptive to change. The initial dash from the starting line could indicate a lack of unit testing and neglect for layering or other best practices. By omitting these details, the team managed to complete features early. However, as the code base became bloated and disorganized, progress began to slow down significantly and the amount of features delivered ground to a halt. A progression like this is likely to be accompanied by an increase in the amount of defects and bad—reckless—technical debt. If the project continues to follow this path, it would probably be better to start over—the refactoring effort required to get it back on track would outweigh the benefits. If the problem was caught early enough, the team and project could recover. It is better to start with Agile development practices in place from the outset, rather than trying to crowbar them in to an unhealthy project.

Backlogs

A backlog is a list of pending items that are yet to be addressed. These items are waiting for their time to be taken from the backlog and acted on until they are complete. Each item in the list has an assigned priority and an estimated required effort, and the list is ordered first by priority and then by effort.

Two backlogs are maintained in Scrum, each with its own distinct purpose: the product backlog and the sprint backlog.

Product backlog

At any point during a product's life, the product backlog contains features that are waiting to be implemented. These features have not been committed to a sprint, so the development team is not actively working on the items on this backlog. The development team—or its key representatives—spends time scoping the effort required on these features in the release planning meeting (covered later in this chapter). This helps to prioritize the items on the product backlog so that they remain in priority order.

The priority of each item is primarily dictated by the value that implementing the feature would represent to the business. This business value must be determined by the owner of the product backlog: the product owner. This person represents the business to the development team and can speak authoritatively for it. The product owner's knowledge of the business and its working practices is vital for assigning the correct business value to any particular feature. If two items on the product backlog have the same relative business value, their priority is decided based on the relative effort required. Given two features of high business value, if one is estimated to require a small effort and another a large effort, it makes business sense to implement the smaller feature first. This is because smaller features pose less of a risk; the probable range of time required to implement a small feature will not vary as much as that of a larger feature. Also, the return on investment (ROI) is larger for a feature that requires less effort than for one of equal value that requires more.

When the business wants to release a new version of the product, the product backlog can be consulted to determine which features are most valuable to the release. This can occur in one of two ways. Either the business sets an absolute deadline for the release and commits to the amount of work likely to be accomplished in that timeframe, given the effort estimates attached, or the business selects the features that are required for the release and the likely release date is determined from the estimates.

Aside from features, the product backlog can also contain defects that must be fixed but that have not yet found their way into a sprint. Just like features, defects will have some assigned business value.

The estimate of effort required for a defect is difficult to ascertain, because there is less known about the cause of defects and time might be required to find an estimate.

The product backlog should reflect the open nature of Agile reporting. It should be visible to everyone so that anyone can contribute ideas, offer suggestions, or indicate possible surprises along the way. It is also important that this list remain authoritative, containing the true state of the product backlog at any time. Poor decisions are often made due to poor information, and an out-of-date product backlog could be disastrous if key release-planning decisions are ill-informed.

Sprint backlog

The sprint backlog contains all of the user stories that are to be completed in the coming sprint. At the start of the sprint, the team selects enough work to fill a sprint based on their current velocity and the relative size of the user stories that are yet to be developed. The priority of the stories is assigned by the product owner. After the stories are committed to the sprint, the team can start to break down each story into tasks that have real-world time estimates in hours. Each individual then elects to implement enough tasks to fill his or her time during the sprint.

The sprint backlog and all of the time estimates are owned by the team. No one outside of the development team can add items to the sprint backlog, nor can they reliably estimate the relative effort or absolute hours required to complete work. The team alone is responsible for the sprint backlog, but they must take work from the product backlog in priority order.

The sprint

The iterations of a Scrum project are called *sprints*. Sprints should last between one and four weeks. Two-week sprints are most popular. A shorter sprint might leave too little time to accomplish the sprint goals, and a longer sprint might cause the team to lose focus.

Sprints are generally referred to by their index number, starting with sprint zero. Sprint zero is intended to prepare the development environment for the whole team, and to carry out some preliminary planning meetings before the first actual sprint begins. There will probably not be any points associated with sprint zero, but a lot can be achieved in those first weeks to make the transition to Scrum easier during subsequent sprints.

The temptation is to align sprints to the working week by starting them on a Monday and ending them on a Friday. The trouble with this is that the sprint retrospective (which will be covered shortly) involves quite a lot of time in meetings, and there is nothing more energy-sapping than sitting in meetings on a Friday afternoon. Some people also tend to leave early on Fridays, and concentration levels are likely to dip before the weekend. Similarly, no one looks forward to starting their week with meetings, so it is best to avoid this and start your sprints around midweek: Tuesday, Wednesday, or Thursday.

The following is an explanation of all of the meetings that form part of each sprint, in order, unless otherwise stated.

Release planning

At some point before the sprint begins, the release of the software must be planned. This involves the customer, the product owner, and a representative of the development team deciding on a release date and prioritizing and sizing the features that are to be included.

Feature estimation

Features can involve a lot of effort, even on the smaller end of the scale. Thus, any attempts to predict the amount of effort required will be off by a wide margin. For this reason, feature effort can be stated in common T-shirt sizes:

- Extra-large (XL)

- Large (L)

- Medium (M)

- Small (S)

- Extra-small (XS)

Tip Estimating in "T-shirt sizes" such as this prevents mathematical equivalence of stories. Two 2-point stories should equal a single 4-point story. But two Small stories might or might not equate to a single Medium story—their relative size is neither clear nor precise. If you do want to maintain an equivalence, your features should be measured in points.

Feature priority

It might be difficult to predict how many features can fit into a release, which is why feature priority is so important. For a specific release, all features can be given one of three priorities:

- Required (R)

- Preferred (P)

- Desired (D)

Required features are the most important parts of a release. Preferred features are the features that should be tackled if any time is available before the deadline looms. Desired features have the lowest priority. These features are not essential—but the customer would certainly like to have them implemented.

In addition, business stakeholders should number the features so that the development team can be sure to implement each feature in priority order.

Sprint planning

The expected outcome of sprint planning is to estimate user stories. As with all parts of the Scrum process, there are variations of the story estimation process. This section discusses planning poker, which is one of the more common ways to generate discussion, and affinity estimation, a quicker way to estimate the relative size of stories. Affinity estimation is better when there are a large number of stories to estimate. For an individual sprint, it is possible to use planning poker if there are only a few stories to estimate, or to use affinity estimation if there is a larger number of stories or if time is short.

Planning poker

The planning poker session involves the whole development team—business analysts, developers, and test analysts—including the Scrum master and the product owner. For every user story that is currently on the product backlog, a small scope explanation is given, and then everyone is asked to vote on its size in story points.

In order to avoid a lot of small-scale differences, it is best to limit the voting options. For example, a common choice is a modified Fibonacci scale: 1, 2, 3, 5, 8, 13, 20, 40, and 100. Regardless of the scale chosen, the choices should be limited overall and the gaps between the options should increase in size as the number of points goes up. At the lower end of the scale, zero can be added to represent "no work required," for a story that might have been obviated by other work. At the upper end of the scale, team members can vote that a story is too big to implement within a sprint and must be vertically split further before being taken off the board to develop.

A few decks of playing cards double well as voting cards, but you can also fashion voting cards from spare index cards or even just scribble numbers on pieces of scrap paper. When it comes time to vote, everyone should show their cards at the same time, to avoid being influenced by the choices of others. It is unlikely that consensus will be achieved all the time, and there could be some large divergences between individual estimates. This is perfectly normal—there are sure to be a couple of outliers who deviate from the modal vote. Each of these voters should be asked to justify his or her choice in light of the general consensus. For example, if someone votes a 1 when the modal vote was 8, that person would be asked—politely, of course—to explain why they think the story requires that much less effort. Similarly, voters who vote above the mode should be asked to explain their reasons, too. All that is occurring here is that a discussion is generated about how much effort the team believes is required to carry a story to its conclusion.

After the justifications have been aired, a revote might be necessary because other people could have been persuaded that their vote was actually too big or too small and that the outlier was in fact correct. Eventually, consensus should be achieved, with all parties agreeing on a suitable number of story points. Each story should be estimated until the number of points assigned reaches the team's current velocity, which is the maximum amount of work that the team should commit to in each sprint.

Affinity estimation

Affinity estimation is provided as a counterpoint to planning poker, which can take a significant amount of time to generate estimates if there are a lot of stories. Rather than entering into a discussion for each story, the team picks two stories from the top of the product backlog and then decides which is the smaller of the two. The smaller is placed on the left side of a table and the larger on the right.

The team then takes a single story from the product backlog and places it where they believe it should go on the spectrum between the existing smaller and larger stories. It could feasibly be placed to the left of the smaller story, indicating that it is smaller still; to the right of the larger, indicating that it is larger still; on top of the small or large story, indicating that it is roughly the same; or anywhere in between the two stories. This process then continues for each story on the product backlog, until there is no more room in the sprint for extra work.

With the stories grouped together by relative size, the team can start at the leftmost group and proceed toward the rightmost group, allocating points to the stories according to the modified Fibonacci sequence. If there are many stories to estimate, or if time is scarce, this is a good way of achieving a ballpark estimate of relative size.

Daily Scrum

Although there are several meetings that will last a couple of hours, the Scrum process itself is only really visible day to day at the daily Scrum, or "stand-up meeting."

The team should gather around the Scrum board in a horseshoe shape and each person, in turn, should address the whole team. The daily Scrum should not last longer than 15 minutes. To focus the meeting, everyone should answer these three questions:

- What did you do yesterday?

- What will you do today?

- What impediments do you face?

The key issues that the daily stand-up meeting addresses are yesterday's actual progress and today's estimated progress. In discussing what you did yesterday, refer to the Scrum board and feel free to move cards across from one swimlane to another or move your avatar from one card to another, thus keeping the Scrum board current. Outline what you worked on and how the day went. If you do not have anything to do at this point, notify the Scrum master and request a new work item. Impediments include anything that might prevent you from completing your goal for the day. Because you will refer back to what you claim you will be doing today in tomorrow's daily Scrum, it is important to enumerate anything that might prevent you from achieving what you plan to do. The impediment could be directly work related, as in, "I will not be able to continue if the network keeps going down like it did yesterday," or it might be a personal matter, as in "I have an appointment with the dentist at 14:00, so I'm unlikely to complete everything." Regardless, the Scrum master should be taking notes so that she knows how everyone is progressing with their stories.

Niko-niko calendar

A "niko-niko calendar"—also sometimes referred to as a "mood board" (in Japanese, "niko-niko" has a meaning close to "smiley")—provides a good barometer of how the team feels about their progress during the sprint. A table is drawn by the Scrum board, with the days of the sprint across the top and the names of the team members down the side, as shown in Figure 1-12.

FIGURE 1-12 A niko-niko calendar quickly shows who is having a good sprint and who is not.

At the Scrum meeting, each person is asked to place one of three stickers on the board—green, yellow, or red—in their square for the previous day. Each sticker corresponds to an overall summary of how the previous day went: good, okay, or bad, respectively. This will quickly show when team members are having consecutive frustrating days and require help, which they might not otherwise seek.

This is just another metric to improve the feedback loop. If all of your team members are consistently feeling bad about their work, perhaps morale needs to be boosted. Or if one of the team is consistently unhappy but the rest of the team is happy, this could indicate that someone is being left behind or doesn't feel like he/she fits in. Worst of all, if the whole team feels happy when sprints are running late, the code is in a mess, and clients are knocking down the door for their money back—the team has stopped caring!

After everyone has spoken, the meeting is over. One thing to be vigilant against is tangential conversations. It is extremely tempting to try to talk through problems during the Scrum. If someone mentions an impediment of some weird and wonderful behavior in the code base, all of the developers will likely want to hypothesize about the possible causes. Be aware of who needs to be present for such conversations—do the test analysts really need to listen to a discussion on why Microsoft Visual Studio is using the coders' entire available RAM? No, most likely not. Make a note of the problem and ask the appropriate people to take the discussion offline (after the meeting).

Sprint demo

A sprint demo is a key event to put in the sprint calendar. It is a showcase of all of the completed stories—those that have met the definition of done during the sprint—in action in a real environment. The entire development team should be present, and you could also invite other stakeholders to the meeting, such as management or sales team representatives. Anyone who might have an interest in the project's progress should be invited to attend. This further fosters an openness that all projects should have.

Collect all of the completed user stories from the Scrum board and, for each one, explain its scope and what it was intended to achieve as part of the project as a whole. Refer to the feature to which the story belongs, and the change in application behavior that has occurred as a result of its implementation. Proceed to demonstrate this behavior by using a real deployment of the system. Invite questions from the audience, but do be careful about off-topic issues or getting sidetracked by irrelevance. Keep the conversation focused, and offer to talk to people individually after the demo has completed. Any suggestions for improvements should feed back into the product backlog so that they are correctly prioritized and scheduled. It sometimes feels that improvements suggested in the demo are suddenly the most important things to be done, but this is rarely a reflection of reality.

The demo should not be feared—it certainly incentivizes progress. No one wants to cancel a demo because nothing has been completed, but resist the temptation to circumvent the definition of done just to demonstrate something. By being honest about progress, you will not have to hide any problems. Instead, point to the charts and metrics to explain probable causes for the reduced output.

Specifying a time before the demo when code will be locked is also a good idea, to prevent those tempting last-minute changes to try to claim more points. Dedicate a realistic amount of time before the demo to set up the environment and ensure that everyone is ready, and guard against throwing reckless technical debt into the code for a short-term boost.

> *Discipline is the ability to consistently choose perpetual benefit over fleeting temptation.*
>
> *Mike Alexander, Fitness Expert*

Sprint retrospective

When the sprint demo is complete, it is time to take stock of the iteration and gauge opinions about its overall success. For some team members, the sprint might have been a resounding success, whereas for others, it might have been an absolute disaster. The sprint retrospective can help you to distill the elements that went well into actions that bear repeating and to isolate problems so that they can be dealt with. The output from the sprint retrospective should not be written once and forever forgotten. It should be referred to at the end of the next sprint to ensure that requisite changes were made and that mistakes were not repeated.

The following questions should be asked of the team during the retrospective:

- What went well?

- What went badly?

- What do we need to start doing?

- What do we need to stop doing?

- What do we need to continue doing?

- Did we experience any surprises during the sprint?

Starting with the positive, ask each team member to elaborate on what they felt went well about the sprint. Perhaps they were very happy with the progress that was made, or with the quality of the work that was produced.

Next, ask them to explain what went badly in the sprint. Perhaps some tasks were more difficult and involved than first anticipated, thus causing an otherwise simple story to be delayed. Whatever the problem, it is certain that some kind of resolution can be found. There is nothing wrong with candidness, as long as it is accompanied by objectivity. No one should be accusatory against other team members, and all criticism should be given constructively and received gracefully. The goal is an improvement of the process and the product, not blame.

It could be that there are certain things that the team does not currently do that should be introduced to the process. Perhaps there are not yet any formal unit tests to accompany the code, and the team believes that this should be introduced at this stage. As with all suggestions, the Scrum master should be actively taking notes to take action later.

Equally, there could be things that the team is doing that they feel should be stopped. Prime examples are to stop unplanned digressions in meetings and to stop moving stories into the In Progress lane when there is plenty of work already there. This latter problem is quite common and can be solved by putting capacity limits on certain swimlanes. By enforcing that no more than three stories can be in progress at a time, team members are encouraged to help finish work that has already begun rather than start something afresh.

Some things that went well will yield actions that bear repeating. If the sprint demo went well and it was decided that this was due to good preparation beforehand, make a note to continue to do this. It is quite surprising how quickly good habits can be forgotten and bad habits can take their place.

Finally, the team should recall any surprises—good or bad—that were revealed during the sprint. Any bad surprise should result in an action item to avoid such an occurrence in the future, whereas a good surprise could result in behavior that bears repeating.

At least one action item from the retrospective should be prioritized for the next sprint. The outcomes of this meeting should not be forgotten; they should be acted on.

Story point triangulation

Some of the stories during the sprint might have required more or less effort than was estimated by the team during the sprint planning meeting. Taking 5 or 10 minutes at the end of the sprint retrospective to triangulate the estimated stories with the actual effort expended can be rewarding.

After a couple of sprints, there will be statistics available for how long each story actually took in comparison to its story point estimate. For example, you might have a table similar to Table 1-1.

TABLE 1-1 Statistics for the average, minimum, and maximum actual effort compared to user story estimates on a hypothetical project.

Story points	Average actual effort (hours)	Minimum actual effort (hours)	Maximum actual effort (hours)
1	5.5	1	19
2	9.5	2	23
3	17	7.5	40
5	36	20	76
8	56	40	86
13	88	68	154

If a one-point story for a sprint actually took 60 hours to complete, it was probably closer to an eight-point story. As long as there were no mitigating circumstances—such as a lack of developer resources because of absence—the estimate can be safely deemed to have been erroneous. If you claim the eight story points instead, your velocity will not suffer as a result, and the amount of stories that the team can commit to does not decrease.

Focus on the stories that are significantly out of range. If a one-point story fits into the range for a two-point or three-point story, it is unlikely to make a significant difference to take more points.

Scrum calendar

For clarity, a calendar showing the typical Scrum meetings over the course of a sprint is shown in Table 1-2.

Observe that almost a whole day is dedicated to the end of a sprint and the beginning of a new sprint. This is called Sprint Handover Day and, to maintain concentration levels, it is sometimes split between two consecutive days: an afternoon and the following morning. The sprint demo and retrospective would then be held Tuesday afternoon, and the planning meeting for the next sprint would be moved to Wednesday morning.

TABLE 1-2 A possible calendar for organizing the Scrum meetings of a sprint for a hypothetical project.

Date (April 2013)	Time	Type of meeting	Attendees
Tuesday 2nd	13:00-15:30	Sprint planning	Development team; product owner
Wednesday 3rd	09:30-09:45	Daily Scrum	Development team
Thursday 4th	09:30-09:45	Daily Scrum	Development team
Friday 5th	09:30-09:45	Daily Scrum	Development team
Monday 8th	09:30-09:45	Daily Scrum	Development team
Tuesday 9th	09:30-09:45	Daily Scrum	Development team
Wednesday 10th	09:30-09:45	Daily Scrum	Development team
Thursday 11th	09:30-09:45	Daily Scrum	Development team
Friday 12th	09:30-09:45	Daily Scrum	Development team
Monday 15th	09:30-09:45	Daily Scrum	Development team
Tuesday 16th	10:00-11:20 11:30-12:00 13:00-15:30	Sprint demonstration Sprint retrospective Sprint planning	Anyone Development team Development team; product owner

Another interesting point is the timing of the daily Scrum. If it is too early in the day, attendance can be a problem because people could be delayed by traffic or otherwise waylaid. If it is too late, dragging people from their desks when they are already involved in a task is also difficult.

These meetings can be added to Microsoft Outlook or some other calendar program, with the relevant people attached as attendees.

Agile in the real world

Agile processes are not a miracle solution, destined to turn every failing project to profitability and success. The aim of any software development process is to create repeatable success when delivering software, but that software still needs to be written. No amount of documentation can remove the fact that a software product is the result of working source code.

This book teaches developers how to create software solutions that are *adaptive*. This means that they are resilient to the sort of change to which all software is subjected. It is irrational to assume that the first attempt at a solution will meet all of the needs of the customer, so change is inevitable. Agile processes—and Scrum is no exception—aim to embrace this change and seek to ensure that customers are allowed to make alterations to the behavior of the software as it is developed. Otherwise, they would be forced to accept a substandard solution that misses the mark.

Code that is not *adaptive* is *maladaptive*. If code is maladaptive, it does not readily lend itself to change. The estimates that the team assigned to various tasks could be significantly different from reality because the code takes much longer to change than it should. Changing the code might also result in the introduction of defects that will eventually take further time, effort, and resources to be fixed.

The rest of this section addresses some of the issues that Agile frameworks alone cannot solve when you are striving for adaptive code.

Rigidity

Code can display a few different signs of rigidity, each of which needs to be addressed so that changes don't become increasingly difficult, limiting the number of features that can be delivered.

Lack of abstractions

An abstraction hides the details of something, showing instead a much simpler representation. Abstractions are all around us. The steering wheel in your car abstracts the mechanical implementation that eventually turns the wheels in either direction. In fact, there are two common types of steering: rack-and-pinion steering and recirculating-ball steering. In either implementation, the end result is that both of the wheels turn to match how much you have turned the steering wheel, in relative terms. Also, the left and right wheels do not turn the same amount. Because the inside wheel traces a circle of smaller radius than the outside wheel, it must turn more tightly than the outside wheel.

Of course, you do not need to know any of this to drive a car. Sure, the knowledge might help you diagnose problems or explain how the system works, but as an everyday driver, all this is extraneous information that is not vital to you. The abstraction hides as many details as it can and gives you just enough to get by.

In software, abstractions are key. The user interface does not need to know what storage medium is being used to house the user's input. In fact, if it does know this, there is a lack of abstraction, and the user interface becomes hopelessly obsessed with details that it should not be concerned with.

Code with sufficient abstractions will be better organized, easier to understand and communicate to others, and easier to maintain, and it will contain fewer errors.

Too many abstractions

Abstractions are good. But there can be too many abstractions. This is because abstractions are not free. Every abstraction comes with a cost—in lower readability and reasonability. Code should be written to be readable by humans first and foremost. Compilers are the tools that convert your code to executable instructions, but they care little for readability.

Do not write code so that it can be parsed by a compiler. Write code so that it can be understood by a human. Too many abstractions will make your code less readable by others. Overcomplicating a solution is as much a problem for adaptability as a lack of patterns and best practices.

Mixed responsibilities

Often, code gradually grows organically from something small, perhaps even trivial, to something much bigger and more important. Incremental changes are made, one on top of the other, until some critical point is reached when a single change can have many related and unpredictable consequences.

This sort of code contains methods, classes, and possibly even whole modules that have no single discernable purpose. Instead, each fulfills several different responsibilities that cannot be easily separated. In this code, a change that *should* only take a few hours to complete can easily end up taking a day or more of wrestling with the side-effects that one change has on another, ostensibly unrelated, area of the code.

To avoid this, ensure that code at every level—methods, classes, and modules—focuses on one well-defined responsibility.

Untestability

Unit testing has been an established practice for many years now. It is a reliable method of ensuring code correctness that should feel entirely natural to many developers. However, it takes constant discipline and diligence to ensure that code remains testable over the long term.

If code is untestable, it is untested. If code is untested, it *will* contain defects. You must simply assume that untested code contains defects. That is the level of suspicion with which you should treat such code.

The following concepts, and testability in general, are discussed in further detail in Chapter 5, "Testing."

Skyhooks vs. cranes

Daniel C. Dennett wrote in his 1995 book, *Darwin's Dangerous Idea* [emphasis mine]:

> "A **skyhook** is ... an exception to the principle that all design, and apparent design, is ultimately the result of mindless, motiveless mechanicity. A **crane**, in contrast, is a subprocess or special feature of a design process that can be demonstrated to permit the local speeding up of the basic, slow process of natural selection, and that can be demonstrated to be itself the predictable (or retrospectively explicable) product of the basic process."
>
> *Daniel C. Dennett,*
> *Darwin's Dangerous Idea: Evolution and the Meaning of Life, 1995 [Simon & Schuster]*

Sidestepping the religiosity of the content, put simply, a skyhook is a way to explain something without reference to a prior antecedent. Conversely, cranes have explicable antecedents—perhaps until arriving at some primary axiom.

This is a useful analogy in programming, too. Skyhooks are indicative of a deeper problem. All skyhooks should be replaced with appropriate cranes.

The presence of a skyhook in code is difficult to replace with a fake implementation, thereby reducing testability. Examples of skyhooks are:

- Static methods

- Static classes (including singletons)

- Object construction that uses new

- Extension methods

Each of these make testing more difficult[1] by hindering your ability to inject mocks into your code; they are skyhooks and thus they are undesirable. Each is used *ex nihilo*—from nothing.

Luckily, each of these can be replaced with a suitable crane, such as the following, that will facilitate some kind of external injection (that is, it can be used *ex materia*—from something):

- Interfaces

- Dependency injection

- Inversion of control

- Factories

In subsequent chapters of this book, each of these "cranes" of programming is explained in more detail.

Metrics

Source code has been subject to many different metrics through the years, each of which attempts to reduce the complexity of code down to numbers that indicate the health—or otherwise—of the project as a whole.

This might seem rather reductive, but metrics have evolved somewhat since middle-management obsessed over source lines of code (SLOC). Although SLOC correlates well to the effort required—it takes longer to write more lines of code than it does to write fewer—it does not necessarily correlate to the level of functionality of a system. Nor, indeed, is it a reliable measure of a developer's productivity.

---

[1] Difficult, though not impossible. Some mocking frameworks, such as TypeMock (*www.typemock.com*), are able to mock skyhooks. However, this should only be considered if the skyhooks are in third-party, unchangeable code.

Unit test coverage

Unit test coverage is a measurement of the percentage of the code that is covered by unit tests. This ranges from 0 percent, indicating that none of the code is covered by any tests, to 100 percent, where every line of code is covered by at least one unit test. Typically, coverage of 80 percent is considered a minimum acceptable level.

In addition to the unit tests, unit test coverage tools should be run by the continuous integration server, which will compile the code every time it is committed to source control. This will allow you to gain fast feedback on any movements in code coverage.

Test coverage is somewhat misleading, because it is a quantitative measure of the unit tests, as opposed to a qualitative measure. It is easy to increase code coverage with *any* tests, as opposed to the *right* tests.

If test coverage is below 80 percent—or whatever your chosen benchmark is—then it can be incrementally increased over time toward your overall coverage goal. With each increase, the continuous integration build should be configured to fail if the coverage percentage slips backward. This means that no new production code can be added without accompanying unit tests, otherwise the coverage percentage would be diluted and would decline.

Cyclomatic complexity

Cyclomatic complexity is a measure of the number of paths that exist in the code. With each additional branch in the code—*if* statements, loops, or *switch* statements—the cyclomatic complexity increases. As Figure 1-13 shows, a simple *if* statement and inner loop can be modeled as a graph. As the figure shows, the total number of paths through the statement and loop is equal to the cyclomatic complexity of the code.

The edge labeled 1 is the case when the *if* statement has a *false* condition, thus its body is not executed. Edge 2 is when the *if* statement's body is executed, but the contained loop is not. Edge 3 is the case when both the *if* statement and loop are executed.

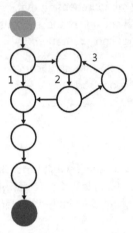

FIGURE 1-13 Each extra path through the code adds further complexity.

As cyclomatic complexity increases, the testing effort required to gain unit test code coverage on each branch also increases. Therefore, it is best to keep branching, and thus cyclomatic complexity, low to avoid extra test code.

To calculate cyclomatic complexity, take the number of edges in the graph, subtract the number of nodes in the graph, and add twice the number of connected components. A *connected component* is a set of nodes that can be traversed by following the edges. Usually there is only one connected component in a single codebase.

Cyclomatic Complexity = # Edges - # Nodes + 2

Refer to Figure 1-13 as an example: there are nine nodes with 10 edges and one connected component. Thus, the code represented by this graph has a cyclomatic complexity measurement of $10 - 9 + 2 \times 1 = 3$.

There is also a statistical correlation between high complexity and defect count. That is, code with more branching tends to have more defects.

Conclusion

This chapter has served as an introduction to the Scrum process. If you have never worked on a Scrum project, I hope that your interest has now been piqued sufficiently to do so. On the other hand, if you do work on a Scrum project, perhaps there were some new ideas in this chapter that you want to use.

Though there is admittedly a lot of ground still not covered in this chapter with respect to Scrum, the rest of the book is dedicated more to the developer's point of view of an Agile project. However, there are plenty of resources available for learning more about Scrum and discovering whether it is a good fit for your company and your projects.

Scrum projects, like any software projects, are vulnerable to failure. Spotting when something is going wrong is a significant part of the battle, but spotting why it is happening can be even harder. The internal machinations of the code might be designed in a way that makes change very difficult—no matter what process is in place for managing this change. The rest of this book will provide advice and guidelines for ensuring that code is adaptive from the bottom up, making change easier and allowing you to focus solely on adding business value with every sprint.

CHAPTER 2

Introduction to Kanban

After completing this chapter, you will be able to

- Create a Kanban board for your current process and continuously improve it.

- Vary work-in-progress limits and classes of service to optimize your productivity.

- Diagnose and resolve problems that Kanban highlights.

- Analyze the efficiency and effectiveness of your workflow.

- Compare and contrast the pros and cons of Kanban versus Scrum.

Kanban is a very simple process with minimal rules and a handful of general guidelines. As with any process, it can be well applied or misapplied, depending on the context. The work itself might be a good fit for Kanban, or it could be a bad fit. Similarly, because a process is performed by people, the team's Agile maturity and discipline play a significant part in Kanban's success.

Kanban was created by the Toyota car manufacturing company in the 1950s. Research into supply chain management in supermarkets resulted in the creation of a feedback loop whereby demand can be used to limit the supply at each phase of production. Toyota identified that supermarkets were supremely efficient in ensuring that stock levels were high enough to consistently meet demand, yet low enough to prevent overstocking.

Since then, Kanban has been reappropriated from the manufacturing world to the software delivery world, with great success.

Kanban quickstart

The best way to find out whether Kanban is right for your team is to try it. No amount of theoretical pondering or anecdotal hearsay can match a healthy dose of experiential evidence. Remember that no two teams are the same, just as no two people are the same. What might have worked with one set of people might not necessarily work again with a different set.

To get you up and running as fast as possible, this section walks you through the basics. Each subsequent part of this chapter goes into more detail.

The information radiator

The Kanban board acts as an information radiator. Anyone within the business should be able to view the Kanban board. Although its viewers might not entirely understand all of the intricacies of the information without additional context, the general progress of cards should be immediately apparent.

> **Note** *Kanban* means *sign board*. Technically, this makes the term *Kanban board* redundant, because the *board* is implied, but *Kanban* is often used to refer to the process itself.

Figure 2-1 shows the simplest example of a Kanban board. It includes only three columns mapping to the phases of work. It is so simple and general that it can apply to any kind of work at all—from household chores such as vacuuming or washing dishes to more complex projects like writing a book. Work is either not yet started, currently in progress, or completed. These states map to the columns To Do, Doing, and Done, respectively.

To Do	Doing	Done

FIGURE 2-1 Kanban boards can be incredibly simple, capturing only a high-level process overview.

The popular online work-tracking software Trello uses this same default set of columns, but they are configurable. Figure 2-2 shows a screenshot from the Trello board that was used to track the progress of writing this book. Trello is a good option for tracking the work of projects that use a simple process.

The columns on the Kanban board represent the stages of work in progress. Place the Kanban board in a prominent position as close to the team as possible. All Agile processes rely on transparency to perform to their potential, and Kanban is no exception. In fact, Kanban often *exposes* deficiencies in process, and these pain points should be made very visible, not hidden away.

FIGURE 2-2 Trello is a popular online service that offers customizable Kanban boards for free.

Consider the analogy of two opposing ways in which code can fail: noisily and obviously through an uncaught exception, or silently and insidiously through an unintended state transition. In the former example, the service or application fails and is unable to function. In the latter example, it continues to run but with unintended consequences that might cause greater harm. You want your process failures to be loud and obvious, and you also want them to be *fast*. It is likely that the early stages of integrating a Kanban process will be painful and will highlight many issues with your process. This is intentional and emphasizes the strength of Kanban to iteratively improve on your process.

Process capture

To start integrating a Kanban process, first capture your *current* process. It does not matter whether you feel that your current process is wrong, too convoluted, or too manual. By capturing your current process, you show how things *are*, rather than focusing on how you want them to be.

At this early stage, ignore the activities that are external to the team and focus solely on the parts of the process that team members perform.

Figure 2-3 shows a basic outline of the process for delivering features into a production environment for a software development team. Each column represents a state that work can be in along its journey to delivery. These states are mutually exclusive; all work wholly resides in one column or another—it cannot straddle columns.

Wait	Analyze	Implement	Verify	Deliver

FIGURE 2-3 A Kanban board customized for a simple software development process.

The column headers have been deliberately chosen to state their purpose. *Backlog* is not as clear as *Wait*. The former is a noun describing a concept of the process that requires further context. The latter is a verb describing the ultimate purpose of the column and the items therein. It is much clearer to the casual observer or those unfamiliar with software development processes to indicate the activity that is performed in each state. Because this is a good example of a common software delivery process, each column—or state—bears further explanation:

- **Wait**   This is the common backlog of work to be started. Work items in this column are not yet in progress but are *possible* options for future work. Whether the items within it are bugs, features, technical improvements, or tasks, the backlog is a container for "stuff" that might or might not eventually be worked on. Items are ordered by priority so that the next item is at the top of the column and proceeds in a first-in-first-out (FIFO) queued fashion.

- **Analyze**   Most items in the backlog are single-sentence ideas or descriptions of the problem at hand. No solutions have been decided, and little detail is present. The Analyze column is where sufficient detail is added to the work so that it becomes ready for development. Although some insight into implementation options might be presented, this column emphasizes *what* needs to be done rather than *how* it is to be done.

- **Implement**   Implementation can now begin, and developers take over to write the code necessary to add new functionality. This is often the slowest part of the software delivery process and, as this chapter will show, there are ways of optimizing your process to maximize throughput despite this.

- **Verify**   Although some degree of unit testing is expected of the developers in the Implement phase, it is likely that manual and/or automated verification forms part of your delivery process. This is the final gate before the work is delivered, so there should be a high bar set to ensure the consistent quality of work products.

- **Deliver**   When you deliver software, you realize the value that, to this point, has been in progress. All work is incomplete until you have passed through this phase of the process.

The Kanban board in Figure 2-4 includes a new and important detail. Except for the Wait column, each column has been further split into two halves. Although each half has a label specific to the sub-state that the column represents, in each state, the leftmost column represents work in progress and the rightmost column represents work that is ready and waiting for the next phase. The leftmost label, therefore, represents the activity that is being performed on the work, whereas the rightmost label represents the result of that activity.

Wait	Analyze		Implement		Verify		Deliver	
	Specifying	Ready for Dev	Coding	Dev Complete	Investigating	Accepted	Deploying	Value Added

FIGURE 2-4 Some phases of a process might have sub-states that represent completion of the parent phase.

Figure 2-5 shows a Kanban board with numbers below some of the column heads or sub-column heads. These numbers represent limits on work in progress (WIP).

One of the key tenets of Kanban is the enforcement of limits on work in progress. Each work item placed under a column header counts toward that column's WIP limit.

Wait	Analyze		Implement		Verify		Deliver	
	3		5		2			
	Specifying	Ready for Dev	Coding	Dev Complete	Investigating	Accepted	Deploying	Value Added
							1	

FIGURE 2-5 Work-in-progress limits can apply to either columns or their sub-columns.

The addition of work items to the board shown in Figure 2-6 shows that the Implement column has reached its WIP limit, and no more items can transition to this state. However, the Analyze column has not yet reached its WIP limit, so another work item can be moved into the Analyze column.

Wait	Analyze		Implement		Verify		Deliver	
	3		5		2			
	Specifying	Ready for Dev	Coding	Dev Complete	Investigating	Accepted	Deploying	Value Added
							1	

FIGURE 2-6 The count of work items in all sub-columns contributes to the column's work-in-progress limit.

Note that the Wait column does not have an associated WIP limit. This allows an infinite number of work items to be placed into the Wait column. Consider the pros and cons of this approach. This allows many new ideas to be captured as work items on the board without limit. But the column can become overloaded and the team overwhelmed by the amount of apparent work that is upcoming. Perhaps limiting the number of items in the Wait column would be a sensible option because, if something is important enough, it will come up again and will eventually be added to the board.

Similar to the Wait column, the Value Added sub-column does not have a WIP limit. The value of this is not so ambiguous, because you do not want to artificially constrain the amount of work that can be delivered. To do so would not make sense, because you want to complete as much work as possible in any particular timeframe.

Limiting work in progress

The purpose of setting limits on work in progress is to maximize the throughput of the team. A software feature is not truly done until it has passed through all phases of delivery: analysis, implementation, testing, and deployment. Therefore, it is inefficient to start specifying many more work items than the developers can feasibly handle. By limiting the work that business analysts can do, you match their progress to that of the slowest step. More often than not, the slowest part of software delivery is implementation.

Protecting against change

Setting WIP limits also protects the team against change. If something occurs during delivery that prevents a feature from being implemented—perhaps a forecasted return on investment (ROI) is discovered to be miscalculated—limiting the amount of work in progress has the advantage of lowering the sunken cost.

Protecting against change is a facet of many software methodologies. Waterfall methodologies protect against change by trying to prevent change from occurring at all. Such processes disallow changes to prior-phase deliverables without significant expense and ceremony. Scrum protects against change by locking the sprint so that new requests for functionality must wait until the next sprint planning meeting to be factored into the plan. Kanban uses WIP limits to protect against change, to mitigate the cost of change. In this way, Kanban could be claimed to embrace change even more than Scrum.

Defining "done"

Each column on the Kanban board aligns to a phase of delivery. No value is realized until changes to software are delivered, most often through deployment of some sort. However, each phase of the process has its own definition of what "done" means, and it is important that all team members are aware of, and agree to, these definitions.

The definition of done can be a checklist of items that must be complete before a work item can move from one column to another. This checklist can be printed out and placed by the column headers on the board for any team member to reference. Some sample checklists are outlined here as a starting point, but do revise these and mold them to your own circumstances. A retrospective (see "Event-driven ceremonies" later in this chapter) is a good opportunity to periodically refine the details of the process.

Analyze: Specifying done

Work items in the Specifying sub-column are considered done when:

- Work has been right-sized so that it is manageable.

- A specification of expected functionality has been provided.

- A specification of behavior under error conditions has been provided.

- User interface mockups are provided where applicable.

- Cross-functional requirements are provided where applicable.

- Key Performance Indicators (KPIs) are generated to assess the added value.

Implement: Coding done

Work items in the Coding sub-column are considered done when:

- Unit test coverage for new code artifacts is at least 80 percent.

- Unit test coverage for existing code artifacts has not decreased.

- All unit tests pass without ambiguity.

- Code has been peer reviewed and accepted.

Verify: Investigating done

Work items in the Investigating sub-column are considered done when:

- Automated acceptance tests pass.

- Functional testing does not uncover defects.

- Functional testing matches the specification of work.

- Existing functionality is intact.

Deliver: Deploying done

Work items in the Deploying sub-column are considered done when:

- Features are deployed across all targets.

- KPIs are measured and indicate an increase in value.

- The features have been in use for at least 24 hours.

- No errors or warnings have been reported.

As you can see, these items are rigorous but also fairly generic. As part of the Analyze: Specifying phase, it is expected that further items would be generated that are tailored to each piece of work.

Event-driven ceremonies

The main event that can cause the scheduling of a meeting is the emptying of a column on the Kanban board. If an in-progress column becomes empty, the team will pull across the next ticket from the column immediately to the left of the empty column. Although the words *meeting* and *ceremony* imply a certain level of pomp and circumstance (and boredom), these meetings need not be formal.

> **Tip** Of course, the threshold for holding a meeting such as this does not have to be an empty column. Instead, the threshold could be set at one or two tickets remaining. This prevents the team from completely running out of work that can be progressed, in favor of buffering to allow some work to continue in parallel.

Meetings of this kind can be held at the Kanban board, rather than in a meeting room, saving on resources and setup time. These meetings also do not have to include everyone who is part of the team. Only invite and include those team members to whom the meeting is relevant, to avoid forcing a context switch on someone who is busily—and happily—making progress on real work.

If the column that is empty is, for example, the Wait column, the team can assemble and create new tickets for the backlog based on the product roadmap. Otherwise, if the empty column is the Implement column, the highest priority ticket from the Analyze column can be pulled into the Coding sub-column. At this point, the state transition of a ticket from Analyze: Complete to Development: Coding might necessitate some initial setup work.

For example, it would be sensible to involve any Quality Assurance team members to help specify acceptance criteria for the ticket, so that the developers know from the outset what "done" truly looks like. The team can also split the ticket into tasks that might relate to the layers of the application, so that suitable experts can assign themselves to front-end, middle-tier, or back-end work. This is also a chance for developers to indicate that a ticket is currently too big because it would require too much effort to complete in one piece. Team members can make compromises on the functionality or implementation of the ticket. All of this happens informally at the Kanban board, with team members amending the tickets and adding checklists.

If you follow an event-driven model for scheduling meetings such as this, the agenda is already set for you and there is no need to force the team into a state of enthusiasm. It is likely to result in more frequent meetings of much shorter length, which are more effective than infrequent, long meetings that are energy sapping and momentum killing.

Be vigilant in identifying other scenarios in which an impromptu meeting would help. Instead of asking the team members to store up their good and bad experiences until the end of the sprint for discussion at the retrospective, have everyone gather around quickly to define an action point. Just be careful to avoid interrupting people constantly and breaking their flow. Development is an act of productive creation, and as such, it requires large blocks of time without interruption. If possible, put a block on all morning or afternoon meetings and interruptions so that at least half of the day is available for pure, productive flow.

Classes of service

The previous section covered the importance of right-sizing work. Although some processes allow for work of differing sizes to be tracked, Kanban works best when work is fairly similar with respect to the effort involved. However, some kinds of work are different from others in ways that make comparisons futile. For example, in software development, fixing bugs is different from adding new features, and adding new features is different from tackling technical debt.

Although Kanban strives to have work of roughly equal size, it cannot control the fact that each ticket will have its own risk profile. Some work is inherently high-risk, whereas other work might be low-risk. It is also unlikely that the risk for a ticket will remain constant over time. It is more likely for the risk to increase over time, to a point where it could either asymptote to infinity or plateau to a constant.

Introducing a class of service to your Kanban process can help when the work has different risk profiles. This enables the team to identify the work that is of high urgency or importance, and to focus their effort there if necessary.

The Kanban board must be able to differentiate between tickets that belong to different classes of service. This can be done by using different-colored sticky notes, or by using markers on the tickets. The latter option is how the Kanban board for this book differentiated between tickets related to code and tickets related to chapter content. The two are very different types of work, thus it makes sense to separate them into different classes of service.

When classes of service have been determined and the board clearly displays the differences, there are a couple of extra features of Kanban that can be used: service level agreements (SLAs) and class WIP limits.

Service level agreements

Kanban allows you to forgo estimation of effort in favor of service level agreements. Recall that Scrum's estimation meetings produce a number of "story points," which equate to a range of the real-time effort involved in completing the story. Instead, Kanban uses statistics to generate a time estimate and a confidence level for that estimate.

If you record the time that it takes for each ticket to be completed, over time, you can calculate the average time taken. Because all of the work has been homogenized, there should not be much deviation in size, but sometimes an uncommonly large ticket might sneak through your checks and balances. Furthermore, the "average" is often a charlatan; it is entirely possible that no one ticket has ever taken an "average" time to complete.

Imagine a team that has completed 20 tickets, with the duration of each—in days—being as follows:

1,1,2,2,3,3,3,4,4,5,5,7,8,8,8,9,9,10,10,18

The total time taken is 120 days. Split between 20 tickets, this equates to an average of precisely 6 days per ticket. However, there has been no single ticket that has taken 6 days so far. This is the fallacy of the average. If you were to give 6 days as your estimate of how long any particular ticket could take, you would have delivered faster 11 times and would have overrun 9 times. At worst, you would have been 300 percent wrong with your estimate! Also, you would never have been precisely accurate.

> **Tip** Of course, estimates are not deadlines. If your managers believe to their core that estimates are merely estimates, many people would envy you. But let's help our misguided colleagues by attaching to our estimates a confidence interval.

If you say you estimate that something will be complete within six days and attach a confidence of 50 percent to that estimate, your stakeholders will be disinclined to treat it as a deadline. But what if you could attach a 95-percent confidence to your estimate? There is margin for error, but it would be a more accurate portrayal of progress.

What you need to find is the number that represents the 95th percentile of your data.

Nearest rank percentile

To find the nearest rank in the list of ticket durations provided earlier in this section, you would use the following formula:

$n = ((p / 100) * N)$

Plugging your values into the formula gives you the following result:

$n = 95/100 * 20$

$n = 19/20 * 20$

$n = 19$

Therefore, the 19th number in the sorted list is your 95th percentile. This results in an estimate of 10 days. Note that this method says nothing of the magnitude of possible overrun if your estimate is wrong. Whether that 20th number was 18 or 180, the long-tail value is ignored in this calculation, so even adding a confidence interval does not give the full picture.

> **Tip** The sample interval here is relatively low. If you can deliver an average of only four tickets per week, it would take five weeks to get a sample size large enough to calculate the 95th percentile.

Now that you can give a more accurate estimate of the time that a ticket might take, you can attach an SLA to your classes of service. For each ticket type, the SLA can state a different 95th percentile estimate for completion.

In the case of defect tickets, a shorter cycle time—and therefore a better SLA—can be given. This highlights the importance of fixing defects over normal feature-delivery work.

Similarly, dedicated refactor or redesign tickets can take longer than standard feature-delivery work. This allows for a longer cycle time and a shorter SLA.

In summary, by separating classes of service, it is possible to treat various work streams differently. This removes what would be outliers if you were to group together work items. SLAs can be attached to classes of service, rather than to the team's work as a whole.

Class WIP limits

Another advantage of separate classes of service is the ability to specify work-in-progress (WIP) limits for each category rather than for any work that arrives in a column.

This is useful when you have some types of work that you want to ensure make some progress without stalling and without dominating the team's time. The best example of this is refactor work. For the uninitiated, refactoring is covered in further detail in Chapter 6, "Refactoring."

Ideally, refactoring would be a consistent part of every ticket that is being developed, included as acceptance criteria on the definition of done. Sometimes the amount of technical debt present in a codebase is so great that it hampers delivery and can overwhelm the team. This can lead to the judicious use of refactor tickets to pay down some specific areas of technical debt. Create a class of service of this refactor work and attach a WIP limit. Kept low, this WIP limit will prevent the entire team from spending a lot of time refactoring at the expense of delivering features. But as long as the WIP limit is greater than zero and the general work's WIP limit is low enough to leave spare developers, the refactoring work should naturally get done.

If there is low level of ambient refactoring that must be done to return the codebase to optimal health and adaptiveness, perhaps only 25 percent of the total WIP limit needs to be assigned to the refactoring class of service.

However, if the codebase is in a particularly unhealthy state whereby adding features is unnecessarily complex, assigning 75 percent of the total WIP limit could make sense. This should not block all feature delivery; it should just limit what can realistically be accomplished while tackling the technical debt.

People as a class of service

If your team is truly a representative vertical slice of functionality through the product, it might include front-end, middle-tier, and data back-end specialists. Some work might cut across all of these disciplines, others might cut across two layers, and others might be isolated to just one layer. Depending on the availability of certain specialists, it might be necessary to specify a class of service that aligns to these layers.

This allows a ticket with front-end user experience and design work attached to it to be treated differently from middle-tier-only work, for example. This front-end work might have a longer SLA as a result, so that you can communicate to stakeholders that any work involving front-end development takes three or four days longer at the 95th percentile. This sort of insight into the process is exactly what Kanban is good at illuminating. Decisions could then be taken to reallocate people to this team to expedite the front-end work.

Similarly, if only one database expert is available in the team, any work that makes it into development that requires this expert will occupy that person for the duration. This should consume the entire WIP limit budget for this person, because they are unable to contribute to any other tickets that involve the data layer. However, middle-tier and front-end work should be unaffected if they are not involved in the completion of the ticket.

Just remember that tickets should not be specifically crafted to align to these layers, because there is typically no discernible value without all layers involved.

Integrating classes of service is an advanced feature of a Kanban framework. It is unlikely that you can capture your current process, map it to a Kanban board, communicate this new way of working, and track all required metrics all at the same time, and even less likely that you could add in classes of service from the outset. Instead, iterate toward this advanced level over time.

Analysis

During the delivery of software products, your process should aid you in making decisions. It should indicate the overall health of your progress. Ideally, the process—or its artefacts—should not only show clearly that something is wrong, but also point to what it is that is wrong.

Kanban generates artefacts that indeed allow for a diagnosis of what is failing on a feature's path to completion. This section introduces the Key Performance Indicators (KPIs) of *lead time* and *cycle time*. The *cumulative flow diagram* is also explained, in addition to how to differentiate between a healthy flow and a range of unhealthy flows.

Lead time and cycle time

Work items start in a backlog column on the Kanban board. This could be a "To Do" column or a "Wait" column. It could even be a generic "Backlog" column. Regardless of its name, such a column is where you place work that has been requested but not yet started. It is possible that anyone can put anything into the backlog at any time. However, how long will it take for items placed on the backlog to be done? You can answer this question by analyzing the team's throughput of work and extracting metrics such as lead time and cycle time.

The backlog itself is prioritized so that items toward the top of the column are of higher priority than those toward the bottom of the column. When an item is added to the backlog, the date that it was placed there should be noted. This can be written directly on the ticket if your Kanban board is physical. Most virtual Kanban board tools will automatically store the date that a work item was added to the backlog.

When there is capacity available in the next column, the ticket is moved into an in-progress column. As earlier examples showed, there can be multiple columns that are collectively classified as in-progress. Generally, the first column on the Kanban board is the backlog, and the final column is reserved for work items that are done. All columns between these two, therefore, are considered in-progress columns. When a work item is moved into the first in-progress column, the date is again written on the card—or otherwise noted.

After all work has been completed for a piece of work, it is finally moved into the done column. This is a column without a work-in-progress limit. so it can hold any number of work items. The definition of done that has been defined for each phase of work in progress should act as a quality gate for whether a ticket is done or not. When the work item enters the done column, a final date is captured on the item.

The time spent in each of the phases of delivery can be calculated by using each of the dates that have been written on the card. The time that a work item was waiting is the difference between the date that the card moved into the first in-progress column and the date that the card first entered the backlog. The time that the work item was in progress is the difference between the date that the card was moved into the done column and the date that work first started for this item. This latter timing for a work item is also known as the *cycle time*. Adding the two timings together produces the work item's *lead time*.

This measurement doesn't have to be particularly precise—the number of days will suffice. Although it is possible to measure both lead time and cycle time in hours, it is less likely that stakeholders will request estimates in hours.

Cycle time = Time spent in progress

Lead time = Time spent waiting in backlog + cycle time

Figure 2-7 shows the progression of a Kanban board over four days. On the first day, three items are added to the To Do column and there is no work in progress and no work done. On the second day, items 1 and 2 move into the Doing column and a new item is added to the To Do column. On the third day, no in-progress work was completed, and two more items were added to the To Do column. On the fourth day, item 1 moves to the Done column, which frees up space in the WIP limit for item 3 to move into the Doing column.

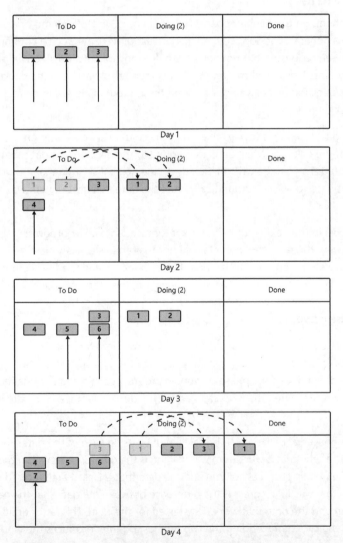

FIGURE 2-7 The movement of tickets across the board as development progresses.

Taking work item 1 as an example, let's calculate its cycle time and the lead time. The cycle time is the difference between the date that work was completed on the ticket and the date that the work was started. On day 4, the work was completed for work item 1; it was moved into the Doing column on day 2. Therefore, the cycle time for this work item is 2 days.

The lead time is the difference between the date that the work was completed on the ticket and the date that the ticket was first added to the backlog column. It is already known from the prior example that work item 1 was completed on day 4 and added to the backlog on day 1; therefore, the lead time for this work item is 3 days.

Cumulative flow diagrams

Let's tabulate the count of work items in each column on each day and then graph the results. This can reveal some interesting patterns that can help you assess the health of the delivery process and diagnose problems that need attention.

Simple example

The data in Table 2-1 shows the count of work items in each column of a simple three-column Kanban board. The columns of the board are the generic workflow To Do, Doing, and Done. Each day of progress is labeled with a number, starting at 1.

TABLE 2-1 The count of work items in each column of a Kanban board, by day.

Day	To Do	Doing	Done
1	3	0	0
2	2	2	0
3	2	2	1
4	2	2	1
5	3	2	2
6	2	2	3
7	2	2	4
8	2	2	4
9	2	2	5
10	2	1	7

By graphing this table of data as a stacked area chart with the number of work items on the y-axis and the day number on the x-axis, you can create the simple cumulative flow diagram shown in Figure 2-8.

FIGURE 2-8 A simple cumulative flow diagram for a simple three-phase process.

Note how the work that is apportioned between To Do, Doing, and Done changes as the days progress. As work items move from To Do to Doing, the mid-gray band increases in size, and as work items move from Doing to Done, the dark-gray band increases in size.

Lead time, cycle time, and work in progress

Taking measurements of parts of a cumulative flow diagram along the x-axis and y-axis provides values for the various metrics used in analyzing the health of a Kanban board. Figure 2-9 shows these measurements on the example cumulative flow diagram.

FIGURE 2-9 How to quickly read the key metrics of process health from a cumulative flow diagram.

The measurements for each metric are taken as follows:

- **Lead time**   Measuring the x-axis distance between the To Do and Done areas gives the lead time of work items.

- **Cycle time**   Measuring the x-axis distance between the Doing and Done areas gives the cycle time of work items.

- **Work in progress**   Measuring the y-axis distance between the Doing and Done areas gives the total number of work items that are currently in progress.

Healthy flow

Returning to the example from earlier in this chapter, Figure 2-10 shows the cumulative flow diagram for a general software delivery process.

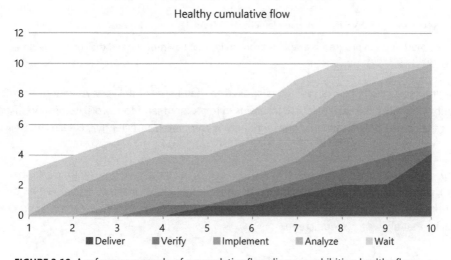

FIGURE 2-10 A reference example of a cumulative flow diagram exhibiting healthy flow.

Let's recap: The Deliver state represents work items that have been completed. The Wait state represents work that is yet to be started. Work in progress, then, is represented by the aggregation of each of the other states: Analyze, Implement, and Verify.

The lead time, cycle time, and work in progress can still be found on this graph by considering all three of those states to be work that is currently underway.

Unhealthy flows

Healthy flows are great, but very few software projects exhibit such smooth running from start to finish. More commonly, one or more unhealthy flows are encountered and, ideally, corrected before causing terminal damage to delivery.

This section shows some of the most common problems with delivery that are easy to spot when visualized on a cumulative flow diagram.

Too much work in progress The first and most common problem is shown in Figure 2-11: too much work in progress. By only day 3, the board is saturated with eight work items, and by day 5, all of the work items are in progress.

FIGURE 2-11 Too much work in progress is a serious problem in a Kanban process, and the cumulative flow diagram will make this obvious.

This happens because of a lack of WIP limits applied to the phases of delivery. At various times there are four work items in Analyze, four work items in Implement, and four work items in Verify. As a result, over the course of 10 days, only one work item is completed sufficiently to reach the Deliver state.

Scope creep Figure 2-12 shows the result of scope creep on a cumulative flow diagram. Kanban is a pull system, which means that work items are only moved into a new phase of delivery when there is capacity, but often the backlog for waiting work items has no limit on capacity. It is this apparently infinite capacity that allows for scope creep.

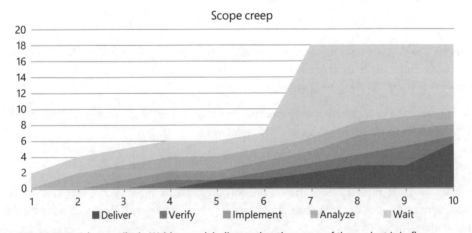

FIGURE 2-12 A huge spike in Waiting work indicates that the scope of the project is in flux.

Up to and including day 6, this cumulative flow diagram looks like an example of a healthy flow. However, on day 7, a surge of new tickets is placed on the Kanban board in the Wait state.

Kanban focuses heavily on the reduction of waste. Placing items in the Kanban board's backlog encourages waste because it increases lead times and has a demoralizing effect on software delivery teams.

Long phase of delivery   It is important to match the overall pace of your software delivery process to the slowest phase of delivery. This is most commonly the Implement phase, when coding occurs.

Figure 2-13 shows the effect of having a long phase of delivery. Note the healthy flow until work items reach the bottleneck.

FIGURE 2-13 Implementation is often the longest part of software delivery.

The remedy to this problem is to apply smaller WIP limits to the bottleneck so that upstream work cannot be pulled into an already overburdened phase of delivery.

Delivery plateau   The delivery plateau is not necessarily a failure of process. In fact, it is more commonly a result of code that is no longer adaptive to the changes required of it. It is the classic problem of accruing technical debt for a short-term gain in delivery efficiency, traded off against striving for code quality, maintainability, and extensibility in the long term. Ideally, this should be identified early enough to allow aggressive refactoring to solve the problem while concurrently delivering features. If this issue is left to stagnate for too long, the code will likely require wholesale rewrites.

Figure 2-14 shows how this problem manifests itself on a cumulative flow diagram.

FIGURE 2-14 If delivery plateaus, a lack of coding best practices is often to blame.

Regulated deployment phase Kanban is best suited to a continuous delivery process whereby each change committed to source control systems could potentially be released as working software. Even compromising mildly, Kanban requires that there be no artificial restrictions on the deployment or release of software products.

Figure 2-15 shows a generally healthy flow of work items with one caveat: the Deliver phase jumps twice in the ten days of work, first on day 5 and second on day 10. Assuming a working week of Monday to Friday, it seems apt to conclude that this team is only allowed to release their code on Fridays.

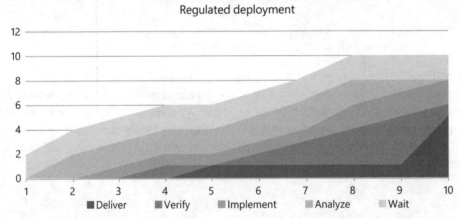

FIGURE 2-15 Artificially waiting for a deployment event slows progress and increases risk.

Such a restriction is common in Scrum but is antithetical to the continuous flow of work items favored by Kanban.

Conclusion

This chapter covered some basics and details of the Kanban approach to Agile software delivery. There are parallels with other Agile methodologies, like Scrum, but also some key differences. There are no distinct iterations in Kanban, just a continuous flow of items coming in and being delivered. Ceremonies, then, happen as and when they are required, rather than at rigidly calendared times.

Scrum's approach to managing change is to timebox the sprint and lock the inputs so that new work arriving after the start of the sprint must wait until the next iteration before being prioritized and scheduled. Kanban allows the addition of new work at any time but only provides service level agreements (SLAs) on how long it will likely take to complete new work. Kanban limits work in progress to ensure that the completion of work is prioritized over starting something anew.

In my experience, Scrum is Agile for *new* teams, while Kanban is Agile for *mature* teams. On a spectrum of experience with Agile methodologies, a team that scores lower would be better suited to the rigid ceremony and discipline of Scrum, whereas a team that scores higher would be better suited to the more *laissez-faire* Kanban. By way of analogy, Scrum can be thought of as the regular rhythmic beat of a regimental marching band. Kanban would therefore be jazz.

Another deciding factor for choosing between Scrum and Kanban as your Agile methodology is the kind of work to which they are to be applied. If the work is part of a project with a finite amount of time and financial resources in place, Scrum is a natural fit because each sprint can be costed individually. If the work is continual without a definite end date (often termed *business as usual* or *BAU*), Kanban will work well.

Foundations of adaptive code

This part of the book gives you a grounding in the principles and practices of writing adaptive code.

Writing code is the central pillar of software development. However, there are many different ways to achieve the goal of working code. Even discounting the selection of platform, language, and framework, there are a multitude of choices presented to a developer who is tasked with implementing even the simplest functionality.

The creation of *successful* software products has always been an obvious focus for the software development industry. In recent decades, software development has emphasized the implementation of patterns and practices that are repeatable and that increase the quality of code. This is because the notion of code quality is no longer separate from the notion of product quality. Over time, poor-quality code will degrade the quality of the product. At the very least, it will delay the delivery of working software.

To produce high-quality software, developers must strive to ensure that their code is maintainable, readable, and tested. In addition to this, a new requirement has emerged that suggests that code should also be *adaptive to change*.

The chapters in this part of the book present modern software implementation patterns and practices. I named these practices *adaptive* because this reflects their ability to change direction quickly. Adaptive code instructs software development teams how to write code that is able to change direction and remain innovative, maintainable, readable, and robust.

CHAPTER 3

Dependencies and layering

After completing this chapter, you will be able to

- Manage complex dependencies from method level to system level.

- Identify areas where dependency complexity is greatest and use tools to reduce complexity.

- Decompose your code into smaller, more adaptive pieces of functionality that promote reuse.

- Apply layering patterns where they are most useful.

- Understand how dependencies are resolved and debug dependency problems.

- Hide implementations behind simple interfaces.

All software has dependencies. Each dependency is either a first-party dependency within the same code base, a third-party dependency on an external assembly, or a dependency on the Microsoft .NET Framework. Except for trivial solutions, all solutions make use of all three types of dependency.

A dependency abstracts functionality away from calling code. You don't need to worry too much about what a dependency is doing, much less *how* it is doing it, but you should ensure that all dependencies are correctly managed. When a dependency chain is poorly managed, developers force dependencies that need not exist. This tangles the code into knots with complex assembly references. You might have heard the adage that "the most correct code is that which is not written." Similarly, the best-managed dependency is that which does not exist.

To keep your code adaptive to change, you must manage your dependencies. This applies at all levels of the software—from architectural dependencies between subsystems to implementation dependencies between individual methods. A poorly architected application can slow down the delivery of working software, even halt it entirely in the worst case.

Not enough emphasis can be placed on how important it is to take a purist approach to dependency management. If you compromise on such an important issue, you might notice a temporary increase in velocity, but the long-term effects are potentially fatal to the project. It is an all-too-familiar story: The short-lived productivity boost disappears as the amount of code and number of modules increases. The code becomes rigid and fragile, and progress slows to a crawl. In terms of Scrum artifacts and metrics, the sprint burndown chart flatlines because no story points are claimed. With Kanban, the cumulative flow diagram diverges and work is stuck in the Implementation column. For as long as the problem is unaddressed, the feature burnup chart follows suit because no features are completed. Even the bug count increases. When the dependency structure is incomprehensible, a change in one module can cause a direct side effect in another, seemingly unrelated module. Testing for regression defects such as this is nearly impossible, because the code does not lend itself to simple unit tests.

Effective dependency management requires discipline, awareness, and vigilance. There are established patterns that help you arrange your application in the short term so that it can adapt to changes in the long term. Layering is one of the most common architectural patterns, and this chapter elaborates on the different layering options available, in addition to other methods of dependency management.

Dependencies

What is a dependency? Generically, a *dependency* is a relationship between two distinct entities whereby one cannot perform some function—or perhaps exist—without the other. A good analogy of this is that one person can be said to be *financially dependent* on another. Often, in legal documents, you are required to state whether you have any dependents—that is, whether anyone depends on you for their living expenses and other basic necessities. This typically refers to a spouse or children.

Transferring this definition to code, the entities are often assemblies: assembly A uses another assembly, B, and thus you can say that A *depends on* B. A common way of stating this relationship is that A is the *client* of B, and B is the *service* of A. Without B, A cannot function. However, it is very important to note that B is *not* dependent on A and, as you will learn, *must not* and *cannot* depend on A. This client/service relationship is shown in Figure 3-1.

FIGURE 3-1 In any dependency relationship, the dependent is referred to as the *client*, and the entity that is being depended on is the *service*.

Throughout this book, code is discussed from the point of view of the *client* and the *service*. Although some services are hosted remotely, such as services created by using Windows Communication Foundation (WCF), this is not a prerequisite to code being termed a service. All code is service code and all code is client code, depending on the perspective from which you are approaching the code. Any class, method, or assembly can call other methods, classes, and assemblies; thus the code is a client. The same class, method, or assembly can also be called by other methods, classes, and assemblies; thus the code is also a service.

A simple example

Let's look at how a dependency behaves in a practical situation. This example is a very simple console application that prints a message to the screen. It's the universal "Hello World!" example. This example is necessarily trivial to distill the problems with dependencies down to their essence.

You can follow the steps here manually or retrieve the solution from GitHub. See the appendix, "Adaptive tools," for basic instructions on using Git and the accompanying sample code.

1. Open Microsoft Visual Studio and create a new console application, as shown in Figure 3-2. I have called mine SimpleDependency, but the name is not important.

FIGURE 3-2 The Add New Project dialog box in Visual Studio allows you to select from many different project templates.

2. Add a second project to the solution, this time a class library. I have called mine MessagePrinter.

3. Right-click the console application's *References* node and select Add Reference.

4. In the Add Reference dialog box, navigate to Projects and select the class library project.

You have now created a dependency from one assembly to another, as shown in Figure 3-3. Your console application depends on your class library, but the class library does not depend on your console application The console application is the client, and the class library is the service. Although this application does nothing at the moment, build the solution and navigate to the project's bin directory—this is where the executable file is.

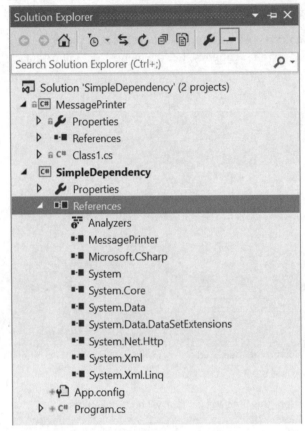

FIGURE 3-3 The referenced assemblies for any project are listed under its *References* node.

The bin directory contains the SimpleDependency.exe file, but it also contains the Message-Printer.dll file. This was copied into the bin directory by the Visual Studio build process because it was referenced as a dependency by the executable. Let's perform an experiment, but first a slight modification to the code is needed. Because this is a console application that does nothing, it will initialize and shut down before you have any time to react. Open the console application's Program.cs file.

Listing 3-1 shows the addition (in bold) inside the Main method. This is the entry point to the application that currently does nothing and exits quickly. By inserting a call to Console.Read-Key(), you ensure that the application waits for the user to press a key before it terminates.

LISTING 3-1 The call to ReadKey prevents the console application from exiting immediately.

```
namespace SimpleDependency
{
  class Program
  {
    static void Main(string[] args)
    {
      Console.ReadKey();
    }
  }
}
```

Rebuild the solution and run the application. As expected, it shows the console window, waits for you to press a key on the keyboard, and then terminates after you do so. Place a breakpoint on the `Console.ReadKey()` line, and debug the solution from Visual Studio.

When the application pauses at the breakpoint, you can view the assemblies that have been loaded into memory for this application. To do this, you can use the menu bar to select Debug > Windows > Modules. Figure 3-4 shows the list of modules that have been loaded for the application.

FIGURE 3-4 When you are debugging, the Modules window shows all of the currently loaded assemblies.

Did you notice something strange? There is no mention of the class library that was created. For this example, shouldn't `MessagePrinter.dll` be loaded? Actually, no—this is exactly the expected behavior. Here's why: the application isn't using anything from inside the `MessagePrinter` assembly, so the .NET runtime does not load it.

Just to prove conclusively that the dependent assembly is not really a prerequisite, navigate again to the console application's `bin` directory and delete `MessagePrinter.dll`. Run the application again, and it will continue happily without raising an exception.

Let's repeat this experiment a couple more times to truly find out what is happening. First, add a using MessagePrinter directive to the top of the Program.cs file. This imports the Message-Printer namespace. Do you think this is enough to cause the Common Language Runtime (CLR) to load the module? It is not. The dependency is again ignored, and the assembly is not loaded. This is because the using statement for importing a namespace is just syntactic sugar that only serves to reduce the amount of code you need to write. Rather than writing out the entire namespace whenever you want to use a type from inside it, you can import the namespace and reference the types directly. The using statement generates no instructions for the CLR to execute.

This next experiment builds on the previous, so you can leave the using statement in place. First, create a MessagePrintingService in the MessagePrinter assembly, as shown in Listing 3-2.

LISTING 3-2 A simple class to introduce a real dependency.

```
namespace MessagePrinter
{
  public class MessagePrintingService
  {
    public void PrintMessage()
    {
      Console.WriteLine("Hello World!");
    }
  }
}
```

Next, in Program.cs, before the call to Console.ReadLine(), construct an instance of the MessagePrintingService and call the PrintMessage method, as shown in Listing 3-3.

LISTING 3-3 Introducing a dependency by calling an instance method.

```
using System;
using MessagePrinter;

namespace SimpleDependency
{
  class Program
  {
    static void Main()
    {
      var service = new MessagePrintingService();
      service.PrintMessage();
      Console.ReadKey();
    }
  }
}
```

The Modules window now shows that the `MessagePrinter.dll` assembly has been loaded, because there is no way to construct an instance of the `MessagePrintingService` without pulling the contents of the assembly into memory.

You can prove this if you delete the `MessagePrinter.dll` from the `bin` directory and run the application again. An exception is thrown this time.

```
Unhandled Exception: System.IO.FileNotFoundException: Could not load file or assembly
'MessagePrinter, Version=1.0.0.0, Culture=neutral, PublicKeyToken=null' or one of its
dependencies. The system cannot find the file specified.
```

Framework dependencies

The dependency shown in the previous section is called a *first-party* dependency. Both the console application and the class library on which it depends belong to the same Visual Studio solution. This means that the dependency should always be accessible, because the dependency project can always be rebuilt from the source code if necessary. It also means that you can modify the source code of first-party dependencies.

Both projects have other dependencies in the form of .NET Framework assemblies. These are not part of the project but are expected to be available. Each .NET Framework assembly is built for a specific version of the framework: 1, 1.1, 2, 3.5, 4, 4.5, and so on. Some .NET Framework assemblies are new to a particular version and cannot be referenced by projects that are using an earlier version of the .NET Framework. Other assemblies change from version to version of the .NET Framework.

The `SimpleDependency` project has several references to the .NET Framework, as shown earlier in Figure 3-3. Many of these dependencies are defaults that are added to all console application projects. The example application doesn't use them, so they can be safely removed. In fact, for both projects, everything except `System` and `System.Core` are superfluous, so they can be removed from the references list. The application will still run correctly.

By removing unnecessary framework dependencies, you make it easier to visualize the dependencies required by each project.

Framework assemblies always load

It is worth noting that, unlike other dependencies, references to .NET Framework assemblies will always cause those assemblies to load. Even if you are not really using an assembly, it will still load at application startup. Fortunately, if multiple projects in the solution all reference the same assembly, only one instance of this assembly is loaded into memory (per AppDomain), and it is shared among all dependents.

The default references for a project vary depending on the project type. Each project type has a project template that lists the references required. This is how a Windows Forms application references the System.Windows.Forms assembly, whereas a Windows Presentation Foundation application references WindowsBase, PresentationCore, and PresentationFramework.

Listing 3-4 shows the references for a console application. All Visual Studio project templates are located under the Visual Studio installation directory root /Common7/IDE/ProjectTemplates/ and are grouped by language.

LISTING 3-4 Part of a Visual Studio project template for conditionally referencing different assemblies.

```
<ItemGroup>
  <Reference Include="System"/>
  $if$ ($targetframeworkversion$ >= 3.5)
  <Reference Include="System.Core"/>
  <Reference Include="System.Xml.Linq"/>
  <Reference Include="System.Data.DataSetExtensions"/>
  $endif$
  $if$ ($targetframeworkversion$ >= 4.0)
  <Reference Include="Microsoft.CSharp"/>
  $endif$
  <Reference Include="System.Data"/>
  <Reference Include="System.Xml"/>
</ItemGroup>
```

There is some logic in these files that can alter how the template generates a real project instance. Specifically, the references differ depending on the version of the .NET Framework that is being used for the resulting project. Here, the Microsoft.CSharp assembly is referenced only if the project is targeting .NET Framework 4 or higher. This makes sense, because it is normally required only if you use the dynamic keyword that was introduced in the .NET Framework 4.

Third-party dependencies

The final type of dependency is that of assemblies developed by third-party developers. Typically, if something is not provided by the .NET Framework, you can implement a solution yourself by creating first-party dependencies. This could be a laborious task depending on the size of the solution required. Instead, you can elect to use third-party solutions. As an example, you are unlikely to want to implement your own Object/Relational Mapper (ORM), because such a large piece of infrastructural code could take months to be functional and years to be complete. Instead, you could look first to Entity Framework, which is part of the .NET Framework. If that did not meet your needs, you could look instead at NHibernate, which is a mature ORM library that has been extensively tested.

The main reason to use a third-party dependency is to exchange the effort required for implementing some features or infrastructure for the effort of integrating something that is already written and suitable for the job. Do not forget that this integration effort could still be significant, depending on the structure of both your first-party code and the interface of the third-party code. When your aim is to deliver increments of business value on an iterative basis—as in Agile—using third-party libraries allows you to maintain this focus.

The simplest way to organize dependencies that are external to your project and the .NET Framework is to create a solution folder called Dependencies under the Visual Studio solution of a project and to add the .dll files to that folder. When you want to add references to these assemblies to the projects of the solution, you can do so by browsing to the files in the Reference Manager dialog box (shown in Figure 3-5).

FIGURE 3-5 Third-party references can be stored in a Dependencies folder in the Visual Studio solution.

The other advantage of this approach is that all of the external dependencies are stored in source control. This allows other developers to receive the dependencies just by retrieving the latest version of the source from a central repository. This is a much simpler approach than requiring all of the developers to install or download the files themselves.

A better way to organize third-party dependencies is demonstrated later in this chapter, in the "Dependency management with NuGet" section. In brief, the NuGet dependency management tool manages a project's third-party dependencies for you, including downloading a package containing all relevant artifacts, referencing assemblies, and upgrading library versions.

Modeling dependencies in a directed graph

A *graph* is a mathematical construct that consists of two distinct elements: nodes and edges. An edge can only exist between two nodes and serves to connect them in some way. Any node can be connected to any number of the other nodes in a graph. A graph can be one of several types, depending on variations in the graph's properties. For example, the graph in Figure 3-6 shows edges that are directionless: the edge between nodes A and C is neither from A to C nor from C to A—the presence of the edge is all that matters. This is called an *undirected graph*.

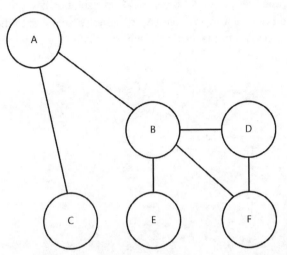

FIGURE 3-6 A graph consists of nodes that are connected by edges.

If, as in Figure 3-7, the edges have arrowheads at one end, you can determine the direction of the edges. There is an edge from A to C, but not an edge from C to A. This is called a *directed graph*, or a *digraph*.

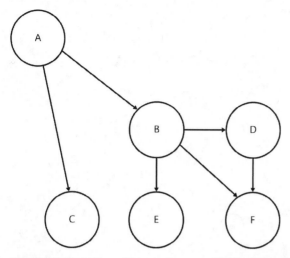

FIGURE 3-7 The edges of this graph are specifically directed, so there is no edge (B,A), yet the edge (A,B) exists.

There are many areas of software engineering in which graphs are excellent models, but graphs are particularly applicable to modeling code dependencies. As you have already learned, dependencies consist of two entities with a direction applied from the dependent code to the dependency. You can think of the entities as nodes and draw a directed edge from dependent to dependency. When you extend this to the rest of the entities, you form a *dependency digraph*.

This structure can be applied at several different granularities, as Figure 3-8 shows. The nodes in the graph could represent the classes in a project, different assemblies, or groups of assemblies that form a subsystem. In all cases, the arrows between the nodes represent the dependencies between components. The source of the arrow is the dependent component and the target of the arrow is the dependency.

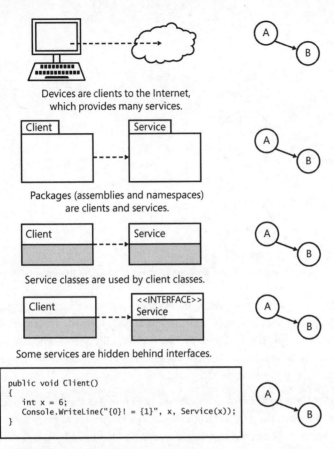

Devices are clients to the Internet, which provides many services.

Packages (assemblies and namespaces) are clients and services.

Service classes are used by client classes.

Some services are hidden behind interfaces.

```
public void Client()
{
    int x = 6;
    Console.WriteLine("{0}! = {1}", x, Service(x));
}
```

Even down at the method level, a method that calls another method is the client of a service.

FIGURE 3-8 Dependencies at all levels can be modeled as graphs.

For each node at a coarse-grained granularity, there is a set of nodes at a more fine-grained granularity. Inside subsystems are assemblies; inside assemblies are classes; inside classes are methods. This exemplifies how a dependency on a single method can pull in a whole subsystem of chained dependencies.

However, with all of these examples, you do not know what *sort* of dependency you are dealing with (inheritance, aggregation, composition, or association), just that there is a dependency. This is still useful, because managing dependencies only requires knowledge of the binary relationship between two entities: *is there a dependency or not?*

Cyclic dependencies

Another part of graph theory is that directed graphs can form cycles: the ability to traverse from one node back to itself by following the edges. The graphs shown so far are said to be *acyclic digraphs*— containing no cycles. Figure 3-9 shows an example of a *cyclic digraph*. If you start at node D, you can follow the edge to E, then B, and finally, end up back at D again. This is a *cyclic dependency*, sometimes referred to as a *circular dependency*.

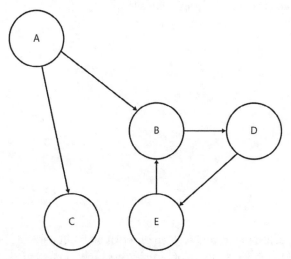

FIGURE 3-9 This digraph contains cycles.

Imagine that these nodes represent assemblies. D has an implicit dependency on anything that its explicit and implicit dependencies also depend on. D depends on E explicitly but B and D implicitly. Therefore, D depends on *itself*.

For assemblies, this is not possible. If you try to set this up in Visual Studio, when you come to assigning the reference from E to B, Visual Studio will not allow this to happen, as Figure 3-10 shows.

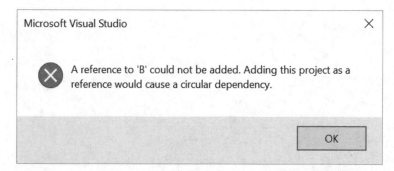

FIGURE 3-10 It is not possible to create a cyclic dependency in Visual Studio.

So, although modeling dependencies as graphs might seem academic, it has clear benefits when you are organizing your dependencies. Cyclic dependencies between assemblies are not a diversion from a purist ideal but are completely disallowed, and their avoidance is mandatory and enforced.

Loops

Loops are specializations of the cycles in digraphs. If a node is connected with an edge to *itself*, that edge becomes a loop. Figure 3-11 shows an example of a graph with a loop.

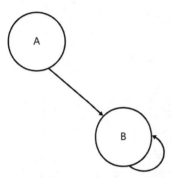

FIGURE 3-11 In this digraph, node B links to itself with a loop.

In practice, assemblies always explicitly self-depend, and such an observation is not particularly noteworthy. However, at the method level, a loop is evidence of *recursion*, as shown in Listing 3-5.

LISTING 3-5 A self-loop in a digraph that represents methods results in recursion.

```
namespace Graphs
{
  public class RecursionLoop
  {
    public void A()
    {
      int x = 6;
      Console.WriteLine("{0}! = {1}", x, B(x));
    }

    public int B(int number)
    {
      if(number == 0)
      {
        return 1;
      }
      else
      {
        return number * B(number - 1);
      }
    }
  }
}
```

The class in Listing 3-4 shows the functional equivalent of the dependency graph in Figure 3-11. Method A calls method B; therefore, you say that method A is dependent on method B. However, more interesting is method B's dependency on itself—B is an example of a recursive function; that is, a function that calls itself.

Managing dependencies

You have learned so far that dependencies are necessary but also must be carefully managed lest they present you with problems later in development. These problems can be quite difficult to back out of after they have manifested themselves. Therefore, it is best to manage your dependencies correctly from the outset and to stay vigilant so that no problems creep in. Poorly managed dependencies can quickly escalate from a small compromise to become an overall architectural problem.

The rest of this chapter is focused on the more practical aspects of continually managing dependencies. This includes avoiding anti-patterns and, more importantly, understanding why these common patterns are *anti*-patterns. Conversely, some patterns are benevolent and should be embraced; these are offered as direct alternatives to the noted anti-patterns.

Patterns and anti-patterns

As an engineering discipline, object-oriented software development is a relatively new endeavor. Over the last few decades, some repeatable collaborations between classes and interfaces have been identified and codified as *patterns*.

There are many software development patterns, each providing a generic solution that can be repurposed to a specific problem domain. Some patterns can be used in conjunction with each other to produce elegant solutions to complex problems. Of course, not all patterns are applicable all the time, and it takes experience and practice to recognize when and where certain patterns might apply.

Some patterns are not so benevolent. In fact, they are quite the opposite. They are considered *anti-patterns*. These patterns harm the adaptability of your code and should be avoided. Some anti-patterns began as patterns before slowly falling out of favor due to perceived negative side effects.

Implementations versus interfaces

Developers who are new to the concept of programming to interfaces often have difficulty letting go of what is behind the interface.

At compile time, any client of an interface should have no idea which implementation of the interface it is using. Such knowledge can lead to incorrect assumptions that couple the client to a specific implementation of the interface.

Imagine the common example in which a class needs to save a record in persistent storage. To do so, it rightly delegates to an interface, which hides the details of the persistent storage mechanism used. However, it would not be right to make any assumptions about which implementation of the interface is being used at run time. For example, casting the interface reference to any implementation is *always* a bad idea.

The new code smell

Interfaces describe *what* can be done, whereas classes describe *how* it is done. Only classes involve the implementation details—interfaces are completely unaware of how something is accomplished. Because only classes have constructors, it follows that constructors are an implementation detail. An interesting corollary to this is that, aside from a few exceptions, you can consider an appearance of the new keyword to be a *code smell*.

Code smells

Saying that code *smells* is a way of saying that some code is *potentially* problematic. The word "potentially" is chosen deliberately because two occurrences of a code smell might not be equally problematic. Unlike anti-patterns, which are more universally considered bad practice, code smells are not necessarily bad practice. Code smells are warnings that something could be wrong and that the root cause might need to be corrected.

Code smells might be indicative of technical debt that will need to be repaid—and the longer the debt remains unpaid, the harder it might be to fix.

There are many different categories of code smell. The use of the new keyword—direct object instantiation—is an example of "inappropriate intimacy." Because constructors are implementation details, their use can cause unintended (and undesirable) dependencies to be required by client code.

Code smells, like anti-patterns, are fixed by refactoring the code so that it has a better, more adaptive design. Although the code might fulfill its requirements, its current design is suboptimal and might cause issues in the future. This is undoubtedly a development task that yields no immediate tangible benefit to the business. As with all refactor work, there appears to be no business value associated with fixing the problem. However, just as financial debt can lead to crippling interest repayments, technical debt can spiral out of control and ruin good dependency management practices, jeopardizing future enhancements and code fixes.

Listing 3-6 shows a couple of examples where directly instantiating an object instance by using the new keyword is a code smell.

LISTING 3-6 An example of how instantiating objects prevents code from being adaptive.

```
public class AccountController
{
    private readonly SecurityService securityService;

    public AccountController()
    {
        this.securityService = new SecurityService();
    }

    [HttpPost]
    public void ChangePassword(Guid userID, string newPassword)
    {
        User userRepository = new UserRepository();
        var user = userRepository.GetByID(userID);
        this.securityService.ChangeUsersPassword(user, newPassword);
    }
}
```

The AccountController class is part of a hypothetical ASP.NET MVC application. Do not worry too much about the specifics; concentrate on the inappropriate object construction, highlighted in bold. The controller's responsibility is to allow the user to perform account queries and commands through MVC controller actions. There is only one command shown: ChangePassword.

There are several problems with this code, and they are caused directly by the two occurrences of new:

- The AccountController is forever dependent on the SecurityService and UserRepository implementations.

- Whatever dependencies the SecurityService and UserRepository have are now implicit dependencies of the AccountController.

- The AccountController is now extremely difficult to unit test—the two classes are impossible to mock with conventional methods.

- The SecurityService.ChangeUsersPassword method requires clients to load User objects.

These problems are addressed in greater detail in the following sections.

Inability to enhance the implementations

If you want to change your implementation of the SecurityService, your two options are to change the AccountController directly to refer to this new implementation or add the new functionality to the existing SecurityService. Throughout this book, you will learn why neither option is preferred. For now, consider that the aim is to never edit either the AccountController or the SecurityService class after they have been created.

Chain of dependency

The SecurityService is also likely to have some dependencies of its own. By having a default constructor, it is making the bold claim that it does not have any dependencies. However, what if the code shown in Listing 3-7 is the implementation of the SecurityService constructor?

LISTING 3-7 The SecurityService has the same problem as the AccountController.

```
public SecurityService()
{
    this.Session = SessionFactory.GetSession();
}
```

This service actually depends on NHibernate, the Object/Relational Mapper, which is being used to retrieve a *session*. The session is NHibernate's analogy for a connection to persistent, relational storage, such as Microsoft SQL Server, Oracle, or MySQL. As explained earlier in this chapter, this means that the AccountController also depends—implicitly—on NHibernate.

Furthermore, what if the signature of the SecurityService constructor changes? That is, what if it suddenly requires clients to provide the connection string to the database that the Session needs? Any client using the SecurityService, including the AccountController, would have to be updated to provide the connection string. Again, this is a change that you should not have to make.

Lack of testability

Testability is a very important concern, and it requires code to be designed in a certain fashion. If it is not, testing is extremely difficult. Unfortunately, neither the AccountController nor the Security-Service is easily tested. This is because you cannot replace their dependencies with fake versions that do not perform any action. For example, when testing the SecurityService, you do not want it to make any connections to the database. That would be needless and slow, and would introduce another large failure point in the test: what if the database is unavailable? There are ways to test these classes by replacing their dependencies at run time with fakes. Tools such as Microsoft Moles and Typemock can hook into constructors and ensure that the objects that they return are fakes. But that is an example of treating the symptoms and not the cause.

More inappropriate intimacy

The AccountController.ChangePassword method creates a UserRepository class to retrieve a User instance. It only needs to do this because that is what the SecurityService.ChangeUsersPassword method demands of it. Without a User instance, the method cannot be called. This is indicative of a badly designed method interface. Instead of requiring all clients to retrieve a User, the SecurityService should, in this case, retrieve the User itself. The two methods would then look like Listing 3-8.

LISTING 3-8 An improvement is made to all clients of SecurityService.

```
[HttpPost]
public void ChangePassword(Guid userID, string newPassword)
{
    this.securityService.ChangeUsersPassword(userID, newPassword);
}
//...
public class SecurityService
{
    public void ChangeUsersPassword(Guid userID, string newPassword)
    {
        var userRepository = new UserRepository();
        var user = userRepository.GetByID(userID);
        user.ChangePassword(newPassword);
    }
}
```

This is definitely an improvement for the AccountController, but the ChangeUsersPassword method is still directly instantiating the UserRepository.

Alternatives to object construction

What would improve the AccountController and SecurityService—or any other example of inappropriate object construction? How can they be made demonstrably correct so that none of the aforementioned problems apply? There are a few options, all complementary, that you can choose from.

Coding to an interface

The first and most important change that you should make is to hide the implementation of SecurityService behind an interface. This allows the AccountController to depend only on the interface, and not on the implementation, of SecurityService. The first refactor is to extract an interface out of SecurityService, as shown in Listing 3-9.

LISTING 3-9 Extracting an interface from SecurityService.

```
public interface ISecurityService
{
    void ChangeUsersPassword(Guid userID, string newPassword);
}
//...
public class SecurityService : ISecurityService
{
    public ChangeUsersPassword(Guid userID, string newPassword)
    {
        //...
    }
}
```

The next step is to update the client so that it no longer depends on the SecurityService class, but rather on the ISecurityService interface. Listing 3-10 shows this refactor applied to the AccountController.

LISTING 3-10 The AccountController now uses the ISecurityService interface.

```
public class AccountController
{
    private readonly ISecurityService securityService;

    public AccountController()
    {
        this.securityService = new SecurityService();
    }

    [HttpPost]
    public void ChangePassword(Guid userID, string newPassword)
    {
        securityService.ChangeUsersPassword(user, newPassword);
    }
}
```

This example is not yet complete—you are still dependent on the SecurityService implementation because of its constructor. The concrete class is still being instantiated in the constructor of AccountController. To separate the two classes completely, you need to make a further refactor: introduce *dependency injection* (DI).

Using dependency injection

This is a large topic that cannot be covered in a small amount of space. In fact, Chapter 12, "Dependency injection," is devoted to the subject, and there are entire books dedicated to it. Luckily, DI is not particularly complex or difficult, so the basics can be covered here from the point of view of classes that make use of DI. Listing 3-11 shows another refactor that has been applied to the constructor of the AccountController class. The constructor is the only change here, highlighted in bold. It is a very minor change as far as this class is concerned, but it makes a huge difference to your ability to manage dependencies. Rather than constructing the SecurityService class itself, the Account-Controller now requires some other class to provide it with an ISecurityService implementation. Not only that, a precondition has been introduced to the constructor that prevents its clients from passing in a null value for the securityService parameter. This ensures that, when you use the securityService field in the ChangePassword method, you are guaranteed to have a valid instance and do not have to check for null anywhere else.

```
public class AccountController
{
    private readonly ISecurityService securityService;

    public AccountController(ISecurityService securityService)
    {
        if(securityService == null) throw new ArgumentNullException("securityService");

        this.securityService = securityService;
    }

    [HttpPost]
    public void ChangePassword(Guid userID, string newPassword)
    {
        this.securityService.ChangeUsersPassword(user, newPassword);
    }
}
```

The SecurityService also needs to follow suit and apply dependency injection. Listing 3-12 shows how it looks after refactoring.

LISTING 3-12 Dependency injection is a ubiquitous pattern that can be applied liberally almost everywhere.

```
public class SecurityService : ISecurityService
{
    private readonly IUserRepository userRepository;

    public SecurityService(IUserRepository userRepository)
    {
        if(userRepository == null) throw new ArgumentNullException("userRepository");
        this.userRepository = userRepository;
    }

    public ChangeUsersPassword()
    {
        var user = userRepository.GetByID(userID);
        user.ChangePassword(newPassword);
    }
}
```

Just as the AccountController enforces its dependency on a valid ISecurityService instance, so too does the SecurityService enforce its dependency on a valid IUserRepository—by throwing an exception if it is given a null reference on construction. Similarly, the UserRepository class dependency has been entirely removed, in favor of an IUserRepository interface.

Resolving dependencies

Knowing how to arrange your projects and the dependencies that they have will not help when it comes to debugging a dependency between assemblies. Sometimes assemblies are not available at run time and it becomes necessary to find out why.

Assemblies

The Common Language Runtime (CLR), which is the virtual machine that the .NET Framework uses to execute code instructions, is a software product like any other and has been programmed to behave in a predictable and logical way when hosting applications. A good grounding in the theory and practice of how assemblies are resolved and how errors in resolution can be fixed is very useful. A little knowledge can go a long way when you need to track down a problem with finding assemblies.

Resolution process   The assembly resolution process is an important facet of the CLR. This covers the gap between adding a reference to an assembly or project and having the application running with this assembly loaded. There are several steps involved, and little more is needed than an overview so that, when something goes wrong during the process, you can reason about the probable causes of the problem.

Figure 3-12 shows the assembly resolution process as a flow chart. This flow chart is at a high level and does not include every detail, but there is enough to show the headline items in the process. The process is as follows:

- The CLR uses a just-in-time (JIT) model to resolve assemblies. As was already proven earlier in the chapter, the references contained in an application are not resolved as you start up the application, but rather when you first make use of a feature of that assembly—literally just in time.

- Each assembly has an identity that is a composite of its name, version, culture, and public key token. Features such as binding redirects can change this identity, so determining it is not quite as simple as it might seem.

- When the assembly's identity has been established, the CLR is able to determine whether it has already attempted to resolve this dependency previously during the current execution of the application.

- Asking this question causes the CLR to branch depending on the answer. If you have attempted to resolve this assembly, that process has either already succeeded or failed. If it succeeded, the CLR can use the assembly that has already been loaded, and it exits early. If not, the CLR knows that it need not continue attempting to resolve this assembly because it will fail.

- Alternatively, if this is the first attempt to resolve the assembly, the CLR first checks the global assembly cache (GAC). The GAC is a machine-wide assembly repository that allows multiple versions of the same assembly to be executed in the same application. If the assembly is found in the GAC, the resolution process is successful and the discovered assembly is loaded. So you now know that, because the GAC is searched first, the presence of an applicable assembly in the GAC will take precedence over an assembly on the file system.

- If the assembly could not be found in the GAC, the CLR starts probing a variety of directories in search of it. The directories searched depend on the `app.config` settings. If there is a `code-Base` element in the `app.config`, that location is checked and—if the assembly is not found—no other locations are subsequently checked. However, the default is for the application's root directory to be searched, which is typically the `/bin` folder that relates to the entry point or web application. If the assembly cannot be found there, the resolution process fails and an exception is thrown by the CLR. Typically, this results in the termination of the application.

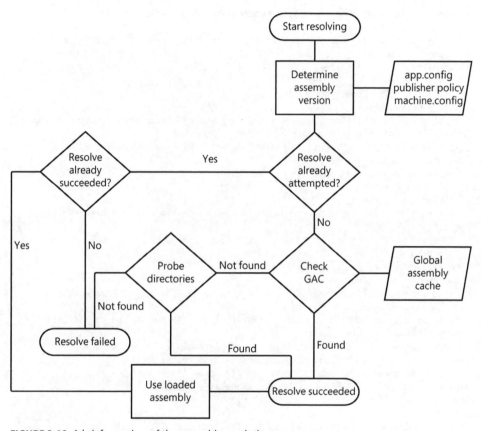

FIGURE 3-12 A brief overview of the assembly resolution process.

The Fusion log This is a very useful tool for debugging failed attempts by the CLR to bind to an assembly at run time. Rather than trying to step through the application in the Visual Studio debugger, it is better to turn Fusion on and read the log file that results.

To enable Fusion you must edit the Windows registry, as shown in the following code.

```
HKLM\Software\Microsoft\Fusion\ForceLog 1
HKLM\Software\Microsoft\Fusion\LogPath C:\FusionLogs
```

The ForceLog value is a DWORD, whereas the LogPath is a string. You can set the LogPath to whatever path you choose. An example of a failed binding is shown in Listing 3-13.

LISTING 3-13 Sample output from Fusion for a failed attempt to bind an assembly.

```
*** Assembly Binder Log Entry  (6/21/2013 @ 1:50:14 PM) ***

The operation failed.
Bind result: hr = 0x80070002. The system cannot find the file specified.

Assembly manager loaded from:  C:\Windows\Microsoft.NET\Framework64\v4.0.30319\clr.dll
Running under executable  C:\Program Files\1UPIndustries\Bins\v1.1.0.242\Bins.exe
--- A detailed error log follows.

=== Pre-bind state information ===
LOG: User = DEV\gmclean
LOG: DisplayName = TaskbarDockUI.Xtensions.Bins.resources, Version=1.0.0.0, Culture=en-US,
    PublicKeyToken=null (Fully-specified)
LOG: Appbase = file:///C:/Program Files/1UPIndustries/Bins/v1.1.0.242/
LOG: Initial PrivatePath = NULL
LOG: Dynamic Base = NULL
LOG: Cache Base = NULL
LOG: AppName = Bins.exe
Calling assembly : TaskbarDockUI.Xtensions.Bins, Version=1.0.0.0, Culture=neutral,
    PublicKeyToken=null.
===
LOG: This bind starts in default load context.
LOG: No application configuration file found.
LOG: Using host configuration file:
LOG: Using machine configuration file from C:\Windows\Microsoft.NET\Framework64
    \v4.0.30319\config\machine.config.
LOG: Policy not being applied to reference at this time (private, custom, partial, or
    location-based assembly bind).
LOG: Attempting download of new URL file:///C:/Program Files/1UPIndustries/
    Bins/v1.1.0.242/en-US/TaskbarDockUI.Xtensions.Bins.resources.DLL.
LOG: Attempting download of new URL file:///C:/Program Files/1UPIndustries/
    Bins/v1.1.0.242/en-US/TaskbarDockUI.Xtensions.Bins.resources/
    TaskbarDockUI.Xtensions.Bins.resources.DLL.
LOG: Attempting download of new URL file:///C:/Program Files/1UPIndustries/Bins/
    v1.1.0.242/en-US/TaskbarDockUI.Xtensions.Bins.resources.EXE.
LOG: Attempting download of new URL file:///C:/Program Files/1UPIndustries/
    Bins/v1.1.0.242/en-US/TaskbarDockUI.Xtensions.Bins.resources/
    TaskbarDockUI.Xtensions.Bins.resources.EXE.
LOG: All probing URLs attempted and failed.
```

After the registry is edited, all attempts, successful or otherwise, to resolve an assembly by any managed application will be written to the logs. This is obviously a lot of log files, which can be good, but it can start to become a needle-in-a-haystack sort of problem.

Luckily, Fusion has a UI application, shown in Figure 3-13, which makes it slightly easier to find the right file for your application, rather than scouring the file system.

FIGURE 3-13 Fusion has a user interface for finding the log file for your application.

Not all dependencies require assembly references. One alternative is to deploy the service code as a hosted service. This requires inter-process or inter-network communication, but it minimizes the assembly references required between client and server, as the next section examines.

Services

In comparison to assemblies, the coupling of a client to a hosted service can be much looser, which is beneficial but also comes at a cost. Depending on your application's requirements, you could have the client know a lot or a little about the location of the service. Also, you can vary how the service is implemented so that it has very few requirements. With each of these options, there are different tradeoffs to be considered.

Known endpoint When the location of the service is known to clients at compile time, you can create a service proxy on the client side. This proxy can be created in at least two ways: by using Visual Studio to add a service reference to a project, and by creating the service proxy yourself via the ChannelFactory class in the .NET Framework.

Adding a service reference in Visual Studio is very easy: just select Add Service Reference on the shortcut menu for the project. All the Add Service Reference dialog box needs is the location of the Web Services Definition Language (WSDL) file, which provides a metadata description of the service, its data types, and available behavior. Visual Studio then generates a set of proxy classes for this service, saving a lot of time. It can even generate asynchronous versions of the service methods to mitigate against blocking. However, the tradeoff of using this method is the loss of control over the code that is generated. The code that Visual Studio generates is unlikely to match up to your in-house coding standards, which might be a problem depending on how strict those standards are. Another issue is that the generated service proxy does not lend itself to unit testing: it does not generate any interfaces, just implementing classes.

An alternative to adding a service reference is to create a service proxy yourself in code. This method is best used when the client has access to the interface of the service and can reuse it directly by reference. Listing 3-14 shows an example of creating a service proxy by using the ChannelFactory class.

LISTING 3-14 The ChannelFactory class allows you to create a service proxy.

```
var binding = new BasicHttpBinding();
var address = new EndpointAddress("http://localhost/MyService");
var channelFactory = new ChannelFactory<IService>(binding, address);
var service = channelFactory.CreateChannel();
service.MyOperation();
service.Close();
channelFactory.Close();
```

The ChannelFactory class is generic, and its constructor requires the interface for the service proxy that you want it to create. Because this code also requires a Binding and an Endpoint-Address, you must furnish the ChannelFactory with the full address/binding/contract (ABC). In this example, the IService interface is the same interface that the service implements. What you receive from ChannelFactory.CreateChannel is a proxy that, for each call made, will call the equivalent method on the server-side implementation. Because the same interface is used, client-side classes can require this interface as a constructor parameter to be resolved by dependency injection, and the client classes instantly become testable. In addition, they don't have to know that they are calling a remote service.

Service Discovery Sometimes you might know the binding type of a service or its contract, but not the address where it is hosted. In this case, you can use Service Discovery, which was introduced to Windows Communication Foundation (WCF) in the .NET Framework 4.

Service Discovery comes in two flavors: managed and ad hoc. In managed mode, a centralized service called a discovery proxy is well known to clients, which directly send it queries for finding other services. This is the less interesting mode, because it introduces a single point of failure (SPOF): if the discovery proxy is not available, clients cannot access *any* other services because they are not discoverable.

Ad hoc mode obviates the need for a discovery proxy by using multicast network messages. The default implementation of this uses the User Datagram Protocol (UDP), with each discoverable service listening on a specified IP address[1] for queries. Clients effectively ask the network whether there is a service that matches its query criteria—a contract or binding type, for example. In this scenario, if one of the services is unavailable, only that service cannot be discovered, whereas the rest will respond to requests. Listing 3-15 shows how to host a discoverable service programmatically, and Listing 3-16 shows how to add discoverability to a service via configuration.

---

[1] The IP address used is 239.255.255.250 (IPv4) or [FF02::C] (IPv6). The port used is 3702. This is set by the WS-Discovery standard, so it is not configurable.

LISTING 3-15 Programmatically hosting a discoverable service.

```
class Program
{
    static void Main(string[] args)
    {
        using (ServiceHost serviceHost = new ServiceHost(typeof(CalculatorService)))
        {
            serviceHost.Description.Behaviors.Add(new ServiceDiscoveryBehavior());

            serviceHost.AddServiceEndpoint(typeof(ICalculator), new BasicHttpBinding(),
    new Uri("http://localhost:8090/CalculatorService"));
            serviceHost.AddServiceEndpoint(new UdpDiscoveryEndpoint());

            serviceHost.Open();
            Console.WriteLine("Discoverable Calculator Service is running...");
            Console.ReadKey();
        }
    }
}
```

LISTING 3-16 Hosting a discoverable service via configuration.

```
<system.serviceModel>
    <behaviors>
      <serviceBehaviors>
        <behavior>
          <serviceMetadata httpGetEnabled="true" httpsGetEnabled="true"/>
          <serviceDebug includeExceptionDetailInFaults="false"/>
        </behavior>
        <behavior name="calculatorServiceDiscovery">
          <serviceDiscovery />
        </behavior>
      </serviceBehaviors>
      <endpointBehaviors>
        <behavior name="calculatorHttpEndpointDiscovery">
          <endpointDiscovery enabled="true" />
        </behavior>
      </endpointBehaviors>
    </behaviors>
    <protocolMapping>
        <add binding="basicHttpsBinding" scheme="https" />
    </protocolMapping>
    <serviceHostingEnvironment aspNetCompatibilityEnabled="true"
    multipleSiteBindingsEnabled="true" />
    <services>
      <service name="ConfigDiscoverableService.CalculatorService"
    behaviorConfiguration="calculatorServiceDiscovery">
        <endpoint address="CalculatorService.svc"
    behaviorConfiguration="calculatorHttpEndpointDiscovery"
    contract="ServiceContract.ICalculator" binding="basicHttpBinding" />
        <endpoint kind="udpDiscoveryEndpoint" />
      </service>
    </services>
  </system.serviceModel>
```

To become discoverable, all a service needs to do is add the `ServiceDiscovery` behavior and host a `DiscoveryEndpoint`. In this example, the `UdpDiscoveryEndpoint` is used for receiving multicast network messages from clients.

> **Note** Service Discovery in WCF complies with the WS-Discovery standard. This makes it interoperable with different platforms and languages, not just the .NET Framework.

Clients make use of the `DiscoveryClient` class to find a discoverable service, which also needs a `DiscoveryEndpoint`. The `Find` method is then called with a configured `FindCriteria` instance, which describes the attributes of the service to be found. `Find` returns a `FindResponse` instance that contains an `Endpoints` property—a collection of `EndpointDiscoveryMetadata` instances, one per matching service. Listing 3-17 shows these steps to find a discoverable service.

LISTING 3-17 Service Discovery is a good way to decouple code.

```
class Program
{
    private const int a = 11894;
    private const int b = 27834;

    static void Main(string[] args)
    {
        var foundEndpoints = FindEndpointsByContract<ICalculator>();

        if (!foundEndpoints.Any())
        {
            Console.WriteLine("No endpoints were found.");
        }
        else
        {
            var binding = new BasicHttpBinding();
            var channelFactory = new ChannelFactory<ICalculator>(binding);
            foreach (var endpointAddress in foundEndpoints)
            {
                var service = channelFactory.CreateChannel(endpointAddress);
                var additionResult = service.Add(a, b);
                Console.WriteLine("Service Found: {0}", endpointAddress.Uri);
                Console.WriteLine("{0} + {1} = {2}", a, b, additionResult);
            }
        }

        Console.ReadKey();
    }

    private static IEnumerable<EndpointAddress> FindEndpointsByContract
    <TServiceContract>()
    {
        var discoveryClient = new DiscoveryClient(new UdpDiscoveryEndpoint());
        var findResponse = discoveryClient.Find(new
    FindCriteria(typeof(TServiceContract)));
        return findResponse.Endpoints.Select(metadata => metadata.Address);
    }
}
```

Bear in mind that with UDP (User Datagram Protocol), as opposed to TCP, there is no guarantee of message delivery. It is possible for datagrams to be lost in transmission, so either the request might not reach a viable service or the response might not make it back to the client. In either scenario, it would appear to the client that there wasn't a service available to handle the request.

> **Tip** When hosting a discoverable service in Internet Information Services (IIS) or Windows Process Activation Service (WAS), ensure that you use the Microsoft AppFabric AutoStart functionality. Discoverability depends on the availability of the service, meaning that it must be running in order to receive queries from clients. AppFabric AutoStart allows the service to run when the application is started in IIS. Without AutoStart, the service is not started until the first request is made.

RESTful services   The most compelling reason to create RESTful services (REST: REpresentational State Transfer) is the very low dependency burden expected of clients. All that is needed is an HTTP client, which is commonly provided by the frameworks and libraries of languages. This makes RESTful services ideal for developing services that need to have wide-ranging, cross-platform support. For example, both Facebook and Twitter have REST APIs for various queries and commands. This ensures that clients can be developed for a large number of platforms: Windows Phone 10, iPhone, Android, iPad, Windows 10, Linux, and much more. Having a single implementation that can service all of these clients would be more difficult without the very low dependency requirements that REST allows.

The ASP.NET Web API is used for creating REST services that use the .NET Framework. Similar to the ASP.NET MVC framework, it allows developers to create methods that map directly to web requests. The Web API provides a base controller class called ApiController. You inherit from this controller and add methods named like the HTTP verbs: GET, POST, PUT, DELETE, HEAD, OPTIONS, and PATCH. Whenever an HTTP request arrives using one of these verbs, the corresponding method is called. Listing 3-18 shows an example of a service that implements all of these verbs.

LISTING 3-18 Almost all of the HTTP verbs are supported by the ASP.NET Web API.

```
public class ValuesController : ApiController
{
    public IEnumerable<string> Get()
    {
        return new string[] { "value1", "value2" };
    }

    public string Get(int id)
    {
        return "value";
    }

    public void Post([FromBody]string value)
    {
    }
```

```
        public void Put(int id, [FromBody]string value)
        {
        }

        public void Head()
        {
        }

        public void Options()
        {
        }

        public void Patch()
        {
        }

        public void Delete(int id)
        {
        }
    }
```

Listing 3-19 shows the client code for accessing the GET and POST methods of this service, using the `HttpClient` class. Although this is by no means the only way to access REST services in the .NET Framework, it relies on only the framework itself.

LISTING 3-19 Clients can use the `HttpClient` class to access RESTful services.

```
class Program
{
    static void Main(string[] args)
    {
        string uri = "http://localhost:7617/api/values";

        MakeGetRequest(uri);
        MakePostRequest(uri);

        Console.ReadKey();
    }

    private static async void MakeGetRequest(string uri)
    {
        var restClient = new HttpClient();
        var getRequest = await restClient.GetStringAsync(uri);

        Console.WriteLine(getRequest);
    }

    private static async void MakePostRequest(string uri)
```

```
    {
        var restClient = new HttpClient();
        var postRequest = await restClient.PostAsync(uri,
                new StringContent("Data to send to the server"));

            var responseContent = await postRequest.Content.ReadAsStringAsync();
            Console.WriteLine(responseContent);
    }
}
```

Just to emphasize the point that multiple clients can be written with equally low dependency requirements, Listing 3-20 shows a Windows PowerShell 3 script for accessing the GET and POST methods of the service.

LISTING 3-20 Accessing the REST service from Windows PowerShell 3 is extremely trivial.

```
$request = [System.Net.WebRequest]::Create("http://localhost:7617/api/values")
$request.Method ="GET"
$request.ContentLength = 0

$response = $request.GetResponse()
$reader = new-object System.IO.StreamReader($response.GetResponseStream())
$responseContent = $reader.ReadToEnd()
Write-Host $responseContent
```

This code uses the `WebRequest` object from the .NET Framework to call the RESTful service. This class is the superclass of the `HttpRequest` class. The `Create` method is a factory method that returns an `HttpRequest` instance because an `http://` URI was provided.

Dependency management with NuGet

Dependency management can be greatly simplified with the use of dependency management tools. Such tools are responsible for following dependency chains to ensure that all dependent artifacts are available. They also manage the versioning of dependencies: you can specify that you want to depend only on specific versions of dependencies, and the dependency management tools do the rest.

NuGet is a package management utility for the .NET Framework. NuGet refers to a dependency as a *package*, but the tool is not limited to assemblies. NuGet packages can also include configuration, scripts, and images—almost anything you need. One of the most compelling reasons to use a package manager such as NuGet is that it has knowledge of a package's dependencies and will bring the entire dependency chain with it when a project references a package.

As of Visual Studio 2013, NuGet is fully integrated as the default package management utility.

Consuming packages

NuGet adds some new commands to the shortcut menu in the Solution Explorer window of Visual Studio. From there, you can open the NuGet package management window and add a reference to a dependency.

For this example, I'm going to add a dependency to RiakClient, the .NET Framework client driver for the Riak NoSql key/value store. Figure 3-14 shows the NuGet package management window.

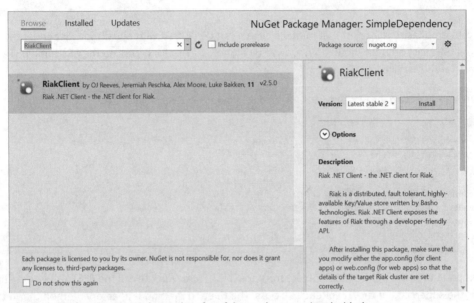

FIGURE 3-14 NuGet packages have a lot of useful metadata associated with them.

Whenever a package is selected in the list, the information pane on the right shows some metadata about the package. This includes its unique name in the gallery, the author or authors of the package, the version of the package, the date it was last published, a description of the package, and any dependencies that it has. The dependencies are very interesting, because they show what else is going to be installed as a result of referencing this package, in addition to the required or supported versions of the dependencies. RiakClient, for example, requires at least version 9.0.1 of Newtonsoft.Json, the popular .NET Framework JSON/class serializer, and at least version 2.0.0.668 of protobuf-net. Both of these packages could have dependencies of their own.

When you choose to install this package, NuGet will first try to download all the files and place them in a `packages/` folder under the solution's root folder. This allows you to put this entire directory into source control, exactly as you did earlier with a `dependencies/` folder. NuGet then references the downloaded assemblies in the project where you want to use this library. Figure 3-15 shows the references for the project after RiakClient is added.

FIGURE 3-15 The target package and all of its dependencies are referenced by the project.

In addition to making the references, NuGet also creates a `packages.config` file that contains information about which packages—and which versions—are referenced by the project. This is useful when it comes to upgrading or uninstalling packages, which is also something that NuGet is able to do.

Riak also needs some default configuration before it is ready to be used. So not only has NuGet downloaded and referenced a lot of assemblies, it has also edited your `app.config` to include some sensible default values for required settings that Riak needs. Listing 3-21 shows the current state of the `app.config` after RiakClient is installed.

LISTING 3-21 NuGet has added a new `configSection` to the `app.config` specifically for RiakClient.

```
<configuration>
  <configSections>
      <section name="riakConfig" type="RiakClient.Config.RiakClusterConfiguration,
RiakClient" />
    </configSections>
    <startup>
      <supportedRuntime version="v4.0" sku=".NETFramework,Version=v4.6.2" />
    </startup>
```

```
<riakConfig nodePollTime="5000" defaultRetryWaitTime="200" defaultRetryCount="3">
    <nodes>
        <node name="riak1" hostAddress="riak-host1" pbcPort="8087" poolSize="20" />
        <node name="riak2" hostAddress="riak-host2" pbcPort="8087" poolSize="20" />
        <node name="riak3" hostAddress="riak-host3" pbcPort="8087" poolSize="20" />
        <node name="riak4" hostAddress="riak-host4" pbcPort="8087" poolSize="20" />
        <node name="riak5" hostAddress="riak-host5" pbcPort="8087" poolSize="20" />
    </nodes>
    </riakConfig>
</configuration>
```

Clearly, this is a great timesaver because you haven't had to search the Riak site for a download of the RiakClient package or any of its dependencies. Everything has been put into a state where you can concentrate on developing. And when it comes time to upgrade RiakClient to the next version, you can also use NuGet to automatically update all of the packages that depend on it in the entire solution.

Producing packages

NuGet also allows you to create packages. You might want to create packages for publication on the official NuGet package gallery so that other developers can use them, or you might want to host your own package feed for first-party dependencies. Figure 3-16 shows the NuGet Package Manager, which can be used to create your own packages. In this package, I have configured RiakClient to be a dependency, so it will also depend on Newtonsoft.Json and protobuf-net, implicitly. I have added a library artifact that is targeted specifically to the .NET Framework 4.6.2 and a Windows PowerShell script that is instructed to run during installation. This could feasibly be used to do almost anything—thanks to the flexibility of Windows PowerShell.

FIGURE 3-16 The NuGet Package Manager makes it very easy to construct your own packages.

Each package has an XML file that details the metadata that is shown in the installation window. Listing 3-22 shows some of the syntax of this file.

LISTING 3-22 The package XML definition, including metadata.

```xml
<package xmlns="http://schemas.microsoft.com/packaging/2010/07/nuspec.xsd">
    <metadata>
        <id>MyTestPackage</id>
        <version>1.0.0</version>
        <authors>Gary McLean Hall</authors>
        <requireLicenseAcceptance>false</requireLicenseAcceptance>
        <description>My package description.</description>
        <dependencies>
            <dependency id="RiakClient" version="1.0.1" />
        </dependencies>
    </metadata>
</package>
```

NuGet is such a productivity and organizational bonus that it is painful to return to manually managing third-party dependencies, if a package does not exist for a particular library. In fact, NuGet is not only for third-party dependencies. When a solution becomes large enough, it is advisable to split the solution into multiple parts, sliced by layer. The assemblies for each layer can then be packaged by using NuGet and consumed by layers above. This keeps solutions small and easy to work with.

Chocolatey

The best way to describe Chocolatey is that it is a package management tool, just like NuGet, but its packages are applications and tools, not assemblies. Developers with some Linux knowledge will find that Chocolatey is like `apt-get`, which is Debian's and Ubuntu's package manager. Again, many of the benefits of package management apply: simplified installation, dependency management, and ease of use.

The following Windows PowerShell script can be used to download and install Chocolatey.

```
@powershell -NoProfile -ExecutionPolicy unrestricted -Command "iex ((new-object
    net.webclient).DownloadString('https://chocolatey.org/install.ps1'))" && SET
    PATH=%PATH%;%systemdrive%\chocolatey\bin
```

After Chocolatey is installed, you can use the command line to search for and install various applications and tools. The installation procedure will have already updated the command-line path to include the `chocolatey.exe` application. Much like Git, Chocolatey has subcommands such as `list` and `install`, but these also have synonyms that can be used as shortcuts: `clist` and `cinst`, respectively. Listing 3-23 shows a sample Chocolatey session that finds the package name for Filezilla, the FTP client, and then installs it.

LISTING 3-23 First you search the packages for the application that you want, and then you install it.

```
C:\dev> clist filezilla
ferventcoder.chocolatey.utilities 1.0.20130622
filezilla 3.7.1
filezilla.commandline 3.7.1
filezilla.server 0.9.41.20120523
jivkok.tools 1.1.0.2
kareemsultan.developer.toolkit 1.4
UAdevelopers.utils 1.9
C:\dev> cinst filezilla
Chocolatey (v0.9.8.20) is installing filezilla and dependencies. By installing you accept
the license for filezilla and each dependency you are installing.
. . .
 This Finished installing 'filezilla' and dependencies - if errors not shown in console,
none detected. Check log for errors if unsure.
```

As long as no errors were reported by Chocolatey, the requested package is now installed. Be aware that Chocolatey *should* have altered your system PATH so that any new binaries can be executed from the command line, but it does not always do so. There are a lot of packages available via Chocolatey, and the convenience that it provides is a compelling reason to use it.

Layering

To this point, this chapter has looked primarily at managing dependencies at the assembly level. This is a natural first step to organizing your application, because all classes and interfaces are contained in assemblies, and how they reference each other is a common concern. When correctly organized, your assemblies will contain classes and interfaces that only pertain to a single group of related functionality. Taken in aggregate, however, how can you ensure that groups of assemblies are also correctly organized?

Groups of two or more interrelated assemblies form *components* of the software system that is being developed. It is equally important—if not more so—that these components interact in a similarly well-defined and structured fashion. As Figure 3-17 shows, components are not physical artifacts of deployment, like assembly dynamic-link libraries (DLLs), but are logical groupings of assemblies that share a similar theme.

FIGURE 3-17 By grouping related assemblies together, you can define logical components.

There are three assemblies included in the diagram: Views, Controllers, and ViewModels. Each assembly contains two classes that serve different purposes and might require different dependencies. Although classes and assemblies are constructs provided by the .NET Framework, the User Interface package that groups everything is logical. The three assemblies might be located in the solution in a folder called `User-Interface`, but there is nothing preventing you or others from polluting this layer with other projects that do not belong. Nothing, that is, except diligence and vigilance.

In dependency management, components are no different from other programming constructs at lower levels. As with methods, classes, and assemblies, you can consider layers to be another node in the dependency graph shown earlier in this chapter. Thus, the same rules apply: keeping the digraph acyclic and ensuring a single responsibility.

Layering is an architectural pattern that encourages you to think of software components as horizontal layers of functionality that build on each other to form a whole application. Components are layered, one on top of another, and the dependency direction must always point downward. That is, the bottom layer of the application has no dependencies, and each layer upward depends on the layer immediately below it. At the top of the stack is the user interface. If the application is a service, the top layer will be the API that clients will use to interact with the system.

Common layering patterns

There are several common layering patterns from which to choose for any project. Each one presented here should be used as a guide to be tailored to the specific requirements and restrictions of your situation. The differentiating factor between the layering patterns is simply the *number* of layers used. This section starts with a simple architecture made up of only two layers, then inserts a third layer in between, and finally, extrapolates to an arbitrary number of layers.

The number of layers required correlates to the complexity of the solution; the complexity of the solution correlates to the complexity of the problem. Therefore, the more complex the problem, the more inclined you might be to invest in a multilayered architecture. Complexity, in this instance, is measured by many factors: the time constraints placed on the project, its required longevity, how frequently the requirements might change, and the importance that the development team places on patterns and practices, to name only a few.

Because this book is about adapting to changes in requirements, I advocate doing the *simplest thing possible first*, and refactoring toward something more complex *only when required*. This has positive effects on projects. First, it allows you to deliver something as soon as possible. Feedback should be sought early and frequently in software development. Trying to deliver the perfect solution is pointless if the customer's idea of perfection differs from the development team's idea of perfection. Developing a multilayer solution takes longer than a simple two-layer solution, delaying that all-important feedback loop.

Layers vs. tiers

The difference between layers and tiers is the difference between the logical organization and physical deployment of code. Logically, you could separate an application into three or four *layers*, but physically deploy it into one *tier*. The number of tiers is somewhat related to the number of machines that the application is deployed to. If you deploy to a single machine, you are deploying an application in one tier. If you deploy the application to two machines, split by at least two layers, you are deploying to two tiers.

With every tier that you deploy to, you accept that you are crossing a network boundary, and with that comes a temporal cost: it is expensive to cross a processing boundary within the same machine, but it is much more expensive to cross a network boundary. Crossing a network boundary also introduces an inevitable failure point: networks are unreliable and *will* fail. However, deploying in tiers has a distinct advantage because it allows you to scale your applications. If you deploy a web application that consists of a user interface layer, a logic layer, and a data access layer onto a single machine—thus a single tier—that machine now has a lot of work to do, and the number of users you can support will necessarily be lower. Were you to split the application's deployment into two tiers—putting the database on one tier and the user interface and logic layers on another—you could actually scale the user interface layer both *horizontally* and *vertically*.

To scale vertically, you increase the power of the computer by adding memory or processing units. This allows the single machine to achieve more by itself. However, you can also scale horizontally by adding completely new machines that perform exactly the same task. There would be multiple machines to host the web user interface code and a load balancer that would direct clients to the least busy machine at any point in time. Of course, this is not a panacea to supporting more concurrent users on a web application. This requires more care with data caching and user authentication, because each request made by a user could be handled by a different machine.

Two layers

A two-layered solution is the simplest step forward from having no discernable layering. It is useful only in a narrow set of circumstances, but it is extremely quick to implement. The only two layers included are the user interface layer and the data access layer. Remember that this does not limit you to just two *assemblies*, but two logical *groups* of assemblies: one focusing directly on the user interface, the other on data access.

Figure 3-18 shows the two layers as packages in a UML diagram, each layer containing assemblies relating to those layers. The only dependency shown is directed from the user interface layer down to the data access layer. This is the only way that the dependencies can ever be directed in any layered architecture.

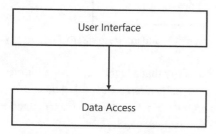

FIGURE 3-18 A two-layered application consists of the UI components and the data access components.

User interface   The user interface layer is responsible for:

- Providing a way for the user to interact with the application (for example, desktop windows and controls, a webpage, or a console application's command line or menu).

- Presenting data and information to the user.

- Receiving requests from the user in the form of queries or commands.

- Validating input that the user has entered.

The user interface layer can vary in its implementation. It could be a Windows Presentation Foundation (WPF) client packed with fancy graphics and animation, a set of webpages that the user navigates through, or a simple console application that uses command-line switches or a simple menu for the user to select a command or query to execute.

> **Note** In some cases, the user interface could be replaced with a set of services that surface functionality to clients elsewhere. There isn't really a user interface, but the two-layer architecture is still apparent, with the UI layer being replaced by an API layer.

The user interface layer sits on top of the data access layer and can make use of it. However, as discussed previously in relation to assembly references, the user interface layer should not make direct reference to any of the data access layer's implementation assemblies. There should be a strict separation between the interface and implementation assemblies of the two layers. This makes the layering diagram look a little more like Figure 3-19.

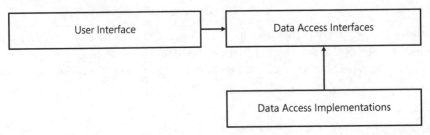

FIGURE 3-19 The two layers are separated into implementation assemblies and interface assemblies.

Each layer is the combination of an abstraction of the functionality that a higher layer depends on, along with an implementation of this abstraction. If a layer above starts referencing part of the implementation of a layer, that layer is called a *leaky abstraction*. The dependencies of that layer's implementation will begin to leak into layers further up the stack, resulting in avoidable dependencies.

Data access   The responsibilities of the data access layer are:

- Servicing queries for data.

- Serializing and deserializing object models to and from a relational model.

The implementation of the data access layer can be just as varied as that of the user interface layer. This layer typically includes some kind of persistent data store that could include a relational database such as Microsoft SQL Server, Oracle, MySQL, or PostgreSQL or a document database such as MongoDB, RavenDB, or Riak. In addition to the data storage mechanism, there is likely to be one or more supporting assemblies for executing queries or insert/update/delete commands by calling stored procedures, or for mapping data to a relational database via Entity Framework or NHibernate.

Data access layers should be hidden behind interfaces that do not depend on any of these technology choices. As with all interfaces, there should be no reference to a third-party dependency, thus keeping clients separated from the choice of implementation.

A well-designed data access layer is reusable across multiple applications. If two different user interfaces require the same data but present it in different forms, the same data access layer can be shared between them. Imagine an application that runs across multiple platforms: Windows 10 and Windows Phone 10. Both have different user interface requirements, but each could use the same data access layer.

As with any architecture, using only two layers has some tradeoffs that must be considered carefully before adoption. The two-layer architecture is a good choice when:

■ There is little or no logic to the application beyond some trivial validation. This can easily be encapsulated in either the data access layer or the user interface layer.

■ The application performs mainly CRUD operations on data. Creating, reading, updating, and deleting data becomes more difficult with every additional layer placed between the user interface and the data itself.

■ Time is short. If only a prototype or a bootstrap needs to be developed, limiting the number of layers can save a lot of time, and the feasibility of a proof of concept can be ascertained.

However, the two-layer architecture has some obvious drawbacks and is a bad choice when:

■ There is significant logic in the application, or logic is subject to change. Any logic placed in the user interface layer or data access layer is technically a pollution of that layer and decreases its flexibility and maintainability.

■ The application is certain to outgrow two layers within one or two sprints. Any concessions made to obtain quick feedback are not worth the investment if that architecture will only last a matter of weeks.

The two-layer architecture is still very much a viable alternative. Too many developers are enchanted by the latest architectural trend and overlook simpler designs. This causes an otherwise trivial application to receive feedback too late and makes it fragile and hard to maintain. Often, the simplest thing possible is the right thing to do.

Three layers

The three-layer architecture adds an extra layer between the user interface and the data access layer. This is the logic layer. The addition of the logic layer allows the application to encapsulate more complex processing. The logic layer, like the data access layer, can be reused across multiple applications, so it need not be implemented multiple times. Figure 3-20 shows the typical three-layer architecture.

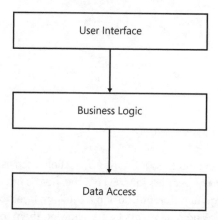

FIGURE 3-20 The third layer contains processing or business logic for the application.

Again, like the data access layer, the logic layer provides interface and implementation assemblies to clients, to avoid a leaky abstraction.

 Note Although the three-layer architecture is very common for web applications, it is typically deployed in only two *tiers*. One node handles the database, and another node handles almost everything else: the user interface, the logic, and even part of the data access.

Business logic   The business logic layer's responsibilities are to:

- Handle commands from the user interface layer.

- Model the business domain to capture business processes, rules, and workflow.

The logic layer might be a command processor that receives commands from the user via the user interface layer and, by collaborating with the data access layer, solves a specific problem or executes a particular task. It could also be a fully developed domain model that aims to map a business's processes into software. For the latter, it is common for the data access layer to include an Object/Relational Mapping (ORM) component so that the logic layer can be implemented directly into classes, possibly by using domain-driven design (DDD). In a domain model, there should be no dependencies, either further down the stack or via some implementation-specific technology. For example, the domain model's assemblies should have no dependencies on an ORM library. Instead, a separate mapping assembly should be created that is implementation-specific and instructs the ORM how to map to the domain model. This allows the domain model's core classes to be reused without depending on the ORM, and the ORM could be replaced without affecting the domain model or its clients. Figure 3-21 shows a possible implementation of a logic layer that uses a domain model.

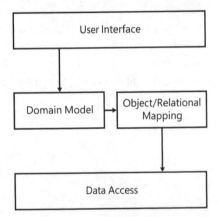

FIGURE 3-21 The assemblies of a domain model collaborate to form a logic layer.

The addition of a logic layer is necessary when there is complex logic in the application, such as business rules that aim to reflect the real-world workflows of people's jobs. Even if the logic is not particularly complex but changes often, this is a good argument for introducing a separate layer for encapsulating this behavior. It simplifies the user interface and data access layers, allowing them to concentrate fully on their only purpose.

Cross-cutting concerns

Sometimes a component's responsibilities are not easily limited to a single layer. Functions such as auditing, security, and caching can permeate through the entire application, because they are applicable at *every* layer. Tracing the code's actions at each method call and return, for example, is a useful debugging tool when the application has been deployed and if the Visual Studio debugger cannot be attached to step through the code. You can manually produce an output of the values of parameters as they are passed around, and the return values of various methods, as shown in Listing 3-24.

LISTING 3-24 Manually applying cross-cutting concerns quickly swamps the real intent of the code.

```
public void OpenNewAccount(Guid ownerID, string accountName, decimal openingBalance)
{
    log.WriteInfo("Creating new account for owner {0} with name '{1}' and an opening
    balance of {2}", ownerID, accountName, openingBalance);

    using(var transaction = session.BeginTransaction())
    {
        var user = userRepository.GetByID(ownerID);
        user.CreateAccount(accountName);
        var account = user.FindAccount(accountName);
        account.SetBalance(openingBalance);

        transaction.Commit();
    }
}
```

This is laborious and error-prone, and it instantly pollutes every method with irrelevant boilerplate code, increasing the noise-to-signal ratio. Instead, you can factor out such cross-cutting concerns into encapsulated functionality and apply them to the code in a much less invasive fashion. The most common way of adding functionality non-invasively is through aspect-oriented programming.

Aspect-oriented programming (AOP) is the application of cross-cutting concerns—or aspects—to multiple layers in the code. The .NET Framework has several AOP libraries to choose from (search NuGet for *AOP*), but the examples given here are for PostSharp, which has a free Express version, though with reduced functionality. Listing 3-25 shows tracing code factored out into a PostSharp aspect and applied as an attribute to some methods.

LISTING 3-25 Aspects are a great way to implement cross-cutting concerns.

```
[Logged]
[Transactional]
public void OpenNewAccount(Guid ownerID, string accountName, decimal openingBalance)
{
    var user = userRepository.GetByID(ownerID);
    user.CreateAccount(accountName);
    var account = user.FindAccount(accountName);
    account.SetBalance(openingBalance);
}
```

The two attributes decorating the OpenNewAccount method provide the same functionality as shown in Listing 3-24, but the intent of the method is clearer. The Logged attribute writes information about the method call to a log, including parameter values. The Transactional attribute wraps the method in a database transaction and commits the transaction on success or rolls back the transaction on failure. The key here is that both of these attributes are generic enough to be applied to *any* method, not specifically this one, so they can be reused many times.

Asymmetric layering

All of the users' requests to an application occur through the provided user interface. However, the path that the requests follow after that is not necessarily always the same. The layering could be asymmetrical, depending on the type of request being made. This is motivated by the need to be pragmatic and to consider whether the layering in place is overkill or even insufficient for some requests.

A pattern of asymmetric layering that has rapidly gained popularity in the last few years is Command/Query Responsibility Segregation (CQRS). Before discussing CQRS, which is an architectural pattern, a grounding in its method-level influencer, command/query separation, is required.

Command/query separation

Bertrand Meyer, in his book *Object-Oriented Software Construction* (Prentice Hall, 1997), used the phrase *command/query separation (CQS)* to explain that all object methods should be one of only two things: a *command* or a *query*.

Commands are imperative calls to action, requiring the code to *do* something. These methods are allowed to change the state of a system but should not also return a value. Listing 3-26 shows an example of a CQS-compliant command method, followed by one that is noncompliant.

LISTING 3-26 CQS-compliant and non–CQS-compliant command methods.

```
// Compliant command
Public void SaveUser(string name)
{
    session.Save(new User(name));
}
// Non-compliant command
public User SaveUser(string name)
{
    var user = new User(name);
    session.Save(user);
    return user;
}
```

Queries are requests for data, requiring the code to *get* something. These methods return data to calling clients but should not also change the state of a system. Listing 3-27 shows an example of a CQS-compliant query method, followed by one that is noncompliant.

LISTING 3-27 CQS-compliant and non–CQS-compliant query methods.

```
// Compliant query
Public IEnumerable<User> FindUserByID(Guid userID)
{
    return session.Get<User>(userID);
}
// Non-compliant query
public IEnumerable<User> FindUserByID(Guid userID)
{
    var user = session.Get<User>(userID);
    user.LastAccessed = DateTime.Now;
    return user;
}
```

Commands and queries are thus differentiated by the presence of a return value. If a method returns a value (and is CQS-compliant) you can safely assume that it does not change any state of the object. The advantage here is that you can reorder query calls knowing that they have no other effect on the object. A method having no return value (and that is CQS-compliant) indicates that you can assume that it does change the state of the object. For these calls, you would have to be more careful in your call order.

Command/Query Responsibility Segregation

The Command/Query Responsibility Segregation pattern is attributed to Greg Young. The pattern is the application of CQS at an architectural level and is an example of asymmetric layering. Commands and queries follow much the same rules as with CQS, but CQRS goes one step further: it acknowledges that commands and queries might need to follow different paths through the layering in order to be best handled.

An example of where minimal CQRS can be applied is when you are developing a three-layer architecture with a domain model. In this instance, the domain model is only ever used by the commanding side of the application, with a much simpler two-layer architecture used for the querying side. Figure 3-22 exemplifies this design.

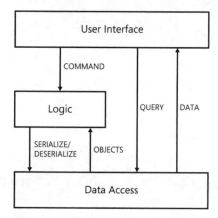

FIGURE 3-22 Domain models should only be used for handling commands.

Querying data often needs to be fast and is allowed to provide few guarantees of transactional consistency: phantom reads or nonrepeatable reads can be an acceptable tradeoff for increased responsiveness. Command processing, though, is often required to have transactional consistency, hence the differing layers in place to handle commands and queries. Sometimes, the data access layers can also differ between commands and queries. A fully ACID-compliant (*ACID* stands for atomic, consistent, isolated, durable) database might be needed for commands, whereas simple document storage might suffice for queries. The document storage would be updated asynchronously by events published from the command layer, giving eventual consistency to the query reads.

Conclusion

This chapter has shown how the organization of dependencies presents a significant challenge when creating software applications. The long-term health, adaptability, and possibly the viability of a project relies on sound management of dependencies. A mess of spaghetti-like interdependencies will occur if developers create classes that reference each other without careful consideration, which can seriously affect a team's ability to deliver business value in a consistent, predictable fashion.

Dependencies must be managed at all levels, from individual classes and methods interacting with each other, through assembly references, to the high-level architecture of components. Developers must be constantly vigilant that spurious dependencies do not leak outside of their method, class, assembly, or layer.

In some ways, this chapter underpins a lot of the content of the rest of this book. The content provides a solid foundation for maintainable, adaptive code that is reinforced with each chapter. If your assemblies are a spaghetti of references, and your layers do not hide their infrastructural dependencies, your code will become harder to test, amend, and understand, no matter what other patterns or practices you attempt to follow.

CHAPTER 4

Interfaces and design patterns

After completing this chapter, you will be able to

- Define interfaces and identify the ways in which they differ from classes.

- Apply design patterns, such as the Adapter and Strategy patterns, by using interfaces.

- Understand an interface's versatility through duck-typing, mixins, and fluent interfaces.

- Identify the limitations of interfaces and implement workarounds.

- Spot common anti-patterns and abuses of interfaces.

The interface is a powerful construct in Microsoft .NET Framework development. Although the `interface` keyword is very simple, what it represents is a very powerful paradigm. When used correctly, interfaces provide your code with the extension points that make it adaptive. However, some uses of interfaces are not so good, yet they remain in common use.

This chapter provides a reminder of the differences between classes and interfaces and describes how best to use the two together, both to protect client code from implementation changes and to facilitate polymorphism.

It also covers the versatility of interfaces and how they are a ubiquitous tool in modern software solutions. This chapter demonstrates some powerful design patterns that, when applied correctly (in conjunction with other patterns in this book) yield code that is very flexible and able to adapt to the changing requirements that Agile projects embrace.

However, interfaces alone are no panacea. A judicious sprinkling of interfaces can certainly help a project, but the interfaces must be applied in the correct manner. This chapter also explores some of the common abuses of interfaces.

What is an interface?

An interface defines the behavior that a class has, but not *how* this behavior is implemented. An interface stands as a separate construct from a class, but it requires a class to provide the working code to fulfill the interface.

An interface is defined by its syntax—that is, the language-construct side of the interface: the `interface` keyword and everything that this implies and entails. But interfaces are also defined by their features: the concepts that they represent and enable.

Syntax

Interfaces are defined by using the `interface` keyword. They can contain properties, methods, and events, just as classes can. However, no element of an interface can be given an access modifier: the implementing class must implement an interface as `public`. Listing 4-1 shows the declaration of an interface, along with a possible implementation.

LISTING 4-1 Declaring and implementing an interface.

```
public interface ISimpleInterface
{
    void ThisMethodRequiresImplementation();

    string ThisStringPropertyNeedsImplementingToo
    {
        get;
        set;
    }

    int ThisIntegerPropertyOnlyNeedsAGetter
    {
        get;
    }

    event EventHandler<EventArgs> InterfacesCanContainEventsToo;
}
// . . .
public class SimpleInterfaceImplementation : ISimpleInterface
{

    public void ThisMethodRequiresImplementation()
    {

    }

    public string ThisStringPropertyNeedsImplementingToo
    {
        get;
        set;
    }

    public int ThisIntegerPropertyOnlyNeedsAGetter
    {
        get
        {
            return this.encapsulatedInteger;
        }
        set
```

```
        {
            this.encapsulatedInteger = value;
        }
    }

    public event EventHandler<EventArgs> InterfacesCanContainEventsToo = delegate { };

    private int encapsulatedInteger;
}
```

The .NET Framework does not support the concept of multiple inheritance of classes, but it does support multiple interface implementation for a single class.

There is no limit imposed on the number of interfaces that a class can implement; the number of interfaces that really make sense on one class is more of a practical concern. Listing 4-2 extends the prior example to implement a second interface on the implementing class.

LISTING 4-2 Multiple interfaces can be implemented by a single class.

```
public interface IInterfaceOne
{
    void MethodOne();
}
// . . .
public interface IInterfaceTwo
{
    void MethodTwo();
}
// . . .
public class ImplementingMultipleInterfaces : IInterfaceOne, IInterfaceTwo
{
    public void MethodOne()
    {
    }

    public void MethodTwo()
    {
    }
}
```

There can be multiple interfaces implemented on a single class, and a single interface can be implemented by different classes.

Multiple inheritance

Some languages support the concept of inheriting from multiple base classes. C++, in particular, allows this construct. However, .NET Framework languages do not permit it, and the compiler will generate a warning if a class attempts to inherit from two or more classes, as Figure 4-1 shows.

 2   Class 'TheInterface.AttemptedMultipleInheritance' cannot
have multiple base classes: 'TheInterface.BaseClassOne'
and 'BaseClassTwo'

FIGURE 4-1 Multiple inheritance is prevented by the compiler.

Diamond inheritance problem

One reason that multiple inheritance is disallowed is because of the diamond inheritance problem. This problem occurs when two or more classes are inherited by the same class. If each of those base classes contains identical methods, which one should be used? Figure 4-2 shows a Unified Modeling Language (UML) diagram of the problem.

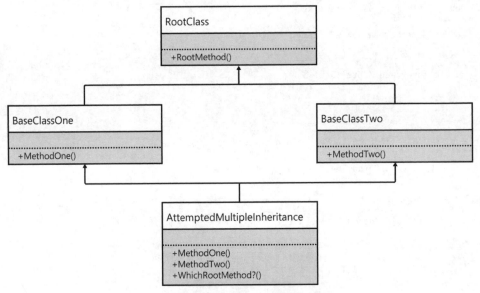

FIGURE 4-2 A UML diagram showing the diamond inheritance problem.

In this case, which version of `RootMethod()` should class `AttemptedMultipleInheritance` inherit—the one that `BaseClassOne` inherited from `RootClass`, or the one that `BaseClassTwo` inherited from `RootClass`? Because of this ambiguity, the .NET Framework does not allow multiple inheritance of classes.

Explicit implementation

Interfaces can also be implemented *explicitly*. Explicit interface implementation differs from implicit interface implementation, which is what was shown in the previous examples. Listing 4-3 shows the same example class from before, but this time it implements its interface explicitly.

LISTING 4-3 Implementing an interface explicitly.

```
public class ExplicitInterfaceImplementation : ISimpleInterface
{
    public ExplicitInterfaceImplementation()
    {
        this.encapsulatedInteger = 4;
    }

    void ISimpleInterface.ThisMethodRequiresImplementation()
    {
        encapsulatedEvent(this, EventArgs.Empty);
    }

    string ISimpleInterface.ThisStringPropertyNeedsImplementingToo
    {
        get;
        set;
    }

    int ISimpleInterface.ThisIntegerPropertyOnlyNeedsAGetter
    {
        get
        {
            return encapsulatedInteger;
        }
    }

    event EventHandler<EventArgs> ISimpleInterface.InterfacesCanContainEventsToo
    {
        add { encapsulatedEvent += value; }
        remove { encapsulatedEvent -= value; }
    }

    private int encapsulatedInteger;
    private event EventHandler<EventArgs> encapsulatedEvent;
}
```

To use an explicitly implemented interface, clients must have a reference to an instance of the interface—a reference to an implementation of the interface will not suffice. Listing 4-4 explores this in further detail.

LISTING 4-4 When implemented explicitly, the interface methods are not visible on class instances.

```
public class ExplicitInterfaceClient
{
    public ExplicitInterfaceClient(ExplicitInterfaceImplementation
        implementationReference, ISimpleInterface interfaceReference)
    {
        // Uncommenting this will cause compilation errors.
        //var instancePropertyValue =
        //implementationReference.ThisIntegerPropertyOnlyNeedsAGetter;
        //implementationReference.ThisMethodRequiresImplementation();
        //implementationReference.ThisStringPropertyNeedsImplementingToo = "Hello";
        //implementationReference.InterfacesCanContainEventsToo += EventHandler;

        var interfacePropertyValue =
            interfaceReference.ThisIntegerPropertyOnlyNeedsAGetter;
        interfaceReference.ThisMethodRequiresImplementation();
        interfaceReference.ThisStringPropertyNeedsImplementingToo = "Hello";
        interfaceReference.InterfacesCanContainEventsToo += EventHandler;
    }

    void EventHandler(object sender, EventArgs e)
    {

    }
}
```

Explicit implementation is useful when you want to avoid a signature clash, when the class already possesses a method signature that must be implemented by an interface.

Every method that can be defined in the .NET Framework has a specific method signature. This signature helps to distinguish methods as unique and to differentiate methods that have been overridden. A method's signature consists of its name and its parameter list. Note that a method's access level, return value, abstract, or sealed status all affect the method signature. Listing 4-5 shows a variety of method signatures, some of which clash. Method signatures clash if they are equal in all aforementioned criteria. No class, interface, or struct can contain methods with clashing signatures.

LISTING 4-5 Some of these methods have the same signature.

```
public class ClashingMethodSignatures
{
    public void MethodA()
    {

    }

    // This would cause a clash with the method above:
    //public void MethodA()
    //{

    //}
```

```
    // As would this: return values are not considered
    //public int MethodA()
    //{
    //    return 0;
    //}

    public int MethodB(int x)
    {
        return x;
    }

    // There is no clash here: the parameters differ.
    // This is an overload of the previous MethodB.
    public int MethodB(int x, int y)
    {
        return x + y;
    }
}
```

Properties, because they don't have parameter lists, are differentiated solely on their name. Thus, two properties' signatures clash if they possess the same name.

Imagine the class shown in Listing 4-6, which is needed to implement the aforementioned interface, InterfaceOne.

LISTING 4-6 The interface that this class needs to implement will cause method signature collisions.

```
public class ClassWithMethodSignatureClash
{
    public void MethodOne()
    {
    }
}
```

First, because the method signatures are the same, you need to add only the interface implementation notation to the class declaration, as shown in Listing 4-7.

LISTING 4-7 Implicitly implementing the interface will allow reuse of the existing methods.

```
public class ClassWithMethodSignatureClash : IInterfaceOne
{
    public void MethodOne()
    {
    }
}
```

Whenever a client calls the interface methods on this class, the same methods that are already in place will be used. An example of where this can be useful is when you are implementing the Model-View-Presenter (MVP) pattern in Windows Forms and adding an IView interface that requires a Close method to be implemented on a Form. Listing 4-8 shows this in practice.

LISTING 4-8 Sometimes the presence of a clashing method can be neatly capitalized on.

```
public interface IView
{
    void Close();
}
// . . .
public partial class Form1 : Form, IView
{
    public Form1()
    {
        InitializeComponent();
    }
}
```

However, if the class needs to provide different method bodies for the interface implementation, the class should implement the interface explicitly, avoiding the method signature clash. Listing 4-9 shows a class with clashing methods that provides different implementations of those methods.

LISTING 4-9 Explicitly implementing an interface to avoid clashing method signatures.

```
public class ClassAvoidingMethodSignatureClash : IInterfaceOne
{
    public void MethodOne()
    {
        // original implementation
    }

    void IInterfaceOne.MethodOne()
    {
        // new implementation
    }
}
```

In a similar situation, if a class needs to implement two different interfaces that are unrelated but that both contain a method with the same signature, you can implement them both implicitly and share the same method implementation. Or, as shown in Listing 4-10, you can implement them both explicitly—for clarity—to demarcate which implementation belongs to which interface.

LISTING 4-10 When implementing two interfaces with a common method signature, only explicit implementation is sufficient.

```
public class ClassImplementingClashingInterfaces : IInterfaceOne, IAnotherInterfaceOne
{
    void IInterfaceOne.MethodOne()
    {

    }

    void IAnotherInterfaceOne.MethodOne()
    {

    }
}
```

Polymorphism

The ability to use an object of one type and have it implicitly act as if it were of a different type is called *polymorphism*. Client code can interact with an object as if it is one type when it is actually another. This programmatic sleight of hand is one of the most important tenets of object-oriented programming and underpins some of the most elegant, adaptive solutions to programming problems.

Figure 4-3 shows an interface representing the behavior of vehicles, and some possible implementing classes for cars, motorcycles, and speedboats. Note that each of these three vehicle types is quite distinct, but they all exhibit the same behavior due to their unifying interface.

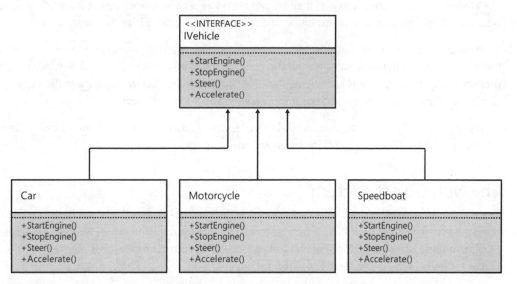

FIGURE 4-3 Interfaces pass on their behavior to implementing classes, enabling polymorphism.

In this example, vehicles are assumed to have an engine that can be started and stopped, some provision for steering, and the ability to accelerate. Polymorphism allows client code to hold a reference to an IVehicle interface and treat all concrete types as if they were the same. The details of how a car steers or accelerates compared to a motorcycle, or how a speedboat engine is started and stopped compared to a train, is irrelevant to the client. And this is a very good thing. In reality, we are all clients to this interface whenever we use a vehicle. Sure, a real interface for a vehicle is more nuanced than what is shown here, but the principle is the same. Do you need to know how the engine of your car works in order to start and stop the engine? No, not at all. Those are all implementation details that can have no bearing on your knowledge of driving. That is good interface design.

The design patterns and interface features that make up the rest of this chapter all facilitate the creation of adaptive code. Polymorphism enables each pattern to be useful for any class that fulfils an expected interface, whether it has already been written or is yet to be conceived.

Adaptive design patterns

Design patterns were popularized by the Gang of Four[1] book, *Design Patterns* (Addison-Wesley Professional, 1994). Despite the fact that this book is more than 20 years old (which is at least four ice ages in software development terms), it is still relevant today. Some of the patterns have crossed over to be reclassified as anti-patterns, but others are used frequently and enhance the adaptability of code.

Good design patterns are reusable collaborations between interfaces and classes that can be applied repeatedly in many different scenarios, across projects, platforms, languages, and frameworks. As with most notable best practices, design patterns are another theoretical tool that it is better to know than not know. They can be overused, and they are not always applicable, sometimes overcomplicating an otherwise simple solution with an explosion of classes, interfaces, indirection, and abstraction.

In my experience, design patterns tend to be either underused or overused. In some projects, there are not enough design patterns and the code suffers from a lack of discernable structure. Other projects apply design patterns too liberally, adding indirection and abstraction where the benefit is negligible. The balance is in finding the right places to apply the right patterns.

The specific design patterns contained in this chapter—and, by extension, in this book—have been selected for their ability to help create adaptive code.

The Null Object pattern

The Null Object pattern is one of the most common design patterns—and it is one of the easiest to comprehend and implement. Its purpose is to allow you to avoid throwing a NullReference-Exception and writing a plethora of null object-checking code. The UML class diagram in Figure 4-4 shows how the Null Object pattern is applied.

---

[1] So called because of its four authors: Erich Gamma, Richard Helm, Ralph Johnson, and John Vlissides.

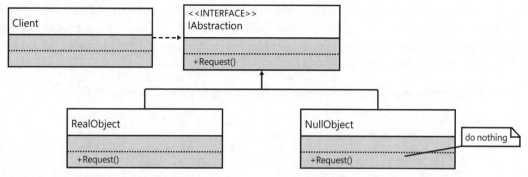

FIGURE 4-4 The Null Object pattern demonstrated as a UML class diagram.

Listing 4-11 shows some typical code that can throw a `NullReferenceException`.

LISTING 4-11 If you don't check return values for `null`, there's a chance of throwing a `NullReferenceException`.

```
class Program
{
    static IUserRepository userRepository = new UserRepository();

    static void Main(string[] args)
    {
        var user = userRepository.GetByID(Guid.NewGuid());
        // Without the Null Object pattern, this line could throw an exception
        user.IncrementSessionTicket();
    }
}
```

Every client that calls `IUserRepository.Get(Guid uniqueID)` is in danger of throwing a `null` reference. In practice, this means that every client must check that the return value is not `null`, to avoid attempting to dereference `null`, causing a `NullReferenceException` to be thrown. This would make the client shown previously look more like the code in Listing 4-12.

LISTING 4-12 Is checking against `null` really the responsibility of *all* clients?

```
class Program
{
    static IUserRepository userRepository = new UserRepository();

    static void Main(string[] args)
    {
        var user = userRepository.GetByID(Guid.NewGuid());
        if(user != null)
        {
            user.IncrementSessionTicket();
        }
    }
}
```

Checking for `null` values indicates that you are placing too much unnecessary burden on all of the clients of `IRepository`. The more clients that use this method, the greater the probability of forgetting a `null` reference check. Instead, you should change the source of the problem to perform the check for you, as shown in Listing 4-13.

LISTING 4-13 The service code should implement the Null Object pattern.

```
public class UserRepository : IUserRepository
{
    public UserRepository()
    {
        users = new List<User>
        {
            new User(Guid.NewGuid()),
            new User(Guid.NewGuid()),
            new User(Guid.NewGuid()),
            new User(Guid.NewGuid())
        };
    }

    public IUser GetByID(Guid userID)
    {
        IUser userFound = users.SingleOrDefault(user => user.ID == userID);
        if(userFound == null)
        {
            userFound = new NullUser();
        }
        return userFound;
    }

    private ICollection<User> users;
}
```

First, this code attempts to retrieve the `User` from the in-memory collection, which is no change from the previous usage shown in Listing 4-12. Now, though, you check whether the `User` instance returned is actually a `null` reference. If it is, you return a special subclass of the `IUser` type: the `NullUser`. This subclass overrides the `IncrementSessionTicket` method to do precisely nothing, as shown in Listing 4-14. In fact, a proper `NullUser` implementation overrides *all* methods to do as close to nothing as possible.

LISTING 4-14 The `NullUser` method implementations all do nothing.

```
public class NullUser : IUser
{
    public void IncrementSessionTicket()
    {
        // do nothing
    }
}
```

Additionally, whenever a method or property of the `NullUser` object is expected to return a reference to another object, it should return a special Null Object implementation of *those* types, too. In other words, all Null Object implementations should return recursive Null Object implementations. This removes the need for any `null` reference checking in clients.

This also has the added benefit of reducing the number of unit tests that you need to write. Previously, when each client had to implement the check, there would also be concomitant unit tests to confirm that the check was in place. Instead, the repository implementation is unit tested to ensure that it returns the `NullUser` implementation.

Cascading nulls

C# 6 introduced a *cascading nulls operator*, also called the *null-conditional operator* and the *safe navigation operator*. This allows the following code snippet to be simplified from this:

```
if(person != null && person.Details != null && person.Detail.Age > 30)
{
    // . . .
}
```

To this:

```
if(person?.Details?.Age > 30)
{
    // . . .
}
```

The `?.` operator thus becomes a way of safely dereferencing any object and, at worst, being handed a `default(T)` of the property type. This has proven to be a useful addition to the language, but I am reluctant to use this as an alternative to a proper Null Object implementation, for a couple of reasons.

First, there are too many instances in which a default value of a type is simply not going to suffice. The previous example of using a sensible user name to avoid throwing a `NullReference-Exception` illustrates that the alternative is not a default value but something more meaningful to the application.

Second, the null coalescing requires all clients of the code to be programmed with the possibility of `null` in mind. Part of the reason to use the Null Object pattern is to obviate `null` checking and give you the freedom to dereference with impunity. If you reject the Null Object pattern in favor of the Cascading Nulls syntax, you open yourself up to forgetting to dereference again.

Given a proper Null Object implementation, this example could be written succinctly as shown here.

```
if(person.Details.Age > 30)
{
    // . . .
}
```

This, surely, offers the most benefit: client code that is less obfuscated but that is safe from the perils of a `NullReferenceException`.

The IsNull property anti-pattern

Sometimes the Null Object pattern involves adding a Boolean `IsNull` property to the interface. All real implementations of this interface return the value `false` for this property. The Null Object implementation of the interface returns `true`. Listing 4-15 shows how this might work, given the previous example.

LISTING 4-15 The `IsNull` property is true only for Null Object implementations.

```
public interface IUser
{
    void IncrementSessionTicket();

    bool IsNull
    {
        get;
    }
}
// . . .
public class User : IUser
{
    // . . .
    public bool IsNull
    {
        get
        {
            return false;
        }
    }

    private DateTime sessionExpiry;
}
// . . .
public class NullUser : IUser
{
    public void IncrementSessionTicket()
    {
        // do nothing
    }

    public bool IsNull
    {
        get
        {
            return true;
        }
    }
}
```

The problem with this property is that it causes logic to spill out of the objects whose purpose is to encapsulate behavior. For example, `if` statements will start to creep into client code to differentiate between real implementations and the Null Object implementation. This defeats the whole purpose of the pattern, which is to avoid exposing this logic to its various clients. Listing 4-16 is a typical example of this problem.

LISTING 4-16 Logic based on the `IsNull` property makes this an anti-pattern.

```
static void Main(string[] args)
{
    var user = userRepository.GetByID(Guid.NewGuid());
    // Without the Null Object pattern, this line would throw an exception
    user.IncrementSessionTicket();

    string userName;
    if(!user.IsNull)
    {
        userName = user.Name;
    }
    else
    {
        userName = "unknown";
    }

    Console.WriteLine("The user's name is {0}", userName);

    Console.ReadKey();
}
```

This can easily be fixed by encapsulating the name of a null user inside the `NullUser` class, as in Listing 4-17.

LISTING 4-17 With proper encapsulation, the `IsNull` property is obsolete.

```
public class NullUser : IUser
{
    public void IncrementSessionTicket()
    {
        // do nothing
    }

    public string Name
    {
        get
        {
            return "unknown";
        }
    }
}
```

```
// . . .
static void Main(string[] args)
{
    var user = userRepository.GetByID(Guid.NewGuid());
    // Without the Null Object pattern, this line would throw an exception
    user.IncrementSessionTicket();

    Console.WriteLine("The user's name is {0}", user.Name);

    Console.ReadKey();
}
```

The Adapter pattern

The Adapter pattern allows you to provide an object instance to a client that has a dependency on an interface that your instance does not implement. An `Adapter` class is created that fulfills the expected interface of the client but that implements the methods of the interface by delegating to different methods of another object. It is typically used when the target class cannot be altered to fit the desired interface. This could be because it is sealed or because it belongs to an assembly for which you do not have the source. You can implement the Adapter pattern in two ways: by using the Class Adapter pattern or by using the Object Adapter pattern.

The Class Adapter pattern

Figure 4-5 shows the collaborating classes and interfaces used in the Class Adapter pattern.

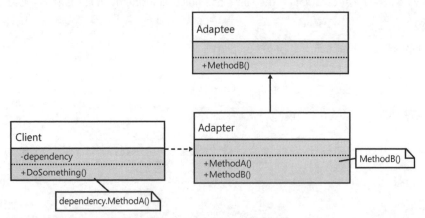

FIGURE 4-5 The UML class diagram for the Class Adapter pattern.

The Class Adapter pattern makes use of inheritance for the adapter—a subclass of the target class needs to be adapted to fit the expected interface of clients. Listing 4-18 shows how this works in practice.

LISTING 4-18 The Class Adapter pattern uses implementation inheritance.

```
public class Adaptee
{
    public void MethodB()
    {

    }
}
// . . .
public class Adapter : Adaptee
{
    public void MethodA()
    {
        MethodB();
    }
}
// . . .
class Program
{
    static Adapter dependency = new Adapter();
    static void Main(string[] args)
    {
        dependency.MethodA();
    }
}
```

This is the less common of the two types of Adapter pattern, mostly because developers are told to favor composition over inheritance. This is because inheritance, which is *whitebox* reuse, makes the subclass dependent on the implementation of a class, rather than merely on its interface. Composition, which is *blackbox* reuse, limits the dependency to the interface, so that the implementation can vary without adversely affecting clients.

Tip The terms *whitebox reuse* and *blackbox reuse* refer to an ability to see into the implementation or have the implementation hidden from inspection, respectively.

The Object Adapter pattern

The Object Adapter pattern uses composition to delegate from the methods of the interface to those of a contained, encapsulated object. Figure 4-6 shows the collaborating classes and interfaces used in the Object Adapter pattern.

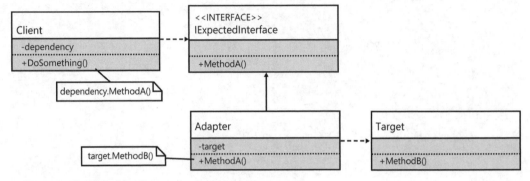

FIGURE 4-6 The UML class diagram for the Object Adapter pattern.

Listing 4-19 shows how this works in practice.

LISTING 4-19 The adaptor accepts the target class as a constructor parameter and delegates to it.

```
public interface IExpectedInterface
{
    void MethodA();
}
// . . .
public class Adapter : IExpectedInterface
{
    public Adapter(TargetClass target)
    {
        this.target = target;
    }

    public void MethodA()
    {
        target.MethodB();
    }

    private TargetClass target;
}
//
public class TargetClass
{
    public void MethodB()
    {

    }
}
```

```
//  . . .
class Program
{
    static IExpectedInterface dependency = new Adapter(new TargetClass());
    static void Main(string[] args)
    {
        dependency.MethodA();
    }
}
```

This is the more common form of the Adapter pattern. The main method uses an IExpected-Interface but, rather than provide a "real" implementation of this interface, an adapter to a different class—TargetClass—is applied. This adapter fulfills the requirements of an IExpectedInterface—a MethodA method—but it delegates this call to TargetClass, rather than doing anything directly itself.

The Strategy pattern

The Strategy pattern allows you to change the desired behavior of a class based on one or more supplied "strategies." Figure 4-7 shows the UML class diagram for the Strategy pattern.

FIGURE 4-7 The UML class diagram of the Strategy pattern.

The Strategy pattern is used whenever a class needs to exhibit variant behavior depending on the state of an object. If this behavior can change at run time depending on the current state of the class, the Strategy pattern is a perfect fit for encapsulating this variant behavior. Listing 4-20 shows how to create the Strategy pattern and use it in a class.

LISTING 4-20 The Strategy pattern in action.

```csharp
public interface IStrategy
{
    void Execute();
}
// . . .
public class ConcreteStrategyA : IStrategy
{
    public void Execute()
    {
        Console.WriteLine("ConcreteStrategyA.Execute()");
    }
}
// . . .
public class ConcreteStrategyB : IStrategy
{
    public void Execute()
    {
        Console.WriteLine("ConcreteStrategyB.Execute()");
    }
}
// . . .
public class Context
{
    public Context()
    {
        currentStrategy = strategyA;
    }

    public void DoSomething()
    {
        currentStrategy.Execute();

        // swap strategy with each call
        currentStrategy = (currentStrategy == strategyA) ? strategyB : strategyA;
    }

    private readonly IStrategy strategyA = new ConcreteStrategyA();
    private readonly IStrategy strategyB = new ConcreteStrategyB();

    private IStrategy currentStrategy;
}
```

With every call that is made to `Context.DoSomething()`, the method first delegates to the current strategy and then swaps between strategy A and strategy B. The next call delegates to the newly selected strategy before again swapping back to the original strategy.

The way the strategies are selected is an implementation detail—it does not alter the net effect of the pattern: that the behavior of the class is hidden behind an interface whose implementations are used to perform the real work.

Further versatility

The utility of interfaces is not limited to design patterns. There are some other, more-specialized uses of interfaces that are worth investigation. Though these features are not generally applicable, there are situations in which they are the right tool for the job.

Just as with design patterns, their *overuse* can be detrimental to the readability and maintainability of code. It is a difficult balancing act to find the correct number of collaborating patterns and techniques to solve a problem concisely, so exercise caution when using interfaces in the following ways.

Duck-typing

C# is a statically typed language, whereas duck-typing is more commonly found in dynamically typed languages. Duck-typing uses the "duck test":

> *When I see a bird that walks like a duck and swims like a duck and quacks like a duck, I call that bird a duck.*
>
> —*James Whitcomb Riley*

Applied to types in a programming language, the duck test suggests that, as long as an object exhibits the *behavior* of a certain interface, it should be treated as that interface. Unfortunately, this is not true by default in C#. Observe the example in Listing 4-21.

LISTING 4-21 Although the object Swan fulfills all of the methods of an IDuck, it is, in fact, *not* an IDuck.

```
public interface IDuck
{
    void Walk();

    void Swim();

    void Quack();
}
// . . .
public class Swan
{
    public void Walk()
    {
        Console.WriteLine("The swan is walking.");
    }

    public void Swim()
    {
```

```
            Console.WriteLine("The swan can swim like a duck.");
    }

    public void Quack()
    {
        Console.WriteLine("The swan is quacking.");
    }
}
// . . .
class Program
{
    static void Main(string[] args)
    {
        var swan = new Swan();

        var swanAsDuck = swan as IDuck;

        if(swan is IDuck || swanAsDuck != null)
        {
            swanAsDuck.Walk();
            swanAsDuck.Swim();
            swanAsDuck.Quack();
        }
    }
}
```

The is predicate and the as cast return false and null, respectively. The Common Language Runtime (CLR) does not consider a Swan as being an IDuck, even though it contains the same methods as the interface. A type must *implement* the interface via interface inheritance.

There are a couple of tricks that you can employ to enable the Swan class to be usable as an instance of the IDuck interface *without* having to implement it. Either you take advantage of the dynamic typing extensions in newer versions of the CLR, or you make use of a third-party library called *Impromptu Interface*.

Using the Dynamic Language Runtime

As of version 4, the .NET Framework was no longer strictly statically typed. With the introduction of the dynamic keyword, and some supporting types, you can avoid the CLR's static typing and switch to the dynamic typing of the Dynamic Language Runtime (DLR). An example of dynamic typing in C# is shown in Listing 4-22.

LISTING 4-22 The DLR can be used for duck-typing.

```
class Program
{
    static void Main(string[] args)
    {
        var swan = new Swan();
```

```
        DoDuckLikeThings(swan);

        Console.ReadKey();
    }

    static void DoDuckLikeThings(dynamic duckish)
    {
        if (duckish != null)
        {
            duckish.Walk();
            duckish.Swim();
            duckish.Quack();
        }
    }
}
```

Notice, however, that the method parameter is of type dynamic. Not only do you need to target the .NET Framework 4, dynamic typing needs to be designed into clients specifically. On both counts, this is sometimes infeasible. You can't, for example, simply start creating all methods to take dynamic parameters everywhere, or you would be better off using a dynamically typed .NET Framework language, such as IronPython[2].

Using Impromptu Interface

Impromptu Interface is a .NET Framework library that can be installed via NuGet. After it is installed, you can use the ActLike<T>() method to pass in your Swan and receive an IDuck instance that delegates to your instance. Listing 4-23 shows how this works.

LISTING 4-23 Impromptu Interface allows duck-typing in C#.

```
class Program
{
    static void Main(string[] args)
    {
        var swan = new Swan();

        var swanAsDuck = Impromptu.ActLike<IDuck>(swan);

        if(swanAsDuck != null)
        {
            swanAsDuck.Walk();
            swanAsDuck.Swim();
            swanAsDuck.Quack();
        }

        Console.ReadKey();
    }
}
```

---

[2] http://ironpython.net/

What the `ActLike` method is doing is creating a new type at run time by using Reflection Emit. This is a powerful part of the .NET Framework Reflection API that allows the creation of new types at run time. This new type fulfills the `IDuck` interface, but it also contains the Swan instance as an encapsulated field. Whenever one of the `IDuck` interface methods is called, the new type delegates to the Swan instance. It is, in effect, a run-time version of the Adapter pattern. Impromptu Interface is an automatic way of creating an Object Adapter.

CLR duck-typing support

Interestingly, the CLR already supports duck-typing. Unfortunately, this is only for one uncommon case: implementing something that is enumerable. A type that is the target of the `foreach` loop must conform to a certain interface, but that interface is not formalized and can be implemented *ad hoc* on the target class. In the example in Listing 4-24, the `Duck` class is the target of a `foreach` loop.

LISTING 4-24 The CLR implicitly supports duck-typing for enumerable types.

```
class Program
{
    static void Main(string[] args)
    {
        var duck = new Duck();

        foreach (var duckling in duck)
        {
            Console.WriteLine("Quack {0}", duckling);
        }

        Console.ReadKey();
    }
}
```

The Duck does not implement any interface, but the `GetEnumerator()` method is required by the `foreach` loop, as the compiler instructs, as shown in Figure 4-8.

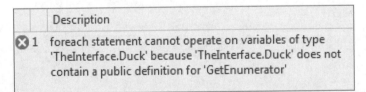

		Description
⊗	1	foreach statement cannot operate on variables of type 'TheInterface.Duck' because 'TheInterface.Duck' does not contain a public definition for 'GetEnumerator'

FIGURE 4-8 Without requiring a specific interface, the compiler complains that a public method is missing from the class.

When you implement this method with a `void` return type, you receive a new error stating that this type does not support some other required methods and properties, as shown in Figure 4-9.

	Description
1	foreach requires that the return type 'void' of 'TheInterface.Duck.GetEnumerator()' must have a suitable public MoveNext method and public Current property

FIGURE 4-9 The return type of the GetEnumerator method must also match an implicit contract.

Thus, the `Duck.GetEnumerator()` method must return a type that exposes a MoveNext property. Listing 4-25 shows the Duck implementation:

LISTING 4-25 Any class can be enumerable, providing it fulfills an implicit interface

```
public class Duck
{
    public DuckEnumerator GetEnumerator()
    {
        return new DuckEnumerator();
    }
}
```

The implementation of the DuckEnumerator and its implicit interface is shown in Listing 4-26.

LISTING 4-26 Completing the implied interface of the DuckEnumerator class.

```
public class DuckEnumerator
{
    int i = 0;

    public bool MoveNext()
    {
        return i++ < 10;
    }

    public int Current
    {
        get
        {
            return i;
        }
    }
}
```

At this point, you have successfully implemented the implicit interface that the `foreach` requires—duck-typing in action!

Mixins

An extension of duck-typing is the concept of the *mixin*. A mixin is a class that contains the implementations from multiple other classes, without using implementation inheritance. As you have already learned, multiple implementation inheritance is not supported by C#, so you must look at other solutions for implementing mixins.

One trivial but limited way of implementing mixins is to use extension methods. This allows you to add methods to a type that has already been defined, which can be very useful. An alternative is to use a third-party library such as Re-motion Re-mix, which operates much like Impromptu Interface in that it generates a new type at run time that contains all of the interfaces you specify and acts as a multifaceted adapter.

Using extension methods

Since the .NET Framework 3.5, extension methods have allowed the addition of new functionality to already existing types. Without needing to access the source of a type, nor requiring the type to be a `partial` definition, you can extend a type. Listing 4-27 shows the interface that will be enhanced in this section, along with a pair of trivial extension methods.

LISTING 4-27 Extension methods can enhance an existing interface.

```
public interface ITargetInterface
{
    void DoSomething();
}
// . . .
public static class MixinExtensions
{
    public static void FirstExtensionMethod(this ITargetInterface target)
    {
        Console.WriteLine("The first extension method was called.");
    }

    public static void SecondExtensionMethod(this ITargetInterface target)
    {
        Console.WriteLine("The second extension method was called.");
    }
}
```

Now, whenever a client has access to an `ITargetInterface` instance, and it also references the `MixinExtensions` class, these two extension methods will be available. Any number of extension methods can be created, spread across multiple static classes. Listing 4-28 shows another pair of extension methods; this time they take extra parameters.

LISTING 4-28 Extension methods can take parameters.

```
public static class MoreMixinExtensions
{
    public static void FurtherExtensionMethodA(this ITargetInterface target, int
        extraParameter)
    {
        Console.WriteLine("Further extension method A was called with argument {0}",
            extraParameter);
    }

    public static void FurtherExtensionMethodB(this ITargetInterface target, string
        stringParameter)
    {
        Console.WriteLine("Further extension method B was called with argument {0}",
            stringParameter);
    }
}
```

These extension methods can be called just like any other by any client, as in Listing 4-29.

LISTING 4-29 Clients have access to extension methods as if they were declared directly on the target interface.

```
public class MixinClient
{
    public MixinClient(ITargetInterface target)
    {
        this.target = target;
    }

    public void Run()
    {
        target.DoSomething();
        target.FirstExtensionMethod();
        target.SecondExtensionMethod();
        target.FurtherExtensionMethodA(30);
        target.FurtherExtensionMethodB("Hello!");
    }

    private readonly ITargetInterface target;
}
```

There are a few notable limitations to this approach to mixins. The first is the testability of the client. As Chapter 5, "Testing," will show, static classes do not lend themselves to be easily mocked. This makes all clients of these extension methods more difficult to properly unit test.

Worse still, also due to extension methods being static classes, they cannot hold any extra per-instance state related to the object. Sure, there are workarounds, such as storing a static dictionary that maps instances to some extra values, but this is not ideal.

Notice also that the extension methods are all targeting the same interface, and that all instances to be enhanced must implement this interface. True mixins, on the other hand, implement multiple different interfaces and act as aggregate adapters.

Using Re-motion Re-mix

An alternative way of implementing mixins is by using a third-party library such as Re-motion Re-mix. Re-mix allows you to specify, via run-time configuration, which classes to combine when creating a new instance of a certain target class. As with Impromptu Interface, it generates a new type on the fly that fulfills all of the interfaces present on the mixins requested, with each instance of this type delegating to an instance of the mixin whenever an interface method is called. The interfaces, and some sample implementations, are shown in Listing 4-30.

LISTING 4-30 The disparate interfaces to be combined as a mixin.

```csharp
public interface ITargetInterface
{
    void DoSomething();
}
// . . .
public class TargetImplementation : ITargetInterface
{
    public void DoSomething()
    {
        Console.WriteLine("ITargetInterface.DoSomething()");
    }
}
// . . .
public interface IMixinInterfaceA
{
    void MethodA();
}
// . . .
public class MixinImplementationA : IMixinInterfaceA
{
    public void MethodA()
    {
        Console.WriteLine("IMixinInterfaceA.MethodA()");
    }
}
// . . .
public interface IMixinInterfaceB
{
    void MethodB(int parameter);
}
```

```
// . . .
public class MixinImplementationB : IMixinInterfaceB
{
    public void MethodB(int parameter)
    {
        Console.WriteLine("IMixinInterfaceB.MethodB({0})", parameter);
    }
}
// . . .
public interface IMixinInterfaceC
{
    void MethodC(string parameter);
}
// . . .
public class MixinImplementationC : IMixinInterfaceC
{
    public void MethodC(string parameter)
    {
        Console.WriteLine("IMixinInterfaceC.MethodC(\"{0}\")", parameter);
    }
}
```

Note that there is no single class that implements all of these interfaces. Instead, the next step is to configure Re-mix so that, when it is asked for an instance of `TargetImplementation`, it will return a mixin containing all of the interfaces and classes combined. Listing 4-31 shows such a configuration.

LISTING 4-31 Instructing Re-mix how to construct `TargetImplementation` instances.

```
var config = MixinConfiguration.BuildFromActive()
    .ForClass<TargetImplementation>()
    .AddMixin<MixinImplementationA>()
    .AddMixin<MixinImplementationB>()
    .AddMixin<MixinImplementationC>()
    .BuildConfiguration();

MixinConfiguration.SetActiveConfiguration(config);
```

Unfortunately, you cannot simply call new on the `TargetImplementation` and expect a mixin. Instead, you have to ask Re-mix to create a `TargetImplementation` instance so that it can build a new type to your specification and instantiate it. Listing 4-32 shows how it can do that—and luckily, it is simple.

LISTING 4-32 Re-mix is in charge of creating mixins.

```
ITargetInterface target = ObjectFactory.Create<TargetImplementation>(ParamList.Empty)
```

One of the limitations of Re-mix is that you do not—and cannot—know the exact type of the instance returned by `ObjectFactory.Create`. All you know is that it is an instance of a *subclass* `TargetImplementation`. This is sort of bad news for clients, because the only interface you can guarantee that `TargetImplementation` fulfills at compile time is `ITargetInterface`. Clients of the mixin, therefore, must type-sniff by using `is` and `as` to cast the mixin to the desired interface. Listing 4-33 highlights this problem.

LISTING 4-33 Type-sniffing is bad practice but necessary for using mixins.

```
public class MixinClient
{
    public MixinClient(ITargetInterface target)
    {
        this.target = target;
    }

    public void Run()
    {
        target.DoSomething();

        var targetAsMixinA = target as IMixinInterfaceA;
        if(targetAsMixinA != null)
        {
            targetAsMixinA.MethodA();
        }

        var targetAsMixinB = target as IMixinInterfaceB;
        if(targetAsMixinB != null)
        {
            targetAsMixinB.MethodB(30);
        }

        var targetAsMixinC = target as IMixinInterfaceC;
        if(targetAsMixinC != null)
        {
            targetAsMixinC.MethodC("Hello!");
        }
    }

    private readonly ITargetInterface target;
}
```

Applying mixins to a solution works best when type-sniffing is already present or necessary. This is true with some libraries and frameworks. For example, Prism (the Windows Presentation Foundation/Model-View-Viewmodel library) makes use of type-sniffing, and the functionality required of client classes can be segregated into different implementations and recombined via mixins.

Fluent interfaces

An interface is said to be *fluent* if it returns itself from one or more of its methods. This allows clients to chain calls together, as shown in Listing 4-34.

LISTING 4-34 Fluent interfaces allow method chaining.

```
public class FluentClient
{
    public FluentClient(IFluentInterface fluent)
    {
        this.fluent = fluent;
    }

    public void Run()
    {
        // without using fluency
        fluent.DoSomething();
        fluent.DoSomethingElse();
        fluent.DoSomethingElse();
        fluent.DoSomething();
        fluent.ThisMethodIsNotFluent();

        // using fluency
        fluent.DoSomething()
            .DoSomethingElse()
            .DoSomethingElse()
            .DoSomething()
            .ThisMethodIsNotFluent();
    }

    private readonly IFluentInterface fluent;
}
```

This improves readability because it avoids repeated references to the instance of the interface. It is an increasingly popular way to implement configuration or finite state machines, as described in Chapter 10, "Interface segregation."

Fluent interfaces are easy to implement, too. All the class has to do is return this from the method. Because the class is already an implementation of the interface, by returning this, the class returns only the interface portion of itself, thus hiding the rest of the implementation. Listing 4-35 shows the definition of the IFluentInterface and the implementation used in this example.

LISTING 4-35 Implementing a simple fluent interface is easy.

```
public interface IFluentInterface
{
    IFluentInterface DoSomething();

    IFluentInterface DoSomethingElse();

    void ThisMethodIsNotFluent();
}
// . . .
public class FluentImplementation : IFluentInterface
{
    public IFluentInterface DoSomething()
    {
        return this;
    }

    public IFluentInterface DoSomethingElse()
    {
        return this;
    }

    public void ThisMethodIsNotFluent()
    {

    }
}
```

Note that one of the methods of the interface is not fluent—it returns `void`. If a method returns anything but an interface, it is not fluent. Any chaining of methods that a client does will be halted by a call to a method that is not fluent.

Conclusion

In this chapter, you have learned what interfaces are and why they are such a key facet of writing adaptive code. They are catalysts for polymorphism, which allows you to encapsulate variation in families of classes. They are the root around which design patterns grow. And yet they actually *do* nothing.

Remember, interfaces are useless without accompanying implementations. But without interfaces, implementations—and their associated dependencies—would infiltrate and pollute your code, making it hard to maintain and extend. A well-placed interface acts as a firewall between the dirty implementation details of service code and a clean, well-organized client.

Interfaces also have other, more-specialized features, such as duck-typing and mixins. These are seldom used, but when applied in the right context, they can simplify otherwise convoluted code and add an extra dimension of adaptability.

The groundwork laid in this chapter will be of great importance as you experience the ubiquity of the interface throughout the rest of the book.

CHAPTER 5

Testing

After completing this chapter, you will be able to

- Define different kinds of application testing and choose between techniques.

- Write code in a test-first fashion, focusing on implementing only that which the tests demand.

- Understand the different types of testing that can improve aspects of a software product.

- Diagnose problems created by testing anti-patterns, which reduce code adaptiveness.

Software quality is not limited to the quality of the code and how adaptive it is to change. It is also a measure of how accurately the software fulfills its requirements. *Testing* is the umbrella of practices that can be used to ensure this kind of software quality.

Unit testing is the discipline of writing code that tests other code. Unit tests are source code, thus they can be compiled and executed. As each unit test runs, it reports the test's success or failure with a simple true or false, often a green or a red visual indicator. If all of the unit tests pass, the production code that they test is considered to be working, meeting its requirements. If even a single unit test fails—out of possibly thousands—the production code overall is deemed not to be meeting its requirements.

When you unit test as early as possible in the process—that is, before you write any production code—you create a safety net to catch any subsequent errors when you change code. If a unit test transitions from a passing state to a failing state, you know that the last change you made is responsible for breaking the code. The process of writing unit tests and then improving code toward better design creates a positive feedback loop whereby the code quality increases while you simultaneously make progress with implementing new features.

Unit testing

To some degree, unit testing should be considered a mandatory part of every programmer's daily discipline. An idealized situation is when production code—the code that forms the basis of the software product—is *entirely* the result of the tests that were written to verify the application's behavior. Later in this chapter, you will learn how this can be achieved through test-driven development, but bear in mind that the aim is to balance the pragmatic with the purist. It is better to ship something and accept some prudent technical debt than it is to be late for the sake of gilding a working solution. That said, every project is unique in its tolerance for timeliness versus completeness.

There are some recognized unit testing patterns and guidelines that will result in repeatable success. These patterns and guidelines are no longer new but expected, tried, and tested. The arrangement and naming of unit tests and, most of all, how to ensure the testability of the code are all primary concerns. If these concerns are neglected, unit tests will no longer be synchronized with the code that they test, test failures will be tolerated, and the safety net will wither and break.

Arrange, Act, Assert

Every unit test is composed of three distinct parts:

- The **arrange**ment of the preconditions of the test

- The performance of the **act** that is being tested

- The **assert**ion that the expected behavior occurred

These three parts form the *Arrange, Act, Assert* (AAA) pattern. Every test that you write should follow this pattern so that other people can read your unit tests.

> **Note** Some readers might be more familiar with this pattern expressed as *Given, When, Then*. This is directly analogous to Arrange, Act, Assert, but it goes like this: *given* some preconditions, *when* the target of the test is executed, *then* some expected behavior should have occurred.

Arranging the preconditions

Before you can execute the action that you need to test, you must set up the scenario that you are testing. For some tests, this will be as simple as constructing the system under test (SUT). The SUT is the class that you are testing. Without a valid instance of the class, you will not be able to test any of its methods.

> **Tip** Static methods do not require an instance to be tested. In cases where your SUT is a static method, you can test directly through the class. Be advised, though: static methods are often a poor design choice. Static methods should have minimal dependencies, because they are very difficult to mock, as you will see later in this chapter.

Listing 5-1 shows a minimal Arrange section of a test for an Account class that represents a customer's balance and transactions. For this example, I use MSTest[1].

---

[1] MSTest is a convenient choice for unit tests—hence its use for the examples in this chapter—but it is not a great choice. NUnit and XUnit are better alternative testing frameworks that rely on external dependencies.

This chapter will continue to build on this example for the Act and Assert parts of the test, too. The test method's name, `AddingTransactionChangesBalance()`, succinctly describes the intent of the test—to ensure that whenever a transaction is added to the account, the balance of the account is changed to include this new transaction.

LISTING 5-1 Constructing the SUT is a common first step in arranging a unit test.

```
[TestClass]
public class AccountTest
{
    [TestMethod]
    public void AddingTransactionChangesBalance()
    {
        // Arrange
        var account = new Account();
    }
}
```

The Arrange step taken here is simple enough. The only precondition to this test is a new instance of the Account class. You create this directly in your test by calling the new operator. From here, you can move on to the next step in the AAA pattern.

Performing the testable act

Now that you have the system under test ready to be acted on, you can execute the method that you are testing. Each test's Act phase should consist of just one interaction with the system under test—one method call or property getter or setter, for instance. This ensures that the tests are simple to both read and write and have clearly delineated execution paths.

Listing 5-2 shows the addition of the Act part of the test. In keeping with the test method's name, the test calls the `account.AddTransaction()` method.

LISTING 5-2 Every Act phase should consist of only one interaction with the SUT.

```
[TestClass]
public class AccountTest
{
    [TestMethod]
    public void AddingTransactionChangesBalance()
    {
        // Arrange
        var account = new Account();

        // Act
        account.AddTransaction(200m);
    }
}
```

The test has passed a value into the AddTransaction method. This represents the monetary amount of the transaction that you are adding to the account. It is a decimal value, meaning that it has very high precision, but there is no currency value associated with this amount. For simplicity, the assumption is that all accounts and transactions are in US dollars.

With the Arrange and Act phases complete, you can move on to the final part of the test.

Asserting the expectations

Both of the phases up to this point have really been a preamble to the crux of this and every unit test: the assertion. This is the part that will give you the green indicator of success or the red indicator of failure of the test as a whole. The test method name is again the reference point for the assertion that you are making—that the account balance has changed. In this case, the assertion is going to be a comparison of an *actual* value and an *expected* value. This is a common kind of assertion in state-based tests, which are tests whose assertions depend on the state of the SUT. This particular assertion requires the actual and expected values to be equal.

The Balance property of the Account class will be queried for the actual value, and you will provide the expected value as a constant. This means that you must have prior knowledge of the expected value, which is a key factor to consider when writing tests. Rather than deriving the expected value in code, you should know what the expected value is ahead of time. In this scenario, it is easy. Given a new account, whose opening balance is zero, if you add $200.00 to that account, what should the expected balance be?

$0.00 + $200.00 = $200.00

Thus, you can write your Assert phase and complete your AAA test, as shown in Listing 5-3.

LISTING 5-3 An assertion of expected behavior has been added to the unit test.

```
[TestClass]
public class AccountTest
{
    [TestMethod]
    public void AddingTransactionChangesBalance()
    {
        // Arrange
        var account = new Account();

        // Act
        account.AddTransaction(200m);

        // Assert
        Assert.AreEqual(200m, account.Balance);
    }
}
```

This test is now ready to compile and run. By running the test, you can verify whether or not the system under test behaves as expected.

Running the tests

When the test is complete, you need to run it by using a unit test runner. Unit tests are contained in test projects whose output is assemblies, not executables. This means that the test projects cannot be run by themselves but must instead be provided as input to a unit test runner. Microsoft Visual Studio supports MSTest unit tests with its integrated test runner, whereas some other kinds of unit tests require plugins to provide integrated support in Visual Studio.

In Visual Studio, you can run MSTest unit tests by selecting one of the options from the Test > Run menu. For now, you can select the All Tests option, which is aliased to the keyboard shortcut Ctrl+R, A. The output of running the `AddingTransactionChangesBalance` unit test is shown in Figure 5-1.

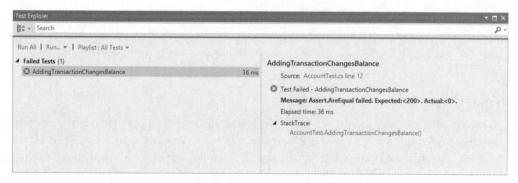

FIGURE 5-1 Running the unit test in the Visual Studio integrated MSTest unit test runner.

The test runner shows a master-details view of the unit tests that you have chosen to run. The list of tests is enumerated in the left pane, with more details about the selected test shown in the right pane. You can tell that the test took only a few milliseconds to execute, which is not much at all. This is precisely one of the advantages of writing unit tests—it does not take long to run thousands of unit tests, compared to the effort required to test manually.

However, notice that the test assertion has *failed* because the expected value of 200 did not match the actual value provided. The `account.Balance` property was used for the actual value of the assertion, and it returned 0.

This is because the `AddTransaction` method is not yet implemented. Listing 5-4 shows the minimal `Account` class implementation that was required up to this point.

LISTING 5-4 The system under test does not need to be completely implemented before the unit test.

```
public class Account
{
    public void AddTransaction(decimal amount)
    {

    }

    public decimal Balance
    {
        get;
        private set;
    }
}
```

As you can tell, this class does nothing with the provided transaction amount in the `AddTransaction` method, and the `Balance` is just a default auto-property, though with a private setter. To make this test pass, you have to implement the `Account` class so that it meets your current expectations.

Test-driven development

To implement a unit test, you do not need a complete implementation of the system under test. In test-driven development (TDD), it is preferential *not* to have a working system under test before you write the unit tests. When you use a TDD approach to writing software, you write the unit tests and the production code in tandem, with a failing test written for every expected behavior exhibited by every method of every class in the production code. The failing test fails only because the production code does not exist yet. The test states—via assertions—that the production code should act in some way, but because it does not yet, the test fails. After the production code is implemented in the simplest way possible to satisfy the test's requirements, the test will succeed.

Red, green, refactor!

What has been produced so far with the `AddingTransactionChangesBalance()` test is the first part of a three-phase process called *red, green, refactor*.

1. Write a failing test that targets the expected behavior of the SUT.

2. Implement just enough of the SUT so that the new test passes without breaking existing successful tests.

3. If any refactoring can be done on the SUT to improve its design or overall quality, now is the time to do so.

The first phase generates a failing test, which test runners indicate with a red icon. The second phase makes that failing test succeed, turning the icon green. The third phase allows you to incrementally improve the production code piece by piece without fear of breaking its functionality. Refactoring is covered in more detail in Chapter 6, "Refactoring."

To turn the failing test from red to green (from failure to success), you need to look at the second phase of the process: *implement just enough of the SUT so that the test passes*. Because this is currently the only test, you need not concern yourself with breaking any existing successful tests.

The test asserts that the balance is 200 after a transaction for that amount is added to a new account. Listing 5-5 shows the bare minimum needed to make the unit test pass.

LISTING 5-5 Always do the bare minimum when transitioning a test from red to green.

```
public class Account
{
    public Account()
    {
        Balance = 200m;
    }

    public void AddTransaction(decimal amount)
    {

    }

    public decimal Balance
    {
        get;
        private set;
    }
}
```

The changed code is highlighted in bold. To transition the test from red to green, the code has introduced a default constructor to the Account class that initializes the Balance property to 200m. To prove that this works—that the test now passes—Figure 5-2 shows a screenshot of the Visual Studio test runner after the failing test was rerun.

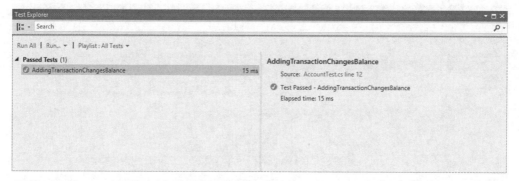

FIGURE 5-2 The test does, indeed, now pass—but is it correct?

Before you pat yourself on the back and move on to the final, refactoring phase, you should assess whether this is the correct way to implement the expected behavior that the test specified. You can prove that it is *not* the correct implementation by adding another expectation in the form of another unit test.

This new test defines the expected value for the `Balance` field given a newly created `Account` object. Recall that the expected value of the `Balance` field was calculated after a transaction of $200 was added to the account. This included the *assumption* that an unspecified opening balance was *zero*. This is an expected behavior, just like any other, so you should write a test that asserts that your expectations of the code are correctly implemented. Listing 5-6 shows the AAA pattern applied to such a unit test.

LISTING 5-6 The Arrange part of this test is omitted.

```
[TestMethod]
public void AccountsHaveAnOpeningBalanceOfZero()
{
    // Arrange

    // Act
    var account = new Account();

    // Assert
    Assert.AreEqual(0m, account.Balance);
}
```

First, notice that the name of the test method is again descriptive of the expected behavior that it asserts. In this case, though, the Arrange part of the unit test is blank, meaning that this part of the AAA syntax is optional. The part of the SUT that is being tested is the behavior of its default constructor, which is the only interaction with the SUT as part of the Act phase. The assertion, finally, codifies the previously stated assumption that a new `Account` will have a balance of 0m.

The fact that this unit test fails, even though the first unit test passes, indicates that the implementation of the expectations of the first unit test was erroneous. Figure 5-3 shows the output from the MSTest runner.

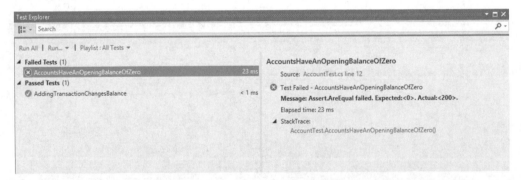

FIGURE 5-3 The second unit test fails because of the implementation of the first unit test's expectations.

From this position, if you undo your previous changes to the Account class, you will transition your failing *opening balance* test from red to green, while correctly causing your *adding transaction* test to fail again. By doing this, you have proven that you have the correct implementation of the `Account` class for the *opening balance* test, but the wrong implementation for the *adding transaction* test.

The effect of adding each new test is that further constraints are created on viable implementations of the SUT. Each test carries with it an expectation of behavior, and each expectation requires balancing in the SUT. The simplest possible implementation to ensure that both tests pass is shown in Listing 5-7.

LISTING 5-7 Both tests now pass with this implementation, but is it correct?

```
public class Account
{
    public void AddTransaction(decimal amount)
    {
        Balance = 200m;
    }

    public decimal Balance
    {
        get;
        private set;
    }
}
```

The balance of a new account will be zero on creation but will change to 200m when `Add-Transaction` is called. Of course, despite the fact that both tests now pass, intuition should tell you that this is absolutely wrong. The point of writing the simplest thing first—rather than jumping directly to the obvious correct solution—is to derive coded assertions from your intuition. Can you write another unit test that fails and proves that this implementation is not right? Listing 5-8 shows an example.

LISTING 5-8 This test is identical to the prior version but has a different amount value.

```
[TestMethod]
public void Adding100TransactionChangesBalance()
{
    // Arrange
    var account = new Account();

    // Act
    account.AddTransaction(100m);

    // Assert
    Assert.AreEqual(100m, account.Balance);
}
```

This test method does the same job as the first, which tested adding a transaction, but it adds a transaction of $100 rather than $200. Although the difference in test assertion is small, it is sufficient to prove that the Account.AddTransaction method is wrong.

As expected, this new test fails. If you alter the Account class so that the value 100m is hardcoded into the AddTransaction method, you will fail the original test and transition this test from red to green. Instead, you can now implement the correct solution, as Listing 5-9 shows.

LISTING 5-9 All three tests pass with this implementation, but it is *still* wrong!

```
public class Account
{
    public void AddTransaction(decimal amount)
    {
        Balance = amount;
    }

    public decimal Balance
    {
        get;
        private set;
    }
}
```

With this implementation in place and all three of your unit tests passing—all having previously failed—the sun is shining and everything is right in the world. Except that it isn't! Again, the expectations of the AddTransaction method do not match up to the reality of the implementation. A fourth unit test highlights the problem, as Listing 5-10 shows.

LISTING 5-10 This unit test should finally help crack the AddTransaction method.

```
[TestMethod]
public void AddingTwoTransactionsCreatesSummationBalance()
{
    // Arrange
    var account = new Account();
    account.AddTransaction(50m);

    // Act
    account.AddTransaction(75m);

    // Assert
    Assert.AreEqual(125m, account.Balance);
}
```

This test points to the correct functionality of the AddTransaction method—at least for the moment. The point is that, with requirements changing and new features being added, you need to codify the expectations of your classes so that you can rely on existing unit tests to form a safety net. Without this, you could easily make a change to your code that appears to work in the narrow circumstances under which you are manually testing it, but that breaks under unusual input or breaks something unrelated elsewhere.

The test you have added asserts that an account's balance is the summation of all of its transactions. Previously, your most correct implementation would set the balance to the value of the last transaction that occurred, meaning that this test will fail and your implementation is not yet right. Listing 5-11 shows the implementation of the AddTransaction method that allows all four unit tests to pass.

LISTING 5-11 This implementation is so far the best for AddTransaction.

```
public class Account
{
    public void AddTransaction(decimal amount)
    {
        Balance += amount;
    }

    public decimal Balance
    {
        get;
        private set;
    }
}
```

After the transition from red to green for each unit test, you had the opportunity to refactor the implementation of the SUT, but this example was very simple. This phase of the process becomes more important with each new method added to the SUT. Refactoring in this manner is covered in more detail in the next chapter.

If you have never written unit tests before, this might seem like taking the scenic route on a drive—why not just head straight for the destination by implementing the production code? The reason will be made clear throughout this chapter, but the short answer is that writing your tests first helps to prevent over-engineering a solution and provides a suite of regression tests to prevent breaking existing functionality.

More complex tests

The previous example involved unit testing a class that forms part of the domain model of an application in a test-first manner. As described in Chapter 3, "Dependencies and layering," the domain model is an implementation of a business logic layer that sits between the user interface and the data access layers.

Specification

For the next set of tests, which build on this `Account` class, you will test a different part of the business logic layer: a service. The user interface for this hypothetical application could be tethered to any framework—ASP.NET MVC, Windows Presentation Foundation (WPF), or Windows Forms—and your service should be reusable regardless of the framework. This means that the service will contain no dependency specific to any of these frameworks, but it will depend on the `Account` class, though indirectly. Figure 5-4 shows the dependencies between the layers and classes that will form this example.

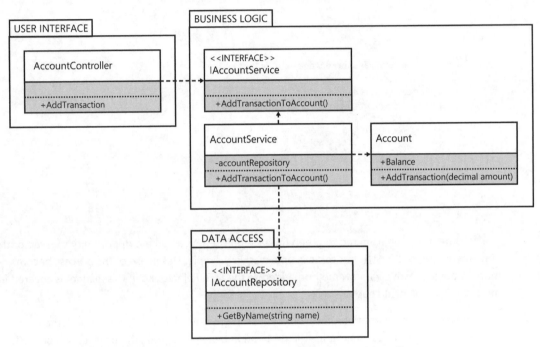

FIGURE 5-4 The dependencies and implementations that form the subsystem you will now test.

The Unified Modeling Language (UML) diagram shows the three packages that make up the three-layered architecture that you will create. The user interface will contain Model-View-Controller (MVC) controllers, although these could be view models or presenters for Model-View-ViewModel (MVVM) or Model-View-Presenter (MVP), respectively. Specifically, the `AccountController` will have a handler for the user interface action of adding a transaction to an account. This controller has a dependency on the interface of the `AccountService` that you are preparing to implement.

The `AccountService` lives in the business logic layer, along with its interface and the domain model, represented by the `Account` class that was previously implemented. Note that the packages represent the logical layers of the application, as opposed to mapping directly to Visual Studio projects and, therefore, to assemblies. The `AccountService` will require some way to retrieve `Account` instances from whichever persistent storage mechanism you are using. Because you are using a domain model in the business logic layer, the data access layer is implemented by using an Object/Relational Mapper (ORM).

A repository interface is used to hide the specific persistence logic from client code. The IAccountRepository is responsible for returning Account instances. The service depends on this interface because it will need to retrieve an account as part of its implementation.

Designing the test

The tests for the AccountService.AddTransactionToAccount method are written by using TDD and AAA, exactly as before. First, you need to think of what to expect of the method: that it delegates to the correct Account instance's AddTransaction method, passing in the correct value for the transaction amount. Let's specify the Arrange, Act, and Assert phases:

- **Arrange** Ensure that there is an available instance of the SUT—the AccountService class.

- **Act** Call the AddTransactionToAccount method.

- **Assert** The SUT calls the AddTransaction method on an Account instance, passing in the correct amount value.

Listing 5-12 shows a first attempt at writing this test.

LISTING 5-12 The first attempt at this new test is incomplete.

```
[TestClass]
public class AccountServiceTests
{
    [TestMethod]
    public void AddingTransactionToAccountDelegatesToAccountInstance()
    {
        // Arrange
        var sut = new AccountService();

        // Act
        sut.AddTransactionToAccount("Trading Account", 200m);

        // Assert
        Assert.Fail();
    }
}
```

Everything looks fine until you get to the assertion. You need to assert that a certain method is called on an object and a particular value is passed in, but how do you assert that? This is where *test doubles* come in.

Test doubles

Sometimes you need to provide your system under test with a dependency. This dependency can be another class or an externality such as the filesystem, a database, or a web service. Often, passing in these dependencies to your system under test can make your tests brittle and prone to intermittent failure. It also prevents the tests from being true *unit* tests, because they require external dependencies to pass. *Test doubles* are fake implementations that achieve the goal of fulfilling a dependency and might also aid your ability to assert against various class interactions. There are five different subcategories of test double:

- **Dummies** This is the simplest of all test doubles. Dummies are intended to fulfil parameter lists and have no special behavior. Often, real implementations are used as dummies and might be primitive types, which are nevertheless required to turn a unit test green.

- **Spies** A spy records the calls that have been made to its methods, along with the parameters that were supplied to each call. The record of these calls can then be used in assertions to ensure that certain calls were made.

- **Stubs** A stub is a dependency that is required by the system under test and that will return a pre-supplied answer whenever queried. Stubs are most useful at the seams of an application, where external dependencies are required. Instead of depending on a database, you can depend on a stub that can return dummy data.

- **Fakes** A fake is very similar to a stub, but the intent is subtly different. Fakes are not supplied with any preconceived responses to queries, but are instead closer to real implementations with some necessary concession to avoid an external dependency. Personally, I make a distinction between a manually implemented mock and a mock that is supplied by a mocking framework: manual mocks are called *fakes*.

- **Mocks** Whereas stubs and fakes provide test doubles for dependencies that are indirect queries, mocks are test doubles for dependencies that have indirect commands. Mocks are useful to determine whether a command was executed on a dependency of the system under test.

Manual test fakery

Continuing the example from above, the first requirement before you can write your assertion is an Account instance to assert against. The IAccountRepository interface will be used by the Account-Service to retrieve the Account that it will interact with, so you cannot just give the AccountService such an instance. Instead, you need to give the AccountService an IAccountRepository—but you do not have any implementations available. Because you depend on interfaces, instead of classes, you can write a fake implementation of an interface that will be sufficient only for the test. Listing 5-13 shows such a class, which lives in the unit testing assembly.

LISTING 5-13 A very simple implementation of a repository that is only for testing purposes.

```
public class FakeAccountRepository : IAccountRepository
{
    public FakeAccountRepository(Account account)
    {
        this.account = account;
    }

    public Account GetByName(string accountName)
    {
        return account;
    }

    private Account account;
}
```

You can now create an account service implementation. Listing 5-14 shows the new implementation of the AccountService class.

LISTING 5-14 The present state of the AccountService class.

```
public class AccountService : IAccountService
{
    public AccountService(IAccountRepository repository)
    {
        this.repository = repository;
    }

    public void AddTransactionToAccount(string uniqueAccountName, decimal
transactionAmount)
    {

    }

    private readonly IAccountRepository repository;
}
```

The unit test can now be completed, with new Arrange criteria:

- Ensure that there is an Account instance available to assert against.

- Ensure that there is a fake IAccountRepository instance available to pass to the service on construction.

These criteria, and the correct assertion, form the failing test in Listing 5-15.

LISTING 5-15 This test fails for the right reasons: the `AccountService` is not yet implemented.

```
[TestClass]
public class AccountServiceTests
{
    [TestMethod]
    public void AddingTransactionToAccountDelegatesToAccountInstance()
    {
        // Arrange
        var account = new Account();
        var fakeRepository = new FakeAccountRepository(account);
        var sut = new AccountService(fakeRepository);

        // Act
        sut.AddTransactionToAccount("Trading Account", 200m);

        // Assert
        Assert.AreEqual(200m, account.Balance);
    }
}
```

As shown in this listing, first you create an account that has an opening balance of zero. You then create an instance of your fake account repository, passing your account into it. Because the fake implements the interface of an account repository, the fake can be passed to the `AccountService` class, your SUT.

After calling the method that is the target of the test, you then assert that the account has the expected balance of 200m. As demonstrated by Figure 5-5, this assertion fails because the target method has not yet been implemented.

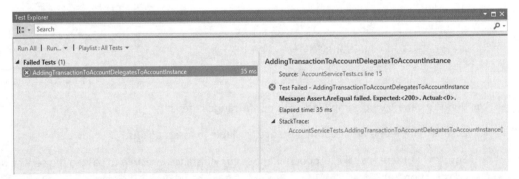

FIGURE 5-5 Continuing the red-to-green transition, you have your failing test.

Now that you have a unit test that specifies some behavior that is missing from your production code, you can do the simplest thing possible to make the unit test pass, as shown in Listing 5-16.

LISTING 5-16 This implementation of the AccountService makes the test pass.

```
public class AccountService : IAccountService
{
    public AccountService(IAccountRepository repository)
    {
        this.repository = repository;
    }

    public void AddTransactionToAccount(string uniqueAccountName, decimal
    transactionAmount)
    {
        var account = repository.GetByName(uniqueAccountName);
        account.AddTransaction(transactionAmount);
    }

    private readonly IAccountRepository repository;
}
```

The unit test has guided you into doing the right thing in this implementation. You had to use the repository to retrieve the account, and you had to call the AddTransaction method on that account to mutate the read-only Balance property. If anyone subsequently breaks this method so that it no longer matches the expectations set out in the unit test, you will know about it very quickly.

Mocking frameworks

It requires little power of the imagination to realize that creating mocks can quickly become laborious. Imagine all of the permutations of unit tests that you might write, and all of the different interfaces that your SUTs might need. This is a lot of extra code just to support your unit tests.

There is another way to mock the IAccountRepository, but it requires the use of an external mocking framework. One positive aspect of writing fakes is that you can write them in isolation without requiring any third-party dependencies. However, mocking frameworks are commonplace nowadays, and there are many to choose from. The following example uses one of the most popular: Moq. This is variously pronounced *Moh-kyoo* and *Mok*.

By using NuGet, you can quickly add your reference to Moq by searching for its package on the online feed. The magic behind Moq is that it can create dynamic proxies of any interface that you ask it to mock. You will edit your existing test to use a Moq mock instead of your manual fake, as shown in Listing 5-17.

LISTING 5-17 Mocking frameworks such as Moq allow you to create mocks very easily.

```
[TestMethod]
public void AddingTransactionToAccountDelegatesToAccountInstance()
{
    // Arrange
    var account = new Account();
    var mockRepository = new Mock<IAccountRepository>();
    mockRepository.Setup(r => r.GetByName("Trading Account")).Returns(account);
    var sut = new AccountService(mockRepository.Object);

    // Act
    sut.AddTransactionToAccount("Trading Account", 200m);

    // Assert
    Assert.AreEqual(200m, account.Balance);
}
```

The changes to the test are highlighted in bold. Rather than instantiating your own fake repository, you now create a new Mock<IAccountRepository> object. This object is very powerful and allows you to set all sorts of expectations and behavior on your mocked interfaces. This class does not implement your interface, so, unlike your fake, it is not directly a viable instance of the IAccountRepository. This is because the Common Language Runtime (CLR) does not allow classes to inherit from generic parameters. Instead, there is a composition relationship between the mock and the proxy instance that it creates. The Object property allows you to access the underlying mocked interface, which is passed in to the AccountService in this example.

Before you provide your mock to the SUT, you need to specify how it should behave. By default, Moq defines *loose* mocks, which means that all of their return values are default. The default for any reference type is null, and this applies to the Account class. The alternative to the loose mock is the *strict* mock, which will throw an exception whenever it is faced with a method call or property access that you have not already specified. Neither of these options is what you need, so you have to set up some expected behavior manually.

The Setup method of a Mock instance is very clever. It accepts a lambda expression that provides an instance of the underlying mocked type as a context parameter. By calling a method on the type, you specify that you want something to happen when the method is called, with the exact arguments provided. What you choose to specify depends on your test situation. Moq lets you set the following expectations on a method call:

- Call some other lambda expression.

- Return a specific value.

- Throw a specified type of exception.

- Verify that this method was called.

Mocks and test over-specification

Testing with mocks is a common but potentially onerous practice. Tests that rely on mocks can easily become *over-specified*. An over-specified test is fragile, but you can avoid this fragility by changing what you assert. The problem arises when the test includes intimate knowledge of *how* the system under test (SUT) works. In other words, a test is over-specified when it has knowledge of the SUT's *implementation* rather than its expected *behavior*.

A unit test that uses mocks might need to know how the SUT is implemented. However, you should always remember that a unit test is a specification of expected behavior, so you should avoid introducing tests against implementation details. This might include calls to other interfaces on which the SUT might depend. If you assert that a method on an interface must be called, the test has become wedded not to a certain behavior but to a specific implementation.

Over-specified tests are undesirable because they prevent refactoring of the production code that they test. A suite of passing unit tests accompanying a method or class is a signal that the implementation of the method or class can be altered with impunity: the only way that the tests will fail is if the expected behavior of the code is broken. Over-specified tests do not provide such a guarantee, because they will fail if the implementation of the method or class has changed—even if the expected behavior remains intact.

There are two options for avoiding test over-specification when testing with mocks. The first is to test behavior only. State-based tests are the best example of testing expected behavior. If a method accepts data as input and returns altered data as output, the method can be treated as a black box for testing purposes. If the method accepts inputs A, B, and C and returns outputs X, Y, and Z, it is irrelevant to the test how it arrived at such answers. The method can then be refactored without breaking the unit tests.

The second option is less attractive but is sometimes the only option. You can treat the unit test and the implementation that it tests as one atomic unit: if one changes, so must the other. This is akin to accepting that the unit test is over-specified and planning to throw away the unit test along with the production implementation when refactoring. This isn't quite as wasteful as it might seem. As you'll see in Part III, "SOLID code," SOLID code yields smaller, more directed classes that are never altered anyway.

For this test, you want the second option: return a specified value. The fluent interface of the `Mock.Setup` method call allows you to chain the call to the `Returns` method. This improves readability and reduces what is already becoming a rather large Arrange phase of the test. The `Returns` method is given the `Account` instance that you have already created, and with this you have completed setting your expectations of this mock. In brief, you have given the mock the following instruction:

When the `GetByName` method is called for this `IAccountRepository` instance, and the account name provided is `"Trading Account"`, return this instance of the `Account` class.

When you run your test again it will pass, just as before, as proven by Figure 5-6.

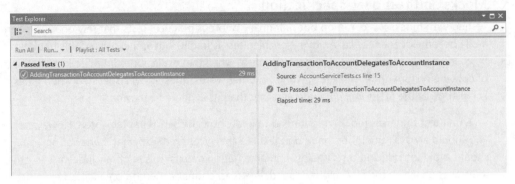

FIGURE 5-6 After being mocked with stubs, the test passes again.

Before you rejoice, you need to acknowledge that you have cheated. You have edited a unit test and not transitioned it from red to green. The test was already successful and, perhaps despite the change, it is still successful. In order to fail this test and then verify that it only passes as a result of a correctly implemented SUT, you should remove the code inside the AddTransactionToAccount method. When you do so, the test will fail, and reinstating the code causes the test to succeed. This is an important part of the unit test editing process that avoids false positives—that is, it prevents you from writing a test that succeeds despite not being implemented correctly.

Testing all control flows

Your first attempt at completing a working `AccountService` by using a TDD approach has been successful. There are potential problems that will require further tests to ensure that this method is much more robust. So far, you have tested only the *Happy Path*: the execution path through the code that yields no errors and causes no problems. There are a few gaps that need to be addressed:

- What if the account repository is a `null` reference?

- What if the repository cannot find the account?

- What if the account method throws an exception?

With each extra test that you write, you either uncover a defect that exists in your implementation (if the test fails) or you add extra confidence that your implementation is robust (if the test succeeds).

Under what circumstances might the account repository be a `null` reference? This will occur only if the `AccountService` is constructed with a `null` passed in as its constructor parameter. Because a valid account repository is a required dependency for the account service, you could say that this is a *precondition* of the constructor. Thus, you can write the test in Listing 5-18.

This test is slightly different from the previous ones; the assertion is not in the usual place. MSTest requires you to apply the `ExpectedExceptionAttribute` to the test method with a parameter describing the type of exception that you require.

LISTING 5-18 No Arrange and no Assert, yet this is a valid test pattern for exceptions.

```
[TestMethod]
[ExpectedException(typeof(ArgumentNullException))]
public void CannotCreateAccountServiceWithNullAccountRepository()
{
    // Arrange

    // Act
    new AccountService(null);

    // Assert
}
```

What this test is specifying is that you expect an `ArgumentNullException` to be thrown if you construct an `AccountService` with a `null` reference for the `IAccountRepository` instance. This is precisely the precondition that you need, to ensure that in any method of the account service, you always have a valid instance of the repository and do not need to handle the case where it is `null`. This test fails for the right reasons, as shown here.

```
Test method ServiceTests.AccountServiceTests.CannotCreateAccountServiceWithNullAccountRepository
    did not throw an exception. An exception was expected by attribute
    Microsoft.VisualStudio.TestTools.UnitTesting.ExpectedExceptionAttribute defined on the test
    method.
```

To make this test pass, you need to implement the precondition. The manual approach is shown in Listing 5-19.

LISTING 5-19 Passing a `null` account repository into the constructor will cause an exception.

```
public AccountService(IAccountRepository repository)
{
    if (repository == null)
    {
        throw new ArgumentNullException("repository", "A valid account
    repository must be supplied.");
    }

    this.repository = repository;
}
```

The added lines are in bold. This is an example of failing fast. Without this precondition, an exception would eventually be thrown, but it would be a `NullReferenceException` and it would occur whenever you first try to access the `null` repository.

With your constructor test passing, you can move on to the next test case: when the repository cannot find the account. Assume that your repository does not implement the Null Object pattern, which, as described in Chapter 4, "Interfaces and design patterns," would mean that it never returned a `null` object or threw an exception if the repository could not find the account requested. Instead, your repository should return a `null` reference for the account. Listing 5-20 shows the unit test that enforces the expected behavior for this case.

LISTING 5-20 No expected exception attribute and no assertion!

```
[TestMethod]
public void DoNotThrowWhenAccountIsNotFound()
{
    // Arrange
    var mockRepository = new Mock<IAccountRepository>();
    var sut = new AccountService(mockRepository.Object);

    // Act
    sut.AddTransactionToAccount("Trading Account", 100m);

    // Assert
}
```

The Assert phase of this test is blank, and there is no `ExpectedException` attribute, either. This is because your expectations are that there should *not* be an exception thrown during the Act phase of the test. If an exception is thrown at that point, the test fails. If an exception is not thrown—and there are no other assertions that could potentially fail—the test will *pass*, by default.

In the Arrange phase of the test, you mock the repository and pass it to the SUT (avoiding the precondition by providing a valid instance of the repository) but set up no expectations. This means that the call to `IAccountRepository.GetByName()` will return `null`. The next thing that you do with this return value is attempt to call `Account.AddTransaction()`. Because the instance is `null`, this causes a `NullReferenceException` and this test fails. To transition this test to green, you need to prevent this exception from being thrown in your method, as Listing 5-21 shows.

LISTING 5-21 The `if` statement protects this method from a `NullReferenceException`.

```
public void AddTransactionToAccount(string uniqueAccountName, decimal transactionAmount)
{
    var account = repository.GetByName(uniqueAccountName);
    if (account != null)
    {
        account.AddTransaction(transactionAmount);
    }
}
```

By adding a simple `if` statement that ensures that the account is not `null` before attempting to use it, you prevent the exception from being thrown, and the test passes.

Now, let's implement the final required test case. This test involves the behavior expected of the account service when the call to the account's `AddTransaction` method throws an exception. To avoid leaking dependencies between layers, it is good practice to wrap an exception thrown at a lower layer in a new exception for this layer. Figure 5-7 exemplifies this principle.

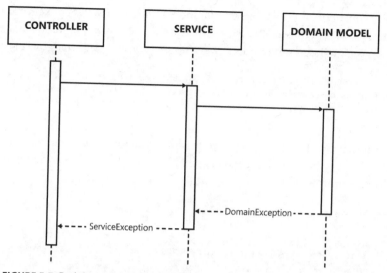

FIGURE 5-7 Each layer defines an exception type for wrapping exceptions at lower levels.

The exceptions that the domain model throws will be specific to that layer. If the service layer allows this to propagate up to the controller, the controller will need knowledge of the Domain-Exception type to catch and handle these exceptions. This introduces a dependency between the controller and the domain model layer, which should be avoided. Instead, the service will catch the domain model exceptions and *wrap* them in ServiceException instances before throwing them up to the controller. Due to the controller's dependency on the service layer, it is able to catch the exceptions that it defines. It is important to acknowledge that the ServiceException contains the DomainException as an inner exception—without this, valuable context about the original exception is lost: the entry point of the application might be able to unwrap this exception in a global exception handler, for example. Listing 5-22 shows the unit test required to enforce this behavior between your collaborating classes.

LISTING 5-22 The mock account is told to throw an exception when called.

```
[TestMethod]
[ExpectedException(typeof(ServiceException))]
public void AccountExceptionsAreWrappedInThrowServiceException()
{
    // Arrange
    var account = new Mock<Account>();
    account.Setup(a => a.AddTransaction(100m)).Throws<DomainException>();
    var mockRepository = new Mock<IAccountRepository>();
    mockRepository.Setup(r => r.GetByName("Trading Account")).Returns(account.Object);
    var sut = new AccountService(mockRepository.Object);

    // Act
    sut.AddTransactionToAccount("Trading Account", 100m);

    // Assert
}
```

The expected exception attribute is used to assert that the SUT throws a `ServiceException`, whereas the account mock is told to throw a `DomainException`. Therefore, it is up to the SUT to convert one to the other. The method does not do this, so this test correctly fails, with this message:

```
Test method ServiceTests.AccountServiceTests.AccountExceptionsAreWrappedInThrowServiceException
  threw exception Domain.DomainException, but exception Services.ServiceException was expected.
  Exception message: Domain.DomainException: Exception of type 'Domain.DomainException' was
  thrown.
```

The expected exception attribute has determined that the exception thrown is not of the correct type compared to that which was specified. The code in Listing 5-23 shows the changes required to the AddTransactionToAccount method.

LISTING 5-23 The try/catch block is introduced to map one exception with another.

```
public void AddTransactionToAccount(string uniqueAccountName, decimal transactionAmount)
{
    var account = repository.GetByName(uniqueAccountName);
    if (account != null)
    {
        try
        {
            account.AddTransaction(transactionAmount);
        }
        catch(DomainException)
        {
            throw new ServiceException();
        }
    }
}
```

Although the introduction of the try/catch block transitions your test from red to green, there is an expectation missing, which means that this is still incomplete.

Writing tests for defect fixes

Imagine that you receive a defect report relating to the current example code. The report states:

> *I received a* `ServiceException` *when adding a transaction to my account.*

You proceed to reproduce the problem and discover the exception that is thrown—this is the proximate cause. But, because the DomainException has been replaced with the ServiceException, it is very difficult to understand the ultimate cause of the error. The original expectation that the new exception should wrap the existing one has not been fulfilled because an assertion is missing from the unit tests.

When a defect arises in this manner, the first thing to do is to write a failing unit test that captures two things: the exact reproduction steps required to force the defect to occur, and the expected behavior that is not currently enforced. Listing 5-24 shows both of these elements in a unit test that fails.

LISTING 5-24 Manually asserting against the thrown exception.

```
[TestMethod]
public void AccountExceptionsAreWrappedInThrowServiceException()
{
    // Arrange
    var account = new Mock<Account>();
    account.Setup(a => a.AddTransaction(100m)).Throws<DomainException>();
    var mockRepository = new Mock<IAccountRepository>();
    mockRepository.Setup(r => r.GetByName("Trading Account")).Returns(account.Object);
    var sut = new AccountService(mockRepository.Object);

    // Act
    try
    {
        sut.AddTransactionToAccount("Trading Account", 100m);
    }
    catch(ServiceException serviceException)
    {
        // Assert
        Assert.IsInstanceOfType(serviceException.InnerException, typeof(DomainException));
    }
}
```

For this test, the ExpectedException attribute alone is insufficient. You need to examine the InnerException property of the thrown exception and assert that it is a DomainException. This proves that the domain exception is wrapped, preserving the original error that occurred. All software defects can be viewed as the result of a missing unit test: an incomplete specification of expected behavior. Listing 5-25 shows how to make the test pass by editing the production code.

LISTING 5-25 The original exception is now wrapped properly by the new exception.

```
public void AddTransactionToAccount(string uniqueAccountName, decimal transactionAmount)
{
    var account = repository.GetByName(uniqueAccountName);
    if (account != null)
    {
        try
        {
            account.AddTransaction(transactionAmount);
        }
        catch(DomainException domainException)
        {
            throw new ServiceException("Adding transaction to account failed",
  domainException);
        }
    }
}
```

By making this test pass, you can then go back and reproduce the original exception from the defect report and, this time, determine the ultimate cause of the problem.

Test setup

Let's take stock of the tests you have written so far. Each has progressively become more complex, with more code required to set up your expectations. It would be nice if you could factor this out somewhere in order to clean up the tests and shorten them a little. MSTest, like other unit testing frameworks, allows special initialization and shutdown methods that are called at the start and end of every test, respectively. The initialization method can be given any name, but it must be tagged with the TestInitialize attribute.

The code to put into this method is the code common to nearly all of the unit tests: instantiating the mock objects. You can store mock objects as private fields in the class so that they are still available to each test. You can also do the same with the SUT, because that only requires the mock repository as a constructor parameter and its construction doesn't depend on anything specific to each unit test. Listing 5-26 shows the changes required to the test class to support the setup method.

LISTING 5-26 The mock objects and the SUT can be constructed in a setup method.

```
[TestClass]
public class AccountServiceTests
{

    [TestInitialize]
    public void Setup()
    {
        mockAccount = new Mock<Account>();
        mockRepository = new Mock<IAccountRepository>();
        sut = new AccountService(mockRepository.Object);
    }

    private Mock<Account> mockAccount;
    private Mock<IAccountRepository> mockRepository;
    private AccountService sut;
}
```

With these objects constructed as part of a test initialization method, which is called individually for each test method, you can simplify some of the unit test code by removing this object construction. Listing 5-27 shows the changes made to the most recent unit test, AccountExceptionsAreWrappedInThrowServiceException.

LISTING 5-27 This test is a little shorter and a little easier to read.

```
[TestMethod]
public void AccountExceptionsAreWrappedInThrowServiceException()
{
    // Arrange
    mockAccount.Setup(a => a.AddTransaction(100m)).Throws<DomainException>();
    mockRepository.Setup(r => r.GetByName("Trading Account")).Returns(mockAccount.Object);

    // Act
    try
    {
        sut.AddTransactionToAccount("Trading Account", 100m);
    }
    catch(ServiceException serviceException)
    {
        // Assert
        Assert.IsInstanceOfType(serviceException.InnerException, typeof(DomainException));
    }
}
```

Three lines might not be a huge amount of code to remove, but the cumulative effect on all of the unit tests is more readable code. You know that, by convention, any variable with the prefix mock will be a mocked object, whereas the variable sut is your system under test.

Unit-testing patterns

Tests, just like production code, can become unwieldy and unreadable. And, just like production code, tests are read many more times than they are written—by all sorts of people. Someone once said that you should write code as if the next person to read it is a psychopath who knows where you live. Of course, this is hyperbolic and pithy, but there is a nugget of truth in there. Be considerate of the poor souls who must read your code in the future: help them to do their job, do not hinder them.

Writing maintainable tests

Given that test readability is at least as important as production code readability, how do you diagnose readability problems with existing tests, and what options are available to you for improving the readability of tests?

First, there are tactical changes that can be made to tests that improve the line-by-line readability of the tests. Second, there are strategic—or structural—changes that can influence the readability in a larger way.

Prioritize consistency

Arguing on the Internet is a complete and utter waste of time and energy. It is futile and illogical. Yet, despite being a category of people who rely on their keen sense of logic, software developers often argue on the Internet. From the pedantry of the perfect sort algorithm to "best language" flame wars, developers cannot help but launch themselves headlong into pointless arguments.

The truth is, on a practical level, you have infinite choices available to you. You cannot hope to critically evaluate all of them at all times; therefore, a better heuristic is needed. The first principle that should be upheld in any codebase is *consistency*. This applies to a multitude of areas.

Do not argue with each other over the relative benefits of preceding underscores for class field names versus ubiquitous use of `this`. Instead, be consistent, and follow the example already set by the code. Any time lost arguing is better spent making real, actual, tangible progress.

This applies throughout the codebase. Test code, however, generates the most heated of debates.

This is all very well in a brownfield project that is already internally consistent, but what about greenfield projects or projects that are ambiguous about their patterns? For greenfield projects, make a decision that is most agreeable and stick to it. When a project's code already exhibits a mixture of naming conventions or applicable patterns, choose the most common example and slowly normalize the rest of the code to match.

Maintain a reasonable test fixture per class ratio

A 1:1 ratio of test fixture to production class should suffice in most cases. Using a single test fixture to exercise more than one system under test is confusing and breaks the Principle of Least Astonishment. This is much the same as putting multiple classes in a single file: it is something that should be avoided lest others have difficulty navigating the code.

> **Tip** The *Principle of Least Astonishment* is a guideline recommending that you choose the simplest, most obvious choice when presented with a decision. It aims to make life easier for those who come after you—perhaps even a future version of yourself who might be astonished at an odd decision!

Name the system under test

Although abbreviations should generally be avoided when writing code, naming the variable that represents the system under test `sut` at least benefits from being consistent. Even if an alternative name is chosen, such as `target`, a consistent name across all tests allows the next readers of your code to orient themselves quickly.

Name your test methods carefully

"There are two hard things in computer science: cache invalidation, naming things, and off-by-one errors."

Unknown

A colleague of mine is a great advocate of intentional bad variable names. If the purpose of a class, method, or variable is unclear, he names it `Fred`. It's important to note that he never commits his code until all rogue `Fred`s have been removed, but some `Fred`s can live an hour until they are renamed. The point is, naming is quite a bit more difficult than it seems.

As you will learn later in this chapter, in the "The testing quadrant" section, unit tests are for the development team, not the business. Therefore, the names of unit tests need not be readable by business analysts or product owners, unlike wider-scoped acceptance tests. However, `Status_code_500_should_throw_invalid_operation_exception` is not a good name—on multiple levels.

First, the test leaks too much implementation knowledge, which does not aid the reader. Instead, the intent of the test should be the focus of the name. Communicate the *intent* of the test, not the *implementation*.

`Account_service_failure_is_propagated_to_client` is a better name for the same test. It doesn't rely on the implementation of the test, and it grounds itself in the context of the code in question.

The Builder pattern for tests

There are two types of verboseness in the writing of code: that which complicates and that which clarifies. The former is apparent when a method deals directly with details at too low of a level. The latter is a result of descriptive variable and method naming, using the tools at your disposal to clearly state intent.

Unit tests are code statements much like any others. Therefore, they are subject to at least the same rules as production code. Tests can become unwieldy for many reasons—most commonly because the code to be tested is not particularly testable. In this scenario, the tests circle around the problem, trying to contrive ways and means of creating tests. But even very testable code can have tests that lack clarity and concision.

The Builder pattern

The Builder pattern is a creational Gang of Four (GoF) design pattern. This means that it is useful for encapsulating and abstracting the creation of objects. It is distinct from the more common Factory pattern in that a Builder pattern contains methods of customizing the creation of an object. Figure 5-8 shows a UML diagram for a general Builder design pattern.

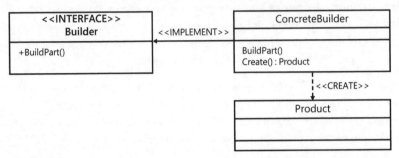

FIGURE 5-8 The Builder pattern decouples complex construction of a product from its use.

Whenever an object can be configured in multiple ways across multiple dimensions, the Builder pattern can simplify your creation code and clarify the intent.

Clarifying unit test intent

Let's revisit a test from earlier in the chapter and improve its clarity of intent by applying the Builder pattern. The Moq mock from the "Testing with mocks" section is repeated here as Listing 5-28.

LISTING 5-28 The Moq mock (shown earlier in Listing 5-17).

```
[TestMethod]
public void AddingTransactionToAccountDelegatesToAccountInstance()
{
    // Arrange
    var account = new Account();
    var mockRepository = new Mock<IAccountRepository>();
    mockRepository.Setup(r => r.GetByName("Trading Account")).Returns(account);
    var sut = new AccountService(mockRepository.Object);

    // Act
    sut.AddTransactionToAccount("Trading Account", 200m);

    // Assert
    Assert.AreEqual(200m, account.Balance);
}
```

The Arrange, Act, and Assert sections are labeled, and the Arrange section is five lines long. This is within an acceptable range: after about seven or eight lines, it becomes important to reduce the number of lines of code. Instead, the problem with this Arrange section is that the *intent* of the code is unclear. Careful reading of each line is needed to understand what this code is doing. Effectively, this test is "skipping an abstraction": reaching through a layer of indirection that would clarify and, possibly, summarize the intent of this code. The Builder pattern can be such a layer.

The product

Much like the Factory pattern, the Builder pattern generates a *product*. This is the result of describing some configuration options to the builder and asking it to create an object. When applied to the context of tests, the Builder pattern can generate products for any or all of the supporting objects required by the test. For this example in particular, the Builder pattern will be used to generate the familiar system under test (SUT): the AccountService.

The Builder

Listing 5-29 shows the AccountServiceBuilder class. It is designed with a fluent interface, meaning that its methods return the builder and can thus be chained together. It is common to have a Build() or Create() method that acts as the final command in the fluent chain. The result is a constructed product, the AccountService.

LISTING 5-29 The builder encapsulates the details of constructing test objects.

```
public class AccountServiceBuilder
{
    private readonly AccountService _accountService;
    private readonly Mock<IAccountRepository> _mockAccountRepo;

    public Mock<Account> MockAccount
    {
        get;
        private set;
    }

    public AccountServiceBuilder()
    {
        _mockAccountRepo = new Mock<IAccountRepository>();
        _accountService = new AccountService(_mockAccountRepo.Object);
    }

    public AccountServiceBuilder WithAccountCalled(string accountName)
    {
        MockAccount = new Mock<Account>();
        _mockAccountRepo.Setup(r =>
            r.GetByName("Trading Account")).Returns(MockAccount.Object);

        return this;
    }

    public AccountServiceBuilder AddTransactionOfValue(decimal transactionValue)
    {
        MockAccount.Setup(a => a.AddTransaction(200m)).Verifiable();
```

```
        return this;
    }

    public AccountService Build()
    {
        return _accountService;
    }
}
```

The test

Plugging the AccountServiceBuilder into the unit test produces the code in Listing 5-30. The Arrange section of the test is only one line of code shorter, at four lines, but that is not the sole aim of the Builder pattern. The builder has provided test writers with a domain-specific language (DSL) with which to construct tests.

LISTING 5-30 The Arrange section of this test has a clearer intent thanks to the Builder pattern.

```
[TestClass]
public class AccountServiceTests
{
    private AccountServiceBuilder _accountServiceBuilder;

    [TestInitialize]
    public void TestInitialize()
    {
        _accountServiceBuilder = new AccountServiceBuilder();
    }

    [TestMethod]
    public void AddingTransactionToAccountDelegatesToAccountInstance()
    {
        // Arrange
        var sut = _accountServiceBuilder
            .WithAccountCalled("Trading Account")
            .AddTransactionOfValue(200m)
            .Build();

        // Act
        sut.AddTransactionToAccount("Trading Account", 200m);

        // Assert
        _accountServiceBuilder.MockAccount.Verify();
    }
}
```

The code can be read sequentially, and the intent is clear. Taking the extraneous noise away from the code gives this piece of prose:

Account service builder, with account called "Trading Account", add transaction of value 200.0.

This is how the test setup should read. There is far more clarity in what you can expect from the system under test. Look back again at the original Arrange section of this test and see how it compares. The details of mock setup—implementation details—cloud the *intent* of the code. Look at the placement of the parameterized values: 200m and "Trading Account". They are lost within the noise of mock initialization. With the use of the Builder pattern, the tests now have far more clarity of intent.

> **Tip** Another advantage of the Builder pattern is that it leads to more declarative tests. No test should ever have a cyclomatic complexity greater than 1, meaning that tests should be completely linear with no branching. An if statement or a for, foreach, or while loop will cause the cyclomatic complexity of a test to exceed 1. The Builder pattern helps with this by converting imperative construction and initialization to declarative.

Writing tests first

What has been presented so far in this chapter are the merits of unit testing with a test-driven development (TDD) approach. But is this, strictly speaking, test-driven development? Software development is fraught with overloaded terms whose meaning is subjective or shifts over time. Consider the word "service," for example. That means a multitude of different things in different situations. This book alone uses the term in a number of different contexts. And context is the key. Without context, there is no basis for discussion, no environment in which debate can exist.

TDD might not necessarily be a subjective term, but its meaning has shifted. The modern standards and practices that are upheld as "software engineering" have trickled through the industry, and their meaning has been distorted or mistaken.

What is TDD?

Test-driven development has a purist and a pragmatist interpretation. Even those terms are loaded: a purist never yields from his or her myopic, idealistic vision of how things ought to be; the pragmatist is a maverick who cuts corners and dilutes the code in the name of delivery. Of course, both of these descriptions are hyperbolic caricatures.

The "purist" idea of TDD is that it is a *design* tool—that developers should approach the keyboard without forethought of the production code they might implement. Instead, they are the proverbial blank slates, prepared to discover their design as they progress. This progress is guided by writing *failing unit tests*.

The "pragmatic" idea of TDD is that developers write the unit tests first. The distinction is subtle. With purist TDD, there are more constraints to the process. The goal of both TDD styles is the same: generate production code that has been verified as meeting requirements with unit tests. However, pragmatic TDD has fewer rules governing how to achieve this goal. With pragmatic TDD, the only rule is this: write tests first.

Therefore, pragmatic TDD should be renamed *test-first development*. I will use the TFD acronym only for the purposes of brevity. Ideally, purist TDD should be renamed test-driven *design*. By correcting the nomenclature, we can have a more meaningful discussion about the relative pros and cons. Behaviors might also change: if your hiring manager is testing for test-driven design but the real work to be done suits test-first development, a realignment of terminology could help you find candidates better suited to the work.

Test-driven design

TDD is a design exercise. It is most applicable when the design of production code is unknown and can emerge organically through the red, green, refactor process of writing unit tests.

Keith Braithwaite of Zuhlke, an engineering services company, terms this sort of testing "TDD as if you meant it." Using the following rules can help to teach test-driven design to developers who have only done test-first development.

1. Write exactly one new test. It should be the smallest test which seems to point in the direction of a solution.

2. Run the test to make sure it fails.

3. Make the test from (1) pass by writing the least amount of implementation code you can IN THE TEST METHOD.

4. Refactor to remove duplication or otherwise as required to improve the design. Be strict about the refactorings. Only introduce new abstractions (methods, classes, etc) when they will help to improve the design of the code. Specifically:

   a. ONLY Extract a new method if there is sufficient code duplication in the test methods. When extracting a method, initially extract it to the test class (don't create a new class yet).

   b. ONLY create a new class when a clear grouping of methods emerges and when the test class starts to feel crowded or too large.

3. Repeat the process by writing another test (go back to step 1).

This is quite a restrictive set of rules, but they are not arbitrary. These rules of test-driven design are intended to generate just enough design to pass the unit tests, and no more. This naturally prevents over-engineering. Over-engineering occurs when code is made pointlessly adaptive—that is, it can be extended in ways that it will never need. This is *speculative generality*, which is discussed in further detail in Chapter 8, "The open/closed principle."

TDD necessarily requires a greenfield approach to the solution. This is why it is so applicable to code katas and domain-driven development (DDD). In both scenarios, there is no code already available for you to hang your new functionality from. There is a problem space that is ill-defined and perhaps constantly changing. Without becoming a domain expert in the field, you need a design tool that will guide you through the process of capturing labyrinthine requirements in working, verified code. TDD, as defined here, fits the bill perfectly.

> **Tip** A *code kata* is a practice or training exercise for learning a new language, technique, or skill. The term *kata* originally referred to an individual training exercise for martial arts such as karate. Some code katas can be found at *http://www.codekatas.org*.

Test-first development

TFD overlaps TDD in some key areas. Tests are obviously written first. The red, green, refactor process is adhered to. But TFD is not a design exercise. The design has already been formed or is forming elsewhere: in the developer's head.

Class, responsibility, and collaboration (CRC) sessions can be used to generate a design for a component. After the existence of classes and methods—and the interactions between them—have been determined, there isn't a lot left but to fill in the blanks. By the time you come to write the unit tests and make them pass with production code, you are already familiar with your design.

Even without an explicit design session such as CRC, it is possible to think of a design without proving it is necessary with unit tests. In fact, it is possible to consider many different designs and to implicitly trade them off against each other before deciding to implement them. This could take the form of a pair-programming session, when a lot of discussion takes place about the relative merits of naming conventions, method implementation, and other issues.

The grey area where TDD and TFD diverge is whether, when the tests are written, the developer focuses strictly on implementing just enough to make the test pass. For example, if a class or method is created as part of the process of turning a red test green, this is contrary to the rules of TDD. Classes and methods are design constructs that should only occur as a grouping mechanism for related functionality. This is part of the refactor phase of unit testing.

To this point, no color is added to this discussion to differentiate either TDD or TFD as being objectively better or worse. The trade-off appears to be this: Fewer developers have enough experience with TDD, or design in general, to consistently find success with this method. But TFD has the tendency to generate overwrought designs that are littered with mechanical decision-making. TDD is misunderstood; TFD is understood. TDD produces just enough design; TFD produces whatever design is in the developer's head.

Further testing

Unit testing is not the only kind of testing that provides value. If only unit tests were used, only the lowest-level details of the code would be verified. By now, it should be clear that software exists at different levels of granularity, and unit tests deal only with the most granular elements.

There are two ubiquitous diagrams that explain the differences between tests at various levels. The testing pyramid reminds you of the relative number of tests that you should aim to maintain. The testing quadrant diagram explains that tests can be useful to different stakeholders and for different reasons.

The testing pyramid

Figure 5-9 shows the *testing pyramid*. It is likely that you have seen this before. It is a useful reference when discussing the relative quantity of tests that are used to verify a system.

FIGURE 5-9 The testing pyramid shows the relative quantity of different types of tests.

Above the top level of the pyramid is a cloud of uncertainty, which represents the manual testing that exercises the system. This can take the form of written checklists that require a real user interacting with the system to verify correctness. There should be few of these, because they are not repeatable without manual intervention, which is costly and time-consuming.

Below the manual tests are the acceptance tests. These tests could be implemented in an automated user interface suite such as Selenium. They are intended to replicate the interactions of a user and assert against the expectations. There should only be a few of these tests, because they are large and difficult to maintain. If these tests are to be relevant, the entire system must be deployed into a test environment that closely represents a live environment.

The middle tier of the pyramid contains component-level integration tests. These could take the form of API tests in which a service is treated as a black box. For a variety of data inputs, the tests assert that the correct responses are returned. There are likely to be more of these kinds of tests than automated UI tests, but not so many that they become neglected and brittle.

The bottom tier of the pyramid is the largest and represents the unit tests.

There are no absolute numbers that can be applied to these layers. The pyramid simply maintains that one layer should be relatively smaller or larger than another. An order of magnitude might be a good guideline to follow, because it allows the actual number to remain relative. If there are hundreds of unit tests for a system, there should be only tens of component-level tests and only a handful of automated user interface tests. The numbers can scale up or down from there, with the smallest systems not requiring high-level tests at all.

Testing pyramid anti-patterns

Sketching the testing pyramid for a system can be a useful diagnostic tool for problems with the code's adaptability. If mapping the relative quantity of tests at each level forms a shape other than a pyramid, there are too many or too few of a category of tests.

The hourglass

Figure 5-10 shows what happens when a test pyramid is too top-heavy: it becomes an hourglass.

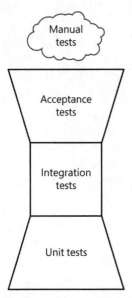

FIGURE 5-10 When it has too many integration and acceptance tests, code is difficult to change.

When there are too many high-level tests, developers are burdened with the maintenance effort of ensuring that these tests run to completion. They also must write new tests, often at a rate at which the cost outweighs the benefit. Recall that testing gives you confidence that something is working.

After you reach your confidence threshold, the marginal extra confidence generated by continuing to add tests is not worth the effort. It is better to stop and focus on the quality and maintainability of the existing tests.

The snowcone

Figure 5-11 shows what happens when the test pyramid becomes fully inverted: the cloud of uncertainty at the top has grown to gargantuan proportions, and there are almost no unit tests in sight.

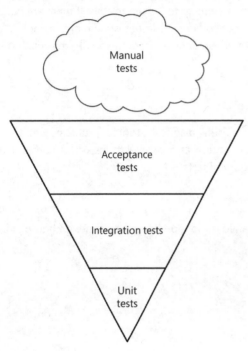

FIGURE 5-11 When the relative quantities of tests are inverted, the pyramid becomes a snowcone.

When the majority of testing effort is manual, this indicates that you have an untestable codebase. Work should begin promptly to refactor the code so that it is inherently testable. To factor in such work, use a combination of the golden master technique (see Chapter 6, "Refactoring") and Kanban's class of service (see Chapter 2, "Introduction to Kanban").

Manual tests are not as reliable as automated tests because of the fallibility of the person executing the test script. Such repetitive, monotonous work quickly becomes demotivating. Work to automate what you can so that the manual tests can be cheaply repeated whenever necessary.

The testing quadrant

The testing covered in the testing pyramid exists at different granularities, from coarse-grained user interface tests to fine-grained unit tests. The test quadrant provides a complementary view of tests: they are applicable to different stakeholders and for different reasons.

To readers who are already somewhat familiar with the testing quadrant—after all, it is quite an old idea—the version presented in Figure 5-12 might look different. Software consultant Gojko Adzic admirably refreshed the testing quadrant to make it more relevant to the current state of the art. This figure is reproduced with the permission of Gojko Adzic.

FIGURE 5-12 The testing quadrant helps categorize the audience and purpose of different test categories.

As with all quadrant-based models, there are two axes to consider. On the vertical axis, the intended audience of the tests is addressed: technologists or business. On the horizontal axis, the test purpose is addressed: expectation verification (quantitative) versus analytical (qualitative) outcomes.

Business/Quantitative

Businesses tend to have service level agreements (SLAs) with their customers and clients. These are formalized, quantifiable standards with which the business must comply or be liable for providing the client some form of compensation. Availability is a common SLA criterion, whereby the business promises to keep a service available with 99.9% uptime. Because this is measurable and has a direct effect on the business, tests for these sorts of standards live in this quadrant.

Business/Qualitative

Subjective concerns such as usability are found in this quadrant. The emphasis here is less on the technologies involved and more on the business impact of the software. A/B and multivariate testing, which allow for multiple versions of components to be evaluated through experimentation, are an emerging trend across the wider software spectrum. Rather than focus-group testing whether your users prefer cornflower blue or ocean blue, the two blues can be A/B tested and the statistical signifi-cance of conversion uplift can be measured.

Technology/Quantitative

Unit tests reside in this quadrant, as do integration tests. These tests support the development team in quantifying how closely the system meets its requirements. Statistics such as unit test pass percent-age, code coverage, and cyclomatic complexity indicate the overall health of a system.

Technology/Qualitative

Here you focus on architectural capabilities for which you might not have quantifiable requirements. Load testing focuses on the resource usage that a system exhibits under various amounts of load. For a service, this is likely to include throughput statistics and response time curves as more users concurrently access the system. Assessing the security of a system is also a qualitative activity; this is assessed through penetration testing. The attack vectors of a system are difficult to quantify, so a more analytical approach is needed.

The testing quadrant shows that there are different categories of each kind of test. Although this book primarily focuses on the low-level details of unit test implementation and design, the adaptability of your code also relies on having the right amount of the right type of tests.

Testing for prevention and cure

All of the testing discussed so far has dealt with testing for prevention. That is, effort is expended up front to ensure that new functionality works as expected and that no existing functionality has been regressed.

This is standard practice. But it is not without cost. Every test written takes time and effort. Confidence is the currency of tests. The equation to bear in mind is this:

effort < confidence

If your efforts do not generate the requisite test confidence, they are too costly and you should focus your effort elsewhere. Of course, all projects have a target confidence that calibrates their tolerance for failure. The software embedded in a pacemaker requires far more confidence than that which powers a commercial software-as-a-service solution. Following the correlation of effort and confidence, the effort that can be expended to ensure the correct working of a pacemaker is thus much higher.

But, if you are not writing such mission-critical software, what are your options for reducing the effort and increasing the confidence?

Figure 5-13 shows how software typically makes its way from development through to a live environment.

FIGURE 5-13 Software can be deployed to many environments for testing before reaching a live environment.

With each phase of the process, your confidence in the functional correctness and robustness of the software increases. By exercising the code at different scopes and in different environments, you generate feedback that the code is working or is broken. After the code is released and verified in a live environment, your confidence is at its highest. What if you could find a shortcut from development to live? Your confidence would increase dramatically, yet the effort required would be minimal.

"But," you say, "without those incremental increases in confidence, we would fail in live so much more!"

Good.

There should never be a fear of failure in software development. If your culture is to fear failure, you cannot innovate. Instead, embrace the fact that you will fail, that you will roll back some releases. Failure is a better teacher than success. What you must do is shift your focus from Mean Time Before Failure (MTBF) toward Mean Time To Recovery (MTTR).

MTBF is a great measurement for systems in which you require a high level of confidence. It shows that the system is robust and has been very rigorously exercised. But as you now know, that level of confidence is expensive and is anathema to innovation.

MTTR, however, not only allows for failure, it prepares for it. Consider the possibility that you have a system with an MTBF of 100 days and an MTTR of 1 day. Thus, in aggregate, every three years, the system is unavailable for a day.

Compare this with a system that has an MTBF of 10 days and an MTTR of 1 hour. This system fails 10 times as often as the last! However, when it fails, it is operable again in only one hour: twenty-four times faster than the other system.

System 1 has an uptime of 99.99%.

System 2 has an uptime of over 99.995%.

You are enabled to fail fast by focusing on MTTR. This lets you loosen your grip on MTBF and innovate faster.

How do you decrease MTTR?

When a service fails in a live environment, you must do something with it to put it back in a workable state. But first, you need to know that it isn't working. Through a mixture of logging and alerting, you can monitor the health of your systems.

Logging is passive. If logging was the only option available, there would be a lot of time wasted polling the logs to see if something was going wrong. This is infeasible for most systems, because they could generate so much logging data that trying to discern a failure would become nearly impossible.

Alerting is active. When logging is in place, you can set acceptable boundaries that a variety of metrics should stay inside. If a metric breaches one of the boundaries, alerting can generate an event that informs you to start looking at specific parts of the logs and to take action.

Examples of metrics are service throughput, response time, and machine resource usage such as percentage of RAM, CPU, and disk that have been used. Other metrics might be domain-specific: a fall in conversion percentage or overall completed transactions, for example.

With monitoring and alerting, you can increase your confidence that you will spot an issue in your live environment, and this is the first step toward recovery.

Conclusion

This chapter has covered a variety of unit testing patterns and practices that will allow you to change your codebase without fear of breaking existing functionality.

Each unit test you write should represent an expectation of the code. Although as code they are technical artifacts, unit tests enforce real-world behavior in objects, just as those objects encapsulate real-world concepts.

When you diligently follow a test-first approach, you write no new production code without first constructing a failing unit test. Then you write the simplest production code possible to transition the unit test from a red failure state to a green success state. Taken to its logical conclusion, the production code becomes a natural side effect of fulfilling the expectations of its unit tests.

When you unit test code, you give yourself a firm foundation to subsequently alter the production code to make it clearly more adaptive to future requirements. The refactoring of code is an incremental process of improving the code's design. The next chapter dives deeper into refactoring.

CHAPTER 6

Refactoring

After completing this chapter, you will be able to

- Understand the importance of unit testing and its role in enabling refactoring.

- Refactor production code to improve its overall design.

- Safely improve the design of old codebases which do not have accompanying unit tests.

Refactoring is the process of incrementally improving the design of existing code. It is analogous to writing various drafts of code, much like I have written various drafts of this book. By acknowledging that we developers rarely get things right the first time, refactoring frees us to do the simplest thing first, and gradually, through incremental improvements, arrive at a better solution later.

The freedom to refactor with impunity is made possible by unit testing. Together, unit testing and refactoring form a mutually beneficial relationship, whereby unit testing enables refactoring and refactoring improves the design of code.

Introduction to refactoring

Your code will be more robust if you follow a test-driven development (TDD) process that writes a failing unit test before moving on to implement the expected behavior. However, this code might not be as organized or understandable as it could be. There are many times during the course of writing code when you should stop writing unit tests and code, and instead focus on *refactoring*.

Refactoring is the process of improving the design of existing code—after it has already been written. Each refactor differs in size and scope. A refactor could be a small tweak to a variable name to aid clarity, or it could be a more sweeping architectural change such as splitting user interface logic from domain logic when the two have become inappropriately intimate.

Changing existing code

In this chapter, you are going to make incremental changes to a class that will, at every step, improve the code in some meaningful way. The `Account` class you worked with in Chapter 5, "Testing," is the target for refactoring, but it has gained a new method since its previous use: `CalculateReward-Points`. Like many companies, your clients want to reward customer loyalty through the accumulation of reward points. These points are earned by the customer, depending on a variety of criteria.

Listing 6-1 shows the new Account class.

LISTING 6-1 The new class tracks reward points in addition to the account's balance.

```
public class Account
{
    public Account(AccountType type)
    {
        this.type = type;
    }

    public decimal Balance
    {
        get;
        private set;
    }

    public int RewardPoints
    {
        get;
        private set;
    }

    public void AddTransaction(decimal amount)
    {
        RewardPoints += CalculateRewardPoints(amount);
        Balance += amount;
    }

    public int CalculateRewardPoints(decimal amount)
    {
        int points;
        switch(type)
        {
            case AccountType.Silver:
                points = (int)decimal.Floor(amount / 10);
                break;
            case AccountType.Gold:
                points = (int)decimal.Floor((Balance / 10000 * 5) + (amount / 5));
                break;
            case AccountType.Platinum:
                points = (int)decimal.Ceiling((Balance / 10000 * 10) + (amount / 2));
                break;
            default:
                points = 0;
                break;
        }
        return Math.Max(points, 0);
    }

    private readonly AccountType type;
}
```

The most important changes to the class are summarized thus:

- A new property tracks the number of reward points that the customer has linked to this account.

- Each account has a type code that indicates the tier of the account: Silver, Gold, or Platinum.

- Whenever a transaction is added to the account, the customer earns reward points.

- The number of reward points earned is dependent on multiple factors, which complicate the calculation method:

  - **The account type**   More points are earned at higher tiers.

  - **The amount of the transaction**   The more customers spend, the more points they earn.

  - **The current balance of the account**   The Gold and Platinum tiers give customers more points for keeping their balances high.

Assuming that this code has been written alongside its unit tests, those tests will help greatly by ensuring that changes do not affect the specified behavior. This is an important point—refactoring changes the *arrangement* of the code, not the *outcome*. If you tried to refactor without unit tests, how would you know if you inadvertently broke the expected behavior? You would not fail fast but much later at run time during testing or, worse, after deployment.

Replacing "magic numbers" with constants

The first refactor is a simple but nonetheless important improvement to the readability of the code. There are a lot of "magic numbers" littering the CalculateRewardPoints method. Six distinct numbers are used without any context as to what they mean or why they are required. To the person who wrote the code, their significance might be obvious because that person has prior knowledge of what it all means. In reality, that will probably only be true for a week, perhaps two, before the person's memory starts to fade and they lose track of what that 5, or that 2, means. Listing 6-2 shows the changes made to the class as a result of this refactor.

LISTING 6-2 This code is more readable to people unfamiliar with it.

```
public class Account
{
    public int CalculateRewardPoints(decimal amount)
    {
        int points;
        switch(type)
        {
            case AccountType.Silver:
                points = (int)decimal.Floor(amount / SilverTransactionCostPerPoint);
                break;
            case AccountType.Gold:
                points = (int)decimal.Floor((Balance / GoldBalanceCostPerPoint) + (amount
    / GoldTransactionCostPerPoint));
                break;
```

```
            case AccountType.Platinum:
                points = (int)decimal.Ceiling((Balance / PlatinumBalanceCostPerPoint) +
    (amount / PlatinumTransactionCostPerPoint));
                break;
            default:
                points = 0;
                break;
        }
        return Math.Max(points, 0);
    }

    private const int SilverTransactionCostPerPoint = 10;
    private const int GoldTransactionCostPerPoint = 5;
    private const int PlatinumTransactionCostPerPoint = 2;

    private const int GoldBalanceCostPerPoint = 2000;
    private const int PlatinumBalanceCostPerPoint = 1000;
}
```

Each of the "magic numbers" has been replaced with an equivalent variable. There is a set of three variables for the cost-per-point denominator of the transaction amount, one per account type. Then there are two variables for the cost-per-point denominator of the balance amount, for the Gold and Platinum account types, which are the only two account types that offer this incentive.

Note that the constant zero (0) has not been refactored. Zero and 1 do not have to be factored out as constant variables, but if it improves readability and comprehension, feel free to do so.

The benefit of this refactor is that the code is now understandable to people who are unfamiliar with it, because you have explained what the values mean through the variable names. It would not be an improvement if you merely replaced the "magic numbers" with variables named A, B, or X. Try to choose variable names that concisely explain their purpose. Never be afraid of verbosity, and take every opportunity to self-document code through variable, class, and method names.

Replacing a conditional expression with polymorphism

The next refactor is more involved. The switch statement, which alters the CalculateRewards algorithm depending on the account type, is problematic for two reasons. First, it adversely affects readability but, more pressingly, it introduces a maintenance burden. Imagine that you are given a new requirement at some time in the future: a new account type. It has been decided that not enough people are meeting the criteria for the Silver account, so you need to create a new Bronze account. To add the Bronze account, you would need to edit the Account class and add tests to it. Editing existing code in this way, after it has been verified and deployed, should be avoided. Instead, you should look to other ways that you can extend code so that it is adaptable without being editable. This is covered in more detail in Chapter 8, "The open/closed principle."

What you are aiming to achieve is to make it easier to add a new account type while improving the readability of the code. For this, you will take advantage of polymorphism. You will model the account types as different subclasses of the Account class. The Gold account type will be represented by the

GoldAccount class, the Silver account type by the `SilverAccount` class, and the Platinum account type by the `PlatinumAccount` class. The first step is to define these classes, as shown in Listing 6-3.

LISTING 6-3 Each account type is now a distinct class.

```
public class SilverAccount
{
    public int CalculateRewardPoints(decimal amount)
    {
        return Math.Max((int)decimal.Floor(amount / SilverTransactionCostPerPoint), 0);
    }

    private const int SilverTransactionCostPerPoint = 10;
}
// …
public class GoldAccount
{

    public decimal Balance
    {
        get;
        set;
    }

    public int CalculateRewardPoints(decimal amount)
    {
        return Math.Max((int)decimal.Floor((Balance / GoldBalanceCostPerPoint) + (amount /
  GoldTransactionCostPerPoint)), 0);
    }

    private const int GoldTransactionCostPerPoint = 5;
    private const int GoldBalanceCostPerPoint = 2000;
}
// …
public class PlatinumAccount
{

    public decimal Balance
    {
        get;
        set;
    }

    public int CalculateRewardPoints(decimal amount)
    {
        return Math.Max((int)decimal.Ceiling(
            (Balance / PlatinumBalanceCostPerPoint) +
            (amount / PlatinumTransactionCostPerPoint)), 0);
    }

    private const int PlatinumTransactionCostPerPoint = 2;
    private const int PlatinumBalanceCostPerPoint = 1000;
}
```

Note that, at this stage, the original Account class has not been changed. These classes have been created as standalone classes. The unit tests for these classes would mirror the expectations of the CalculateRewardPoints class, but with a different system under test (SUT) for each account type. The algorithms for determining the reward points due on the Platinum and Gold account classes have a dependency on the current balance; that has been included so that these classes compile in isolation. The Balance property is also publicly settable, which enables unit testing with different values. The UML class diagram in Figure 6-1 explains how these classes are related.

FIGURE 6-1 The Account class will become abstract with an abstract CalculateRewardPoints method.

This is merely an objective on the way to completing the goal of replacing the switch statement, of course. It is important not to do too much all at once, so that you can verify that you are on the right track with a succession of smaller changes. The next change, in Listing 6-4, is to link all four classes into an inheritance hierarchy.

LISTING 6-4 The complexity has been removed from the Account class.

```
public abstract class AccountBase
{
    public decimal Balance
    {
        get;
        private set;
    }

    public int RewardPoints
    {
        get;
        private set;
    }

    public void AddTransaction(decimal amount)
    {
        RewardPoints += CalculateRewardPoints(amount);
        Balance += amount;
    }

    public abstract int CalculateRewardPoints(decimal amount);
}
```

Without the `switch` statement, there is no reason for this class to be aware of its "type" anymore, so the constructor has been removed, too. The class is abstract due to the abstract calculation method, but this means that you can no longer instantiate it and, consequently, you can no longer test it.

Indiana Jones and the aggressive refactor

At the start of the Indiana Jones movie, *Raiders of the Lost Ark*, the hero is deep in a Peruvian cave attempting to recover a small idol. He is aware that there are booby-traps set that will be triggered by the weighted switch on which the idol sits. He fills a cloth bag with sand and tries to use this as a proxy for the idol. His theory is that if he substitutes the sandbag for the idol quickly enough, he will prevent the switch from being tripped and the booby-trap will not fire.

Unfortunately for Indy, his plan fails and he is chased from the cave by a giant boulder. As initiating incidents go, it's one of the most memorable. But there is a technique in there that can be applied to redesigning: *parallel implementations*.

The golden idol is represented by the existing class or method, and the bag of sand is analogous to the new design. Implementing the new design in parallel allows the client code to be updated right at the last minute, effectively swapping out the golden idol for the bag of sand. The old design can then be removed, safely and entirely.

The refactor of the `Account` classes is an example of an aggressive refactor that requires intermediate objectives via parallel implementations. Note that the compelling advantage of parallel implementation is that, throughout the whole process, progress can be saved at any time for later resumption. Refactoring should not prevent you from committing to source control at regular intervals. Aim to commit every 10 to 15 minutes.

An object instance is needed for the unit tests to work, so the next step is to link the three account types as subclasses of this base. A useful naming convention—similar to prefixing interface names with a capital *I*—is to suffix abstract classes with *Base*. This a quick clue that the class cannot be instantiated and has associated subclasses.

When the three subclasses are created, you can remove the `Balance` property from the `GoldAccount` and `PlatinumAccount` because they will inherit the `Balance` and `AddTransaction` members from this base. Listing 6-5 shows all three classes after this step.

LISTING 6-5 Complete the refactor by inheriting from the base class.

```
public class SilverAccount : AccountBase
{
    public override int CalculateRewardPoints(decimal amount)
    {
        return Math.Max((int)decimal.Floor(amount / SilverTransactionCostPerPoint), 0);
    }

    private const int SilverTransactionCostPerPoint = 10;
}
```

```
// . . .
public class GoldAccount : AccountBase
{
    public override int CalculateRewardPoints(decimal amount)
    {
        return Math.Max((int)decimal.Floor((Balance / GoldBalanceCostPerPoint) + (amount /
    GoldTransactionCostPerPoint)), 0);
    }

    private const int GoldTransactionCostPerPoint = 5;
    private const int GoldBalanceCostPerPoint = 2000;
}
// . . .
public class PlatinumAccount : AccountBase
{
    public override int CalculateRewardPoints(decimal amount)
    {
        return Math.Max((int)decimal.Ceiling(
            (Balance / PlatinumBalanceCostPerPoint) +
            (amount / PlatinumTransactionCostPerPoint)), 0);
    }

    private const int PlatinumTransactionCostPerPoint = 2;
    private const int PlatinumBalanceCostPerPoint = 1000;
}
```

The refactor is now complete. From this point, it is easy to add a new account type by creating a subclass of the AccountBase and providing an implementation of the required CalculateReward-Points method. No existing code would have to be changed; you would just have to write a few unit tests to exercise the new algorithm for calculating reward points.

Replacing a constructor with a factory method

During the course of improving the Account class, there has probably been an adverse effect else-where in the code. Clients of the class were expecting to construct the account objects by using the Account constructor, and to pass in the type of account required. What will you now provide them by way of creating the correct account subclass for their situation?

The AccountType enumeration can be reused as a parameter to a new factory method on the AccountBase. Whereas a constructor, in conjunction with the new operator, returns an instance of the type in which it resides, a factory method is able to return many different types of object, all of which belong to the same inheritance hierarchy. Listing 6-6 shows such a factory method implemented on the base class.

LISTING 6-6 The switch statement returns, but in simplified form.

```
public abstract class AccountBase
{
    public static AccountBase CreateAccount(AccountType type)
```

```
    {
        AccountBase account = null;
        switch(type)
        {
            case AccountType.Silver:
                account = new SilverAccount();
                break;
            case AccountType.Gold:
                account = new GoldAccount();
                break;
            case AccountType.Platinum:
                account = new PlatinumAccount();
                break;
        }
        return account;
    }
}
```

There are two key features of the factory method that alleviate the burden on clients. First, it is `static`, meaning that clients call it on the type, rather than on an instance of that type. Second, the return type is the base class, allowing you to hide the subclass accounts from clients. In fact, you can hide them to the degree that they are `internal` and therefore invisible outside of this assembly. This disallows clients from directly constructing the subclasses, eliminating the new operator as a potential code smell (see Chapter 3, "Dependencies and layering"). Listing 6-7 compares how a client would interact with the account before and after the refactor.

Although a `switch` statement still remains, it is far simpler in this instance and facilitates the prior refactor where it was replaced with polymorphism.

LISTING 6-7 How the Account creates a new account before and after the refactor.

```
public void CreateAccount(AccountType accountType)
{
    var newAccount = new Account(accountType);
    accountRepository.NewAccount(newAccount);
}
// . . .
public void CreateAccount(AccountType accountType)
{
    var newAccount = AccountBase.CreateAccount(accountType);
    accountRepository.NewAccount(newAccount);
}
```

This code is an example of how a client—in this case, the Account—would construct a new account before and after the refactor. The difference is negligible, but note that the new operator has been removed and replaced with the static call to the factory method. This is a common way to replace something very rigid with something much more adaptive. Factory methods open up many more possibilities because of what they can return, compared to methods that always return the same type.

Observant readers will note that the choice of a static factory method is suboptimal—it is a skyhook rather than a crane and thus affects the testability and adaptability of the code. A better implementation would place the `CreateAccount` method on a suitable interface, as explored in the next section.

Replacing a constructor with a factory class

There is an alternative to the factory method: the factory class. In fact, you do not need to couple clients to the implementation of a standalone factory; you can just give them the interface, as in Listing 6-8.

LISTING 6-8 The account factory hides the implementation details of creating an account instance.

```
public interface IAccountFactory
{
    AccountBase CreateAccount(AccountType accountType);
}
```

The interface of the method is actually identical to that of the factory method, except for the fact that it is an instance method. The implementation *could* be identical to the previous method body, meaning that it has perfect knowledge of all of the different types of accounts. The `Account`, and other clients, would then require this interface as a constructor parameter, as shown in Listing 6-9.

LISTING 6-9 The service now receives a factory as a constructor parameter and uses it to create the account.

```
public class Account
{
    public Account(IAccountFactory accountFactory, IAccountRepository
    accountRepository)
    {
        this.accountFactory = accountFactory;
        this.accountRepository = accountRepository;
    }

    public void CreateAccount(AccountType accountType)
    {
        var newAccount = accountFactory.CreateAccount(accountType);
        accountRepository.NewAccount(newAccount);
    }

    private readonly IAccountRepository accountRepository;
    private readonly IAccountFactory accountFactory;
}
```

This service is starting to look as it should: an orchestration of more fine-grained interfaces designed to achieve a larger goal for the user interface layer. It is, for reasons of brevity and clarity, missing some guard clauses on the constructor, to prevent null dependencies, and some try/catch blocks on the `CreateAccount` method, to marshal domain exceptions to service exceptions.

A new account type

At this point, can you be confident enough that a request for a new account type results in minimal changes to existing code? Yes and no. In one case, you can trivially add an account, but in another, you will find that your current model makes some wrong assumptions that form *technical debt*.

A new reward account

Imagine that your client wants to add another kind of account—a Bronze account—that earns half of the reward points that the Silver account does. There are only two changes that need to be made to support this in the domain layer. First, you need to create a new subclass of the AccountBase class, as in Listing 6-10.

LISTING 6-10 The Bronze account is added as a new account type.

```
internal class BronzeAccount : AccountBase
{
    public override int CalculateRewardPoints(decimal amount)
    {
        return Math.Max((int)decimal.Floor(amount / BronzeTransactionCostPerPoint), 0);
    }

    private const int BronzeTransactionCostPerPoint = 20;
}
```

This is a simple change that involves new unit tests to provide your expectations, and a new class that provides the algorithm for calculating reward points for this class.

Whether you have a factory class or a factory method, you need to change it to support your new account type, along with the enumeration that defines possible account types to be created. Listing 6-11 shows how a factory class would change to support the new Bronze account.

LISTING 6-11 The switch statement has a new case added to it that handles creating Bronze accounts.

```
public AccountBase CreateAccount(AccountType accountType)
{
    AccountBase account = null;
    switch (accountType)
    {
        case AccountType.Bronze:
            account = new BronzeAccount();
            break;
        case AccountType.Silver:
            account = new SilverAccount();
            break;
        case AccountType.Gold:
            account = new GoldAccount();
            break;
```

```
        case AccountType.Platinum:
            account = new PlatinumAccount();
            break;
    }
    return account;
}
```

Before moving on to the next new account for the client, is there any way you can refactor this method so that you do not have to amend it for every account? You cannot use the refactor detailed earlier in the "Replacing a conditional expression with polymorphism" section, because this is a result of such a refactor. Instead, is there a way to construct an `AccountBase` from an `accountType` name without directly referencing each value and subclass? Listing 6-12 provides the answer.

LISTING 6-12 If the accounts follow a certain naming convention, this factory will suffice for all account subclasses.

```
public AccountBase CreateAccount(string accountType)
{
    var objectHandle = Activator.CreateInstance(null, string.Format("{0}Account",
  accountType));
    return (AccountBase)objectHandle.Unwrap();
}
```

Note that the enumeration has been dropped in favor of a more flexible string value. This could be a problem, because any string value could be provided, rather than only those that match valid account types. Of course, this is the point of the exercise.

This sort of refactor is a little risky because it is in danger of creating a leaky abstraction of the factory—it might not work in all required scenarios. Several things have to be true before this sort of code is viable:

- Each account type must follow a naming convention of *[Type]Account*, where the *[Type]* prefix is the value of the enumeration.

- Each account type must be contained in the same assembly as this factory method.

- Each account type must have a public default constructor—the types cannot be parameterized with any values.

Due to these constraints, this usually means that you have refactored too much, and it causes problems later when one of these constraints needs to be circumvented. Proceed with caution.

Code smell: Refused bequest

Sometime after the launch of the new reward card scheme, the client's marketing department asks how many people are assigned to each account type. Your answer leads them to conclude that they have a 100-percent uptake in the reward card scheme: that every single customer has either a Bronze, Silver, Gold, or Platinum reward card. But this is not so. There was no provision made for creating an account that was *not* part of the reward card scheme, thus everyone was given a Bronze account by default. As a result of this conversation, another new account type is required: the Standard account.

This account serves a different purpose—it does not earn any reward points. There are two ways of modeling this. First, you can create a new AccountBase subclass, shown in Listing 6-13, which does nothing in its CalculateRewardPoints override but return zero, effectively accumulating no points.

LISTING 6-13 A simple account without any reward point calculation.

```
internal class StandardAccount : AccountBase
{
    public override int CalculateRewardPoints(decimal amount)
    {
        return 0;
    }
}
```

The alternative solution is to acknowledge that not all accounts have reward points and, in fact, there are two different types in the domain model. In such a circumstance, rather than provide a "default implementation" for the CalculateRewardPoints method, the subclass effectively *refuses* what the superclass has *bequeathed* to it—hence the code smell "refused bequest." In the prior example, the StandardAccount has refused to implement the interface rather than to ignore it, whereas the next refactor will refuse the interface altogether.

Replacing inheritance with delegation

In practice, this means that you need to split the AccountBase class into two parts. Some of the interface will remain on the account, with some of it moving to a new class hierarchy to represent reward cards. In this way, the inheritance of accounts is replaced with delegation to reward cards.

The first change is to introduce a new IRewardCard interface to define the properties and behavior of each reward card, as shown in Listing 6-14.

LISTING 6-14 The reward points and their calculation have moved away from the Account class.

```
public interface IRewardCard
{
    int RewardPoints
    {
        get;
    }

    void CalculateRewardPoints(decimal transactionAmount, decimal accountBalance);
}
```

Previously, these two members were part of the AccountBase class, but they have been moved out because they are wholly dependent on the presence of reward cards. Note that the interface of CalculateRewardPoints has changed in two ways. First, there is no longer a return value on this method, because it is expected to mutate the RewardPoints property directly. Second, you must pass in the account balance as a parameter to this method because it is no longer available. This is an important side effect of splitting the two objects up in this manner: any context not directly encapsulated by the reward card object will need to be handed to it. This might cause the interface of this method to change in the future.

Listing 6-15 shows the implementations of this interface for the Bronze and Platinum cards after the refactor.

LISTING 6-15 Examples of the reward card implementations.

```
internal class BronzeRewardCard : IRewardCard
{
    public int RewardPoints
    {
        get;
        private set;
    }

    public void CalculateRewardPoints(decimal transactionAmount, decimal accountBalance)
    {
        RewardPoints += Math.Max((int)decimal.Floor(transactionAmount /
    BronzeTransactionCostPerPoint), 0);
    }
    private const int BronzeTransactionCostPerPoint = 20;
}
// . . .
internal class PlatinumRewardCard : IRewardCard
{
    public int RewardPoints
    {
        get;
        private set;
    }

    public void CalculateRewardPoints(decimal transactionAmount, decimal accountBalance)
    {
        RewardPoints += Math.Max((int)decimal.Ceiling(
            (accountBalance / PlatinumBalanceCostPerPoint) +
            (transactionAmount / PlatinumTransactionCostPerPoint)), 0);
    }

    private const int PlatinumTransactionCostPerPoint = 2;
    private const int PlatinumBalanceCostPerPoint = 1000;
}
```

These classes are very similar to their previous incarnation, with an extra local RewardPoints property.

As shown in Listing 6-16, the Account class is no longer abstract and therefore no longer requires the Base suffix. For construction, it accepts an IRewardCard instance and delegates to this when adding a transaction. Overall, this account looks more like it used to before the initial requirement for capturing reward points.

LISTING 6-16 Each account contains a reward card.

```
public class Account
{
    public Account(IRewardCard rewardCard)
    {
        this.rewardCard = rewardCard;
    }

    public decimal Balance
    {
        get;
        private set;
    }

    public void AddTransaction(decimal amount)
    {
        rewardCard.CalculateRewardPoints(amount, Balance);
        Balance += amount;
    }

    private readonly IRewardCard rewardCard;
}
```

To model a Standard account—an account without a reward card—you can either pass in null for the reward card constructor dependency (and protect against a NullReferenceException by testing for null before delegating) or you can model a NullRewardCard. The latter would be an implementation of the Null Object pattern that would not accumulate any reward points when CalculateRewardPoints was called.

Aggressive refactoring

Code is never *done*. Code can be working, good enough, sufficient, valuable, and producing revenue. But it is rarely, if ever, complete. Often, code is found in a certain state, but it is only a snapshot of a transitioning form. Code is always on a journey from where it is now to some unknown place in the future. When code is *considered* finished, there is the temptation to label it pejoratively. It becomes "stupid," "unreadable"—a figure of ridicule. Worse still, you might start to consider its authors as stupid or bad coders, or even malevolent forces, spitefully making your life a waking nightmare.

If you instead consider code as perpetually unfinished, you are better able to break the inertia to change. No code is ever sacred. Code can be underdeveloped and in need of some engineering discipline, or overwrought and in need of simplification. Different parts of the code might exhibit each property, perhaps in startling proximity. Never be afraid to roll your sleeves up and set about *improving* something. Even if you revert your changes, you will learn something, guaranteed. Better still, use your skills as an adaptive code ninja to aggressively refactor it into a better shape.

Aggressive refactoring is what normal refactoring should be but rarely is. Refactoring should be continuous and diligent. It should also occur at different scopes. The refactors discussed so far in this chapter are somewhat tactical. This is fine, but it will result in code that is clean at the lowest levels but that lacks a discernible structure. Capturing magic numbers in constant variables is a noble undertaking, but it will not result in code that can absorb the functionality of endless new requirements.

For this, a new phase is needed in the development process: *redesign*.

Red, green, refactor...redesign

Refactoring implies the fourth conceptual stage, *redesign*, but developers often stop short of refactoring so much. There are also nuanced differences in the rules for refactoring versus redesigning.

When you are refactoring, the unit tests protect against a misstep by specifying the expected behavior of the code. If the refactor goes wrong and you inadvertently change the behavior of the code in addition to its design, the unit test fails. Recovery is simple: revert the changes and try again.

When you are redesigning, the unit tests will no longer apply as valid tests of the design. Changing the name of a production class or method, either manually or by automated tools, is a refactor, not a redesign. Replacing that class with an entirely new class, whose methods accept different parameters and return different outputs, is a redesign. The difference is that the unit tests must change in order to be effective.

The steps for redesigning, and therefore aggressive refactoring, are twofold. First, the tests must change first to reflect the new design. Second, the production code to satisfy the new design must be created in parallel.

Changing the tests first ensures that you are still doing test-first development (not to be confused with test-driven design; see Chapter 5). Implementing the new production code in parallel ensures that you do not break the existing code for any length of time. Try to avoid committing code that is broken to source control. If the code was broken at any time during the redesign, it could not be committed to source control. This would put you in the awkward situation of needing to redesign code all in one sitting without any pauses or breaks. This is not enforceable, because the work of a developer is fraught with constant interruptions and context switches.

Making legacy code adaptive

Legacy code is code without tests.

- Michael Feathers, Working Effectively with Legacy Code

All examples of refactoring up to this point have assumed that the code that is the target of your refactors has sufficient tests to protect against a refactoring mistake. What if there are no unit tests?

In his great book, *Working Effectively with Legacy Code* (Prentice Hall, 2014), Michael Feathers asserts that legacy code is not simply code from a bygone era written in Cobol or some such arcane language. No, the differentiating factor that distinguishes legacy code is that it does not have any unit tests that verify its behavior.

Such code makes refactoring more difficult, because there is no guarantee against an inevitable mistake that could alter the behavior and the structure of the code. Furthermore, the omission of tests also correlates with poor code design, so legacy code is both perilous to refactor and in desperate need of refactoring! This lack of design is what makes it so difficult to retrofit unit tests so that the code can be safely refactored.

The golden master technique

Michael Feathers solves this problem with two types of tests: characterization tests and a golden master.

Characterization tests are intended to capture the current behavior of the system. The goal is not to be exhaustive, mapping the range of all possible inputs to the domain of all possible outputs. Instead, the goal is to capture the general ebb and flow of the code's runtime execution.

When the characterization tests have been created, the system's current behavior is stored, perhaps as log messages in a file. This file is now your expectation for the system, and the output of the characterization tests is disabled. These expectations can form the basis of test assertions. The golden master will run the system and capture a current view of the characterization tests. From here, changes can be made to the system, and the output of the characterization tests compared against the golden master. Any deviation from the expected paths will result in a test failure. With a green, passing test, you have given yourself some confidence that your refactoring efforts have not altered the behavior of the legacy code.

Only when the expected behavior of the system has changed do you regenerate the golden master by re-running the characterization tests. During the normal course of regression testing, the generation of the golden master is disabled, but the assertion of current behavior versus expected behavior remains enabled.

Of course, this technique lacks the precision of true unit tests, but the idea is that each refactor is more of a redesign. This will generate a parallel design that is implemented by using a test-first process. As the suite of unit tests grows, so does your confidence that the application is still functional.

The trade processor

Listing 6-17 shows a class called TradeProcessor that you want to refactor. This code is *legacy code*, by the Michael Feathers definition: it does not have any accompanying tests.

LISTING 6-17 Changing code without tests is perilous without first introducing some tests.

```
public class TradeProcessor
{
    public void ProcessTrades(System.IO.Stream stream)
    {
        // read rows
        var lines = new List<string>();
        using(var reader = new System.IO.StreamReader(stream))
        {
            string line;
            while((line = reader.ReadLine()) != null)
            {
                lines.Add(line);
            }
        }

        var trades = new List<TradeRecord>();

        var lineCount = 1;
        foreach(var line in lines)
        {
            var fields = line.Split(new char[] { ',' });

            if(fields.Length != 3)
            {
                Console.WriteLine("WARN: Line {0} malformed. Only {1} field(s) found.",
 lineCount, fields.Length);
                continue;
            }

            if(fields[0].Length != 6)
            {
                Console.WriteLine("WARN: Trade currencies on line {0} malformed: '{1}'",
 lineCount, fields[0]);
                continue;
            }

            int tradeAmount;
            if(!int.TryParse(fields[1], out tradeAmount))
            {
                Console.WriteLine("WARN: Trade amount on line {0} not a valid integer:
 '{1}'", lineCount, fields[1]);
            }

            decimal tradePrice;
            if (!decimal.TryParse(fields[2], out tradePrice))
```

```
            {
                Console.WriteLine("WARN: Trade price on line {0} not a valid decimal:
    '{1}'", lineCount, fields[2]);
            }

            var sourceCurrencyCode = fields[0].Substring(0, 3);
            var destinationCurrencyCode = fields[0].Substring(3, 3);

            // calculate values
            var trade = new TradeRecord
            {
                SourceCurrency = sourceCurrencyCode,
                DestinationCurrency = destinationCurrencyCode,
                Lots = tradeAmount / LotSize,
                Price = tradePrice
            };

            trades.Add(trade);

            lineCount++;
        }

        using (var connection = new System.Data.SqlClient.SqlConnection("Data
    Source=(local);Initial Catalog=TradeDatabase;Integrated Security=True"))
        {
            connection.Open();
            using (var transaction = connection.BeginTransaction())
            {
                foreach(var trade in trades)
                {
                    var command = connection.CreateCommand();
                    command.Transaction = transaction;
                    command.CommandType = System.Data.CommandType.StoredProcedure;
                    command.CommandText = "dbo.insert_trade";
                    command.Parameters.AddWithValue("@sourceCurrency", trade.
    SourceCurrency);
                    command.Parameters.AddWithValue("@destinationCurrency", trade.
    DestinationCurrency);
                    command.Parameters.AddWithValue("@lots", trade.Lots);
                    command.Parameters.AddWithValue("@price", trade.Price);

                    command.ExecuteNonQuery();
                }

                transaction.Commit();
            }
            connection.Close();
        }

        Console.WriteLine("INFO: {0} trades processed", trades.Count);
    }

    private static float LotSize = 100000f;
}
```

This code is more procedural than object-oriented. It is a long recipe for transforming data that is in one format—a stream—into another format—a relational database. It might have started life as a prototype or a spike, or just a very quick-and-dirty solution. But, as is common, it is now to be repurposed into a more robust and full-featured solution. If you were to encounter code like this, the temptation might be to hack away at it until it is in better shape: more object-oriented, with extension points, and more testable. That would be a good idea, but the execution would be perilous: without the safety net of tests to indicate mistakes, the refactor would be prone to the most insidious type of failure: silent failure. The prerequisite step to refactoring code without tests is to capture its current behavior as best you can.

Characterization tests

The first objective is to gather the outcomes of the code given a variety of inputs. By defining and supplying a range of inputs, you can ascertain the domain of outputs. This could be a manual process involving running the application many times and recording the outputs for any provided inputs. But, of course, this doesn't scale well and will take a long time to execute. Instead, it is better to automate the process in the form of *characterization tests*.

Despite the name, you will not implement the characterization tests as unit tests. This is because you will not run the characterization tests all the time. The output of a characterization test is the set of current behaviors given certain inputs. These will then become your expectations when you create a golden master test. Your expectations will change infrequently and only when you are ready to add functionality to the code or change its current behavior. Implementing characterization tests as unit tests would cause you either to erroneously regenerate the expectations every time you run all tests, or comment out the characterization test for most of the development, only uncommenting it when an expectation has failed. This is prone to error. Instead, the characterization tests will be implemented as a running console application. Listing 6-18 shows the first characterization test.

LISTING 6-18 An initial characterization test written as a standalone console application.

```
class Program
{
    static void Main(string[] args)
    {
        var inputs = new List<string>()
        {
            "empty-file.txt"
        };

        var originalConsoleOut = Console.Out;

        foreach (var input in inputs)
        {
            var tradeStream = Assembly.GetExecutingAssembly()
                .GetManifestResourceStream(typeof(Program), input);

            using (var streamWriter = new StreamWriter(
                File.OpenWrite($"expectation-{input}")))
```

```
        {
            Console.SetOut(streamWriter);

            var tradeProcessor = new TradeProcessorService();
            tradeProcessor.ProcessTrades(tradeStream);
        }
    }

    Console.SetOut(originalConsoleOut);

    Console.ReadKey();
    }
}
```

This code captures anything that is written to the console by the ProcessTrades method and redirects it to an output file. Although it is possible that many input and output pairs will be generated, only one is currently provided: an empty file. A few more examples will be added soon, and these output files will later supply your golden master tests with their expectations. As you can tell, this is a coarse-grained way to scaffold some tests onto untested—and likely untestable—code. It would be great if you could mock out the database interaction that is embedded in the TradeProcessor class, but that is not possible without potentially breaking the functionality. Code that exhibits even more complexity than this sample is often much riskier to refactor without first creating a safety net.

Running this one characterization test generates an output file with the following contents.

```
INFO: 0 trades processed
```

Table 6-1 shows some more input and output pairs for the characterization test.

TABLE 6-1 Characterization test inputs and expected outputs.

Name	Input	Output
Empty file		`INFO: 0 trades processed`
One field	`Test`	`WARN: Line 1 malformed. Only 1 field(s) found.` `INFO: 0 trades processed`

Malformed currency pair	`Test,123,abc`	`WARN: Trade currencies on line 1 malformed:`
		`'Test'`
		`INFO: 0 trades processed`

Trade volume invalid	`GBPUSD,xyz,abc`	`WARN: Trade amount on line 1 not a valid integer: 'xyz'`
		`WARN: Trade price on line 1 not a valid decimal: 'abc'`
		`INFO: 1 trades processed`

Trade amount invalid	`GBPUSD,100,abc`	`WARN: Trade price on line 1 not a valid decimal: 'abc'` `INFO: 1 trades processed`
Correct format	`GBPUSD,1000,0.81`	`INFO: 1 trades processed`

This set of inputs and outputs is not exhaustive, nor could it be. The more tests you can capture, the more confidence you can have when refactoring, so a single input and output pair is unlikely to be sufficient. But there are diminishing returns when capturing many esoteric inputs.

Instrumenting legacy code

Legacy code is often not as helpful as it is in this example; there might not even be any console output to capture. Even the minimal foundations required to support characterization tests might, in practice, necessitate some edits to the existing code without tests in place. This is a common reality because most legacy code was never intended to be tested. Therefore, you might need to add some console logging at certain points in the class or method to be refactored. Typically, this logging is added around branching and looping expressions in addition to parts of the code that generate side effects like writing to a database or raising an event.

It is not wholly disingenuous to claim that these changes are not *changes*. They are not *amendments*; but *appendments*. There is still a risk of breaking functionality when appending changes; it is just less likely that they will be detrimental to the existing code than altering an existing line.

A golden master

With a set of characterization tests run, you can now turn your attention to creating a golden master test. This test will take the outputs of the characterization tests and use them as expectations to assert against. These will be implemented as unit tests and can be run as usual. Remember, though, that these tests are not, strictly speaking, unit tests, because they depend on externalities such as the filesystem. Therefore, they are neither isolated enough nor fast enough to be considered unit tests. Listing 6-19 shows the golden master test.

LISTING 6-19 The golden master test.

```
public class GoldenMaster
{
    private static string CharacterizationTestOutput =
        Path.Combine("../../../", "CharacterizationTests/bin/Debug/");

    [Fact]
    public void OutputStillMatchesCharacterization()
    {
        var inputsAndExpectations = new Dictionary<string, string>()
        {
            { "empty-file.txt", "expectation-empty-file.txt" },
            { "one-field.txt", "expectation-one-field.txt" },
            { "malformed-currency-pair.txt", "expectation-malformed-currency-pair.txt"
},

            { "trade-volume-invalid.txt", "expectation-trade-volume-invalid.txt" },
```

```
                { "trade-amount-invalid.txt", "expectation-trade-amount-invalid.txt" },
                { "correct-format.txt", "expectation-correct-format.txt" }
            };

            var originalConsoleOut = Console.Out;

            foreach (var pair in inputsAndExpectations)
            {
                var input = typeof(CharacterizationTest).Assembly
                    .GetManifestResourceStream(typeof(CharacterizationTest), pair.Key);
                var expectation = File.ReadAllText(
                    Path.Combine(CharacterizationTestOutput, pair.Value));

                string actual = null;
                using (var memoryStream = new MemoryStream())
                using (var streamWriter = new StreamWriter(memoryStream))
                {
                    Console.SetOut(streamWriter);

                    var tradeProcessor = new TradeProcessor();
                    tradeProcessor.ProcessTrades(input);

                    streamWriter.Flush();

                    memoryStream.Seek(0, SeekOrigin.Begin);
                    actual = new StreamReader(memoryStream).ReadToEnd();
                }

                Assert.Equal(expectation, actual);
            }

            Console.SetOut(originalConsoleOut);
        }
    }
```

The test itself will run the TradeProcessor with each configured input file and capture the output string in memory. It will then compare that actual result with the expected result that was generated by the characterization test. This is repeated for each input and output pair, as long as there are no breaking changes to the code.

Note how fragile this method of testing is: a change to a logging line will break the test but will not break the real behavior of the TradeProcessor. This is a false negative result. Conversely, you could change any part of the database interaction and the golden master test will still pass, despite the TradeProcessor no longer functioning as it should. This is a false positive result. Therefore, golden master tests are not replacements for real unit tests: they do not give you the same level of confidence that you have avoided introducing a regression bug through refactoring.

In the next chapter, you will refactor this code to follow the first of five SOLID principles: single responsibility.

Conclusion

Refactoring and unit testing are interdependent practices that are vital to the creation and maintenance of adaptive code. Code is in a constant state of flux and should never truly be considered absolute. Aside from adding new features as requirements shift, code should be aggressively refactored so that it has a better chance of standing the test of time. With aggressive refactoring—redesigning—the code will exhibit good design at its lowest levels, but new knowledge about the problem space will never be incorporated into the code. Consider the number of times that you "finish" a project and wish—weeks, months, or years later—that you could revise it because you finally "understand the requirements" or have learned a new technique that would have simplified the solution. Through consistent and diligent refactoring and redesigning, code is able to remain adaptive long into the future. Do not be tempted by the siren song of a system rewrite!

With this chapter complete, the Agile foundation part of this book is closed. Next, you will look at SOLID code and how it will help to further increase the adaptability of your code.

SOLID code

SOLID is the acronym for a set of practices that, when implemented together, make code adaptive to change. The SOLID practices were introduced by Bob Martin almost 15 years ago. Even so, these practices are not as widely known as they could be—and perhaps should be.

In this part, a chapter is devoted to each of the SOLID principles:

- **S**   The single responsibility principle

- **O**   The open/closed principle

- **L**   The Liskov substitution principle

- **I**   The interface segregation principle

- **D**   The dependency inversion principle

Even taken in isolation, each of these principles is a worthy practice that any software developer would do well to learn. When used in collaboration, these patterns give code a completely different structure—one that lends itself to change.

However, take note that these patterns and practices, just like all others, are merely tools for you to use. Deciding when and where to apply any pattern or practice is part of the art of software development. Overuse leads to code that is adaptive, but on too fine-grained a level to be appreciated or useful. Overuse also affects another key facet of code quality: readability. It is far more common for software to be developed in teams than as an individual pursuit. Thus, judiciously selecting when and where to apply each pattern, practice, or SOLID principle is imperative to ensure that the code remains comprehensible in the future.

CHAPTER 7

The single responsibility principle

After completing this chapter, you will be able to

- Understand the importance of the single responsibility principle.

- Identify classes that have too many responsibilities.

- Write modules, classes, and methods that have a single responsibility.

- Refactor monolithic classes into smaller classes with single responsibilities.

- Use design patterns to separate responsibilities.

The single responsibility principle (SRP) instructs developers to write code that has one *and only one* reason to change. If a class has more than one reason to change, it has more than one responsibility. Classes with more than a single responsibility should be broken down into smaller classes, each of which should have only one responsibility and reason to change.

This chapter explains that process and shows you how to create classes that have only a single responsibility but are still useful. Through a process of delegation and abstraction, a class that contains too many reasons to change should delegate one or more responsibilities to other classes.

It is difficult to overstate the importance of delegating to abstractions. It is the lynchpin of adaptive code and, without it, developers would struggle to adapt to changing requirements in the way that Scrum, Kanban, and other Agile frameworks demand.

Problem statement

To better explain the problem with having classes that hold too many responsibilities, this section explores an example. Listing 7-1 shows the `TradeProcessor` introduced in Chapter 6, "Refactoring." Recall that this class reads records from a file and updates a database, and some characterization tests were added around it to capture its current behavior. This created a Golden Master test, which can be used as a safety harness to protect somewhat against inadvertent behavioral changes when refactoring.

Despite its small size, this sort of code is common and often needs to cope with new features and changes to requirements.

LISTING 7-1 An example of a class with too many responsibilities.

```
public class TradeProcessor
{
    public void ProcessTrades(System.IO.Stream stream)
    {
        // read rows
        var lines = new List<string>();
        using(var reader = new System.IO.StreamReader(stream))
        {
            string line;
            while((line = reader.ReadLine()) != null)
            {
                lines.Add(line);
            }
        }

        var trades = new List<TradeRecord>();

        var lineCount = 1;
        foreach(var line in lines)
        {
            var fields = line.Split(new char[] { ',' });

            if(fields.Length != 3)
            {
                Console.WriteLine("WARN: Line {0} malformed. Only {1} field(s) found.",
lineCount, fields.Length);
                continue;
            }

            if(fields[0].Length != 6)
            {
                Console.WriteLine("WARN: Trade currencies on line {0} malformed: '{1}'",
lineCount, fields[0]);
                continue;
            }

            int tradeAmount;
            if(!int.TryParse(fields[1], out tradeAmount))
            {
                Console.WriteLine("WARN: Trade amount on line {0} not a valid integer:
'{1}'", lineCount, fields[1]);
            }

            decimal tradePrice;
            if (!decimal.TryParse(fields[2], out tradePrice))
            {
                Console.WriteLine("WARN: Trade price on line {0} not a valid decimal:
'{1}'", lineCount, fields[2]);
            }
```

```
            var sourceCurrencyCode = fields[0].Substring(0, 3);
            var destinationCurrencyCode = fields[0].Substring(3, 3);

            // calculate values
            var trade = new TradeRecord
            {
                SourceCurrency = sourceCurrencyCode,
                DestinationCurrency = destinationCurrencyCode,
                Lots = tradeAmount / LotSize,
                Price = tradePrice
            };

            trades.Add(trade);

            lineCount++;
        }

        using (var connection = new System.Data.SqlClient.SqlConnection("Data
Source=(local);Initial Catalog=TradeDatabase;Integrated Security=True"))
        {
            connection.Open();
            using (var transaction = connection.BeginTransaction())
            {
                foreach(var trade in trades)
                {
                    var command = connection.CreateCommand();
                    command.Transaction = transaction;
                    command.CommandType = System.Data.CommandType.StoredProcedure;
                    command.CommandText = "dbo.insert_trade";
                    command.Parameters.AddWithValue("@sourceCurrency", trade.
SourceCurrency);
                    command.Parameters.AddWithValue("@destinationCurrency", trade.
DestinationCurrency);
                    command.Parameters.AddWithValue("@lots", trade.Lots);
                    command.Parameters.AddWithValue("@price", trade.Price);

                    command.ExecuteNonQuery();
                }

                transaction.Commit();
            }
            connection.Close();
        }

        Console.WriteLine("INFO: {0} trades processed", trades.Count);
    }

    private static float LotSize = 100000f;
}
```

This is more than an example of a class that has too many responsibilities; it is also an example of a single *method* that has too many responsibilities. By reading the code carefully, you can discern what this class is trying to achieve:

1. It reads every line from a Stream parameter, storing each line in a list of strings.

2. It parses out individual fields from each line and stores them in a more structured list of Trade-Record instances.

3. The parsing includes some validation and some logging to the console.

4. Each TradeRecord is enumerated, and a stored procedure is called to insert the trades into a database.

The responsibilities of the TradeProcessor are reading streams, parsing strings, validating fields, logging, and database insertion. The single responsibility principle states that this class, like all others, should have only a single reason to change. However, the reality of the TradeProcessor is that it will change under the following circumstances:

- When you decide not to use a Stream for input but instead read the trades from a remote call to a web service.

- When the format of the input data changes, perhaps with the addition of an extra field indicating the broker for the transaction.

- When the validation rules of the input data change.

- When the way in which you log warnings, errors, and information changes. If you are using a hosted web service, writing to the console would not be a viable option.

- When the database changes in some way—perhaps the insert_trade stored procedure requires a new parameter for the broker, too, or you decide not to store the data in a relational database and opt for document storage, or the database is moved behind a web service that you must call.

For each of these changes, this class would have to be modified. Furthermore, unless you maintain a variety of versions, there is no possibility of adapting the TradeProcessor so that it is able to read from a different input source, for example. Imagine the maintenance headache when you are asked to add the ability to store the trades in a web service, but only if a certain command-line argument was supplied.

Refactoring for clarity

The first task on the road to refactoring the TradeProcessor so that it has one reason to change is to split the ProcessTrades method into smaller methods so that each one focuses on a single responsibility. Each of the following listings shows a single method from the refactored TradeProcessor class, followed by an explanation of the changes.

First, Listing 7-2 shows the ProcessTrades method, which now does nothing more than delegate to other methods.

LISTING 7-2 The ProcessTrades method is very minimal because it delegates work to other methods.

```
public void ProcessTrades(System.IO.Stream stream)
{
    var lines = ReadTradeData(stream);
    var trades = ParseTrades(lines);
    StoreTrades(trades);
}
```

The original code was characterized by three distinct parts of a process—reading the trade data from a stream, converting the string data in the stream to TradeRecord instances, and writing the trades to persistent storage. Note that the output from one method feeds into the input to the next method. You cannot call StoreTrades until you have the trade records returned from the ParseTrades method, and you cannot call ParseTrades until you have the lines returned from the ReadTradeData method.

Taking each of these methods in order, let's look at ReadTradeData, in Listing 7-3.

LISTING 7-3 ReadTradeData encapsulates the original code.

```
private IEnumerable<string> ReadTradeData(System.IO.Stream stream)
{
    var tradeData = new List<string>();
    using (var reader = new System.IO.StreamReader(stream))
    {
        string line;
        while ((line = reader.ReadLine()) != null)
        {
            tradeData.Add(line);
        }
    }
    return tradeData;
}
```

This code is preserved from the original implementation of the ProcessTrades method. It has simply been encapsulated in a method that returns the resultant string data as a string enumeration. Note that this makes the return value read-only, whereas the original implementation unnecessarily allowed subsequent parts of the process to add further lines.

The ParseTrades method, shown in Listing 7-4, is next. It has changed somewhat from the original implementation because it, too, delegates some tasks to other methods.

LISTING 7-4 ParseTrades delegates to other methods to limit its complexity.

```
private IEnumerable<TradeRecord> ParseTrades(IEnumerable<string> tradeData)
{
    var trades = new List<TradeRecord>();
    var lineCount = 1;
    foreach (var line in tradeData)
    {
        var fields = line.Split(new char[] { ',' });

        if(!ValidateTradeData(fields, lineCount))
        {
            continue;
        }

        var trade = MapTradeDataToTradeRecord(fields);

        trades.Add(trade);

        lineCount++;
    }
    return trades;
}
```

This method delegates validation and mapping responsibilities to other methods. Without this delegation, this section of the process would still be too complex, and it would retain too many responsibilities. The ValidateTradeData method, shown in Listing 7-5, returns a Boolean value to indicate whether any of the fields for a trade line are invalid.

LISTING 7-5 All of the validation code is in a single method.

```
private bool ValidateTradeData(string[] fields, int currentLine)
{
    if (fields.Length != 3)
    {
        LogMessage("WARN: Line {0} malformed. Only {1} field(s) found.", currentLine,
    fields.Length);
        return false;
    }
```

```
        if (fields[0].Length != 6)
        {
            LogMessage("WARN: Trade currencies on line {0} malformed: '{1}'", currentLine,
fields[0]);
            return false;
        }

        int tradeAmount;
        if (!int.TryParse(fields[1], out tradeAmount))
        {
            LogMessage("WARN: Trade amount on line {0} not a valid integer: '{1}'",
currentLine, fields[1]);
            return false;
        }

        decimal tradePrice;
        if (!decimal.TryParse(fields[2], out tradePrice))
        {
            LogMessage("WARN: Trade price on line {0} not a valid decimal: '{1}'",
currentLine, fields[2]);
            return false;
        }

        return true;
}
```

The only change made to the original validation code is that it now delegates to yet another method for logging messages. Rather than embedding calls to `Console.WriteLine` where needed, the `LogMessage` method is used, shown in Listing 7-6.

LISTING 7-6 The `LogMessage` method is currently just a synonym for `Console.WriteLine`.

```
private void LogMessage(string message, params object[] args)
{
    Console.WriteLine(message, args);
}
```

Returning up the stack to the `ParseTrades` method, Listing 7-7 shows the other method to which it delegates. This method maps an array of strings representing the individual fields from the stream to an instance of the `TradeRecord` class.

LISTING 7-7 Mapping from one type to another is a separate responsibility.

```
private TradeRecord MapTradeDataToTradeRecord(string[] fields)
{
    var sourceCurrencyCode = fields[0].Substring(0, 3);
    var destinationCurrencyCode = fields[0].Substring(3, 3);
    var tradeAmount = int.Parse(fields[1]);
    var tradePrice = decimal.Parse(fields[2]);
```

```
    var tradeRecord = new TradeRecord
    {
        SourceCurrency = sourceCurrencyCode,
        DestinationCurrency = destinationCurrencyCode,
        Lots = tradeAmount / LotSize,
        Price = tradePrice
    };

    return tradeRecord;
}
```

The sixth and final new method introduced by this refactor is StoreTrades, shown in Listing 7-8. This method wraps the code for interacting with the database. It also delegates the informational log message to the aforementioned LogMessage method.

LISTING 7-8 Now that the StoreTrades method is in place, the responsibilities in this class are clearly demarcated.

```
private void StoreTrades(IEnumerable<TradeRecord> trades)
{
    using (var connection = new System.Data.SqlClient.SqlConnection("Data
    Source=(local);Initial Catalog=TradeDatabase;Integrated Security=True"))
    {
        connection.Open();
        using (var transaction = connection.BeginTransaction())
        {
            foreach (var trade in trades)
            {
                var command = connection.CreateCommand();
                command.Transaction = transaction;
                command.CommandType = System.Data.CommandType.StoredProcedure;
                command.CommandText = "dbo.insert_trade";
                command.Parameters.AddWithValue("@sourceCurrency", trade.SourceCurrency);
                command.Parameters.AddWithValue("@destinationCurrency",
    trade.DestinationCurrency);
                command.Parameters.AddWithValue("@lots", trade.Lots);
                command.Parameters.AddWithValue("@price", trade.Price);

                command.ExecuteNonQuery();
            }

            transaction.Commit();
        }
        connection.Close();
    }

    LogMessage("INFO: {0} trades processed", trades.Count());
}
```

Looking back at this refactor, you can see that it is a clear improvement on the original implementation. However, what have you really achieved? Although the new ProcessTrades method is indisputably smaller than the monolithic original, and the code is definitely more readable, you have gained very little by way of adaptability. You can change the implementation of the LogMessage method so that it, for example, writes to a file instead of to the console, but that involves a change to the TradeProcessor class, which is precisely what you wanted to avoid.

This refactor has been an important stepping stone on the path to truly separating the responsibilities of this class. It has been a refactor for clarity, not for adaptability. The next task is to split each responsibility into different classes and place them behind interfaces. What you need is true abstraction to achieve useful adaptability.

Refactoring for abstraction

Building on the new TradeProcessor implementation, the next refactor introduces several abstractions that will allow you to handle almost any change request for this class. Although this running example might seem very small, perhaps even insignificant, it is a workable contrivance for the purposes of this tutorial. Also, it is *very* common for a small application such as this to grow into something much larger. When a few people start to use it, the feature requests begin to increase.

Often, the terms *prototype* and *proof of concept* are applied to such allegedly small applications, and the conversion from prototype to production application is relatively seamless. This is why the ability to refactor toward abstraction is such a touchstone of adaptive development. Without it, the myriad requests devolve into a "big ball of mud"—a class, or a group of classes in an assembly, with little delineation of responsibility and no discernible abstractions. The result is an application that has no unit tests and that is difficult to maintain and enhance, and yet that could be a critical piece of the line of business.

The first step in refactoring the TradeProcessor for abstraction is to design the interface or interfaces that it will use to perform the three high-level tasks of reading, processing, and storing the trade data. Figure 7-1 shows the first set of abstractions.

FIGURE 7-1 The TradeProcessor will now depend on three new interfaces.

Because you moved all of the code from `ProcessTrades` into separate methods in the first refactor, you should have a good idea of where the first abstractions should be applied. As prescribed by the single responsibility principle, the three main responsibilities will be handled by different classes. As you know from previous chapters, you should not have direct dependencies from one class to another but should instead work via interfaces. Therefore, the three responsibilities are factored out into three separate interfaces. Listing 7-9 shows how the `TradeProcessor` class looks after this change.

LISTING 7-9 The `TradeProcessor` is now the encapsulation of a process, and nothing more.

```
public class TradeProcessor
{
    public TradeProcessor(ITradeDataProvider tradeDataProvider, ITradeParser tradeParser,
    ITradeStorage tradeStorage)
    {
        this.tradeDataProvider = tradeDataProvider;
        this.tradeParser = tradeParser;
        this.tradeStorage = tradeStorage;
    }

    public void ProcessTrades()
    {
        var lines = tradeDataProvider.GetTradeData();
        var trades = tradeParser.Parse(lines);
        tradeStorage.Persist(trades);
    }

    private readonly ITradeDataProvider tradeDataProvider;
    private readonly ITradeParser tradeParser;
    private readonly ITradeStorage tradeStorage;
}
```

The class is now significantly different from its previous incarnation. It no longer contains the implementation details for the whole process but instead contains the *blueprint* for the process. The class models the process of transferring trade data from one format to another. This is its only responsibility, its only concern, and the only reason that this class should change. If the process itself changes, this class will change to reflect it. But if you decide you no longer want to retrieve data from a `Stream`, log to the console, or store the trades in a database, this class remains as is.

The interfaces that the `TradeProcessor` now depends on all live in a separate assembly. This ensures that neither the client nor the implementation assemblies reference each other. Also separated into another assembly are the three classes that implement these interfaces, the `StreamTradeData-Provider`, `SimpleTradeParser`, and `AdoNetTradeStorage` classes. Note that there is a naming convention used for these classes. First, the prefixed `I` was removed from the interface name and replaced with the implementation-specific context that is required of the class. So `StreamTradeDataProvider` allows you to infer that it is an implementation of the `ITradeDataProvider` interface that retrieves its data from a `Stream` object. The `AdoNetTradeStorage` class uses ADO.NET to persist the trade data. I have prefixed the `ITradeParser` implementation with the word `Simple` to indicate that it has no dependency context.

All three of these implementations are able to live in a single assembly due to their shared dependencies—core assemblies of the Microsoft .NET Framework. If you were to introduce an implementation that required a third-party dependency, a first-party dependency of your own, or a dependency from a non-core .NET Framework class, you should put these implementations into their own assemblies. For example, if you were to use the Dapper mapping library instead of ADO.NET, you would create an assembly called `Services.Dapper`, inside of which would be an `ITradeStorage` implementation called `DapperTradeStorage`.

The `ITradeDataProvider` interface does not depend on the `Stream` class. The previous version of the method for retrieving trade data required a `Stream` instance as a parameter, but this artificially tied the method to a dependency. When you are creating interfaces and refactoring toward abstractions, it is important that you do not retain dependencies where doing so would affect the adaptability of the code. The possibility of retrieving the trade data from sources other than a `Stream` has already been discussed, so the refactoring has ensured that this dependency is removed from the interface. Instead, the `StreamTradeDataProvider` requires a `Stream` as a constructor parameter, instead of a method parameter. By using the constructor, you can depend on almost anything without polluting the interface. Listing 7-10 shows the `StreamTradeDataProvider` implementation.

LISTING 7-10 Context can be passed into classes via constructor parameters, keeping the interface clean.

```
public class StreamTradeDataProvider : ITradeDataProvider
{
    public StreamTradeDataProvider(Stream stream)
    {
        this.stream = stream;
    }

    public IEnumerable<string> GetTradeData()
    {
        var tradeData = new List<string>();
        using (var reader = new StreamReader(stream))
        {
            string line;
            while ((line = reader.ReadLine()) != null)
            {
                tradeData.Add(line);
            }
        }
        return tradeData;
    }

    private Stream stream;
}
```

Remember that the `TradeProcessor` class, which is the client of this code, is aware of nothing other than the `GetTradeData` method's signature via the `ITradeDataProvider`. It has no knowledge whatsoever of how the real implementation retrieves the data—nor should it.

There are more abstractions that can be extracted from this example. Remember that the original `ParseTrades` method delegated responsibility for validation and for mapping. You can repeat the process of refactoring so that the `SimpleTradeParser` class does not have more than one responsibility. Figure 7-2 shows in Unified Markup Language (UML) how this can be achieved.

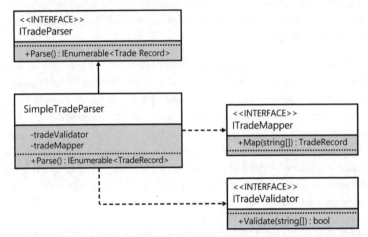

FIGURE 7-2 The `SimpleTradeParser` is also refactored to ensure that each class has a single responsibility.

This process of abstracting responsibilities into interfaces (and their accompanying implementations) is recursive. As you inspect each class, you must determine the responsibilities that it has and factor them out until the class has only one. Listing 7-11 shows the `SimpleTradeParser` class, which delegates to interfaces where appropriate. Its single reason for change is if the overall structure of the trade data changes—for instance, if the data no longer uses comma-separated values and changes to using tabs, or perhaps XML.

LISTING 7-11 The algorithm for parsing trade data is encapsulated in `ITradeParser` implementations.

```
public class SimpleTradeParser : ITradeParser
{
    public SimpleTradeParser(ITradeValidator tradeValidator, ITradeMapper tradeMapper)
    {
        this.tradeValidator = tradeValidator;
        this.tradeMapper = tradeMapper;
    }

    public IEnumerable<TradeRecord> Parse(IEnumerable<string> tradeData)
    {
        var trades = new List<TradeRecord>();
        var lineCount = 1;
        foreach (var line in tradeData)
        {
            var fields = line.Split(new char[] { ',' });
```

```
            if (!tradeValidator.Validate(fields))
            {
                continue;
            }

            var trade = tradeMapper.Map(fields);

            trades.Add(trade);

            lineCount++;
        }
        return trades;
    }

    private readonly ITradeValidator tradeValidator;
    private readonly ITradeMapper tradeMapper;
}
```

The final refactor aims to abstract logging from two classes. Both the `ITradeValidator` and `ITradeStorage` implementations are still logging directly to the console. This time, instead of implementing your own logging class, you will create an adapter for the popular logging library, Log4Net. The UML class diagram in Figure 7-3 shows how this all fits together.

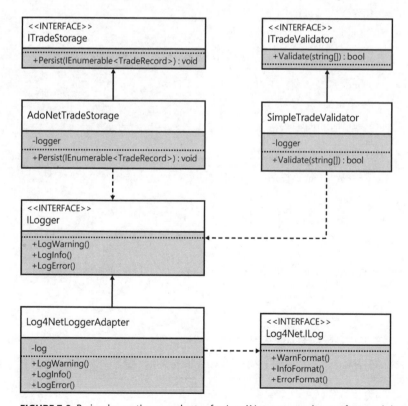

FIGURE 7-3 By implementing an adapter for Log4Net, you need not reference it in every assembly.

The net benefit of creating an adapter class such as Log4NetLoggerAdapter is that you can convert a third-party reference into a first-party reference. Notice that both AdoNetTradeStorage and SimpleTradeValidator both depend on the first-party ILogger interface. But, at run time, both will actually use Log4Net. The only references needed to Log4Net are in the entry point of the application (see Chapter 12, "Dependency injection," for more information) and the newly created Service.Log4Net assembly. Any code that has a dependency on Log4Net, such as custom appenders, should live in the Service.Log4Net assembly. For now, only the adapter resides in this new assembly.

> **Tip** It is not always necessary to convert third-party dependencies into first-party dependencies in this way. For cross-cutting concerns like logging, depending on the circumstances, it might be preferable to depend directly and ubiquitously on the third-party library throughout the codebase.

The refactored validator class is shown in Listing 7-12. It now has no reference whatsoever to the console. Because of the flexibility of Log4Net, you can actually log to almost anywhere now. Total adaptability has been achieved as far as logging is concerned.

LISTING 7-12 The SimpleTradeValidator class after refactoring.

```
public class SimpleTradeValidator : ITradeValidator
{
    private readonly ILogger logger;    public SimpleTradeValidator(ILogger logger)
    {
        this.logger = logger;
    }

    public bool Validate(string[] tradeData)
    {
        if (tradeData.Length != 3)
        {
            logger.LogWarning("Line malformed. Only {1} field(s) found.",
    tradeData.Length);
            return false;
        }

        if (tradeData[0].Length != 6)
        {
            logger.LogWarning("Trade currencies malformed: '{1}'", tradeData[0]);
            return false;
        }

        int tradeAmount;
        if (!int.TryParse(tradeData[1], out tradeAmount))
        {
            logger.LogWarning("Trade amount not a valid integer: '{1}'", tradeData[1]);
            return false;
        }
```

```
        decimal tradePrice;
        if (!decimal.TryParse(tradeData[2], out tradePrice))
        {
            logger.LogWarning("WARN: Trade price not a valid decimal: '{1}'",
  tradeData[2]);
            return false;
        }

        return true;
    }
}
```

At this point, a quick recap is in order. Bear in mind that you have altered nothing as far as the functionality of the code is concerned. This should be proven by the passing of the Golden Master test, which is protecting against refactoring mistakes. Functionally, this code does exactly what it used to do. However, if you wanted to enhance it in any way, you could do so with ease. The added ability to adapt this code to a new purpose more than justifies the effort expended to refactor it.

Tip When refactoring in this way, ensure that new code is written in a test-first fashion so that the Golden Master test is not the only test coverage that is in place.

Referring back to the original list of potential enhancements to this code, this new version allows you to implement each one without touching the existing classes.

- *Request: You decide not to use a `Stream` for input but instead read the trades from a remote call to a web service.*

  - Solution: Create a new `ITradeDataProvider` implementation that supplies the data from the service.

- *Request: The format of the input data changes, perhaps with the addition of an extra field indicating the broker for the transaction.*

  - Solution: Alter the implementations for the `ITradeDataValidator`, `ITradeDataMapper`, and `ITradeStorage` interfaces, which handle the new broker field.

- *Request: The validation rules of the input data change.*

  - Solution: Edit the `ITradeDataValidator` implementation to reflect the rule changes.

- *Request: The way in which you log warnings, errors, and information changes. If you are using a hosted web service, writing to the console would not be a viable option.*

  - Solution: As discussed, Log4Net provides you with infinite options for logging, by virtue of the adapter.

- Request: The database changes in some way—perhaps the `insert_trade` stored procedure requires a new parameter for the broker, too, or you decide not to store the data in a relational database and opt for document storage, or the database is moved behind a web service that you must call.

  - Solution: If the stored procedure changes, you would need to edit the `AdoNetTrade-Storage` class to include the broker field. For the other two options, you could create a `MongoTradeStorage` class that uses MongoDB to store the trades, and you could create a `WebServiceTradeStorage` class to hide the implementation behind a web service.

I hope you are now somewhat convinced that a combination of abstracting via interfaces, decoupling assemblies, aggressive refactoring, and adhering to the single responsibility principle are the foundation of adaptive code.

When you arrive at a scenario in which your code is neatly delegating to abstractions, the possibilities are endless. The rest of this chapter concentrates on other ways in which you can focus on a single responsibility per class.

SRP and the Decorator pattern

The Decorator pattern is excellent for ensuring that each class has a single responsibility. Classes can often do too many things without an obvious way of splitting the responsibilities into other classes. The responsibilities seem too closely linked.

The Decorator pattern's basic premise is that each decorator class fulfills the contract of a type and also accepts one or more of those types as constructor parameters. This is beneficial because functionality can be added to an existing class that implements a certain interface, and the decorator also acts—unbeknownst to clients—as an implementation of the required interface. Figure 7-4 shows a UML diagram of the Decorator design pattern.

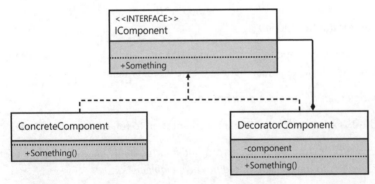

FIGURE 7-4 A UML diagram showing an implementation of the Decorator pattern.

A simple example of the pattern is shown in Listing 7-13, which does not pertain to a specific use of the pattern but provides a canonical example.

LISTING 7-13 A template example of the Decorator pattern.

```
public interface IComponent
{
    void Something();
}
// . . .
public class ConcreteComponent : IComponent
{
    public void Something()
    {

    }
}
// . . .
public class DecoratorComponent : IComponent
{
    private readonly IComponent decoratedComponent;

    public DecoratorComponent(IComponent decoratedComponent)
    {
        this.decoratedComponent = decoratedComponent;
    }

    public void Something()
    {
        SomethingElse();
        decoratedComponent.Something();
    }

    private void SomethingElse()
    {

    }
}
// . . .
class Program
{
    static IComponent component;

    static void Main(string[] args)
    {
        component = new DecoratorComponent(new ConcreteComponent());
        component.Something();
    }
}
```

Because a client accepts the interface shown in the listing as a method parameter, you can provide either the original, undecorated type to that client or you can provide the decorated version. Note that the client will be oblivious: it will not have to change depending on which version it is being provided.

The Composite pattern

The Composite pattern is a specialization of the Decorator pattern and is one of the more-common uses of that pattern. A UML diagram describing the Composite pattern's collaborators is shown in Figure 7-5.

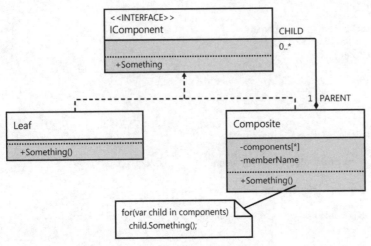

FIGURE 7-5 The Composite pattern closely resembles the Decorator pattern.

The Composite pattern's purpose is to allow you to treat many instances of an interface as if they were just one instance. Therefore, clients can accept just one instance of an interface, but they can be implicitly provided with many instances, without requiring the client to change. Listing 7-14 shows a composite decorator in practice.

LISTING 7-14 The composite implementation of an interface.

```
public interface IComponent
{
    void Something();
}
// . . .
public class Leaf : IComponent
{
    public void Something()
    {

    }
}
// . . .
public class CompositeComponent : IComponent
{
    public CompositeComponent()
    {
        children = new List<IComponent>();
    }
```

```csharp
    public void AddComponent(IComponent component)
    {
        children.Add(component);
    }

    public void RemoveComponent(IComponent component)
    {
        children.Remove(component);
    }

    public void Something()
    {
        foreach(var child in children)
        {
            child.Something();
        }
    }

    private ICollection<IComponent> children;
}
// . . .
class Program
{
    static void Main(string[] args)
    {
        var composite = new CompositeComponent();
        composite.AddComponent(new Leaf());
        composite.AddComponent(new Leaf());
        composite.AddComponent(new Leaf());

        component = composite;
        component.Something();
    }

    static IComponent component;
}
```

In the CompositeComponent class, there are methods for adding and removing other instances of the IComponent. These methods do not form part of the interface and are for clients of the Composite Component class, directly. Whichever factory method or class is tasked with creating instances of the CompositeComponent class will also have to create the decorated instances and pass them in to the Add method; otherwise, the clients of the IComponent would have to change in order to cope with compositions.

Whenever the Something method is called by the IComponent clients, the list of composed instances is enumerated, and their respective Something is called. This is how you reroute the call to a single instance of IComponent—of type CompositeComponent—to many other types.

Each instance that you supply to the CompositeComponent class must implement the IComponent interface—and this is enforced by the compiler due to C#'s strong typing—but the instances need not all be of the same concrete type. Because of the advantages of polymorphism, you can treat all implementations of an interface as instances of that interface. In the example shown in Listing 7-15, the CompositeComponent instances provided are of different types, further enhancing this pattern's utility.

LISTING 7-15 Instances provided to the composite can be of different types.

```
public class SecondTypeOfLeaf : IComponent
{
    public void Something()
    {

    }
}
// . . .
public class AThirdLeafType : IComponent
{
    public void Something()
    {

    }
}
// . . .
public void AlternativeComposite()
{
    var composite = new CompositeComponent();
    composite.AddComponent(new Leaf());
    composite.AddComponent(new SecondTypeOfLeaf());
    composite.AddComponent(new AThirdLeafType());

    component = composite;
    composite.Something();
}
```

Taking this pattern to its logical conclusion, you can even pass in one or more instances of the CompositeComponent interface to the Add method, forming a chain of composite instances in a hierarchical tree structure.

In Chapter 3, "Dependencies and layering," classes were modeled as object graphs. That theme continues here, to further demonstrate how the Composite pattern works. In Figure 7-6, the nodes of the graph represent object instances, and the edges represent method calls.

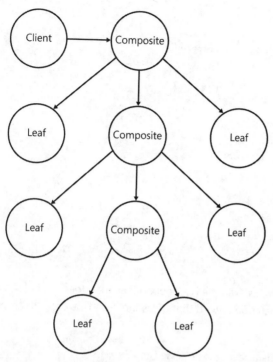

FIGURE 7-6 The object graph notation helps to visualize the runtime structure of the program.

Predicate decorators

The predicate decorator is a useful construct for hiding the conditional execution of code from clients. Listing 7-16 shows an example.

LISTING 7-16 This client will execute only the Something method on even days of the month.

```
public class DateTester
{
    public bool TodayIsAnEvenDayOfTheMonth
    {
        get
        {
            return DateTime.Now.Day % 2 == 0;
        }
    }
}
// . . .
class PredicatedDecoratorExample
```

```
{
    public PredicatedDecoratorExample(IComponent component)
    {
        this.component = component;
    }

    public void Run()
    {
        DateTester dateTester = new DateTester();
        if (dateTester.TodayIsAnEvenDayOfTheMonth)
        {
            component.Something();
        }
    }

    private readonly IComponent component;
}
```

The presence of the DateTester class in this example is a dependency that does not belong in this class. The initial temptation is to alter the code toward that of Listing 7-17. However, that is only a partial solution.

LISTING 7-17 An improvement is to require the dependency to be passed into the class.

```
class PredicatedDecoratorExample
{
    public PredicatedDecoratorExample(IComponent component)
    {
        this.component = component;
    }

    public void Run(DateTester dateTester)
    {
        if (dateTester.TodayIsAnEvenDayOfTheMonth)
        {
            component.Something();
        }
    }

    private readonly IComponent component;
}
```

You now require a parameter of the Run method, breaking the client's public interface and burdening its clients with providing an implementation of the DateTester class. By using the Decorator pattern, you are able to keep the client's interface the same, yet retain the conditional-execution functionality. Listing 7-18 proves that this is not too good to be true.

LISTING 7-18 The predicate decoration contains the dependency, and the client is much cleaner.

```
public class PredicatedComponent : IComponent
{
    public PredicatedComponent(IComponent decoratedComponent, DateTester dateTester)
    {
        this.decoratedComponent = decoratedComponent;
        this.dateTester = dateTester;
    }

    public void Something()
    {
        if(dateTester.TodayIsAnEvenDayOfTheMonth)
        {
            decoratedComponent.Something();
        }
    }

    private readonly IComponent decoratedComponent;
    private readonly DateTester dateTester;
}
// . . .
class PredicatedDecoratorExample
{
    public PredicatedDecoratorExample(IComponent component)
    {
        this.component = component;
    }

    public void Run()
    {
        component.Something();
    }

    private readonly IComponent component;
}
```

Note that this listing has added conditional branching to the code without modifying either the client code or the original implementing class. Also, this example has accepted the DateTester class as a dependency, but you could take this one step further by defining your own predicate interface for handling this scenario generically. After a few changes, the code looks like Listing 7-19.

LISTING 7-19 Defining a dedicated IPredicate interface makes the solution more general.

```
public interface IPredicate
{
    bool Test();
}
// . . .
public class PredicatedComponent : IComponent
```

```
{
    public PredicatedComponent(IComponent decoratedComponent, IPredicate predicate)
    {
        this.decoratedComponent = decoratedComponent;
        this.predicate = predicate;
    }

    public void Something()
    {
        if (predicate.Test())
        {
            decoratedComponent.Something();
        }
    }

    private readonly IComponent decoratedComponent;
    private readonly IPredicate predicate;
}
// . . .
public class TodayIsAnEvenDayOfTheMonthPredicate : IPredicate
{
    public TodayIsAnEvenDayOfTheMonthPredicate(DateTester dateTester)
    {
        this.dateTester = dateTester;
    }

    public bool Test()
    {
        return dateTester.TodayIsAnEvenDayOfTheMonth;
    }

    private readonly DateTester dateTester;
}
```

The TodayIsAnEvenDayOfTheMonthPredicate class converts the original dependent class, DateTester, to that of an IPredicate. This is an example of the Adapter pattern that was discussed earlier, in the "Refactoring for abstraction" section, and in Chapter 4, "Interfaces and design patterns."

Note The .NET Framework, as of version 2.0, contains a Predicate<T> delegate, which models a predicate that accepts a single, generic parameter as context. I did not choose the Predicate<T> delegate for this example for two reasons: First, no context needs to be provided, because the original conditional test accepted no arguments. However, I could have used a Func<bool> delegate to model a context-free predicate, which brings me to the second reason: *delegates are not as versatile as interfaces*. By modeling an IPredicate, I will be able to decorate that interface just the same as any other in the future. In other words, I have defined another extension point that is infinitely decoratable.

Branching decorators

You can extend the predicate decorator further by accepting a decorated instance of the interface to execute something on the false branch of the conditional test, as shown in Listing 7-20.

LISTING 7-20 The branching decorator accepts two components and a predicate.

```
public class BranchedComponent : IComponent
{
    public BranchedComponent(IComponent trueComponent, IComponent falseComponent,
IPredicate predicate)
    {
        this.trueComponent = trueComponent;
        this.falseComponent = falseComponent;
        this.predicate = predicate;
    }

    public void Something()
    {
        if (predicate.Test())
        {
            trueComponent.Something();
        }
        else
        {
            falseComponent.Something();
        }
    }

    private readonly IComponent trueComponent;
    private readonly IComponent falseComponent;
    private readonly IPredicate predicate;
}
```

Whenever the predicate is tested, if it returns `true`, you call the equivalent interface method on the `trueComponent` instance. If it returns `false`, you instead call the interface method on the `falseComponent` instance.

Lazy decorators

The lazy decorator allows clients to be provided with a reference to an interface that will not be instantiated until its first use. Typically, and erroneously, clients are made aware of the presence of a lazy instance because a Lazy<T> is passed to them, as in Listing 7-21.

LISTING 7-21 This client has been given a Lazy<T>.

```
public class ComponentClient
{
    public ComponentClient(Lazy<IComponent> component)
    {
        this.component = component;
    }

    public void Run()
    {
        component.Value.Something();
    }

    private readonly Lazy<IComponent> component;
}
```

This client has no option but to accept that all instances of IComponent that it is provided with will be lazy. However, if you return to a more standard use of the interface, you can create a lazy decorator that prevents the client from knowing that it is dealing with a Lazy<T>, and allows some ComponentClient objects to accept IComponent instances that are not lazy. Listing 7-22 shows this decorator.

LISTING 7-22 LazyComponent implements a lazily instantiated IComponent, but ComponentClient is unaware of this.

```
public class LazyComponent : IComponent
{
    public LazyComponent(Lazy<IComponent> lazyComponent)
    {
        this.lazyComponent = lazyComponent;
    }

    public void Something()
    {
        lazyComponent.Value.Something();
    }

    private readonly Lazy<IComponent> lazyComponent;
}
// . . .
public class ComponentClient
{
```

```
    public ComponentClient(IComponent component)
    {
        this.component = component;
    }

    public void Run()
    {
        component.Something();
    }

    private readonly IComponent component;
}
```

Logging decorators

Listing 7-23 shows a common pattern that occurs whenever code contains extensive logging. The logging code becomes ubiquitous throughout the application, and the signal-to-noise ratio suffers.

LISTING 7-23 Logging code clouds the intent of methods.

```
public class ConcreteCalculator : ICalculator
{
    public int Add(int x, int y)
    {
        Console.WriteLine("Add(x={0}, y={1})", x, y);

        var addition = x + y;

        Console.WriteLine("result={0}", addition);

        return addition;
    }
}
```

Instead of proliferating the logging code throughout the application, you can limit it to one assembly that implements logging decorators, as shown in Listing 7-24.

LISTING 7-24 Logging decorators factor out the logging code, simplifying the main implementation.

```
public class LoggingCalculator : ICalculator
{
    public LoggingCalculator(ICalculator calculator)
    {
        this.calculator = calculator;
    }

    public int Add(int x, int y)
```

```
    {
        Console.WriteLine("Add(x={0}, y={1})", x, y);

        var result = calculator.Add(x, y);

        Console.WriteLine("result={0}", result);

        return result;
    }

    private readonly ICalculator calculator;
}
// . . .
public class ConcreteCalculator : ICalculator
{
    public int Add(int x, int y)
    {
        return x + y;
    }
}
```

Clients of the ICalculator interface will pass in various parameters, and some of the methods themselves will return values, too. Because the LoggingCalculator is in a position to intercept both of these artifacts, it can interrogate them directly. There are limitations to using logging decorators that should be considered. First, any private state contained in the decorated class remains unavailable to the logging decorator, which cannot access this state and write it to a log. Second, a logging decorator would need to be created for every interface in the application—a significant undertaking. For something so common, logging is better implemented as a logging aspect. Aspect-oriented programming (AOP) was covered in Chapter 3.

Profiling decorators

One of the major reasons to choose the .NET Framework as the target platform for developing an application is that it lends itself well to Rapid Application Development (RAD). A working application can be developed in a far shorter time frame than in a lower-level language like, for example, C++. This is for several reasons, including the automatic memory management of the .NET Framework, the rich and varied list of libraries that can be used, and the .NET Framework itself. C# is often deemed fast at development time but slow at run time. C++, on the other hand, is considered to be slow at development time and fast at run time.

Although the .NET Framework can also be fast, bottlenecks do occur. How can you tell which part of the code is slow? By *profiling* the methods of the application, you gather statistics on which parts of the code are slower than others. See the code in Listing 7-25.

LISTING 7-25 This code is (intentionally and artificially) slow.

```
public class SlowComponent : IComponent
{
    public SlowComponent()
    {
        random = new Random((int)DateTime.Now.Ticks);
    }

    public void Something()
    {
        for(var i = 0; i<100; ++i)
        {
            Thread.Sleep(random.Next(i) * 10);
        }
    };

    private readonly Random random
}
```

The component's `Something()` method in this example is slow. *Slow* and *fast*, of course, mean different things to different people at different times. In this case, a slow method is defined as one that takes one second or more to execute. How can you tell that a method is slow? You can time the method to find out how long it took to execute from start to finish, much like in Listing 7-26.

LISTING 7-26 The `System.Diagnostics.Stopwatch` class can time how long a method takes to execute.

```
public class SlowComponent : IComponent
{
    public SlowComponent()
    {
        random = new Random((int)DateTime.Now.Ticks);
        stopwatch = new Stopwatch();
    }

    public void Something()
    {
        stopwatch.Start();
        for(var i = 0; i<100; ++i)
        {
            System.Threading.Thread.Sleep(random.Next(i) * 10);
        }
        stopwatch.Stop();
        Console.WriteLine("The method took {0} seconds to complete",
    stopwatch.ElapsedMilliseconds / 1000);
    }

    private readonly Random random;
    private readonly Stopwatch;
}
```

Here the Stopwatch class from the System.Diagnostics assembly is used to time each method from start to finish. Note that the Something method in the class starts the stopwatch on entry and then stops it on exit.

Of course, this can be factored out into a profiling decorator. The interface as a whole is decorated and, before delegating to the decorated instance, you start the stopwatch. When the delegated method returns, you stop the stopwatch before returning to the calling client. The stopwatch decorator code is shown in Listing 7-27.

LISTING 7-27 The profiling decorator code.

```
public class ProfilingComponent : IComponent
{
    public ProfilingComponent(IComponent decoratedComponent)
    {
        this.decoratedComponent = decoratedComponent;
        stopwatch = new Stopwatch();
    }

    public void Something()
    {
        stopwatch.Start();
        decoratedComponent.Something();
        stopwatch.Stop();
        Console.WriteLine("The method took {0} seconds to complete",
    stopwatch.ElapsedMilliseconds / 1000);
    }

    private readonly IComponent decoratedComponent;
    private readonly Stopwatch stopwatch;
}
```

There is one further change that you could make to the ProfilingComponent class: make it transparently log the profiling. First, you need to factor out the stopwatch code behind an interface so that you can provide multiple implementations, including decorators. This is a common first step when refactoring toward a better separation of responsibilities. Listing 7-28 shows this intermediate step.

LISTING 7-28 Before you can implement a decorator, you must replace concrete implementations with interfaces.

```
public class ProfilingComponent : IComponent
{
    public ProfilingComponent(IComponent decoratedComponent, IStopwatch stopwatch)
    {
        this.decoratedComponent = decoratedComponent;
        this.stopwatch = stopwatch;
    }
```

```
    public void Something()
    {
        stopwatch.Start();
        decoratedComponent.Something();
        var elapsedMilliseconds = stopwatch.Stop();
        Console.WriteLine("The method took {0} seconds to complete", elapsedMilliseconds /
    1000);
    }

    private readonly IComponent decoratedComponent;
    private readonly IStopwatch stopwatch;
}
```

Now that the ProfilingComponent class does not depend directly on the
System.Diagnostics.Stopwatch class, you can vary the implementation of the
IStopwatch class. A LoggingStopwatch decorator is created, as shown in Listing 7-29,
to enhance any further IStopwatch implementations with logging facilities.

LISTING 7-29 The LoggingStopwatch decorator is an IStopwatch implementation that logs and delegates.

```
public class LoggingStopwatch : IStopwatch
{
    public LoggingStopwatch(IStopwatch decoratedStopwatch)
    {
        this.decoratedStopwatch = decoratedStopwatch;
    }

    public void Start()
    {
        decoratedStopwatch.Start();
        Console.WriteLine("Stopwatch started...");
    }

    public long Stop()
    {
        var elapsedMilliseconds = decoratedStopwatch.Stop();
        Console.WriteLine("Stopwatch stopped after {0} seconds",
    TimeSpan.FromMilliseconds(elapsedMilliseconds).TotalSeconds);
        return elapsedMilliseconds;
    }

    private readonly IStopwatch decoratedStopwatch;
}
```

Of course, you need a non-decorator implementation of the IStopwatch interface—
one that acts as a real stopwatch. This is just a case of delegating to the .NET Framework
System.Diagnostics.Stopwatch class, as Listing 7-30 shows.

```
public class StopwatchAdapter : IStopwatch
{
    public StopwatchAdapter(Stopwatch stopwatch)
    {
        this.stopwatch = stopwatch;
    }

    public void Start()
    {
        stopwatch.Start();
    }

    public long Stop()
    {
        stopwatch.Stop();
        var elapsedMilliseconds = stopwatch.ElapsedMilliseconds;
        stopwatch.Reset();
        return elapsedMilliseconds;
    }

    private readonly Stopwatch stopwatch;
}
```

Note that you could have chosen to implement IStopwatch as a subclass of the System.Diagnostics.Stopwatch class and used the existing Start and Stop methods. However, the Start method acts to resume functionality when a stopwatch is stopped, but what you need to do is to call Reset after you call Stop, and retrieve the ElapsedMilliseconds property value in between. This is another example of the Adapter pattern.

Decorating properties and events

So far, you have learned how to decorate the methods of an interface, but what about properties and events? Both of those syntactic elements can also be decorated, as long as you do not use auto-properties or auto-events; you need to explicitly define both in order to decorate them properly.

Listing 7-31 shows the manual creation of a property, but rather than having a backing field, for both the getter and the setter this code delegates to the decorated instance of the interface.

LISTING 7-31 Properties can also use the Decorator pattern, just like methods.

```
public class ComponentDecorator : IComponent
{
    public ComponentDecorator(IComponent decoratedComponent)
    {
        this.decoratedComponent = decoratedComponent;
    }
```

```
    public string Property
    {
        get
        {
            // We can do some mutation here after retrieving the value
            return decoratedComponent.Property;
        }
        set
        {
            // And/or here, before we set the value
            decoratedComponent.Property = value;
        }
    }

    private readonly IComponent decoratedComponent;
}
```

Listing 7-32 shows the manual creation of an event, but rather than having a backing field, for both the adder and remover this code delegates to the decorated instance of the interface.

LISTING 7-32 Events can also use the Decorator pattern, just like methods.

```
public class ComponentDecorator : IComponent
{
    public ComponentDecorator(IComponent decoratedComponent)
    {
        this.decoratedComponent = decoratedComponent;
    }

    public event EventHandler Event
    {
        add
        {
            // We can do something here, when the event handler is registered
            decoratedComponent.Event += value;
        }
        remove
        {
            // And/or here, when the event handler is deregistered
            decoratedComponent.Event -= value;
        }
    }

    private readonly IComponent decoratedComponent;
}
```

Conclusion

The single responsibility principle has a hugely positive impact on the adaptability of code. Compared to equivalent code that does not adhere to the principle, SRP-compliant code leads to a greater number of classes that are smaller and more directed in scope. Where there would otherwise have been a single class or suite of classes with interdependencies and a confusion of responsibility, the SRP introduces order and clarity.

The SRP is primarily achieved through abstracting code behind interfaces and delegating responsibility for unrelated functionality to whichever implementation happens to be behind the interface at run time. Some design patterns are excellent at supporting efforts to strictly regiment the SRP—in particular, the Adapter pattern and the Decorator pattern. The former enables much of your code to maintain first-party references to interfaces under your direct control, although in reality using a third-party library. The latter can be applied whenever some of a class's functionality needs to be removed but it is too tightly coupled with the intent of the class to stand alone.

What this chapter did not cover is how all of these classes are orchestrated at run time. Passing interfaces into constructors was taken for granted in this chapter, but Chapter 12 describes a variety of ways in which this can be accomplished.

CHAPTER 8

The open/closed principle

After completing this chapter, you will be able to

- Understand different interpretations of the open/closed principle.

- Treat SOLID code as append-only.

- Compare and contrast different class extension-point mechanisms.

- Use protected variation as a guideline for extension points.

The oxymoronic nature of the open/closed principle causes some confusion. Its pithy name suggests code that is permissive but at the same time restrictive. The fact that there are several variations of the definition serves only to cloud matters further.

Picking one definition over another and using it alone would be remiss. Rather, this chapter compares each definition and its consequences to try to distill the principle down to its essence. The goal is a very useful guideline that will enable you to create code that is more adaptive to future changes.

Introduction to the open/closed principle

There are two definitions of the open/closed principle that must be examined, the original coining from the 1980s and a more contemporary definition. The latter seeks to elaborate on the former by giving it more context and clarifying the principle's scope.

The Meyer definition

Bertrand Mayer, in his 1988 book, *Object-Oriented Software Construction* (Prentice Hall), defined the open/closed principle (OCP) as follows:

> *Software entities should be open for extension, but closed for modification.*

The Meyer definition is the most commonly cited definition of the principle, but there is a second: the Martin definition.

The Martin definition

Robert C. Martin has defined the OCP in many different writings over the years. A more verbose version has been chosen here to contrast with the brief original:

> *"Open for extension." This means that the behavior of the module can be extended. As the requirements of the application change, we are able to extend the module with new behaviors that satisfy those changes. In other words, we are able to change what the module does.*
>
> *"Closed for modification." Extending the behavior of a module does not result in changes to the source or binary code of the module. The binary executable version of the module, whether in a linkable library, a DLL, or a Java .jar, remains untouched.*
>
> —Robert C. Martin, *Agile Software Development: Principles, Patterns, and Practices*
> (Prentice Hall, 2003)

For both sides of the open/closed principle, Martin explains in further detail what is meant by the key terms from the Meyer definition. For code to be open for extension, Martin explains, developers must be able to respond to changing requirements and support new features. This must be achieved despite modules being closed to modification. Developers must support new functionality without editing the source code—or compiled assembly—of the existing modules.

Before this chapter begins to describe how this is possible, there are exceptions to the restrictive "closed for modification" clause of the OCP that are sometimes cited: changes for fixing bugs or defects and changes that can be made without any client awareness.

Bug fixes

Bugs are a common problem in software, and they are impossible to prevent entirely. When they do occur, you need to respond by fixing the problem code. Of course, this involves a modification to an existing class—that is, unless you are willing to duplicate the class and implement the bug fix on the new version. This sounds needlessly convoluted and runs counter to the guiding principle of erring on the side of pragmatism rather than purity.

The two-step process for fixing a bug is outlined as follows:

1. Write a failing unit test and/or integration test that specifically targets the bug. This requires reliable and repeatable reproduction steps to create the conditions under which the code fails. If the code is legacy code—that is, code without tests—see Chapter 6, "Refactoring," for information about how to implement a golden master test to retrofit some tests. Also, recall the AAA syntax of a unit test introduced in Chapter 5, "Testing." You need to be able to *Arrange* the system under test so that it is in a state that might exhibit the defect, perform the specific *Act* in which the defect resides, and finally *Assert* the *expected* behavior. When you write such a test, the test will initially fail. This demonstrates the fact that bugs are the result of missing tests. If a test is present that captures the defect, the test fails.

2. The source code is *modified* so that the unit test passes. The bug fix exception to the OCP becomes necessary at this juncture because, without it, you would not be able to modify any existing code. Editing the system under test allows you to transition the failing test from red to green—from failure to success. When you ensure that no other tests are failing as a side effect, the bug is fixed.

Client awareness

A more permissive exception to the "closed for modification" rule is that any change to existing code is allowed as long as it does not also require a change to any client of that code. This places an emphasis on how coupled the software modules are, at all levels of granularity: between classes and classes, assemblies and assemblies, and subsystems and subsystems.

If a change in one class forces a change in another, the two are said to be *tightly* coupled. Conversely, if a class can change in isolation without forcing other classes to change, the participating classes are *loosely* coupled. At all times and at all levels, loose coupling is preferable. Maintaining loose coupling limits the impact that the OCP has if you allow modifications to existing code that do not force further changes to clients.

Extension points

Now that the "closed for modification" rule of the OCP is clarified, the "open for extension" rule can be considered. Classes that honor the OCP should be open to extension by containing defined extension points where future functionality can hook into the existing code and provide new behaviors.

Some options for different kinds of extension points are detailed in this section, with their pros and cons explored. These examples continue the `TradeProcessor` example of the previous chapters, this time from the point of view of the client interacting with the class.

Code without extension points

First, what does code look like when it has no extension points? Figure 8-1 shows what happens when a class that has no extension points needs new functionality.

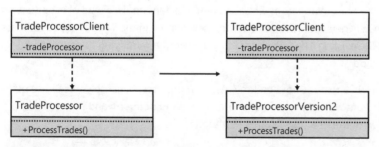

FIGURE 8-1 When there are no extension points, clients are forced to change.

The TradeProcessorClient depends directly on the TradeProcessor class. A new requirement is handed to you, resulting in necessary changes to the TradeProcessor class. Without modifying the original class, you create a new version (TradeProcessorVersion2) that contains the new functionality as specified in your new requirement. Because the client directly depends on the TradeProcessor class, and because of the lack of extension points in the TradeProcessor class, you need to place the new functionality inside a new class. The side effect of this change is that the TradeProcessorClient must be edited so that it depends on the new version of the class. It seems like it would just be easier to allow you to edit the existing TradeProcessor, doesn't it?

If you allow changes to existing code where they have no client impact, you might not have to create an entirely new version of the TradeProcessor. If the ProcessTrades method signature were to change, this would not simply be an implementation change for the class, it would also be an interface change. All interface changes force client changes because clients are tightly coupled to the interfaces of their dependencies.

Virtual methods

An alternative implementation for the TradeProcessor class contains an extension point: the ProcessTrades method is *virtual*. Figure 8-2 shows how the three classes are now arranged.

FIGURE 8-2 The client depends on the TradeProcessor class, which can be extended via inheritance.

Any class that marks one of its members as virtual is open to extension. This type of extension is via *implementation inheritance*. When your requirement for a new feature in the TradeProcessor class arrives, you can subclass the existing TradeProcessor and—without modifying its source code—alter the ProcessTrades method.

The TradeProcessorClient does not need to change in this case, because you can use polymorphism to supply the client with the new version of the TradeProcessor and have it call the subclass's implementation of the ProcessTrades method.

You are somewhat limited in the scope of your reimplementation, however. You have access to the base class—so you can call `TradeProcessor.ProcessTrades()`—but you cannot alter individual lines of the original method. You either call the original method in its entirety, perhaps implementing the new feature before or after the call, or you reimplement it completely. There is no middle ground with a virtual method. Remember, subclasses can access only members from their base class that are marked as protected. If the `TradeProcessor` was created with many private members, you would not have access to them, and altering the original class is, of course, prohibited by the OCP.

Abstract methods

A more flexible extension point that uses implementation inheritance is an *abstract* method. In this case, the `TradeProcessor` is an abstract class that defines a public `ProcessTrades` method, which delegates the work of the processing algorithm to three protected abstract methods. The client has no knowledge of these protected methods and, because they are abstract, no implementation is provided. Figure 8-3 shows the relationships between the classes involved.

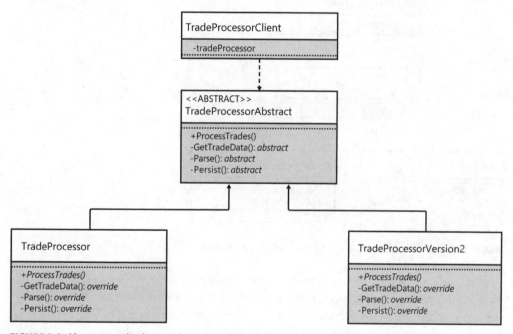

FIGURE 8-3 Abstract methods provide extension points for future subclasses.

Two versions of the trade processor are provided. Both inherit the `ProcessTrades` method directly from the abstract base class, and both provide their own implementations for the abstract methods. The client depends on the abstract base class, so either concrete subclass—or a new subclass for new requirements—could be provided and the OCP would be preserved.

This is an example of the *Template Method pattern*, in which an algorithm is modeled but its general steps are customizable because of delegation to abstract methods. In effect, the base class delegates the individual steps of the process to subclasses.

These methods need not be abstract; they could be virtual. The difference here is mainly the *granularity* of what has been made extensible. Rather than replacing the `ProcessTrades` method in its entirety, you can now replace select parts of the process by overriding the constituent methods.

Interface inheritance

The final type of extension point discussed in this chapter is the alternative to implementation inheritance: *interface inheritance*. Here, the client's dependency on a *class* is replaced with the now-familiar delegation to an *interface*. Figure 8-4 shows the client's dependency on the interface and the two implementations of the interface.

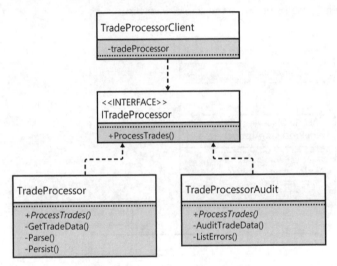

FIGURE 8-4 The client depends on an interface rather than a class.

Interface inheritance is preferable to implementation inheritance. With implementation inheritance, all subclasses—present and future—are *clients*. This prevents modification because, with implementation inheritance, subclasses depend on the *implementation*, too. All implementation changes are thus potentially client-aware changes. This echoes the advice to prefer composition over inheritance and to keep inheritance hierarchies shallow, with few layers of subclassing. If a change is made to add a member at the top of the inheritance graph, that change affects all members of the hierarchy.

Interfaces are also better extension points because they can be decorated with rich object graphs of functionality that touch upon many different contexts. They are more flexible than classes. I don't mean that the `virtual` and `abstract` methods that form the extension points of class inheritance are not useful, but that they do not provide quite the same level of *adaptability* as do interfaces.

"Design for inheritance or prohibit it"

In his book *Effective Java* (Addison-Wesley, 2008), Joshua Bloch has this to say about inheritance:

> *Design and document for inheritance or else prohibit it.*

If you choose to use implementation inheritance as an extension point, you must design and document the class properly so as to protect and inform future programmers who extend the class. Inheritance of classes can be tricky—new subclasses can break existing code in unpredictable ways.

It is very important to note that any class that is not marked with the `sealed` keyword claims to support inheritance. A class does not need to be abstract or to contain virtual methods in order to be subclassed. The `new` keyword can be used to hide inherited members, but this blocks polymorphism, possibly defying expectations.

Prohibiting inheritance by sealing a class communicates a clear message to other programmers who might use the class: inheritance is not just unsupported in this class, it is prevented. This removes the temptation to try to extend the class, so programmers will redirect their efforts to finding an alternative.

Protected variation

You are now armed with several tools with which to implement the OCP. You know under which circumstances you can edit existing classes, and you know that you need to implement extension points in your code in order to support future changes in requirements. You also know that you can use interfaces as extension points to make your code truly adaptable.

The missing ingredient is the knowledge of *when* and *where* to apply this principle. Taken to its logical extreme, should you add extension points everywhere, all the time? Would this make your code infinitely flexible, or is there a law of diminishing returns that applies?

This is where another principle related to the OCP is of vital importance: *protected variation*. Alistair Cockburn coined the term:

> *Identify points of predicted variation and create a stable interface around them.*
> —Alistair Cockburn, Pattern Languages of Program Design, vol. 2 (Addison-Wesley, 1996)

Somewhat confusingly, the definition references *predicted variation*, yet the principle itself is called *protected variation*. However, "predicted variation" is, to my mind, a more accurate term. The two major facets of this definition bear a closer examination.

Predicted variation

The requirements of an individual class should be linked directly to a business client's requirement. If this link is ignored, there is a risk that the class will not serve any purpose that the business client requested. Over the course of a sprint, user stories are taken from the sprint backlog, and developers and the product owner converse. At this point, questions should be asked as to the potential for future, related requirements. This informs the *predicted variation* that can be translated into extension points.

A stable interface

Even if you delegate only to interfaces, clients are still dependent on those interfaces. If the interface changes, the client must also change. A key advantage of depending on interfaces is that they are much less likely to change than implementations. If you place the interface in a separate assembly from its implementation, clients can change without affecting change on the interface's implementations, and implementations can change without affecting clients.

Clearly, it is very important that all interfaces chosen to represent an extension point should be stable. The likelihood and frequency of interface changes should be low, otherwise you will need to amend all clients to use the new version.

Just enough adaptability

There is a "Goldilocks Zone" where code contains just the right amount of extension points—in the right places—to enable change in areas where it is needed without increasing complexity or over-engineering the solution. For any individual problem, there can be too little, too much, or *just enough* adaptability.

Programmers who are beginning their careers tend to write code that is quite procedural, even in object-oriented languages such as C#. They tend to use classes as storage mechanisms for methods, regardless of whether those methods truly belong together. There is no discernible architecture to the code, and there are few extension points (and those that exist might be misplaced). Any changes to requirements necessitate direct changes to the existing class or classes. This is how the original TradeProcessor was organized in Chapter 7, "The single responsibility principle." It was a "god object" that had perfect knowledge of everything to do with the program.

However, sometimes, this is the correct solution. If you assess the predicted variation for a small tool such as the TradeProcessor and conclude that it is very unlikely to change in any way, the original version of the code will suffice. Or perhaps the version that was refactored for clarity would be sufficient. The extra time spent refactoring for abstraction is wasted effort if you never make use of the extension points provided. Not only that, but it is more difficult to reason about the code and what it does, spread over different files and assemblies, with implementations hidden behind interfaces.

At the opposite end of the spectrum is the programmer who has started abstracting code behind interfaces. This programmer has discovered a new hammer, and now everything looks like a nail. The code produced by this programmer is a mass of extension points, most of which will never be used. A significant effort is required to piece together the code, which constantly delegates responsibilities to interfaces, and a significant effort is required to write this code in the first place.

If these two archetypal programmers—and their code—were combined, the result might be a harmonious middle ground where there are sufficient extension points, but where code can be adapted only in areas where requirements are unclear, changeable, or difficult to implement. This comes with experience, however, and it is difficult to arrive at this Zen-like state of predicted variation without first being a naïve beginner and then transitioning to a know-it-all super-abstractor!

Predicted variation versus speculative generality

Software development is an emerging engineering practice that is still finding its feet as a science. Because of this, what is a hard-and-fast rule as opposed to a suggestion, guideline, or best practice is open to interpretation.

Two such guidelines are *predicted variation* and *speculative generality.*

The predicted variation guideline states that you should be explicit in what you allow and disallow to be extended. The speculative generality guideline states that you should beware of trying to preempt how a class might apply to a general problem, lest you create a leaky abstraction.

Both guidelines appear to be at odds with each other, but could it be that they are the two sides of the same coin?

Consider the number of times that you use the `sealed` keyword on a class, or have a class depend directly on another class, rather than an interface. Now compare this to the number of times that you either create an interface dependency or mark a class as `abstract` or a method as `abstract` or `virtual`.

When a class is sealed, you cannot subclass it in the future, and this prevents the class from being used as an extension point. Abstract classes are designed to be extended and cannot be instantiated without first being subclassed. This is also true for abstract methods. Virtual methods provide a meaningful default implementation but can be specialized in some way in the future.

These are all design choices. Some of them are implicit and unintended: you just didn't mark the class as `sealed`; therefore, you can circumvent certain methods in the future. Others are explicit. Ideally, all design choices should be made with an explicit intent.

Do you need so many interfaces?

Interfaces are, by now, a ubiquitous construct in object-oriented programming. There are few cases where interfaces are not relied on to provide extension points. And interfaces are the ultimate extension point: you provide clients with a way of passing a message to some other object and allow infinite possibilities for filling in the blanks of how the message is handled.

There are some cases where the value of this is obvious. Typically, this is at the edges of the application where a decoupling of client and service is required. A common and concrete example of this is data access, such as when client code wants to access some data that is persisted and keyed by identifier. Such a class is furnished with an interface that represents a way of accessing this data. Later, the interface is implemented for some specific data storage mechanism: a relational database, a document store, a key-value cache, file storage on disk, an in-memory dictionary, a mocked-out test double, a service call.... The list goes on.

However, there are cases where interfaces and the myriad possibilities for implementation are unwarranted. Take, for example, the mapping of code from one layer to another. Suppose your code contains a data access layer that retrieves data transfer objects (DTOs) that are implementation-specific. Your domain layer wants to receive some of the data that these DTOs hold in a format that it recognizes. This necessitates the mapping code, but will there be multiple implementations of this code, or just one canonical version for which you explicitly disallow the possibility of extension?

The expected return values from a repository are domain model objects; thus it is up to the specific implementation of the data access layer to convert its own implementation-specific DTOs to domain model types. Therefore, mapping layers conceptually reside with their data access implementations, not in some half-space between data access layer and domain model.

If a specific implementation of a data access layer depends on a specific type of DTO and is of use to a specific domain model, there is no benefit in providing extensible or substitutable mapping code, yet there is a cost: decreased readability.

This is an example of avoiding speculative generality by predicting a *lack* of variation. The two guidelines are not inimical: they are complementary. If the generality you seek is speculative, you have predicted no specific variation. And, if the generality you seek is not speculative, you must have predicted a specific variation.

Conclusion

The open/closed principle is a guideline for the overall design of classes and interfaces and how developers can build code that allows change over time. With each passing sprint, new requirements are inevitable and should be embraced. Acknowledging that change is a good thing is only part of the answer, however. If the code you have produced up until this point is not built to enable change, change will be difficult, time consuming, error prone, and costly.

By ensuring that your code is open to extension but closed to modification, you effectively disallow future changes to existing classes and assemblies, which forces programmers to create new classes that can plug into the extension points. There are two main types of extension points available: implementation inheritance and interface inheritance. Virtual and abstract methods allow you to create subclasses that customize methods in a base class. If classes delegate to interfaces, this provides you with more flexibility in your extension points by virtue of a variety of patterns.

Knowing that you can integrate extension points into code is not sufficient, however. You also need to know when this is applicable. The concept of protected variation suggests that you identify parts of the requirements that are likely to change or that are particularly troublesome to implement, and factor these out behind extension points. Code can be quite rigidly defined, with little scope for extension or elaboration, or it can be very fluid, with myriad extension points ready to handle new requirements. Either of these options can be correct, depending on the specific scenario and context.

CHAPTER 9

The Liskov substitution principle

After completing this chapter, you will be able to

- Understand the importance of the Liskov substitution principle.

- Avoid breaking the rules of the Liskov substitution principle.

- Further solidify your single responsibility principle and open/closed principle habits.

- Create derived classes that honor the contracts of their base classes.

- Use code contracts to implement preconditions, postconditions, and data invariants.

- Write correct exception-throwing code.

- Understand covariance, contravariance, and invariance and where each applies.

Introduction to the Liskov substitution principle

The Liskov substitution principle (LSP) is a collection of guidelines for creating inheritance hierarchies in which a client can reliably use any class or subclass without compromising the expected behavior.

If the rules of the LSP are not followed, an extension to a class hierarchy—that is, a new subclass—might necessitate changes to any client of the base class or interface. Whenever the LSP is followed, clients can remain unaware of changes to the class hierarchy. Whenever there are no changes to the interface, there should be no reason to change any existing code. The LSP, therefore, helps to enforce both the open/closed principle and the single responsibility principle.

Formal definition

The definition of the LSP by prominent computer scientist Barbara Liskov is a bit dry, so it requires further explanation. Here is the official definition:

> *If S is a subtype of T, then objects of type T may be replaced with objects of type S, without breaking the program.*

There are three code ingredients relating to the LSP:

- **Base type** The type (T) that clients have reference to. Clients call various methods, any of which can be overridden—or partially specialized—by the subtype.

- **Subtype** Any one of a possible family of classes (S) that inherit from the base type (T). Clients should not know which specific subtype they are calling, nor should they need to. The client should behave the same regardless of the subtype instance that it is given.

- **Context** The way in which the client interacts with the subtype. If the client doesn't interact with a subtype, the LSP can neither be honored nor contravened.

LSP rules

There are several "rules" that must be followed for LSP compliance. These rules can be split into two categories: contract rules (relating to the expectations of classes) and variance rules (relating to the types that can be substituted in code).

Contract rules

These rules relate to the contract of the supertype and the restrictions placed on the contracts that can be added to the subtype.

- Preconditions cannot be strengthened in a subtype.

- Postconditions cannot be weakened in a subtype.

- Invariants of the supertype—conditions that must remain true—must be preserved in a subtype.

To understand the contract rules, you should first understand the concept of contracts and then explore what you can do to ensure that you follow these rules when creating subtypes. The "Contracts" section later in this chapter covers both in depth.

Variance rules

These rules relate to the variance of arguments and return types.

- There must be contravariance of the method arguments in the subtype.

- There must be covariance of the return types in the subtype.

- No new exceptions can be thrown by the subtype unless they are part of the existing exception hierarchy.

The concept of type variance in the languages of the Common Language Runtime (CLR) of the Microsoft .NET Framework is limited to generic types and delegates. However, variance in these scenarios is well worth exploring and will equip you with the requisite knowledge to write code that is LSP compliant for variance. This will be explored in depth in the "Covariance and contravariance" section later in this chapter.

Contracts

It is often said that developers should *program to interfaces*, and a related idiom is to *program to a contract*. However, beyond the apparent method signatures, interfaces convey a very loose notion of a contract. A method signature reveals little about the actual requirements and guarantees of the method's implementation, as Figure 9-1 shows. In a strongly typed language like C#, there is at least a notion of passing the correct type for an argument, but this is largely where the interface ends and the concept of the contract must begin.

FIGURE 9-1 Method signatures reveal little about the expectations of the implementation.

Methods have an optional return type, a name, and an optional list of formal parameters. Each parameter consists of a type specifier and a name. When calling the method shown in Figure 9-1, you know—from only looking at the signature—that you must pass in three parameters, one of type `float`, one of type `Size<float>`, and another of type `RegionInfo`. You also know that you can save the return value, of type `decimal`, in a variable or otherwise operate on this value after the call has been made.

Note It is not advisable to use the `decimal` type to represent currency values, as is done in Figure 9-1. Instead, a Money value type[1] should be used. Although effort has been taken to ensure that the examples in this book are, as much as possible, relevant to a real-world context and are not just contrivances, some concessions have been made in the interest of brevity.

As a method writer, you can control the names given to parameters and methods. Take extra care to ensure that the method name truly represents the method's purpose and that the parameter names are as descriptive as possible. The `CalculateShippingCost` function's name uses a verb-noun form. Here the verb—the action performed by the method—is `Calculate`, and the noun—the object of the verb—is `ShippingCost`. This noun is, in a sense, the name of the return value. Descriptive names have also been chosen for the parameters: `packageDimensionsInInches` and `packageWeightIn-Kilograms` are self-explanatory parameter names, especially in the context of the method. They form a starting point for documenting the method.

Tip For further information on good variable and method naming and other best practices, Steve McConnell's *Code Complete*[2] (Microsoft Press, 2004) is essential reading.

---

[1] *http://moneytype.codeplex.com/*

[2] *http://www.stevemcconnell.com/cc.htm*

What is missing, though, is the *contract* of the method. For example, the `packageWeightIn-Kilograms` parameter is of type `float`. Consider that clients of this method might infer that *any* `float` value is valid, including a negative value. But, because the parameter represents a weight, a negative value should not be valid. The contract of this method should enforce a weight of greater than zero. For this, the method could implement a *precondition*.

Tip Although contracts as outlined in this chapter add run-time protection against many invalid calls to methods, the importance of good method and parameter naming is hard to exaggerate. If the formal parameters of the `CalculateShippingCost` method did not specify that they are in inches or kilograms, clients could, for example, call the method with values representing centimeters and pounds, respectively.

Preconditions

Preconditions are defined as all the conditions necessary for a method to run reliably and without fault. Most methods require one or more preconditions to be true before being called. By default, interfaces force no such guarantees to be fulfilled by any of the implementers of their methods. Listing 9-1 shows how you can implement a precondition by using a guard clause at the start of a method.

LISTING 9-1 Throwing an exception is an effective way of enforcing precondition contracts.

```
public decimal CalculateShippingCost(
    float packageWeightInKilograms,
    Size<float> packageDimensionsInInches,
    RegionInfo destination)
{
    if (packageWeightInKilograms <= 0f) throw new Exception();

    return decimal.MinusOne;
}
```

The `if` statement at the very start of the method is one way to enforce a precondition, such as the requirement for a positive weight. If the predicate `packageWeightInKilograms <= 0f` is true, an exception is thrown and the method stops executing immediately. This prevents the method from being executed unless all parameters have valid values. You can provide more context to the caller by using a more descriptive exception, as shown in Listing 9-2.

LISTING 9-2 It is important to provide as much context as possible about why the precondition caused a failure.

```
public decimal CalculateShippingCost(
    float packageWeightInKilograms,
    Size<float> packageDimensionsInInches,
    RegionInfo destination)
{
    if (packageWeightInKilograms <= 0f)
        throw new ArgumentOutOfRangeException("packageWeightInKilograms",
            "Package weight must be positive and nonzero");

    return decimal.MinusOne;
}
```

This is an improvement on the first exception that was thrown. In addition to using an exception specifically for out-of-range arguments, this code tells the client which parameter is errant and provides a description of the problem.

You can add more conditions that must be fulfilled by chaining more guard clauses like this together. The changes shown in Listing 9-3 include exceptions that are thrown when the package dimensions are out of range, too.

LISTING 9-3 As many preconditions as necessary can be added to prevent the method from being called with invalid parameters.

```
public decimal CalculateShippingCost(
    float packageWeightInKilograms,
    Size<float> packageDimensionsInInches,
    RegionInfo destination)
{
    if (packageWeightInKilograms <= 0f)
        throw new ArgumentOutOfRangeException("packageWeightInKilograms", "Package weight
    must be positive and non-zero");

    if (packageDimensionsInInches.X <= 0f || packageDimensionsInInches.Y <= 0f)
        throw new ArgumentOutOfRangeException("packageDimensionsInInches",
            "Package dimensions must be positive and nonzero");

    return decimal.MinusOne;
}
```

With these preconditions in place, clients must ensure that the parameters they provide are within valid ranges before calling. One corollary from this is that all the state that is checked in a precondition *must* be publicly accessible by clients. If a client is unable to verify that the method it is about to call will throw an error due to an invalid precondition, the client won't be able to ensure that the call will succeed. Therefore, private state should not be the target of a precondition; only method parameters and the class's public properties should be referenced by preconditions.

Postconditions

Postconditions check whether an object is being left in a valid state as a method is exited. Whenever state is mutated in a method, it is possible for the state to be invalid due to logic errors.

Postconditions can be implemented in the same manner as preconditions, through guard clauses. However, rather than placing the clauses at the start of the method, postcondition guard clauses should be placed at the end of the method after all edits to state have been made, as Listing 9-4 shows.

LISTING 9-4 The guard clause at the end of the method is a postcondition that ensures that the return value is in range.

```
public virtual decimal CalculateShippingCost(float packageWeightInKilograms, Size<float>
    packageDimensionsInInches, RegionInfo destination)
{
    if (packageWeightInKilograms <= 0f)
        throw new ArgumentOutOfRangeException("packageWeightInKilograms", "Package weight
must be positive and non-zero");

    if (packageDimensionsInInches.X <= 0f || packageDimensionsInInches.Y <= 0f)
        throw new ArgumentOutOfRangeException("packageDimensionsInInches",
            "Package dimensions must be positive and nonzero");

    var shippingCost = decimal.One;

    // shipping cost calculation

    if(shippingCost <= decimal.Zero)
        throw new ArgumentOutOfRangeException("return",
            "The return value is out of range");

    return shippingCost;
}
```

By testing state against a predetermined valid range—and throwing an exception if the value falls outside of that range—you can enforce a postcondition on the method. The postcondition here relates not to the state of the object but to the return value. Much like method argument values are tested against preconditions for validity, so are method return values tested against postconditions for validity. If, at the end of the method, the return value is zero or a negative value, the postcondition will detect this and halt execution at the end of the method. This way, clients of this method will never inadvertently receive an invalid value, and they can continue to assume that it will always be valid. Note that the interface of the method does not communicate that the return value will always be nonzero and positive—that is a feature of the interface's contract with clients.

Data invariants

A third type of contract is the data invariant. A *data invariant* is a predicate that remains true for the lifetime of an object; it is true after construction and must remain true until the object is out of scope. Data invariants relate to the expected internal state of the object. An example of a data invariant for the ShippingStrategy call is that the flat rate provided is positive and nonzero. If, as shown in Listing 9-5, the flat rate is set on construction, a simple guard clause in the constructor will prevent an invalid value from being set.

LISTING 9-5 Adding a precondition to a constructor can help protect a data invariant.

```
public class ShippingStrategy
{
    public ShippingStrategy(decimal flatRate)
    {
        if (flatRate <= decimal.Zero)
            throw new ArgumentOutOfRangeException("flatRate", "Flat rate must be positive
    and non-zero");

        this.flatRate = flatRate;
    }

    protected decimal flatRate;
}
```

Because the flatRate value is a protected field, the only opportunity that clients have for setting the value is through the constructor. If flatRate is set to a valid value at this point, it should be valid for the rest of the lifetime of the object because clients have no way of changing this value.

However, if the flatRate variable is instead a publicly settable property, the guard clause would have to be moved to the setter block to protect the data invariant. Listing 9-6 shows the flat rate refactored as a public property, with an accompanying guard clause.

LISTING 9-6 When a data invariant is a public property, the guard clause moves to the setter.

```
public class ShippingStrategy
{
    public ShippingStrategy(decimal flatRate)
    {
        FlatRate = flatRate;
    }

    private decimal flatRate;
    public decimal FlatRate
    {
        get
        {
            return flatRate;
        }
        set
```

```
        {
            if (value <= decimal.Zero)
                throw new ArgumentOutOfRangeException("value",
                    "Flat rate must be positive and nonzero");

            flatRate = value;
        }
    }
}
```

Now clients might be able to change the value of the `FlatRate` property but, because of the `if` statement and exception, the invariant cannot be broken. Furthermore, not even private methods in the `ShippingStrategy` class will be able to set an invalid value—something that is possible when you are using a private field, because there is no way to enforce a valid value at runtime.

> ### Encapsulation vs. contracts
>
> The contracts implemented in this example make sense, but they are necessitated by a poor choice of types for each value. The precondition contract for ensuring that the package weight argument is nonzero and positive is intrinsically linked with the type of the variable: weight should never be zero or negative. This makes weight a candidate for encapsulation into its own type. If, as is likely, another class or method requires a weight, you would need to carry this precondition across to the new code. This is inefficient, hard to maintain, and error-prone. It makes more sense to create a new type and define the precondition with it so that all uses of the `Weight` type must have a nonzero and positive value. It is, in fact, an invariant of the *type* rather than a precondition of the `CalculateShippingCost` method.
>
> Similarly, the flat rate is modeled poorly by the `decimal` type. Instead, this should be promoted to its own value type, and the invariant requiring it to also be nonzero and positive should be applied to this type.

Liskov contract rules

All this method contract coverage is merely preamble to a discussion of some of the tenets of the Liskov substitution principle. The LSP sets rules by which types must inherit contracts. A reminder of the definition of the LSP is shown here:

> *If S is a subtype of T, then objects of type T may be replaced with objects of type S, without breaking the program.*

Where contracts are concerned, this leads to the guidelines that were stated earlier:

- Preconditions cannot be strengthened in a subtype.

- Postconditions cannot be weakened in a subtype.

- Invariants of the supertype must be preserved in a subtype.

If you follow all these rules when creating subclasses of existing classes, substitutability will be retained when you are dealing with contracts.

Whenever a subclass is created, it brings with it all the methods, properties, and fields that make up the parent class. This also includes the contracts inside the methods and property setters. Preconditions, postconditions, and data invariants are all expected to be maintained in the same way that they were in the parent class. Subclasses are, where applicable, allowed to override method implementations, which includes the possibility for changing the contracts. Liskov substitution stipulates that some changes are not allowed, because they could break existing clients that must be able to use the new subclass as if it were an instance of the superclass.

Preconditions cannot be strengthened

Whenever a subclass overrides an existing method that contains preconditions, it must never *strengthen* the existing preconditions. Doing so would potentially break any client code that already assumes that the subclass defines the strongest possible precondition contracts for any method.

Listing 9-7 shows the addition of a new WorldWideShippingStrategy. Due to the large number of similarities in how the classes behave, this new class is implemented as a subclass of the Shipping-Strategy class. The CalculateShippingCost method is overridden to provide a new value that represents the destination of the package being sent via the RegionInfo parameter. Although the ShippingStrategy class did not make any guarantees that the destination of the package would be provided, WorldWideShippingStrategy now requires this parameter to be provided, otherwise it cannot correctly calculate how much it would cost to send the package to that location.

LISTING 9-7 This subclass adds a new guard clause, thus strengthening the preconditions.

```
public class WorldWideShippingStrategy : ShippingStrategy
{
    public override decimal CalculateShippingCost(
        float packageWeightInKilograms,
        Size<float> packageDimensionsInInches,
        RegionInfo destination)
    {
        if (packageWeightInKilograms <= 0f)
            throw new ArgumentOutOfRangeException("packageWeightInKilograms", "Package
weight must be positive and non-zero");

        if (packageDimensionsInInches.X <= 0f || packageDimensionsInInches.Y <= 0f)
            throw new ArgumentOutOfRangeException("packageDimensionsInInches", "Package
dimensions must be positive and non-zero");

        if (destination == null)
            throw new ArgumentNullException("destination", "Destination must be
provided");

        return decimal.One;
    }
}
```

The temptation is to strengthen the preconditions so that you can guarantee that the destination parameter is provided. This creates a conflict that calling code is unable to solve. If a class calls the CalculateShippingCost method of the ShippingStrategy base class, it is free to pass in null for the destination parameter without experiencing a side effect. But if it is calling the Calculate-ShippingCost method of the WorldWideShippingStrategy class, it *must not* pass in null for the destination parameter. Doing so would violate a precondition and cause an exception to be thrown. As demonstrated in earlier chapters, client code should not make assumptions about what type it is acting on. Doing so leads to strong coupling between classes and an inability to adapt to changing requirements.

To demonstrate the problem, examine the unit test shown in Listing 9-8.

LISTING 9-8 When the precondition is strengthened, clients cannot reliably use a WorldWideShippingStrategy where a ShippingStrategy is required.

```
[Test]
public void ShippingRegionMustBeProvided()
{
    strategy.Invoking(s => s.CalculateShippingCost(1f, ValidDimensions, null))
        .ShouldThrow<ArgumentNullException>("Destination must be provided")
        .And.ParamName.Should().Be("destination");
}
```

If the strategy used by this test is of type WorldWideShippingStrategy, the test will pass; no destination is provided but one is required, thus an exception meeting the specification is thrown. If a ShippingStrategy is used instead, this test will fail because no precondition exists to prevent the null value for the destination and no exception will be thrown.

Listing 9-9 shows a refactored set of unit tests that do not attempt to test the same preconditions on both strategy types. A test asserting that the shipping region must be provided is only valid for the WorldWideShippingStrategy. However, regardless of shipping strategy, the precondition that the shipping weight must be positive is always valid, so this is included in a base class of tests that will be run for each shipping strategy class.

LISTING 9-9 These refactored unit tests separately target the two shipping strategy classes.

```
[TestFixture]
public class WorldWideShippingStrategyTests : ShippingStrategyTestsBase
{
    [Test]
    public void ShippingRegionMustBeProvided()
    {
        strategy.Invoking(s => s.CalculateShippingCost(1f, ValidSize, null))
            .ShouldThrow<ArgumentNullException>("Destination must be provided")
            .And.ParamName.Should().Be("destination");
    }
}
```

```
    protected override ShippingStrategy CreateShippingStrategy()
    {
        return new WorldWideShippingStrategy(decimal.One);
    }
}
// . . .
public abstract class ShippingStrategyTestsBase
{
    [Test]
    public void ShippingWeightMustBePositive()
    {
        strategy.Invoking(s => s.CalculateShippingCost(-1f, ValidSize, null))
            .ShouldThrow<ArgumentOutOfRangeException>("Package weight must be positive and
  non-zero")
            .And.ParamName.Should().Be("packageWeightInKilograms");
    }
}
```

Postconditions cannot be weakened

When applying postconditions to subclasses, the opposite rule applies. Instead of not being able to
strengthen postconditions, you cannot weaken them. As for all the Liskov substitution rules relating to
contracts, the reason that you cannot weaken postconditions is because existing clients might break
when presented with the new subclass. Theoretically, if you comply with the LSP, any subclass you create
should be usable by all existing clients without causing them to fail in unexpected ways.

One such example of causing an unexpected failure in an existing client is explored in Listing 9-10.
The unit test and implementation relate to the WorldWideShippingStrategy, the Shipping-
Strategy subclass for international packages.

LISTING 9-10 The new implementation requires a weakening of the postcondition.

```
[Test]
public void ShippingDomesticallyIsFree()
{
    strategy.CalculateShippingCost(1f, ValidDimensions, RegionInfo.CurrentRegion)
        .Should().Be(decimal.Zero);
}
// . . .
public override decimal CalculateShippingCost(float packageWeightInKilograms, Size<float>
  packageDimensionsInInches, RegionInfo destination)
{
    if (destination == null)
        throw new ArgumentNullException("destination", "Destination must be provided");

    if (packageWeightInKilograms <= 0f)
        throw new ArgumentOutOfRangeException("packageWeightInKilograms", "Package weight
  must be positive and non-zero");
```

```
        if (packageDimensionsInInches.X <= 0f || packageDimensionsInInches.Y <= 0f)
            throw new ArgumentOutOfRangeException("packageDimensionsInInches", "Package
    dimensions must be positive and non-zero");

        var shippingCost = decimal.One;

        if(destination == RegionInfo.CurrentRegion)
        {
            shippingCost = decimal.Zero;
        }

        return shippingCost;
    }
```

The unit test asserts that, when the current region is used for the destination—that is, the shipping is domestic—the WorldWideShippingStrategy does not charge for shipping at all. This is reflected in the accompanying implementation. This assertion is, again, in conflict with an existing unit test for the base class that asserts the original postcondition: that the result is always positive and nonzero, as shown in Listing 9-11.

LISTING 9-11 This unit test shows the original unit test, which fails when the strategy is a WorldWide-ShippingStrategy.

```
[Test]
public void ShippingCostMustBePositiveAndNonZero()
{
    strategy.CalculateShippingCost(1f, ValidDimensions, RegionInfo.CurrentRegion)
        .Should().BeGreaterThan(0m);
}
```

A client could easily be broken by this change in behavior due to its assumption of the value of the shipping cost. For example, the client assumes that the shipping cost is always positive and nonzero, as indicated by the postcondition contract of the ShippingStrategy. This client then uses the shipping cost as the denominator in a subsequent calculation. When a switch is made to use the new WorldWideShippingStrategy, the client unexpectedly starts throwing DivideByZeroException errors for all domestic orders.

Had the LSP been honored and the postcondition never weakened, this defect would never have been introduced.

Invariants must be maintained

Whenever a new subclass is created, it must continue to honor all the data invariants that were part of the base class. The violation of this principle is easy to introduce because subclasses have a lot of freedom to introduce new ways of changing previously private data.

Listing 9-12 returns to the previous data invariant example from earlier in the chapter. However, in this instance, the ShippingStrategy accepts the flat rate value as a constructor parameter and maintains this value as a read-only data invariant. The new WorldWideShippingStrategy is introduced, and the means to change the flat rate value is made public through a property.

LISTING 9-12 The subclass breaks the data invariant of the superclass, violating the LSP.

```
[Test]
public void ShippingFlatRateCanBeChanged()
{
    strategy.FlatRate = decimal.MinusOne;

    strategy.FlatRate.Should().Be(decimal.MinusOne);
}
// . . .
public class WorldWideShippingStrategy : ShippingStrategy
{
    public WorldWideShippingStrategy(decimal flatRate)
        : base(flatRate)
    {

    }

    private decimal flatRate;
    public decimal FlatRate
    {
        get
        {
            return flatRate;
        }
        set
        {
            flatRate = value;
        }
    }
}
```

Although the subclass reuses the base class's constructor and guard clause, it does not maintain the data invariant and therefore breaks the Liskov substitution principle. The unit test proves that clients can set the value to a negative number, which should be disallowed by the class if it is to correctly protect its data invariants.

Listing 9-13 shows that when the base class is reworked to disallow direct write access to the flat rate field, the invariant is properly honored by the subclass. This is a very common pattern whereby fields are private but there are protected or public properties that contain guard clauses to centralize the protection of invariants.

```
public class WorldWideShippingStrategy : ShippingStrategy
{
    public WorldWideShippingStrategy(decimal flatRate)
        : base(flatRate)
    {

    }

    public new decimal FlatRate
    {
        get
        {
            return base.FlatRate;
        }
        set
        {
            base.FlatRate = value;
        }
    }
}
// . . .
public class ShippingStrategy
{
    public ShippingStrategy(decimal flatRate)
    {
        if (flatRate <= decimal.Zero)
            throw new ArgumentOutOfRangeException("flatRate", "Flat rate must be positive
    and non-zero");

        this.flatRate = flatRate;
    }

    protected decimal FlatRate
    {
        get
        {
            return flatRate;
        }
        set
        {
            if (value <= decimal.Zero)
                throw new ArgumentOutOfRangeException("value",
                    "Flat rate must be positive and nonzero");

            flatRate = value;
        }
    }
}
```

Tightening the visibility of the field and instead providing access only through the property setter protects the invariant with a guard clause. Doing this in the base class is preferable because it means that all future subclasses are absolved of this responsibility and simply cannot directly write to the field at all.

A new unit test can be created that asserts this new behavior, as shown in Listing 9-14.

LISTING 9-14 With the invariant maintained, this unit test passes.

```
[Test]
public void ShippingFlatRateCannotBeSetToNegativeNumber()
{
    strategy.Invoking(s => s.FlatRate = decimal.MinusOne)
        .ShouldThrow<ArgumentOutOfRangeException>("Flat rate must be positive and non-
    zero")
        .And.ParamName.Should().Be("value");
}
```

If a client tries to set the `FlatRate` property to a negative value, or even to zero, the guard clause prevents the assignment and an `ArgumentOutOfRangeException` is thrown.

Code contracts

Throughout the previous section, the guard clauses that formed the basis of the contracts were all written in long form, using `if` statements and throwing exceptions. It is worth exploring an alternative to these manual guard clauses: code contracts.

Previously a separate library, code contracts were integrated into the .NET Framework 4 main libraries. In addition to being easier to read, write, and comprehend than manual guard clauses, code contracts bring with them the possibility of using static verification and automatic generation of reference documentation.

With static contract verification, code contracts can check for contract violations without executing the application. This helps expose implicit contracts such as null dereferences and problems with array bounds, in addition to the explicitly coded contracts shown throughout this section.

Generating reference documentation relating to the contract of a method or class is important because client code has no other way of knowing the expectations. When more detail is included in the XML comments that form the documentation to methods and classes, clients can view the expectations via IntelliSense. This makes working with classes that use contracts a bit easier.

Preconditions

Preconditions can be written succinctly by using code contracts. You will need to include the `System.Diagnostics.Contracts` namespace, which is part of the `mscorlib.dll` and so should not need an additional assembly reference. The static `Contract` class provides most of the functionality that is required to implement contracts.

> **Note** If you make the decision to use code contracts, the static `Contract` class will permeate throughout much of your code base. This is less of a problem than it is with most static references because code contracts are ubiquitous infrastructure that, it is assumed, will not be removed or replaced. Thus, it is a significant undertaking to undo the decision to use code contracts, and it is best to use them from the outset of a project, or not at all.

Listing 9-15 shows the declarative nature of a code contract precondition.

LISTING 9-15 The `System.Diagnostics.Contracts` namespace can provide guard clauses to methods.

```
using System.Diagnostics.Contracts;

public class ShippingStrategy
{
    public decimal CalculateShippingCost(float packageWeightInKilograms, Size<float>
    packageDimensionsInInches, RegionInfo destination)
    {
        Contract.Requires(packageWeightInKilograms > 0f);
        Contract.Requires(packageDimensionsInInches.X > 0f && packageDimensionsInInches.Y
    > 0f);

        return decimal.MinusOne;
    }
}
```

The `Contract.Requires` method accepts a Boolean predicate value. This represents the state that the method requires to proceed. Note that this is the inverse logic of the predicate used in an `if` statement in manual guard clauses. In that case, the clauses were checking for state that was *invalid* before throwing an exception. With code contracts, the predicate is closer to an *assertion*: that the Boolean value must return `true`, otherwise the contract fails. This example requires that the `packageWeightInKilograms` parameter is nonzero and positive and that the `packageDimensionsInInches` parameter is nonzero and positive for both its X and Y properties.

This version of the `Contract.Requires` method throws an exception when the contract predicate is not met, but the type of exception is a `ContractException`, which does not match the expected exception in the existing unit tests. Therefore, they fail:

```
Expected System.ArgumentOutOfRangeException because Package dimension must be positive and non-
    zero, but found System.Diagnostics.Contracts.__ContractsRuntime+ContractException with message
    "Precondition failed: packageDimensionsInInches.X > 0f && packageDimensionsInInches.Y > 0f"
```

Furthermore, if you run this example while passing in an invalid value for one of the parameters, you will get the message shown in Figure 9-2. This informs you that you have not properly configured code contracts for use.

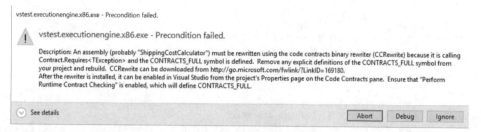

FIGURE 9-2 Code contracts must be configured before use.

After Code Contracts are installed, the property pages of each project include a *Code Contracts* tab through which you can configure code contracts. A minimal working setup is shown in Figure 9-3.

FIGURE 9-3 The property pages for code contracts contain a lot of settings.

When they are configured correctly, the contract preconditions can be rewritten to use an alternative version of the `Contract.Requires` method. Listing 9-16 shows this version.

LISTING 9-16 This version of the `Requires` method accepts the type of the exception to be thrown.

```
public class ShippingStrategy
{
    public decimal CalculateShippingCost(float packageWeightInKilograms, Size<float>
    packageDimensionsInInches, RegionInfo destination)
    {
        Contract.Requires<ArgumentOutOfRangeException>(packageWeightInKilograms > 0f,
    "Package weight must be positive and non-zero");
        Contract.Requires<ArgumentOutOfRangeException>(packageDimensionsInInches.X > 0f &&
    packageDimensionsInInches.Y > 0f, "Package dimensions must be positive and non-zero");

        return decimal.MinusOne;
    }
}
```

This generic version of the `Requires` method accepts the type of exception that you would like the contract to throw when the predicate fails. This, along with the exception message included in a subsequent method parameter, will cause the existing unit tests to pass.

Postconditions

Code contracts also provide a shortcut to defining postconditions. The `Contract` static class contains an `Ensures` method that is the postcondition complement to the precondition's `Requires` method. This method also accepts a Boolean predicate that must be true to progress through to the return statement. It is worth noting that the `return` statement must be the only line that follows a call to `Contract.Ensures`. This makes intuitive sense because, otherwise, it would be possible to further modify state in a way that might break the postcondition.

Listing 9-17 reiterates the `ShippingCostMustBePositive` unit test and includes a rewritten `CalculateShippingCost` implementation that uses the `Contract.Ensures` method as a postcondition.

LISTING 9-17 The Ensures method creates a postcondition that should be true on exiting the method.

```
[Test]
public void ShippingCostMustBePositive()
{
    strategy.CalculateShippingCost(1, ValidSize, null)
        .Should().BeGreaterThan(decimal.MinusOne);
}
// . . .
public class ShippingStrategy
{
    public decimal CalculateShippingCost(float packageWeightInKilograms, Size<float>
```

```
packageDimensionsInInches, RegionInfo destination)
    {
        Contract.Ensures(Contract.Result<decimal>() > 0m);

        Contract.Requires<ArgumentOutOfRangeException>(packageWeightInKilograms > 0f,
"Package weight must be positive and non-zero");
        Contract.Requires<ArgumentOutOfRangeException>(packageDimensionsInInches.X > 0f &&
packageDimensionsInInches.Y > 0f, "Package dimensions must be positive and nonzero");


        return decimal.MinusOne;
    }
}
```

The predicate in this example is a bit different from the ones in prior examples and demonstrates a common use of the postcondition: testing that a return value is within valid bounds. Checking that the shipping cost is positive requires knowledge of the return value. The return value is often, but not always, a local variable that is declared and defined within the method. You could assert that the value you are returning is greater than zero, but this is not foolproof. To access the value that is returned from the method, you can use the `Contract.Result` method to retrieve it. This generic method accepts the return type of the method and returns whichever result is eventually returned by the method. This is how you can ensure that no subsequent lines can replace a valid value with an invalid value without the postcondition failing and an exception being thrown.

Data invariants

It is common for each method in a class to contain its own preconditions and postconditions, but data invariants relate to the whole class. Code contracts allow you to create a private method on the class that contains declarative definitions of the class's invariants. As Listing 9-18 shows, each invariant is defined by an assertion involving a private field of the class.

LISTING 9-18 Data invariants can be protected by a method dedicated to the purpose.

```
public class ShippingStrategy
{
    public ShippingStrategy(decimal flatRate)
    {
        this.flatRate = flatRate;
    }

    [ContractInvariantMethod]
    private void ClassInvariant()
    {
        Contract.Invariant(this.flatRate > 0m, "Flat rate must be positive and non-zero");
    }

    protected decimal flatRate;
}
```

The Contract.Invariant method follows the same pattern as the Requires and Ensures methods in that it accepts a Boolean predicate that must be true to satisfy the contract. In this example, there is also a second string parameter provided that describes the fault if this contract fails, leaving the invariant unprotected. The client can make as many calls to the Invariant method as necessary, so it is best to break the invariants down to their most granular, rather than logically AND them all together with the && operator. This gives you the maximum benefit of knowing exactly which data invariant has been broken.

If this were a normal private method, you would be obliged to call the method at the start and end of every method, to ensure that the invariants were correctly protected. Luckily, you can have code contracts do this on your behalf by marking the method with the ContractInvariantMethodAttribute. Remember that attributes do not require the Attribute suffix, so this has been shortened in the example to ContractInvariantMethod. This informs code contracts that the method must be called when entering and leaving a method, to confirm that the class's data invariants are not being violated. The prerequisites for marking a method as a ContractInvariantMethod are that it must return void and accept no arguments. However, it can be public or private, and you can choose any name to describe the method. Classes can have more than one ContractInvariantMethod, so logically grouping them is also possible. The body of the method must only make calls to the Contract.Invariant method.

Interface contracts

The final feature of code contracts to be covered here is that of *interface contracts*. So far, you have embedded all calls to Contract.Requires, Contract.Ensures, and Contract.Invariant in the class implementation itself. As has been mentioned, the static nature of the Contract class makes this code ubiquitous and difficult to remove or change in favor of an alternative library in the future. This is somewhat contrary to the adaptive codebase that is the ideal, but some infrastructural concessions are justifiable for pragmatic reasons.

A more immediate concern is the reduced readability that occurs when code contracts are liberally applied to classes. In fact, this is not a fault of code contracts but a result of diligently applying contracts in general. Preconditions, postconditions, and data invariants are implemented near the target code, but this tends to adversely affect the noise-to-signal ratio.

An interface contract, such as that shown in Listing 9-19 for the ongoing ShippingStrategy example, can alleviate this problem in addition to providing another helpful feature.

For interface contracts, you need an interface to work with. In this example, the Calculate-ShippingCost method has been extracted into its own IShippingStrategy interface. It is this interface, rather than a single implementation, that is going to have the contract applied to it. This is an important departure from the previous examples because it means that *all* implementations of this interface will acquire the applied contract. This is how you can enhance a simple interface that provides few instructions for implementation and use, to give it more powerful requirements and assurances.

LISTING 9-19 A dedicated class can define preconditions, postconditions, and invariants for every implementation of an interface.

```
[ContractClass(typeof(ShippingStrategyContract))]
interface IShippingStrategy
{
    decimal CalculateShippingCost(
        float packageWeightInKilograms,
        Size<float> packageDimensionsInInches,
        RegionInfo destination);

    float FlatRate { get; }
}
//. . .
[ContractClassFor(typeof(IShippingStrategy))]
public abstract class ShippingStrategyContract : IShippingStrategy
{
    public decimal CalculateShippingCost(float packageWeightInKilograms, Size<float>
    packageDimensionsInInches, RegionInfo destination)
    {
        Contract.Requires<ArgumentOutOfRangeException>(packageWeightInKilograms > 0f,
    "Package weight must be positive and non-zero");
        Contract.Requires<ArgumentOutOfRangeException>(packageDimensionsInInches.X > 0f &&
    packageDimensionsInInches.Y > 0f, "Package dimensions must be positive and non-zero");

        Contract.Ensures(Contract.Result<decimal>() > 0m);

        return decimal.One;
    }

    public float FlatRate { get; private set; }

    [ContractInvariantMethod]
    private void ClassInvariant()
    {
        Contract.Invariant(FlatRate > 0m, "Flat rate must be positive and non-zero");
    }
}
```

When writing an interface contract, you also need a class that is going to implement the methods of the interface but only fill them with uses of the Contract.Requires and Contract.Ensures methods. The abstract ShippingStrategyContract provides this functionality and looks like the prior examples, but what the prior examples lacked was the real functionality of the method. Even in production code, this is the limit of the code contained in a contract class. There is also a Contract-InvariantMethod to house any calls to Contract.Invariant, just as if this class were the real implementation.

To link the interface to the contract class implementation, you unfortunately need a two-way reference via attributes. This is unfortunate because it adds noise to the interface, which it would be nice to avoid. Nevertheless, by marking the interface with the `ContractClass` attribute and the contract class with the `ContractClassFor` attribute, you can write your preconditions, postconditions, and data invariant protection code once and have it apply to all subsequent implementations of the interface. Both the `ContractClass` and `ContractClassFor` attributes accept a Type argument. The `ContractClass` is applied to the interface and has the contract class type passed in, whereas the `ContractClassFor` is applied to the contract class and has the interface type passed in.

This concludes the introduction to code contracts and the foray into the Liskov substitution principle's rules relating to contracts. One final important point needs to be emphasized. Whether they are implemented manually or by using code contracts, if a precondition, postcondition, or invariant fails, *clients should not catch the exception.* Catching an exception is an action that indicates that the client can recover from this situation, which is seldom likely or perhaps even possible when a contract is broken. The ideal is that all contract violations will happen during functional testing and that the offending code will be fixed before shipping. Therefore, it is very important to unit test contracts. If a contract violation is not fixed before shipping and an end user is unfortunate enough to trigger an exception, it is most likely the best course of action to force the application to close. It is advisable to allow the application to fail because it is now in a potentially invalid state. For a web application, this will mean that the global error page is displayed. For a desktop application, the user can be shown a friendly message and be given a chance to report the problem. In all cases, a log should be made of the exception, with full stack trace and as much context as possible.

The next section covers the rest of the LSP's rules—those that apply to covariance and contravariance.

Covariance and contravariance

The remaining rules of the Liskov substitution principle all relate to covariance and contravariance. Generally, *variance* is a term applied to the expected behavior of subtypes in a class hierarchy containing complex types.

Definitions

As previously demonstrated, it is important to cover the basics of this topic before diving in to the specifics of the LSP's requirements for variance.

The prefixes *co-* and *contra-* are mathematical terms that mean *with* and *against*, respectively. *Variance*, in the context of types, measures the behavior of subtypes and their relationship. Therefore, *covariance* is a relationship where subtypes go *with* each other, and *contravariance* is a relationship where subtypes go *against* each other.

Covariance

Figure 9-4 shows a very small class hierarchy of just two types: the generically named Supertype and Subtype, which are named after their respective roles in the inheritance structure. Supertype defines some fields and methods that are inherited by Subtype. Subtype enhances the Supertype by defining its own fields and methods.

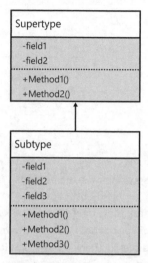

FIGURE 9-4 Supertype and Subtype have a parent/child relationship in this class hierarchy.

Polymorphism is the ability of a subtype to be treated as if it were an instance of the supertype. Thanks to this feature of object-oriented programming, which C# supports, any method that accepts an instance of Supertype will also be able to accept an instance of Subtype without any casting required by either the client or service code, and without any type-sniffing by the service. To the service, it has been handed an instance of Supertype, and this is the only fact it is concerned with. It doesn't care what specific subtype has been handed to it.

Variance enters the discussion when you introduce another type that might use Supertype and/or Subtype through a generic parameter.

Figure 9-5 is a visual explanation of the concept of *covariance*. First, let's define a new interface called ICovariant. This interface is a generic of type T and contains a single method that returns this type, T. Because the out keyword is used before the generic type argument T, this interface is well named because it exhibits *covariant* behavior.

The second half of the class diagram details a new inheritance hierarchy that has been created thanks to the covariance of the ICovariant interface. By plugging in the values for the Supertype and Subtype classes that were defined previously, ICovariant<Supertype> becomes a supertype for the ICovariant<Subtype> interface.

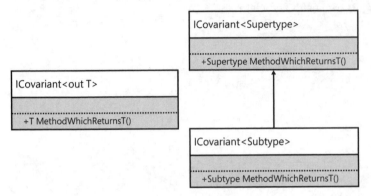

FIGURE 9-5 Due to covariance of the generic parameter, the base-class/subclass relationship is preserved.

Polymorphism applies here, just as it did previously, and this is where it gets interesting. Thanks to covariance, whenever a method requires an instance of ICovariant<Supertype>, you can provide it instead with an instance of ICovariant<Subtype>. This will work seamlessly thanks to the simultaneous interoperating of both covariance and polymorphism.

So far, this is of limited general use. To firm up this explanation, I'll move away from class diagrams and instructive type names to a more real-world scenario. Listing 9-20 shows a class hierarchy between a general Entity base class and a specific User subclass. All Entity types inherit a GUID unique identifier and a string name, and each User has an EmailAddress and a DateOfBirth.

LISTING 9-20 In this small domain, a User is a specialization of the Entity type.

```
public class Entity
{
    public Guid ID { get; private set; }

    public string Name { get; private set; }
}
// . . .
public class User : Entity
{
    public string EmailAddress { get; private set; }

    public DateTime DateOfBirth { get; private set; }
}
```

This is directly analogous to the Supertype/Subtype example, but with a more directed purpose. This small domain is going to have the Repository pattern applied to it. The Repository pattern provides you with an interface for retrieving objects as if they were in memory but that could be loaded from a very different storage medium. Listing 9-21 shows an `EntityRepository` class and its `UserRepository` subclass.

LISTING 9-21 Without involving generics, all inheritance in C# is invariant.

```
public class EntityRepository
{
    public virtual Entity GetByID(Guid id)
    {
        return new Entity();
    }
}
// . . .
public class UserRepository : EntityRepository
{
    public override User GetByID(Guid id)
    {
        return new User();
    }
}
```

This example is not the same as that previously described because of one key difference: in the absence of generic types, C# is not covariant for method return types. In fact, a compilation error is generated due to an attempt to change the return type of the `GetByID` method in the subclass to match the `User` class.

```
error CS0508: 'SubtypeCovariance.UserRepository.GetByID(System.Guid)': return type must be
   'SubtypeCovariance.Entity' to match overridden member
   'SubtypeCovariance.EntityRepository.GetByID(System.Guid)'
```

Perhaps experience tells you that this will not work, but the reason is a lack of covariance in this scenario. If C# supported covariance for general classes, you would be able to enforce the change of return type in the `UserRepository`. Because it does not, you have only two options. You can amend the `UserRepository.GetByID` method's return type to be `Entity` and use polymorphism to allow you to return a `User` in its place. This is dissatisfying because clients of the `UserRepository` would have to downcast the return type from an `Entity` type to a `User` type, or they would have to sniff for the `User` type and execute specific code if the expected type was returned.

Instead, you could redefine `EntityRepository` as a generic class that requires the `Entity` type it intends to operate on via a generic type argument. This generic parameter can be marked `out`, thus covariant, and the `UserRepository` subclass can specialize its parent base class for the `User` type.

Listing 9-22 shows an example of this.

LISTING 9-22 Make base classes generic to take advantage of covariance and allow subclasses to override the return type.

```
public interface IEntityRepository<TEntity>
    where TEntity : Entity
{
    TEntity GetByID(Guid id);
}
// . . .
public class UserRepository : IEntityRepository<User>
{
    public User GetByID(Guid id)
    {
        return new User();
    }
}
```

Rather than maintaining `EntityRepository` as a concrete class that can be instantiated, this code has converted it into an interface that removes the default implementation of `GetByID`. This is not entirely necessary, but the benefits of clients depending on interfaces rather than implementations have been demonstrated consistently, so it is a sensible reinforcement of that policy.

Note also that there is a `where` clause applied to the generic type parameter of the `EntityRepository` class. This clause prevents subclasses from supplying a type that is not part of the `Entity` class hierarchy, which would have made this new version more permissive than the original implementation.

This version prevents the need for `UserRepository` clients to mess around with downcasting because they are guaranteed to receive a `User` object, rather than an `Entity` object, and yet the inheritance of `EntityRepository` and `UserRepository` is preserved.

Contravariance

Contravariance is a similar concept to covariance. Whereas covariance relates to the treatment of types that are used as return values, *contravariance* relates to the treatment of types that are used as method parameters.

Using the same `Supertype` and `Subtype` class hierarchy as previously discussed, Figure 9-6 explores the relationship between types that are marked as contravariant via generic type parameters.

FIGURE 9-6 Due to contravariance of the generic parameter, the base-class/subclass relationship is inverted.

The `IContravariant` interface defines a method that accepts a single parameter of the type dictated by the generic parameter. Here, the generic parameter is marked with the `in` keyword, meaning that it is contravariant.

The subsequent class hierarchy can be inferred, indicating that the inheritance hierarchy has been inverted: `IContravariant<Subtype>` becomes the superclass, and `IContravariant<Supertype>` becomes the subclass. This seems strange and counterintuitive, but it will soon become apparent why contravariance exhibits this behavior—and why it is useful.

In Listing 9-23, the .NET Framework `IEqualityComparer` interface is provided for reference and an application-specific implementation is created. The `EntityEqualityComparer` accepts the previous `Entity` class as a parameter to the `Equals` method. The details of the comparison are not relevant, but a simple identity comparison is used.

LISTING 9-23 The `IEqualityComparer` interface allows the definition of function objects like `Entity-EqualityComparer`.

```
public interface IEqualityComparer<in TEntity>
    where TEntity : Entity
{
    bool Equals(TEntity left, TEntity right);
}
// . . .
public class EntityEqualityComparer : IEqualityComparer<Entity>
{
    public bool Equals(Entity left, Entity right)
    {
        return left.ID == right.ID;
    }
}
```

The unit test in Listing 9-24 explores the affect that contravariance has on the `EntityEquality-Comparer`.

LISTING 9-24 Contravariance inverts class hierarchies, allowing a more general comparer to be used wherever a more specific comparer is requested.

```
[Test]
public void UserCanBeComparedWithEntityComparer()
{
    SubtypeCovariance.IEqualityComparer<User> entityComparer = new
  EntityEqualityComparer();
    var user1 = new User();
    var user2 = new User();
    entityComparer.Equals(user1, user2)
        .Should().BeFalse();
}
```

Without contravariance—the innocent-looking `in` keyword applied to generic type parameters—the following error would be shown at compile time.

```
error CS0266: Cannot implicitly convert type 'SubtypeCovariance.EntityEqualityComparer' to
  'SubtypeCovariance.IEqualityComparer<SubtypeCovariance.User>'. An explicit conversion exists
  (are you missing a cast?)
```

There would be no type conversion from `EntityEqualityComparer` to `IEqualityComparer-<User>`, which is intuitive because `Entity` is the supertype and `User` is the subtype. However, because the `IEqualityComparer` supports contravariance, the existing inheritance hierarchy is inverted and you can assign what was originally a less specific type to a more specific type via the `IEquality-Comparer` interface.

Invariance

Beyond covariant or contravariant behavior, types are said to be invariant. This is not to be confused with the term *data invariant* used earlier in this chapter as it relates to code contracts. Instead, *invariant* in this context is used to mean "not variant." If a type is not variant at all, no arrangement of types will yield a class hierarchy. Listing 9-25 uses the `IDictionary` generic type to demonstrate this fact.

LISTING 9-25 Some generic types are neither covariant or contravariant. This makes them *invariant*.

```
[TestFixture]
public class DictionaryTests
{
    [Test]
    public void DictionaryIsInvariant()
    {
        // Attempt covariance...
        IDictionary<Supertype, Supertype> supertypeDictionary = new Dictionary<Subtype,
  Subtype>();
```

```
        // Attempt contravariance...
        IDictionary<Subtype, Subtype> subtypeDictionary = new Dictionary<Supertype,
    Supertype>();
        }
}
```

The first line of the `DictionaryIsInvariant` test method attempts to assign a dictionary whose key and value parameters are of type `Subtype` to a dictionary whose key and value parameters are of type `Supertype`. This will not work because the `IDictionary` type is not covariant, which would preserve the class hierarchy of `Subtype` and `Supertype`.

The second line is also invalid, because it attempts the inverse: to assign a dictionary of `Supertype` to a dictionary of `Subtype`. This fails because the `IDictionary` type is not contravariant, which would invert the class hierarchy of `Subtype` and `Supertype`.

The fact that the `IDictionary` type is neither covariant nor contravariant leads to the conclusion that it must be invariant. Indeed, Listing 9-26 shows how the `IDictionary` type is declared, and you can tell that there is no reference to the `out` or `in` keywords that would specify covariance and contravariance, respectively.

LISTING 9-26 None of the generic parameters of the `IDictionary` interface are marked with `in` or `out`.

```
public interface IDictionary<TKey, TValue> : ICollection<KeyValuePair<TKey, TValue>>,
    IEnumerable<KeyValuePair<TKey, TValue>>, IEnumerable
```

As previously proven for the general case—that is, without generic types—C# is invariant for both method parameter types and return types. Only when generics are involved is variance customizable on a per-type basis.

Liskov type system rules

Now that you have a grounding in variance, this section can circle back and relate all of this to the Liskov substitution principle. The LSP defines the following rules, two of which relate directly to variance:

- There must be contravariance of the method arguments in the subtype.

- There must be covariance of the return types in the subtype.

- No new exceptions are allowed.

Without contravariance of method arguments and covariance of return types, you cannot write code that is LSP-compliant.

The third rule stands alone as not relating to variance and bears its own discussion.

No new exceptions are allowed

This rule is more intuitive than the other LSP rules that relate to the type system of a language. First, you should consider this: what is the purpose of exceptions?

Exceptions aim to separate the reporting of an error from the handling of an error. It is common for the reporter and the handler to be very different classes with different purposes and context. The exception object represents the error that occurred through its type and the data that it carries with it. Any code can construct and throw an exception, just as any code can catch and respond to an exception. However, it is recommended that an exception only be caught if something meaningful can be done at that point in the code. This could be as simple as rolling back a database transaction or as complex as showing users a user interface for them to view the error details and to report the error.

It is also often inadvisable to catch an exception and silently do nothing, or catch the general `Exception` base type. These two scenarios together are discouraged even more strongly. With the latter scenario, you end up attempting to catch and respond to *everything*, including exceptions that you realistically have no meaningful way of recovering from, like `OutOfMemoryException`, `StackOverflowException`, or `ThreadAbortException`. You could improve this situation by ensuring that you always inherit your exceptions from `ApplicationException`, because many unrecoverable exceptions inherit from `SystemException`. However, this is not a common practice and relies on third-party libraries to also follow this practice.

Listing 9-27 shows two exceptions that have a sibling relationship in the class hierarchy. It is important to note that this precludes the ability to create a single catch block that specifically targets one of the exception types and to intercept both types of exception.

LISTING 9-27 Both exceptions are of type `Exception`, but neither inherits from the other.

```
public class EntityNotFoundException : Exception
{
    public EntityNotFoundException()
        : base()
    {

    }

    public EntityNotFoundException(string message)
        : base(message)
    {

    }
}
//. . .
public class UserNotFoundException : Exception
{
    public UserNotFoundException()
        : base()
    {

    }
```

```
    public UserNotFoundException(string message)
        : base(message)
    {

    }
}
```

Instead, to catch both an `EntityNotFoundException` and a `UserNotFoundException` with a single catch block, you would have to resort to catching the general `Exception`, which is not recommended.

This problem is exacerbated in the potential code taken from the `EntityRepository` and `UserRepository` classes, as shown in Listing 9-28.

LISTING 9-28 Two different implementations of an interface might throw different types of exceptions.

```
public Entity GetByID(Guid id)
{
    Contract.Requires<EntityNotFoundException>(id != Guid.Empty);

    return new Entity();
}
//. . .
public User GetByID(Guid id)
{
    Contract.Requires<UserNotFoundException>(id != Guid.Empty);

    return new User();
}
```

Both classes use code contracts to assert a precondition: that the provided `id` parameter must not be equal to `Guid.Empty`. Each uses its own exception type if the contract is violated. Consider the impact that this would have on a client using the repository. The client would need to catch both kinds of exception and could not use a single catch block to target both exceptions without resorting to catching the `Exception` type. Listing 9-29 shows a unit test that is a client to these two repositories.

LISTING 9-29 This unit test will fail because a `UserNotFoundException` is not assignable to an `EntityNotFoundException`.

```
[TestFixture(typeof(EntityRepository), typeof(Entity))]
[TestFixture(typeof(UserRepository), typeof(User))]
public class ExceptionRuleTests<TRepository, TEntity>
    where TRepository : IEntityRepository<TEntity>, new()
{
    [Test]
    public void GetByIDThrowsEntityNotFoundException()
```

```
    {
        var repo = new TRepository();
        Action getByID = () => repo.GetByID(Guid.Empty);

        getByID.ShouldThrow<EntityNotFoundException>();
    }
}
```

This unit test fails because the `UserRepository` does not, as required, throw an `EntityNotFound-Exception`. If the `UserNotFoundException` was a subclass of the type `EntityNotFoundException`, this test would pass and a single catch block could guarantee catching both kinds of exception.

This becomes a problem of client maintenance. If the client is using an interface as a dependency and calling methods on that interface, it should not know anything about the classes behind that interface. If new exceptions that are not part of an expected exception class hierarchy are introduced, clients must start referencing these exceptions directly. And—even worse—clients must be updated whenever a new exception type is introduced.

Instead, it is important that interfaces have a unifying base class exception that conveys the necessary information about an error from the exception reporter to the exception handler.

Conclusion

On the surface, the Liskov substitution principle is one of the more complex facets of the SOLID principles. It requires a foundational knowledge of both contracts and variance to build rules that guide you toward more adaptive code.

By default, interfaces do not convey rules for preconditions or postconditions to clients. Creating guard clauses that halt the application at run time further narrows the allowed range of valid values for parameters. The LSP provides guidelines specifying that each subclass in a class hierarchy must not strengthen preconditions or weaken postconditions.

Similarly, the LSP suggests rules for variance in subtypes. There should be contravariance of method arguments in subtypes and covariance of return values in subtypes. Additionally, any new exception that is introduced, perhaps with the creation of a new interface implementation, should inherit from an existing base exception. To do otherwise would be to cause an existing client to miss the catch—to fumble the exception and cause an application crash.

If the LSP is violated with respect to these rules, it becomes harder for clients to treat all types in a class hierarchy the same. Ideally, clients would be able to hold a reference to a base type or interface and not alter its own behavior depending on the concrete subclass that it is using at run time. Such mixed concerns create dependencies between sections of the code that are better kept separate. Any violation of the LSP should be considered technical debt and, as demonstrated in prior chapters, this debt should be paid off sooner rather than later.

CHAPTER 10

Interface segregation

After completing this chapter, you will be able to

- Understand the importance of interface segregation.

- Write interfaces with the client code's requirements as a primary concern.

- Create smaller interfaces with more directed purposes.

- Identify scenarios where interface segregation can be used.

- Split interfaces by their implementations' dependencies.

The interface, as earlier chapters have established, is a key tool in the modern object-oriented programmer's toolkit. Interfaces represent the boundaries between the behavior that client code requires and how that behavior is implemented. The interface segregation principle states that interfaces should be *small*.

All members of an interface must be implemented: properties, events, and methods. Unless every client of an interface requires every member, it does not make sense to require every implementation to fulfill a large contract. Bearing in mind the single responsibility principle and how developers can make liberal use of the Decorator pattern, for every member present in an interface, there needs to be a valid analogy for the decoration being implemented.

At their simplest, interfaces contain single methods that serve a single purpose. At this level of granularity, they are akin to delegates, but with the added benefits enabled by interfaces.

A segregation example

This chapter works through a complete example that progresses from a single monolithic interface to multiple smaller interfaces. Along the way, a variety of decorators will be created to demonstrate the benefits of smaller interfaces when writing SOLID code.

A simple CRUD interface

The interface itself is quite simple, with only five methods. It is used to allow clients to interact with persistent storage for an entity through the traditional CRUD operations. *CRUD* stands for *create*, *read*, *update*, and *delete*. These are the common operations that clients need to perform to maintain persistent storage for an entity. Figure 10-1 shows a UML class diagram explaining the operations available to the `ICreateReadUpdateDelete` interface.

```
<<INTERFACE>>
ICreateReadUpdateDelete

+Create()
+ReadOne()
+ReadAll()
+Update()
+Delete()
```

FIGURE 10-1 The initial interface before segregation.

The read operations are split into two methods, one for retrieving a single record from storage and another for reading all records. In code, this interface is as shown in Listing 10-1.

LISTING 10-1 A simple interface for CRUD operations on an entity.

```
public interface ICreateReadUpdateDelete<TEntity>
{
    void Create(TEntity entity);

    TEntity ReadOne(Guid identity);

    IEnumerable<TEntity> ReadAll();

    void Update(TEntity entity);

    void Delete(TEntity entity);
}
```

The `ICreateReadUpdateDelete` interface is generic, allowing reuse across different entity types. However, by making the interface generic, rather than making each individual method generic, you force clients to declare up front which `TEntity` you are dealing with, which clarifies dependencies. If a client wants to perform CRUD operations on more than one entity, it must request multiple `ICreate-ReadUpdateDelete<TEntity>` instances, one for each entity type.

> **Note** Though clients will require an *instance* of `ICreateReadUpdateDelete<TEntity>` per entity type, there could still only be one *implementation* of `ICreateReadUpdateDelete<TEntity>` that would suffice for all concrete `TEntity` types. Such an implementation would also be generic.

Every operation of CRUD is performed by each implementation of the `ICreateReadUpdate-Delete` interface—including any decorator. This would be acceptable for decorators such as logging or transaction handling, as Listing 10-2 shows.

LISTING 10-2 Some decorators apply to all methods.

```csharp
public class CrudLogging<TEntity> : ICreateReadUpdateDelete<TEntity>
{
    private readonly ICreateReadUpdateDelete<TEntity> decoratedCrud;
    private readonly ILog log;

    public CrudLogging(ICreateReadUpdateDelete<TEntity> decoratedCrud, ILog log)
    {
        this.decoratedCrud = decoratedCrud;
        this.log = log;
    }

    public void Create(TEntity entity)
    {
        log.InfoFormat("Creating entity of type {0}", typeof(TEntity).Name);
        decoratedCrud.Create(entity);
    }

    public TEntity ReadOne(Guid identity)
    {
        log.InfoFormat("Reading entity of type {0} with identity {1}",
    typeof(TEntity).Name, identity);
        return decoratedCrud.ReadOne(identity);
    }

    public IEnumerable<TEntity> ReadAll()
    {
        log.InfoFormat("Reading all entities of type {0}", typeof(TEntity).Name);
        return decoratedCrud.ReadAll();
    }

    public void Update(TEntity entity)
    {
        log.InfoFormat("Updating entity of type {0}", typeof(TEntity).Name);
        decoratedCrud.Update(entity);
    }

    public void Delete(TEntity entity)
    {
        log.InfoFormat("Deleting entity of type {0}", typeof(TEntity).Name);
        decoratedCrud.Delete(entity);
    }

}
// . . .
public class CrudTransactional<TEntity> : ICreateReadUpdateDelete<TEntity>
{
    private readonly ICreateReadUpdateDelete<TEntity> decoratedCrud;
    public CrudTransactional(ICreateReadUpdateDelete<TEntity> decoratedCrud)
    {
        this.decoratedCrud = decoratedCrud;
    }

    public void Create(TEntity entity)
```

```
    {
        using (var transaction = new TransactionScope())
        {
            decoratedCrud.Create(entity);

            transaction.Complete();
        }
    }

    public TEntity ReadOne(Guid identity)
    {
        TEntity entity;
        using (var transaction = new TransactionScope())
        {
            entity = decoratedCrud.ReadOne(identity);

            transaction.Complete();
        }
        return entity;
    }

    public IEnumerable<TEntity> ReadAll()
    {
        IEnumerable<TEntity> allEntities;
        using (var transaction = new TransactionScope())
        {
            allEntities = decoratedCrud.ReadAll();

            transaction.Complete();
        }
        return allEntities;
    }

    public void Update(TEntity entity)
    {
        using (var transaction = new TransactionScope())
        {
            decoratedCrud.Update(entity);

            transaction.Complete();
        }
    }

    public void Delete(TEntity entity)
    {
        using (var transaction = new TransactionScope())
        {
            decoratedCrud.Delete(entity);

            transaction.Complete();
        }
    }
}
```

The decorators for logging and transaction management are *cross-cutting concerns*. Irrespective of the method on the interface and, in many cases, irrespective of the interface itself, logging and transaction management could be applied. Thus, to avoid repetitive implementations for multiple interfaces, you can decorate all implementations by using aspect-oriented programming.

Some other decorators apply only to a subset of the methods of a single interface, not to all of them. For example, you might want to prompt the user before you permanently delete an entity from persistent storage—a common requirement. Remember that you do not want to edit an existing class, which would violate the open/closed principle. Instead, you could create a new implementation of an existing interface that clients are already using to perform the delete action, such as the Delete method of the ICreateReadUpdateDelete<TEntity> interface. A confirmation prompt implementation would look like Listing 10-3.

LISTING 10-3 If a decorator targets part of an interface, segregation is an option.

```
public class DeleteConfirmation<TEntity> : ICreateReadUpdateDelete<TEntity>
{
    private readonly ICreateReadUpdateDelete<TEntity> decoratedCrud;
    public DeleteConfirmation(ICreateReadUpdateDelete<TEntity> decoratedCrud)
    {
        this.decoratedCrud = decoratedCrud;
    }

    public void Create(TEntity entity)
    {
        decoratedCrud.Create(entity);
    }

    public TEntity ReadOne(Guid identity)
    {
        return decoratedCrud.ReadOne(identity);
    }

    public IEnumerable<TEntity> ReadAll()
    {
        return decoratedCrud.ReadAll();
    }

    public void Update(TEntity entity)
    {
        decoratedCrud.Update(entity);
    }

    public void Delete(TEntity entity)
    {
        Console.WriteLine("Are you sure you want to delete the entity? [y/N]");
        var keyInfo = Console.ReadKey();
        if (keyInfo.Key == ConsoleKey.Y)
        {
            decoratedCrud.Delete(entity);
        }
    }
}
```

The DeleteConfirmation<TEntity> class decorates only the Delete method, as its name suggests. The other methods are implemented with pass-through delegation to the wrapped interface. *Pass-through* means that there is no decoration for that method: the call is merely *passed through* the decorator to the underlying implementation, almost as if it had been called directly. Despite these pass-through methods apparently doing nothing special, to maintain unit test coverage and ensure that they are delegating properly, test methods should still be written to verify that their behavior is correct. This is laborious when compared to the alternative: interface segregation.

By separating the Delete method from the rest of the ICreateReadUpdateDelete<TEntity> interface, you have two interfaces. This is the interface segregation principle in practice. The code for this is shown in Listing 10-4.

LISTING 10-4 The ICreateReadUpdateDelete interface is split in two.

```
public interface ICreateReadUpdate<TEntity>
{
    void Create(TEntity entity);

    TEntity ReadOne(Guid identity);

    IEnumerable<TEntity> ReadAll();

    void Update(TEntity entity);
}
// . . .
public interface IDelete<TEntity>
{
    void Delete(TEntity entity);
}
```

This allows the confirmation decorator to be replaced with an implementation only for the IDelete<TEntity> interface, as shown in Listing 10-5.

LISTING 10-5 The confirmation decorator is applied only to the interface to which it pertains.

```
public class DeleteConfirmation<TEntity> : IDelete<TEntity>
{
    private readonly IDelete<TEntity> decoratedDelete;

    public DeleteConfirmation(IDelete<TEntity> decoratedDelete)
    {
        this.decoratedDelete = decoratedDelete;
    }

    public void Delete(TEntity entity)
    {
        Console.WriteLine("Are you sure you want to delete the entity? [y/N]");
        var keyInfo = Console.ReadKey();
        if (keyInfo.Key == ConsoleKey.Y)
```

```
        {
            decoratedDelete.Delete(entity);
        }
    }
}
```

This is an improvement, because there is less code overall, without the pass-through decoration methods, so the intent is much clearer. Also, less code means fewer tests.

Before moving on to the next decorator, consider the following refactor that is available for the DeleteConfirmation decorator. You could encapsulate the user interrogation into a simple interface. That way, you could write multiple different implementations of this new interface—one for each user interface type (for example, console, Windows Forms, and Windows Presentation Foundation)—and the decorator would not need to change. You could do this because the DeleteConfirmation class does not currently adhere to the single responsibility principle. As it is now, it contains two reasons to change: the interface that it delegates to has changed, *and* you want to elicit confirmation from the user in a different manner. Asking users whether they want to delete an entity requires a very simple predicate-like interface, as shown in Listing 10-6.

LISTING 10-6 A very simple interface for asking the user to confirm something.

```
public interface IUserInteraction
{
    bool Confirm(string message);
}
```

Caching

The next decorator that you could implement is for the read methods: ReadOne and ReadAll. For both methods, you want to cache the returned value from the decorated implementation and return the contents of the cache in all subsequent requests. Again, with no equivalent analogy for caching the Create or Update methods, the first decorator contains needless methods, as in Listing 10-7.

LISTING 10-7 The caching decorator includes redundant, pass-through methods.

```
public class CrudCaching<TEntity> : ICreateReadUpdate<TEntity>
{
    private TEntity cachedEntity;
    private IEnumerable<TEntity> allCachedEntities;
    private readonly ICreateReadUpdate<TEntity> decorated;

    public CrudCaching(ICreateReadUpdate<TEntity> decorated)
    {
        this.decorated = decorated;
    }
```

```
    public void Create(TEntity entity)
    {
        decorated.Create(entity);
    }

    public TEntity ReadOne(Guid identity)
    {
        if(cachedEntity == null)
        {
            cachedEntity = decorated.ReadOne(identity);
        }
        return cachedEntity;
    }

    public IEnumerable<TEntity> ReadAll()
    {
        if (allCachedEntities == null)
        {
            allCachedEntities = decorated.ReadAll();
        }
        return allCachedEntities;
    }

    public void Update(TEntity entity)
    {
        decorated.Update(entity);
    }

}
```

By applying interface segregation a second time, you can factor out the two methods used for reading data into their own interface, and they can now be decorated separately. The new IRead interface, and its accompanying caching decorator, is shown in Listing 10-8.

LISTING 10-8 The IRead interface is targeted specifically by the ReadCaching decorator.

```
public interface IRead<TEntity>
{
    TEntity ReadOne(Guid identity);

    IEnumerable<TEntity> ReadAll();
}
// . . .
public class ReadCaching<TEntity> : IRead<TEntity>
{
    private Dictionary<Guid, TEntity> cachedEntities = new Dictionary<Guid, TEntity>();
    private IEnumerable<TEntity> allCachedEntities;
    private readonly IRead<TEntity> decorated;
```

```
    public ReadCaching(IRead<TEntity> decorated)
    {
        this.decorated = decorated;
    }

    public TEntity ReadOne(Guid identity)
    {
        var foundEntity = cachedEntities [identity];
        if(foundEntity == null)
        {
            foundEntity = decorated.ReadOne(identity);
            if(foundEntity != null)
                cachedEntities [identity] = foundEntity;
        }
        return foundEntity;
    }

    public IEnumerable<TEntity> ReadAll()
    {
        if (allCachedEntities == null)
        {
            allCachedEntities = decorated.ReadAll();
        }
        return allCachedEntities;
    }

}
```

Before you implement the final decorator, the remaining interface contains only two methods, as Listing 10-9 shows.

LISTING 10-9 The remaining methods can probably be unified.

```
public interface ICreateUpdate<TEntity>
{
    void Create(TEntity entity);

    void Update(TEntity entity);
}
```

The Create and Update methods have identical signatures. Not only that, they serve very similar purposes: the former saves a new entity, and the latter saves an existing entity. You could unify these methods into one Save method, which acknowledges that the distinction between creating and updating is an implementation detail that clients don't need to know about. After all, a client is likely to want to both save and update an entity, so requiring two interfaces that are so similar seems needless when there is a viable alternative. Clients of the interface want to *save* an entity. The refactored interface looks like the one in Listing 10-10.

LISTING 10-10 ISave implementations will either create or update an entity, as appropriate.

```
public interface ISave<TEntity>
{
    void Save(TEntity entity);
}
```

After this refactor, you can add a new decorator that is specific to this interface—audit tracking. Every time a user saves an entity, you want to add some metadata to persistent storage. Specifically, you want to know which user enacted the save and at what time. Listing 10-11 shows the SaveAuditing decorator.

LISTING 10-11 Two ISave interfaces are used by the audit decorator.

```
public class SaveAuditing<TEntity> : ISave<TEntity>
{
    private readonly ISave<TEntity> decorated;
    private readonly ISave<AuditInfo> auditSave;
    public SaveAuditing(ISave<TEntity> decorated, ISave<AuditInfo> auditSave)
    {
        this.decorated = decorated;
        this.auditSave = auditSave;
    }

    public void Save(TEntity entity)
    {
        decorated.Save(entity);
        var auditInfo = new AuditInfo
        {
            UserName = Thread.CurrentPrincipal.Identity.Name,
            TimeStamp = DateTime.Now
        };
        auditSave.Save(auditInfo);
    }

}
```

The SaveAuditing decorator implements the ISave interface, but it also needs to be constructed with two further ISave implementations. The first must match the TEntity generic type parameter of the decorator and is used to do the real work of saving (or, of course, to provide further decoration on the way to doing the real work of saving). The second is an ISave implementation that is specifically for saving AuditInfo types. This class is not shown, but it can be inferred to contain string UserName and DateTime TimeStamp properties. When clients call the Save method, a new AuditInfo instance is created and its properties are set. The real implementation responsible for saving this instance will then persist this new record to storage.

Again, it is worth reiterating that client code has no idea that this is happening; it is entirely un-aware that auditing is occurring and does not need to change because of the decoration. Similarly, the leaf implementation of the `ISave<TEntity>` interface—that is, the non-decorator version that is responsible for the actual work of saving—is also unaware of the decorator and does not need to change to accommodate any specific decoration.

You now have three different interfaces where before you had one, and each has a decorator that provides some different, meaningful, real-world function. Figure 10-2 shows a UML class diagram of the new interfaces and their decorators after segregation.

FIGURE 10-2 Interface segregation allows you to target methods for decoration without redundancy.

Multiple interface decoration

Each decorator so far has maintained a one-to-one relationship with the interface that it enhances. This is true because each decorator implements the interface that it is decorating. But you can use the Adapter pattern (introduced in Chapter 4, "Interfaces and design patterns"), in conjunction with the Decorator pattern to produce multiple decorators while minimizing the code you must write.

The next decorator you will create is intended to publish an event whenever a record is saved or deleted. This notification will allow disparate subscribers to act upon any change to persistent storage. Note that there is no analogous event for reading any records, so the `IRead` interface will not be targeted in this instance.

For this, you first need a mechanism for publishing and subscribing events. Continuing the theme of interface segregation, this is split into the two interfaces shown in Listing 10-12.

LISTING 10-12 Two interfaces for publishing and subscribing to events.

```
public interface IEventPublisher
{
    void Publish<TEvent>(TEvent @event)
        where TEvent : IEvent;
}
// . . .
public interface IEventSubscriber
{
    void Subscribe<TEvent>(TEvent @event)
        where TEvent : IEvent;
}
```

The IEvent interface is extremely simple, containing just a `string Name` property. By using these two interfaces, a decorator can be created, as in Listing 10-13, that publishes a specific event when an entity is deleted.

LISTING 10-13 This decorator publishes an event when an entity is deleted.

```
public class DeleteEventPublishing<TEntity> : IDelete<TEntity>
{
    private readonly IDelete<TEntity> decorated;
    private readonly IEventPublisher eventPublisher;

    public DeleteEventPublishing(IDelete<TEntity> decorated, IEventPublisher
  eventPublisher)
    {
        this.decorated = decorated;
        this.eventPublisher = eventPublisher;
    }

    public void Delete(TEntity entity)
    {
        decorated.Delete(entity);
        var entityDeleted = new EntityDeletedEvent<TEntity>(entity);
        eventPublisher.Publish(entityDeleted);
    }
}
// . . .
public class EntityDeletedEvent<TEntity> : IEvent<TEntity>
{
    public EntityDeletedEvent(TEntity entity) : base("EntityDeleted")
    {
        DeletedEntity = entity;
    }

    public TEntity DeletedEntity
    {
        get;
        private set;
    }
}
```

From here, you have two choices: implementing the equivalent ISave decorator for publishing events on the same class or implementing the ISave decorator in a new class. Listing 10-14 shows the former option, which involves renaming the existing class and adding a new Save method.

LISTING 10-14 Two decorators can be implemented in one class.

```csharp
public class ModificationEventPublishing<TEntity> : IDelete<TEntity>, ISave<TEntity>
{
    private readonly IDelete<TEntity> decoratedDelete;
    private readonly ISave<TEntity> decoratedSave;
    private readonly IEventPublisher eventPublisher;

    public ModificationEventPublishing(IDelete<TEntity> decoratedDelete, ISave<TEntity>
  decoratedSave, IEventPublisher eventPublisher)
    {
        this.decoratedDelete = decoratedDelete;
        this.decoratedSave = decoratedSave;
        this.eventPublisher = eventPublisher;
    }

    public void Delete(TEntity entity)
    {
        decoratedDelete.Delete(entity);
        var entityDeleted = new EntityDeletedEvent<TEntity>(entity);
        eventPublisher.Publish(entityDeleted);
    }

    public void Save(TEntity entity)
    {
        decoratedSave.Save(entity);
        var entitySaved = new EntitySavedEvent<TEntity>(entity);
        eventPublisher.Publish(entitySaved);
    }
}
// . . .
public class EntitySavedEvent<TEntity> : IEvent<TEntity>
{
    public EntitySavedEvent(TEntity entity) : base("EntitySaved")
    {
        SavedEntity = entity;
    }

    public TEntity SavedEntity
    {
        get;
        private set;
    }
}
```

A single class can be the implementation for multiple decorators—but only when the context of the decorator is shared, as in this example. The `ModificationEventPublishing` decorator is implementing the same functionality—event publication—for both interfaces that it implements. It would be unwise, however, to combine decorators for event publishing with those for auditing, for example. This is due to the dependencies involved. One decorator depends on the `IEventPublisher` interface, whereas the other depends on the `AuditInfo` class. It would be better instead to separate those implementations into their own assemblies with their own dependency chains.

Client construction

The design of interfaces—segregated or otherwise—affects the classes that implement the interfaces and the clients that use the interfaces. If clients are to use interfaces, the interfaces must in some way be supplied to the clients. This chapter will continue, for the most part, to manually construct the implementations and provide them to clients via constructor parameters. For an alternative option, see Chapter 12, "Dependency injection."

The way you supply the implementations to clients is partly dictated by the number of implementations of the segregated interfaces. If each interface is given its own implementation, each of those implementations needs to be constructed and supplied to the client. Alternatively, if all the interfaces are implemented in a single class, a single instance is sufficient for all of the related dependencies on the client.

Multiple implementations, multiple instances

Continuing the CRUD example, assume that the `IRead`, `ISave`, and `IDelete` interfaces have all been implemented by different, distinct classes. A client needing to use these interfaces will, because of segregation, require three interfaces, whereas it previously only required one. Such a client is shown in Listing 10-15.

LISTING 10-15 The order-specific controller requires each facet of CRUD as a separate dependency.

```
public class OrderController
{
    private readonly IRead<Order> reader;
    private readonly ISave<Order> saver;
    private readonly IDelete<Order> deleter;

    public OrderController(IRead<Order> orderReader, ISave<Order> orderSaver,
    IDelete<Order> orderDeleter)
    {
        reader = orderReader;
        saver = orderSaver;
        deleter = orderDeleter;
    }
```

```
    public void CreateOrder(Order order)
    {
        saver.Save(order);
    }

    public Order GetSingleOrder(Guid identity)
    {
        return reader.ReadOne(identity);
    }

    public void UpdateOrder(Order order)
    {
        saver.Save(order);
    }

    public void DeleteOrder(Order order)
    {
        deleter.Delete(order);
    }
}
```

This controller works specifically with order entities. This means that each of the interfaces supplied contains the Order class as the generic parameter. If you were to alter any of those declarations to use a different type, the operations provided by that interface would then require that type. For example, if you decided to change the delete interface parameter to IDelete<Customer>, the DeleteOrder method of the OrderController would complain that you were trying to delete an Order with a method that only accepts Customers. This is simply strong typing and generics in action.

Each method of this controller class requires a different interface to perform its function. For clarity, each method maps one-to-one with the operations on the respective interfaces. It is likely that this will not always be the case, of course.

As its name suggests, the OrderController deals only with Order classes. You can make use of the fact that the service interfaces are each generic by implementing a controller that is similarly generic. This is shown in Listing 10-16.

LISTING 10-16 An entity-generic version of the controller class requires an entity-generic version of each CRUD interface.

```
public class GenericController<TEntity>
{
    private readonly IRead<TEntity> reader;
    private readonly ISave<TEntity> saver;
    private readonly IDelete<TEntity> deleter;

    public GenericController(IRead<TEntity> entityReader, ISave<TEntity> entitySaver,
    IDelete<TEntity> entityDeleter)
    {
        reader = entityReader;
        saver = entitySaver;
        deleter = entityDeleter;
    }
```

```
        public void CreateEntity(TEntity entity)
        {
            saver.Save(entity);
        }

        public TEntity GetSingleEntity(Guid identity)
        {
            return reader.ReadOne(identity);
        }

        public void UpdateEntity(TEntity entity)
        {
            saver.Save(entity);
        }

        public void DeleteEntity(TEntity entity)
        {
            deleter.Delete(entity);
        }
}
```

There is little difference between this version of the controller and the prior one, but the impact on the amount of code that you might have to write could be significant. This controller can be instantiated to operate on any entity, and the service interfaces that are required are all forced to agree on the same operation. No longer can you supply different types for each one—such as ISave<Customer>, IRead<Order>, IDelete<LineItem>.

Either version of the controller can be created in much the same way. Listing 10-17 shows how you must instantiate each class that implements the required interfaces before passing them in to the controller's constructor.

LISTING 10-17 Creating the OrderController with separate instances of the dependencies.

```
static OrderController CreateSeparateServices()
{
    var reader = new Reader<Order>();
    var saver = new Saver<Order>();
    var deleter = new Deleter<Order>();

    return new OrderController(reader, saver, deleter);
}
```

By creating classes for each individual segregated interface, the segregation has, in effect, permeated the implementations. The key point to note is that the three parameters to the OrderController class—reader, saver, and deleter—are not just distinct instances, they are also distinct *types*.

Single implementation, single instance

A second approach to implementing segregated interfaces is to implement all of them in one single class. This might at first appear somewhat counterintuitive (after all, what is the point of segregating interfaces just to unify them all again in the implementation?), but there are advantages to this approach. Listing 10-18 shows all three interfaces in a single class.

LISTING 10-18 All interfaces can be implemented in a single class.

```
public class CreateReadUpdateDelete<TEntity> :
    IRead<TEntity>, ISave<TEntity>, IDelete<TEntity>
{
    public TEntity ReadOne(Guid identity)
    {
        return default(TEntity);
    }

    public IEnumerable<TEntity> ReadAll()
    {
        return new List<TEntity>();
    }

    public void Save(TEntity entity)
    {

    }

    public void Delete(TEntity entity)
    {

    }
}
```

Remember, clients are not aware of the existence of this class. At compile time, they are only aware of the individual interfaces, which it requires one by one. To the client, each interface will still only have the members declared on that interface, although the underlying implementation has other operations available. This is how interfaces are used for encapsulation and information hiding—they are analogous to a small window onto the implementing class, masking out what it does not allow the client to see.

Even with this change, the controller from the multiple implementation example is sufficient: it correctly asks for each interface as a separate constructor parameter. What needs to change is how you construct the controller and supply it with those parameters. This is shown in Listing 10-19.

LISTING 10-19 Although it might look unusual, this is an expected side effect of interface segregation.

```
public OrderController CreateSingleService()
{
    var crud = new CreateReadUpdateDelete<Order>();

    return new OrderController(crud, crud, crud);
}
```

First, you only need a single instance of the `CreateReadUpdateDelete` class. It implements all three interfaces, so it suffices for *all three constructor parameters*.

As unusual as that might look—passing in the same instance three times—it makes sense because each parameter requires a different facet of the class. This is a common side effect of the interface segregation principle.

Of the two variations explored, this single implementation for a suite of related—but segregated—interfaces is not as versatile as having multiple implementations. It is most commonly used for the leaf implementation of the interfaces—that is, the implementation that is neither decorator nor adapter. It is the one that does the actual work. The reason for this is that the context is the same across all implementations. Whether you are using NHibernate, ADO.NET, Entity Framework, or some other persistence framework, the leaf implementation is the one that directly uses these libraries. In each case—reading, saving, or deleting—that same library will be used to do the main work.

Some decorators and adapters also apply to the full suite of segregated interfaces, but it is more common for these to be implemented individually only on the appropriate interface.

The Interface Soup anti-pattern

A common mistake is to take the segregated interfaces and reunify them in an aggregate interface for some reason, as Listing 10-20 demonstrates. This is usually done to avoid the odd-looking multiple injection shown earlier.

LISTING 10-20 Interface segregation is wrongly circumvented when all interfaces are thrown together to form a soup.

```
interface IInterfaceSoupAntiPattern<TEntity> : IRead<TEntity>, ISave<TEntity>,
  IDelete<TEntity>
{
}
```

This creates an "interface soup" that is made from constituent interfaces but undermines the benefits of interface segregation. Implementers will again be required to provide implementations of all operations, so there is no scope for targeted decoration.

Splitting interfaces

The ability—or requirement—to decorate interfaces is only one reason that you might want to split a large interface into smaller constituents. However, I view this as a good enough reason for the practice.

Two more utilitarian reasons for interface segregation are based on client need and architectural design.

Client need

Different developers work on different parts of code. Therefore, it is likely that two or more developers will converge at some point, with one using the interface of another. Having detailed, step-by-step instructions for an interface is not only unlikely, but also impractical. Writing any code—especially code that is sufficiently unit tested—takes time. Writing extensive documentation is tedious and time consuming. Instead, it is better to program as defensively as is possible, to prevent other developers—or even yourself in the future—from inadvertently doing something they shouldn't with your interface.

It helps to remember that clients need only what they need. Monolithic interfaces tend to hand too much control to clients. Interfaces with many members allow clients to do more than they perhaps should, clouding the intent and misdirecting the focus.

Functionality

Listing 10-21 shows an interface that allows clients to interact with a user's settings—specifically, the user interface theme that the clients have set for the application. This example is surprising—it is an interface with a single property that, in this scenario, is *still* exposing too much to its client. How can you possibly segregate this further?

LISTING 10-21 The user settings interface allows access to the application's current theme.

```
public interface IUserSettings
{
    string Theme
    {
        get;
        set;
    }
}
```

First, see the implementation in Listing 10-22, which uses the ConfigurationManager class to read and write to the AppSettings section of the configuration files.

LISTING 10-22 An implementation that loads settings from the configuration file.

```
public class UserSettingsConfig : IUserSettings
{
    private const string ThemeSetting = "Theme";

    private readonly Configuration config;

    public UserSettingsConfig()
    {
        config = ConfigurationManager.OpenExeConfiguration(ConfigurationUserLevel.None);
    }

    public string Theme
    {
        get
        {
            return config.AppSettings.Settings[ThemeSetting].Value;
        }
        set
        {
            config.AppSettings.Settings[ThemeSetting].Value = value;
            config.Save();
            ConfigurationManager.RefreshSection("appSettings");
        }
    }
}
```

So far, so what? Well, there are two clients to this interface. One is focused only on *reading* the data, and the other is focused on *writing* the data. Herein lies the problem, as shown in Listing 10-23.

LISTING 10-23 The clients of the interface use the property for different purposes.

```
public class ReadingController
{
    private readonly IUserSettings settings;

    public ReadingController(IUserSettings settings)
    {
        this.settings = settings;
    }

    public string GetTheme()
    {
        return settings.Theme;
    }
}
```

```
// . . .
public class WritingController
{
    private readonly IUserSettings settings;

    public WritingController(IUserSettings settings)
    {
        this.settings = settings;
    }

    public void SetTheme(string theme)
    {
        settings.Theme = theme;
    }
}
```

As is to be expected, the ReadingController only uses the getter of the Theme property, whereas the WritingController only uses the setter of the Theme property. However, due to a lack of segregation, there is nothing to stop the writer from retrieving the theme, nor—which is more problematic—the reader from modifying the theme.

To be truly defensive and eliminate the possibility of interface misuse, you can segregate the read and write portions of the interface, as shown in Listing 10-24.

LISTING 10-24 The interface is split into two parts: one for reading the theme, and one for writing it.

```
public interface IUserSettingsReader
{
    string Theme
    {
        get;
    }
}
// . . .
public interface IUserSettingsWriter
{
    string Theme
    {
        set;
    }
}
```

Although this might look a little odd, it is valid C#. It is perhaps not unusual that an interface can dictate that implementers only supply a getter for a property, but it is slightly more unusual that it requires only a setter.

Each controller is now able to depend only on the interface that it truly requires. As Listing 10-25 shows, the ReadingController is paired with the IUserSettingsReader, and the Writing-Controller is paired with the IUserSettingsWriter.

LISTING 10-25 Each of the two controllers now depends only on the interface that it requires.

```
public class ReadingController
{
    private readonly IUserSettingsReader settings;

    public ReadingController(IUserSettingsReader settings)
    {
        this.settings = settings;
    }

    public string GetTheme()
    {
        return settings.Theme;
    }
}
// . . .
public class WritingController
{
    private readonly IUserSettingsWriter settings;

    public WritingController(IUserSettingsWriter settings)
    {
        this.settings = settings;
    }

    public void SetTheme(string theme)
    {
        settings.Theme = theme;
    }
}
```

Via interface segregation, you have prevented the reader from being able to write the user settings, and you have prevented the writer from being able to read the user settings. Developers are thus not able to accidently dilute the purpose of the controller by mistakenly performing an operation that they should not.

The implementing class, which uses the ConfigurationManager, changes only very subtly, as shown in Listing 10-26.

LISTING 10-26 The UsersSettingsConfig class now implements both interfaces, but clients are unaware.

```
public class UserSettingsConfig : IUserSettingsReader, IUserSettingsWriter
{
    private const string ThemeSetting = "Theme";

    private readonly Configuration config;
```

```
    public UserSettingsConfig()
    {
        config = ConfigurationManager.OpenExeConfiguration(ConfigurationUserLevel.None);
    }

    public string Theme
    {
        get
        {
            return config.AppSettings.Settings[ThemeSetting].Value;
        }
        set
        {
            config.AppSettings.Settings[ThemeSetting].Value = value;
            config.Save();
            ConfigurationManager.RefreshSection("appSettings");
        }
    }
}
```

Other than in the fact that it inherits from both reader and writer interfaces, this class is identical to the previous version. Remember that this same implementation can easily be passed to both the `ReadingController` and the `WritingController`, yet the window provided by the interface means that the `set` and `get` operations, respectively, will not be available.

The requirement that some clients should be able to read without writing is particularly likely. The other scenario, where writers are not allowed to read, is less likely. In this case, instead of total segregation, you can segregate and inherit the interfaces, as shown in Listing 10-27.

LISTING 10-27 Now using methods, the writer inherits from the reader.

```
public interface IUserSettingsReader
{
    string GetTheme();
}
// . . .
public interface IUserSettingsWriter : IUserSettingsReader
{
    void SetTheme(string theme);
}
```

To do this, the `Theme` property had to be converted to `GetTheme` and `SetTheme` methods. This is because the language doesn't cleanly support property inheritance. The `Theme` property is present on both interfaces. Although classes can cleanly implement the `get` and `set` parts of an interface from two different interfaces, this is not the case with interface inheritance. When property names clash through interface inheritance, the compiler warns that the base class property is *hidden* by the subclass property. This would not achieve the result that you want, and the compiler's suggestion that you replace the base class property with the new keyword is not a solution, either—the getter would still not be inherited.

Instead, you can change from properties to methods with the same semantic function. The GetTheme method is the same as Theme.get, and the SetTheme method is the same as Theme.set. Now inheritance works as expected—implementers and clients of the reader interface will only have access to the GetTheme method, and implementers and clients of the writer interface will have access to both the GetTheme and SetTheme methods. Additionally, any implementation of the IUser-SettingsWriter interface is *also* an implementation of the IUserSettingsReader interface.

Listing 10-28 shows a change to the writing controller: it first checks whether the theme has been changed before it tries to set a new theme. This is now acceptable because the user settings writer service is also the user settings reader service. In this case, the two interfaces do not need to be supplied separately to be used.

LISTING 10-28 The writing controller has access to both the getter and setter through one interface.

```
public class WritingController
{
    private readonly IUserSettingsWriter settings;

    public WritingController(IUserSettingsWriter settings)
    {
        this.settings = settings;
    }

    public void SetTheme(string theme)
    {
        if (settings.GetTheme() != theme)
        {
            settings.SetTheme(theme);
        }
    }
}
```

Authorization

Another example of segregation by client need is when a set of operations is only available when the application is in a specific state. For example, the operations that a user can perform are typically different depending on whether that user is logged in or not.

The IUnauthorized interface shown in Listing 10-29 contains operations that can be done by an anonymous, unauthenticated user.

LISTING 10-29 This interface contains only operations that anonymous users can perform.

```
public interface IUnauthorized
{
    IAuthorized Login(string username, string password);

    void RequestPasswordReminder(string emailAddress);
}
```

Note that the Login method returns an interface. It is returned only when the credentials are correct, and it allows clients to perform authorized actions, as shown in Listing 10-30.

LISTING 10-30 After logging in, the user will have access to privileged operations.

```
public interface IAuthorized
{
    void ChangePassword(string oldPassword, string newPassword);

    void AddToBasket(Guid itemID);

    void Checkout();

    void Logout();
}
```

The operations on this interface are available only to a user who has entered his or her credentials and is logged in as authenticated.

Segregating interfaces by client need prevents programmers from doing something they should not. In this case, it prevents them from executing a privileged action with an anonymous user. Of course, there are ways around this, but it is hoped that developers will realize that they are making a very fundamental change to the application to do something that they should not.

Architectural need

Another driver of the interface segregation principle is architectural design. High-level decisions can have a large impact on the low-level organization of the code.

In this example, the decision has been made to have an asymmetric architecture. Like the read/ write split shown earlier, the IPersistence interface shown in Listing 10-31 contains a combination of queries and commands.

LISTING 10-31 This persistence-layer interface contains both commands and queries.

```
public interface IPersistence
{
    IEnumerable<Entity> GetAll();

    Item GetByID(Guid identity);

    IEnumerable<Entity> FindByCriteria(string criteria);

    void Save(Entity entity);

    void Delete(Entity entity);
}
```

The asymmetric architecture that this interface is part of is specifically CQRS: Command/Query Responsibility Segregation. The recurrence of the word *segregation* is no accident here, because this architectural pattern is about to cause you to perform some interface segregation.

A first implementation of the `IPersistence` interface is shown in Listing 10-32.

LISTING 10-32 When commands and queries are handled asymmetrically, the implementation is muddled.

```
public class Persistence : IPersistence
{
    private readonly ISession session;
    private readonly MongoDatabase mongo;

    public Persistence(ISession session, MongoDatabase mongo)
    {
        this.session = session;
        this.mongo = mongo;
    }

    public IEnumerable<Entity> GetAll()
    {
        return mongo.GetCollection<Entity>("entities").FindAll();
    }

    public Entity GetByID(Guid identity)
    {
        return mongo.GetCollection<Entity>("entities").FindOneById(identity.ToBson());
    }

    public IEnumerable<Entity> FindByCriteria(string criteria)
    {
        var query = BsonSerializer.Deserialize<QueryDocument>(criteria);
        return mongo.GetCollection<Entity>("entities").Find(query);
    }

    public void Save(Entity entity)
    {
        using(var transaction = session.BeginTransaction())
        {
            session.Save(entity);

            transaction.Commit();
        }
    }

    public void Delete(Entity entity)
    {
        using(var transaction = session.BeginTransaction())
        {
            session.Delete(entity);

            transaction.Commit();
        }
    }
}
```

There are two very different dependencies here: NHibernate is used for commands, and MongoDB is used for queries. The former is an Object/Relational Mapper used here for storing a domain model. The latter is a document storage library used here for fast querying. This class has two disparate dependencies and therefore two reasons to change. With such different dependencies, it is likely that their respective decorators will also be different. Rather than being split into very small operations, as the entire CRUD interface was earlier in this chapter, this interface will only be split into two parts: commands and queries. Figure 10-3 shows a UML class diagram of how this will be orchestrated.

With the commands and queries split between two interfaces, the implementations can depend on different packages. The commands implementation will depend only on NHibernate, and the queries implementation will depend only on MongoDB.

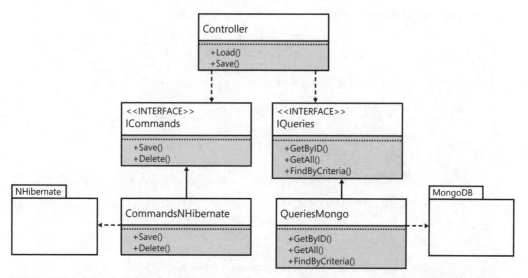

FIGURE 10-3 Splitting interfaces by architectural need allows implementations to have very different dependencies.

Ideally, these two implementations will not only be different classes, but those classes will reside in different packages—assemblies—too. If not, the problem is only partially alleviated because it will be impossible to reuse one implementation without depending on the other, plus the chain of dependencies—the NHibernate or Mongo libraries—that comes with it.

Listing 10-33 shows the interfaces after they have been split. The two can now be implemented separately.

LISTING 10-33 The interface has been split into query and command methods.

```
public interface IPersistenceQueries
{
    IEnumerable<Item> GetAll();

    Item GetByID(Guid identity);

    IEnumerable<Item> FindByCriteria(string criteria);
}
```

```
// . . .
public interface IPersistenceCommands
{
    void Save(Item item);

    void Delete(Item item);
}
```

As shown in Listing 10-34, the queries class is the same implementation as before, except for the commands—and the dependency on NHibernate—being completely excised.

LISTING 10-34 The query implementation depends only on MongoDB.

```
public class PersistenceQueries : IPersistenceQueries
{
    private readonly MongoDatabase mongo;

    public Persistence(MongoDatabase mongo)
    {
        this.mongo = mongo;
    }

    public IEnumerable<Item> GetAll()
    {
        return mongo.GetCollection<Item>("items").FindAll();
    }

    public Item GetByID(Guid identity)
    {
        return mongo.GetCollection<Item>("items").FindOneById(identity.ToBson());
    }

    public IEnumerable<Item> FindByCriteria(string criteria)
    {
        var query = BsonSerializer.Deserialize<QueryDocument>(criteria);
        return mongo.GetCollection<Item>("Items").Find(query);
    }
}
```

Similarly, the commands class contains no queries, nor any reference to MongoDB, as shown in Listing 10-35.

LISTING 10-35 The command implementation depends only on NHibernate.

```
public class PersistenceCommands : IPersistenceCommands
{
    private readonly ISession session;
    public PersistenceCommands(ISession session)
```

```
    {
        this.session = session;
    }

    public void Save(Item item)
    {
        using(var transaction = session.BeginTransaction())
        {
            session.Save(item);

            transaction.Commit();
        }
    }

    public void Delete(Item item)
    {
        using(var transaction = session.BeginTransaction())
        {
            session.Delete(item);

            transaction.Commit();
        }
    }
}
```

Single-method interfaces

Interface segregation taken to its logical conclusion results in very small interfaces. The smaller the interface, the more versatile it becomes. Such interfaces have analogies in the framework: Action, Func, and Predicate. However, delegates are not as versatile as interfaces. Though delegates certainly have their uses, the fact that interfaces can be decorated, adapted, and composed in many ways sets them apart. Because interfaces must be implemented, there can also be extra context provided through other interfaces implemented on the same class, or via constructor parameters.

The simplest interface available has a single method. The simplest method available accepts no parameters and returns no value, as shown in Listing 10-36.

LISTING 10-36 ITask is the simplest interface possible.

```
public interface ITask
{
    void Do();
}
```

This interface is extremely decoratable. Because it returns no value, it can even have an asynchronous fire-and-forget decorator. It can be used whenever a client needs to send a message but does not have any context to provide it, nor does it require any response to be returned.

A step up from this is the action interface, which is analogous to the `Action` delegate in the framework. It takes a generic parameter that dictates the type of its context. The `IAction` interface is shown in Listing 10-37.

LISTING 10-37 The `IAction` interface adds a context parameter.

```
public interface IAction<TContext>
{
    void Do(TContext context);
}
```

This is only slightly more complex than the task. If you introduce a return value, instead of a parameter, you create a function, as shown in Listing 10-38.

LISTING 10-38 `IFunction` interfaces have return values.

```
public interface IFunction<TReturn>
{
    TReturn Do();
}
```

A further specialization of this interface is to require that the function return a Boolean value. This creates a predicate, as shown in Listing 10-39.

LISTING 10-39 `IPredicate` is a function that returns a Boolean value.

```
public interface IPredicate
{
    bool Test();
}
```

The predicate can be used to encapsulate a branching test, such as an `if` statement or the clause of a loop.

Although these interfaces look unassuming, a lot can be achieved by decorating, adapting, and composing several different instances of these interfaces.

Conclusion

This chapter has been dedicated to the art of good interface design. Too often, interfaces are large facades behind which huge subsystems are hidden. At a certain critical mass, interfaces lose the adaptability that makes them so fundamental to developing SOLID code.

There are plenty of reasons why interfaces should be segregated—to aid decoration, to hide functionality from clients, as self-documentation for other developers, or as a side effect of architectural design. Whatever the reason, it is a technique that should be kept at the forefront of your mind whenever you are creating an interface. As with most programming tools, it is easier to start out on the right path than to go back and heavily refactor.

Dependency inversion

After completing this chapter, you will be able to

- Identify the Entourage anti-pattern and work to replace it.

- Apply the Stairway pattern to uphold the dependency inversion principle.

- Design better abstractions.

The dependency inversion principle states:

- High-level modules should not depend on low-level modules. Both should depend on abstractions.

- Abstractions should not depend on details. Details should depend on abstractions.

In practice, dependency inversion introduces abstractions in the form of interfaces that are depended on by client code and that are depended on by implementers.

Often, code does not use enough modularity at the package level to separate dependency chains, so this chapter will address the Entourage anti-pattern and introduce a better solution to package-level modularity via the Stairway pattern.

In this chapter, I also present a method of identifying meaningful and long-lived abstractions that prevents leaky abstractions and the overuse of interfaces. You should exercise diligent dependency management even above the solution level by deploying multiple, single-purpose services that can be composed, or re-composed, to fulfil a use case.

Structuring dependencies

Splitting classes and interfaces into projects is a good practice, but the way that these dependencies are structured can have a profound effect on the quality of your solution's modularity. Too often, dependencies are not structured correctly and follow the Entourage anti-pattern, which does not properly separate interfaces and their implementations.

Instead, projects should be structured in such a way as to follow the Stairway pattern, which will correctly separate interfaces, implementations, and client code. This section presents the problems introduced by the Entourage anti-pattern and how they are solved by applying the Stairway pattern.

The Entourage anti-pattern

The *Entourage anti-pattern* gets its name from the fact that even though you think you are asking for just one simple thing, it brings along all of its friends. This is much like music or film stars who are followed by hangers-on and moochers: their entourage. It is a name that I have created to best describe undesirable dependency management.

The Entourage anti-pattern is a common mistake that is made when developers explain programming to an interface. Rather than providing a full solution, the demonstration commonly stops short of saying, unequivocally, that interfaces and their implementations *should not be in the same assembly*.

The Unified Modeling Language (UML) diagram in Figure 11-1 shows how the `AccountController` example is organized at the package level. The `AccountController` depends on the `ISecurityService` interface, which is implemented by the `SecurityService` class. The diagram also shows the packages—in the .NET Framework, these are assemblies or Microsoft Visual Studio projects—that contain each entity. This is an example of the Entourage anti-pattern: the implementation of an interface in the same assembly as the interface itself. The `SecurityService` should not be in the same assembly as the `ISecurityService` interface that it implements.

FIGURE 11-1 The `AccountController` assembly depends on the `Services` assembly.

You have already learned in Chapter 3, "Dependencies and layering," that the `SecurityService` class has some dependencies of its own, and how the chain of dependencies results in implicit dependencies from client to client. The package diagram in Figure 11-2 displays the full extent of the Entourage problem.

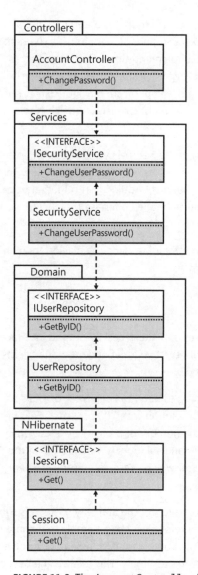

FIGURE 11-2 The AccountController is still at the mercy of too many implementations.

If you build the Controllers project in isolation, you will still find NHibernate in the bin/ directory, indicating that it is still an implicit dependency. Although you have made excellent steps to separate the AccountController *class* from any unnecessary dependencies, it is still not loosely coupled from the implementations in each dependent *assembly*.

There are two problems caused by this anti-pattern. The first issue is that of programmer discipline. You need the interfaces in each of the packages—`Services`, `Domain`, and `NHibernate`—to be marked as `public`. However, you also need the concrete classes—the implementations—to be marked as `public` to make them available for construction at some point (just not inside the client classes). This means that there is nothing to stop an undisciplined or unaware developer from making a direct reference to the implementation. There is a temptation to cut corners and just call `new` on the class to get an instance of it.

Second, what happens if you create a new implementation of the `SecurityService` that, instead of depending on a domain model that is persisted by using NHibernate, uses a third-party service bus, such as `NServiceBus`, to send a command message to a handler? Adding it into the `Services` assembly creates yet another dependency, leading to a bloated, fragile codebase that will be very difficult to adapt to new requirements.

It is a general rule that implementations should be split from their interfaces by placing them in separate assemblies. For this, you can use the Stairway pattern.

The Stairway pattern

The Stairway pattern is the correct way to organize your classes and interfaces. By putting interfaces and their implementations in different assemblies, you can vary the two independently, and clients only need to make a single reference—to the interface assembly.

You might be thinking, "But how many assemblies am I going to need to keep track of? If I split every interface and class into its own assembly, I would have a solution with 200 projects!" Fear not, because applying the Stairway pattern should only increase the number of projects by a few while giving you the benefit of a well-organized and easy-to-understand solution. It is possible that the number of overall projects will *decrease* when you apply the Stairway pattern, if the projects were particularly badly arranged before.

The running example of the `AccountController`, refactored to use the Stairway pattern, is shown in Figure 11-3. Each implementation—that is, each class—only references the assembly that contains the interface on which it is dependent. It does not reference the implementation assembly, not even implicitly. Each implementation class *also* references its interface's assembly. This really is the best of all worlds: interfaces without any dependencies, client code without any implicit dependencies, and implementations that continue the pattern by depending only on other interface assemblies.

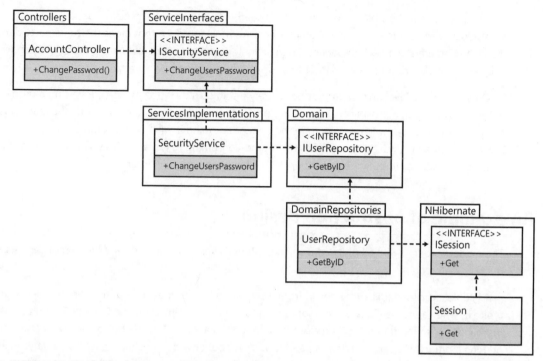

FIGURE 11-3 The Stairway pattern is aptly named.

I now want to focus on one of those benefits in greater detail: interfaces should not have any external dependencies. As far as possible, this should always be adhered to. Interfaces should not have methods or properties that expose any data objects or classes defined in third-party references. Although they can, and certainly will, need to depend on classes and data types from other projects in the solution and common .NET Framework libraries, a reference to infrastructural entities should be avoided. Third-party libraries are commonly used for infrastructure purposes. Even the interfaces from libraries such as Log4Net, NHibernate, and MongoDB are infrastructural dependencies that will tie your interfaces to a specific implementation. This is because those libraries are packaged by using the Entourage anti-pattern, rather than the Stairway pattern. They each provide a single assembly that contains both the interface you *want* to depend on and the implementation that you *do not* want to depend on.

To get around this problem, you can refer instead to your own interfaces for logging, domain persistence, and document storage. You can write a simple interface that hides the third-party dependency behind a first-party dependency. Then, if you ever need to replace the third-party dependency, you can do so by writing a new adapter to your interface for the new library.

On a pragmatic level, this might not be entirely feasible. In instances where converting a third-party dependency to a first-party dependency presents an inordinate amount of work, the team must acknowledge that they will have to retain the dependency and it will become omnipresent. If the library is outgrown, it will be more difficult and time-consuming to replace. This sort of concession is commonly made for *frameworks*, which are much larger than simple libraries.

An example of abstraction design

The modern world—with all of its conveniences, time-savers, cost-cutters, and labor-reducers—is built on *abstractions*.

Multiple layers of detail are removed from view, not to be worried about until absolutely necessary—typically, when a problem arises. Even something as simple as a retractable pen reduces a sophisticated mechanism of spring tension and precision cam motion to a mere click of a button. In the normal course of using a retractable pen, you do not need to worry about how this mechanism works. What you see is the abstraction of that complexity: a push button and its current state. Either the ballpoint is retracted or the ballpoint is revealed. That is, you do not need to know about the inner workings unless you take apart your pen and cannot put it back together again!

Similarly, all of computing is built on abstraction. Computers are a multiplicity of abstractions, all working in harmony to present you with some consistent interfaces like the application windows on your monitor screen and the keyboard, mouse, or touchscreen for interactive input. A network is a simple abstraction in that we talk of ports, IP addresses, and DNS resolution; but that is just the surface. That is what you see and interact with given your requirements and level of expertise. A more modal user might think only in website URLs and email addresses. A network technician must consider more detailed implementation concerns like gateways, routing tables, subnet masks, and transport protocols.

It's all a complex fractal that is best reasoned about with a certain useful level of abstraction.

Software development is the same. When you write code, you feed binary instructions to a CPU so that it does your bidding. But that low level of abstraction does not provide you with the requisite tools to achieve your lofty goals. Instead, layers and layers of abstraction have been added to spare you from the minutiae. In C#, you don't even worry about memory management. Perhaps not as much as you should, but certainly not as much as your C++ colleagues must. Even in C++, there are libraries that abstract the management of memory references so that developers need worry less about the details and more about productivity.

Hopefully, you get the idea that abstraction is useful. This section presents an example that demonstrates a poor abstraction and the steps taken to improve it.

Abstractions

Before this chapter works through an example of creating an abstraction, some context is required to explain the problem domain.

In this example, you are working on computer-aided measurement software that uses a variety of sensors to gain real-world measurements of tangible, physical items. This forms the quality assurance phase of a manufacturing process: if some measured items are outside of a specified tolerance level, the process should indicate that the item is defective.

Although this project is in the early stages, some work has been done to communicate with some of the different types of sensor. So far, there are classes to represent a high-resolution camera that can capture images, a laser that can determine three-dimensional height, and a touch-probe that can detect awkward shapes and forms.

Concretions

The application has a command-line interface through which the user can select a tool, issue commands to the tool, and take a measurement.

At this point in the project, it occurs to you that the tools—and the classes that represent them in code—are similar, but not similar enough to make any abstraction appear obvious.

Tip The code listings for this section are quite long and have been necessarily abridged to save trees. See the accompanying GitHub repository for a full code listing at *www.github.com /AdaptiveCode/AdaptiveCode*.

Listing 11-1 shows the entry point to the application, which accepts commands from the user and forwards any parameters to a handler method.

LISTING 11-1 Interactive command-line interfaces often have a switchboard of command handlers like this.

```
class Program
{
    private delegate void CommandHandler(IEnumerable<string> parameters);
    private Sensor CurrentSensor;

    static void Main(string[] args)
    {
        while (true)
        {
            Console.Write("> ");
            var input = Console.ReadLine() ?? string.Empty;
            var tokens = input.Split(' ');

            if (tokens.Length < 1)
```

```
        {
            Console.WriteLine("Please supply a command");
            continue;
        }

        var command = tokens.First();
        var parameters = tokens.Skip(1);

        var handlers = new Dictionary<string, CommandHandler>
        {
            {"select", SelectTool},
            {"move", Move},
            {"zoom", Zoom},
            {"capture-image", CaptureImage},
            {"measure-height", MeasureHeight},
            {"pitch", Pitch},
            {"roll", Roll},
            {"raise", Raise},
            {"lower", Lower},
            {"get-pressure", GetPressure},
            {"quit", Quit}
        };

        if (!handlers.ContainsKey(command))
        {
            Console.WriteLine($"Unrecognized command: {command}");
        }
        else
        {
            handlers[command].Invoke(parameters);
        }
    }
}
// . . .
}
```

From this code, it is clear that adding a new command is quite simple: implement a new method that matches the CommandHandler delegate and add a command mapping to the handlers dictionary.

Listing 11-2 shows the command handler for the Zoom method, which is available for only the camera sensor.

LISTING 11-2 Command handlers such as the Zoom method must type-sniff for supported classes.

```
private static void Zoom(IEnumerable<string> parameters)
{
    var camera = CurrentSensor as Camera;
    if (camera != null)
    {
        float level;
        if (float.TryParse(obj.FirstOrDefault(), out level))
```

```
        {
            camera.Zoom(level);
        }
        else
        {
            Console.WriteLine(
                "Zooming camera requires a floating-point parameter (eg: 1.5)");
        }
    }
    else
    {
        Console.WriteLine("Must select camera to capture an image!");
    }
}
```

This is indicative of most of the command handlers in the application. The process is:

1. Ensure that the currently selected sensor is a Camera by using type-sniffing.

2. Attempt to validate the required parameters of the command.

3. Send the specific command message to the specific sensor type.

Listing 11-3 shows the implementation of the Camera sensor and its Sensor base class. It does not do much, because this is example code. Pay attention to the exposed public methods, rather than their implementation, because that is of most interest in this example.

LISTING 11-3 The abstract Sensor class and the Camera implementation.

```
public abstract class Sensor
{
    protected readonly string Name;
    protected float X, Y;

    protected Sensor(string name)
    {
        Name = name;
    }

    public virtual void Move(float x, float y)
    {
        X += x;
        Y += y;
    }
}
// . . .
public class Camera : Sensor
{
    private float _zoomLevel;

    public Camera() : base("camera") { }
```

```
        public void Zoom(float level) => _zoomLevel = level;

        public Image Capture()
        {
            return new Bitmap(100, 100);
        }
    }
```

All three of the sensors (Camera, Laser, and TouchProbe) inherit from Sensor, which implies that all sensors are mobile. Unfortunately, as the product owner has just informed you, this is not necessarily true. The company's new heat-detection sensor is static and does not move. If you were to implement a new HeatDetector class as shown in Listing 11-4, you would break the Liskov substitutability principle (see Chapter 9, "The Liskov substitution principle"). The principle states that clients must be able to treat any implementation of a base type in the same manner, without special exceptions.

LISTING 11-4 A hypothetical HeatDetector that would not support the Move method.

```
public class HeatDetector : Sensor
{
    public virtual void Move(float x, float y)
    {
        throw new NotImplementedException("Heat detectors are static!");
    }
}
```

Here are some of the problems with this current design:

- Not all sensors are movable, so the Sensor base class is a premature abstraction.

- The command switchboard depends directly on all of the concretions of the Sensor class: it has intimate knowledge of the Camera, Laser, and TouchProbe classes.

- Unless every sensor exhibits a certain behavior, the command switchboard must use type-sniffing and casting to send messages.

Instead, the following requirements should be met:

- Adding a new sensor type should be much simpler, without type-sniffing.

- No assumptions should be made about the behavior of any particular sensor beyond having an identifying name.

The trouble with "extract interface"

A naive first attempt at creating an abstraction might use a refactoring tool to automatically "extract interface" on each of the sensors, but this is perilous.

None of the sensors exhibit the same method signatures other than the Move method, so three interfaces would be created: ICamera, ILaser, and ITouchProbe, each of which maps to its respective implementation in a 1:1 ratio.

This is dissatisfying because it costs some indirection, which decreases comprehensibility, and it doesn't give any benefits in return.

Instead, what you want to do is to identify the cohesive behaviors between the sensors and capture their *capabilities*.

Abstracting capabilities

Let's look in more detail at the Laser and TouchProbe classes, shown in Listing 11-5.

LISTING 11-5 The Laser and TouchProbe sensors have their own specific commands.

```
public class Laser : Sensor
{
    public Laser() : base("laser") { }

    public float Measure()
    {
        return 0f;
    }
}
// . . .
public class TouchProbe : Sensor
{
    private float _pitch, _roll;
    private float _height;

    public TouchProbe() : base("name")
    {
    }

    public void Pitch(float pitch)
    {
        _pitch += pitch;
    }

    public void Roll(float roll)
    {
        _roll += roll;
    }
```

```
    public void Raise(float height)
    {
        _height += height;
    }

    public void Lower(float height)
    {
        _height -= height;
    }

    public PoundsPerSquareInch GetPressure()
    {
        return new PoundsPerSquareInch(13.2f);
    }
}

public struct PoundsPerSquareInch
{
    public PoundsPerSquareInch(float value)
    {
        Value = value;
    }

    public float Value { get; private set; }
}
```

Between the Camera, Laser, and TouchProbe classes, there is not a lot of commonality in the method naming. However, if you look closely, there is commonality as far as *behavior* is concerned. For example, the Camera class has Zoom functionality, whereas the TouchProbe has Raise and Lower methods. Could these perhaps be treated as equivalents? They both represent movement in the z-axis, so you could unify this behavior and model it as an adjustable height.

Similarly, all of the current sensors are movable in an xy plane, so this could be captured as another capability. The TouchProbe is rotatable. All sensors are measurable.

Consider the words used here: *adjustable, movable, rotatable, measurable*. These are all attributive adjectives that end in *-able* (although *-ible* is also acceptable). The root of each of these words is a verb: *adjust, move, rotate, measure*. These are the behaviors you expect of your sensors. From here, you can extract interfaces that map to capabilities of a sensor, as shown in Listing 11-6.

LISTING 11-6 Extracted interfaces that represent sensor capabilities.

```
public interface IMovable
{
    void Move(float x, float y);
}
// . . .
public interface IRotatable
```

```
{
    void Pitch(float pitch);
    void Roll(float roll);
}
// . . .
public interface IHeightAdjustable
{
    void Raise(float height);
    void Lower(float height);
}
```

These are all of the interfaces for the commands that are supported by the sensors. Querying for a sensor's measurement will take an extra step to create an abstraction, so that will be covered later.

Instead of implementing one large ISensor interface and putting the full union of all sensor commands and queries in there, this allows the creation of a new sensor that will have an intersection of useful capabilities. However, there is still some commonality between all sensors, which is captured in the ISensor interface shown in Listing 11-7.

LISTING 11-7 A unifying interface that all sensors must implement.

```
public interface ISensor
{
    string GetName();
}
```

All sensors have a readable name. This also provides a basis from which you can make use of polymorphism in the client.

Abstracting sealed code

In this example, the code is *redesigned* so that both the sensor classes and the command-line client of the sensors are changed to use the new abstraction. However, it is not always possible to change the target classes. Sometimes these classes are sealed, or they are in a third-party assembly.

In those cases, the abstraction is still possible, but it requires intermediate implementations of the new interfaces: adapters. (See "The Adapter pattern" in Chapter 4, "Interfaces and design patterns.")

Listing 11-8 shows the Camera class after the redesign.

LISTING 11-8 The Camera class opts in to all capabilities that it supports.

```
public class Camera : ISensor, IMovable, IHeightAdjustable
{
    private float _zoomLevel;
    private float _x, _y;

    public Image Capture()
    {
        return new Bitmap(100, 100);
    }

    public string GetName()
    {
        return "camera";
    }

    public void Raise(float height)
    {
        _zoomLevel += height;
    }

    public void Lower(float height)
    {
        _zoomLevel -= height;
    }

    public void Move(float x, float y)
    {
        _x += x;
        _y += y;
    }
}
```

The Camera class implements the set of interfaces that best describe its capabilities. If a new capability was introduced that the camera could fulfil, this class would opt in to the new interface and provide an implementation.

Note that the Zoom method has been replaced with the Raise and Lower methods from the IAdjustableHeight interface, but that the private state that is being manipulated is the zoom level.

Listing 11-9 shows the Laser class after applying the interfaces.

LISTING 11-9 The Laser class supports only movement at this point in time.

```
public class Laser : ISensor, IMovable
{
    private float _x, _y;

    public float Measure()
    {
        return 0f;
    }

    public string GetName()
    {
        return "laser";
    }

    public void Move(float x, float y)
    {
        _x += x;
        _y += y;
    }
}
```

The laser fulfils the criteria of being a sensor, but its only other capability is that it is movable. Note that neither the Camera nor the Laser classes have altered their measurement queries yet. That will be addressed soon.

The final sensor, the TouchProbe, is shown in Listing 11-10.

LISTING 11-10 The TouchProbe class opts in to all of the sensor capabilities.

```
public class TouchProbe : ISensor, IMovable, IRotatable, IHeightAdjustable
{
    private float _x, _y;
    private float _pitch;
    private float _roll;
    private float _height;

    public PoundsPerSquareInch GetPressure()
    {
        return new PoundsPerSquareInch(13.2f);
    }
```

```
public string GetName()
{
    return "touchprobe";
}

public void Move(float x, float y)
{
    _x += x;
    _y += y;
}

public void Pitch(float pitch)
{
    _pitch += pitch;
}

public void Roll(float roll)
{
    _roll += roll;
}

public void Raise(float height)
{
    _height += height;
}

public void Lower(float height)
{
    _height -= height;
}
}
```

The `IMovable` and `IAdjustableHeight` interfaces are reused abstractions, which is a requirement of identifying a good abstraction. The `IRotatable` interface is used only once, though. This is indicative that it is probably not the greatest abstraction ever devised—and so it proves when subjected to even shallow scrutiny.

Rotation can occur along *three* axes, not just two. Rotation around the x, y, and z axes is called *roll*, *pitch*, and *yaw*, respectively. This is not fully represented by the `IRotatable` interface: yaw rotation is missing. But do you need it? If nothing requires such a rotation, there is no benefit in representing a spurious capability.

The improved client

There was a definite purpose to undertaking this endeavor: to improve the client code and make it more resilient to the kind of change that you *can* predict. In this case, the prediction is that there are enough different sensors that all share enough commonality that an abstraction would improve code comprehensibility and extensibility. Listing 11-11 shows the refactored command switchboard.

LISTING 11-11 The command-handler switchboard has been simplified and will change less frequently.

```csharp
class Program
{
    private delegate void CommandHandler(IEnumerable<string> parameters);
    private static ISensor CurrentSensor;

    static void Main(string[] args)
    {
        while (true)
        {
            Console.Write("> ");
            var input = Console.ReadLine() ?? string.Empty;
            var tokens = input.Split(' ');

            if (tokens.Length < 1)
            {
                Console.WriteLine("Please supply a command");
                continue;
            }

            var command = tokens.First();
            var parameters = tokens.Skip(1);

            var handlers = new Dictionary<string, CommandHandler>
            {
                {"select", SelectTool},
                {"move", Move},
                {"measure", Measure},
                {"rotate", Rotate},
                {"adjust-height", AdjustHeight},
                {"quit", Quit}
            };

            if (!handlers.ContainsKey(command))
            {
                Console.WriteLine($"Unrecognized command: {command}");
            }
            else
            {
                handlers[command].Invoke(parameters);
            }
        }
    }
    // . . .
}
```

The main noticeable difference is that the switchboard is shorter; there are fewer commands and handlers. In fact, there is a command handler for each capability, as shown in Table 11-1.

TABLE 11-1 Commands have names and handlers and map to capability interfaces

Command name	Command handler	Capability interface
move	Move	IMovable
measure	Measure	IMeasurable
rotate	Rotate	IRotatable
adjust height	AdjustHeight	IHeightAdjustable

This code is more self-documenting than the original. The relationship between the command name, handler method name, and interface name is much more intuitive, and someone new approaching the code should be able to orient themselves with greater ease.

The handlers have also changed. Listing 11-12 shows the AdjustHeight handler, which is analogous to the old Zoom command, but this is now applicable to any sensor that implements IHeightAdjustable.

LISTING 11-12 Each command handler sniffs for the capability that it requires.

```
private static void AdjustHeight(IEnumerable<string> parameters)
{
    var heightAdjustableSensor = CurrentSensor as IHeightAdjustable;
    if (heightAdjustableSensor == null)
    {
        Console.WriteLine(
            $"Current sensor '{CurrentSensor.GetName()}' is not height adjustable");
        return;
    }

    float height;
    if (obj.Count() >= 2 &&
        float.TryParse(obj.Skip(1).FirstOrDefault(), out height))
    {
        var direction = obj.FirstOrDefault();
        switch (direction)
        {
            case "raise":
            {
                heightAdjustableSensor.Raise(height);
                break;
            }
            case "lower":
            {
                heightAdjustableSensor.Lower(height);
                break;
            }
            default:
            {
                Console.WriteLine(
```

```
              "First parameter to height adjustment must be 'raise' or 'lower'");
            break;
        }
    }
}
else
{
    Console.WriteLine(
"Height adjustment requires two parameters: 'raise'/'lower' and height (eg: 1.5f)");
    }
}
```

Instead of type-sniffing for concretions, this code is sniffing for *capabilities* represented by interfaces. If the currently selected sensor implements the `IHeightAdjustable` interface, this command is valid for this sensor and you can send a message to the sensor.

The benefit of this abstraction bears repeating:

If a new sensor is created and it implements the requisite interfaces, the client can interact with it without requiring changes.

Abstracting queries

The abstractions created so far only cover the commands that are supported by the sensors, not the queries. Listing 11-13 shows the three queries for retrieving a measurement from each of the sensors.

LISTING 11-13 The queries for the current measurement all return disparate types.

```
public Image Capture()
{
    return new Bitmap(100, 100);
}
// . . .
public float Measure()
{
    return 0f;
}
// . . .
public PoundsPerSquareInch GetPressure()
{
    return new PoundsPerSquareInch(13.2f);
}
```

These three method signatures have little in common, but they all represent the same capability: that the sensor is measurable. But what would the unifying behavior inside an `IMeasurable` interface look like?

Stating the client code's requirements might help. Given a sensor, you want to retrieve its current measurement so that you can output it to the console.

Instead of retrieving state and then using it as output, you could ask each sensor to write to the console itself. But, instead of writing to the console directly, it would be a better abstraction to have the sensors write to something more extensible and reusable. In this case, you could ask the sensors to write their measurement to a `Stream`. This would allow you to supply a console output stream, but you would also be able to supply an `HttpResponse.OutputStream`, a `MemoryStream`, or a `FileStream`. However, under these circumstances, you do not want the bytes of the sensor's state to be written; you want a string representation. In this case, a `TextWriter` is a better choice.

In effect, you are replacing a query that requests state and writes it to an output stream with a command that writes directly to the output stream. Listing 11-14 shows the `IMeasurable` interface.

LISTING 11-14 Sensors that can be measured must write their state to a TextWriter.

```
public interface IMeasurable
{
    void WriteMeasurement(TextWriter writer);
}
```

The `WriteMeasurement` method returns void, so it is no longer a query, but a command. This can be implemented by all of the sensors, as shown in Listing 11-15.

LISTING 11-15 The command handler for measurement requires that a sensor implement IMeasurable.

```
private static void Measure(IEnumerable<string> parameters)
{
    var measurableSensor = CurrentSensor as IMeasurable;
    if (measurableSensor == null)
    {
        Console.WriteLine("Current sensor is not measurable!");
        return;
    }

    measurableSensor.WriteMeasurement(Console.Out);
}
```

As usual, you must cast the current sensor to determine whether it is capable of writing its own measurement. If it is, you can pass in the `Console.Out` property to the `WriteMeasurement` method, because this is a `TextWriter`. The question of whether every sensor should implement `IMeasurable` is beyond the scope of this discussion; it is the kind of choice that depends on the context of the specific scenario. Here, the assumption is that some sensors might not be measurable, so each implementation can opt in to the `IMeasurable` interface.

Further abstraction

There is still scope for further abstraction here. The dependency of the command switchboard on concrete types has been limited, but not removed. For practice, you can clone this code sample from the accompanying GitHub repository (*www.github.com/AdaptiveCode/AdaptiveCode*) and try the following exercises:

- Remove all of the dependencies between the command-line client and the concrete sensor types.

- Implement the Command pattern (GoF) to represent the switchboard commands as ICommand implementations, so that a new command can be represented by implementing a new ICommand, without changing the Program class.

- Add more sensors: create the HeatDetection sensor, which cannot move, or a ColorSampler.

- Add more capabilities, such as sensor activation and deactivation or sound detection.

- Each of the sensors are Input/Output (IO) devices, which means that interaction with each of them will result in blocking calls. Convert each of the methods and interfaces to asynchronous by using async/await and Task.

- Try using mixins, as described in Chapter 4, to create reusable data implementations for each of the sensors. This would avoid the repetition of each sensor storing the state associated with each interface. Tip: Because state is involved, extension methods will not suffice, and something like Re-motion Re-mix will be required.

Conclusion

Dependency inversion results in code that is less coupled and modules that are more cohesive. It instructs programmers to provide abstractions that both high-level modules and low-level modules can mutually depend on.

However, finding the correct abstraction for a given scenario is a skill that takes practice. It is not as simple as using an "extract interface" tool, because interfaces themselves are not abstractions.

By applying the dependency inversion principle and designing robust and reusable abstractions, you can make your code more maintainable and extensible. When you do so, your code is easier to comprehend and does not have needless indirection through interfaces that are used only once.

PART IV

Applying adaptive code

This part introduces the practical and theoretical glue that holds together the principle of good design that have been introduced so far.

On the practical side, dependency injection enables the construction of the florid object graphs that adaptive code encourages for solving problems.

In the final chapter, coupling and cohesion are introduced as indicators of software quality. Connascence is a measurement of coupling strength, and examples are given to help you spot problems.

CHAPTER 12

Dependency injection

After completing this chapter, you will be able to

- Understand the importance of dependency injection.

- Use dependency injection as the glue that holds SOLID code together.

- Choose between Poor Man's Dependency Injection, an Inversion of Control container, or convention over configuration.

- Avoid dependency injection anti-patterns.

- Organize your solutions around composition roots and resolution roots.

- Know how the Factory pattern collaborates with dependency injection to manage object lifetimes correctly.

Dependency injection (DI) is a very simple concept with a simple implementation. However, this simplicity belies the importance of the pattern. DI is the glue without which the techniques of the previous SOLID chapters—and much of the Agile foundation chapters—would not be possible.

When something is so simple, yet so important, there is a tendency to overcomplicate. DI is no exception, but there are a number of pitfalls that you should be aware of. These include anti-patterns and general bad practices that subvert the intent of this pattern.

Implemented correctly, dependency injection is invisible to the majority of a project's code. It is limited to a very small amount of the code, often in a single assembly. The trick is to plan for dependency injection from the outset, because integrating it into an established project is difficult and time consuming.

Humble beginnings

The following example highlights the underlying problem that dependency injection solves. Imagine that you are developing a task management application that allows the user to manage a to-do list. In this hypothetical scenario, you are still in the early stages of development, using Windows Presentation Foundation (WPF) for the user interface. So far, you have a main window for the application that does little other than show the current state of your to-do list, which is read from persistent storage.

Figure 12-1 shows this window.

ID	Description	Priority	DueDate	Completed
0	Clean the house	LOW	2/14/2017 11:04:05 AM	☐
1	Pay the bills	HIGH	2/15/2017 11:04:05 AM	☐
2	Wash the dog	MED	2/16/2017 11:04:05 AM	☐
3	Book flights	HIGH	2/16/2017 11:04:05 AM	☐
4	Buy presents	HIGH	2/17/2017 11:04:05 AM	☐
5	Post letters	MED	2/17/2017 11:04:05 AM	☐
6	Write emails	LOW	2/17/2017 11:04:05 AM	☐
7	Read articles	LOW	2/18/2017 11:04:05 AM	☐
8	Skype family	HIGH	2/18/2017 11:04:05 AM	☐
9	Take out wife	HIGH	2/19/2017 11:04:05 AM	☐
10	Write book	HIGH	3/13/2017 11:04:05 AM	☐
				☐

FIGURE 12-1 The task list has some state beyond the task description: priority, due date, and the task's completion state.

Because this is a WPF application, you are using the Model-View-ViewModel (MVVM) pattern to ensure a separation of concerns between the layers. The application strives to use best practices—although dependency injection is still to come. One of the view models is the backing controller for the main window. TaskListController delegates to a TaskService to retrieve all of the tasks. An example of how this is currently accomplished without dependency injection is shown in Listing 12-1.

LISTING 12-1 This controller does not use dependency injection.

```
public class TaskListController
{
    public event PropertyChangedEventHandler PropertyChanged = delegate { };

    private readonly ITaskService taskService;
    private readonly IObjectMapper mapper;
    private ObservableCollection<TaskViewModel> allTasks;

    public TaskListController()
    {
        this.taskService = new TaskServiceAdo();
        this.mapper = new MapperAutoMapper();

        var taskDtos = taskService.GetAllTasks();
        AllTasks = new
ObservableCollection<TaskViewModel>(mapper.Map<IEnumerable<TaskViewModel>>(taskDtos));
    }
```

```
    public ObservableCollection<TaskViewModel> AllTasks
    {
        get
        {
            return allTasks;
        }
        set
        {
            allTasks = value;
            PropertyChanged(this, new PropertyChangedEventArgs("AllTasks"));
        }
    }

}
```

The problems with this approach include:

- Difficulty in unit testing the controller due to a dependency on an implementation.

- Lack of clarity as to what this view model requires—depends on—unless its source is checked.

- Implied dependency from this class to the dependencies of the service.

- Lack of flexibility in providing alternative service implementations.

The rest of this section investigates these problems in greater depth by comparing the original class with a refactored version that uses dependency injection, as shown in Listing 12-2. (The changes have been highlighted in bold.)

LISTING 12-2 After refactoring, this controller uses dependency injection.

```
public class TaskListController : INotifyPropertyChanged
{
    public event PropertyChangedEventHandler PropertyChanged = delegate { };

    private readonly ITaskService taskService;
    private readonly IObjectMapper mapper;
    private ObservableCollection<TaskViewModel> allTasks;

    public TaskListController(ITaskService taskService, IObjectMapper mapper)
    {
        this.taskService = taskService;
        this.mapper = mapper;
    }

    public void OnLoad()
    {
        var taskDtos = taskService.GetAllTasks();
        AllTasks = new
  ObservableCollection<TaskViewModel>(mapper.Map<IEnumerable<TaskViewModel>>(taskDtos));
    }
```

```
public ObservableCollection<TaskViewModel> AllTasks
{
    get
    {
        return allTasks;
    }
    set
    {
        allTasks = value;
        PropertyChanged(this, new PropertyChangedEventArgs("AllTasks"));
    }
}

}
```

To unit test the first class in isolation, the TaskService would need to be mocked. However, it is unlikely that the TaskService can be mocked by conventional means. It is not likely to be a proxiable class, nor should you be forced to make it so. The second class accepts an ITaskService, which is an interface, rather than a class. This is more testable because interfaces are always proxiable.

> **Note** A class is said to be *proxiable* if an alternative implementation—known as a *proxy*—can be provided to the client. In C#, classes are only proxiable if they declare all their methods as virtual. Interfaces, on the other hand, are always proxiable.

If a class arbitrarily constructs classes inside its methods, you cannot know externally what it requires in order to function correctly. The first example, without DI, is a black box of dependencies. You can only discover what it needs by opening the class file and reading it. The class declares none of its dependencies as part of its interface or method signatures. The second example, with DI, clearly states that it needs an implementation of the task service in order to function. This is discoverable from client code by using IntelliSense, which is a feature of Microsoft Visual Studio.

When a dependency exists between class A and class B, if class B has a dependency on class C, it follows that class A is implicitly dependent on class C. This is how the Entourage anti-pattern manifests and leads to an interconnected web of dependencies that are very difficult to rectify. If you ensure that your interfaces generalize—that is, that they correctly abstract their behavior—a class that depends on an interface does not depend on anything further. This holds true even though implementations of the interface might depend on something heavy and external, such as a database. This is the Stairway pattern correctly applied.

When objects are instantiated directly, you also lose a possible extension point that an interface would otherwise provide. You cannot inherit from the TaskService and enhance its methods—even if they are declared virtual—because you would have to amend the controller to directly construct a new instance of this subclass. Interfaces lend themselves to all sorts of interesting patterns that can be used to provide alternative implementations or enhance the existing implementation. Additionally, as you have learned, this can be done after the initial version of the class has been written, before new requirements have been discovered. *This is the key to code adaptability.*

The Task List application

Figure 12-2 shows the package-level and class-level organization that you are aiming for with the Task List application.

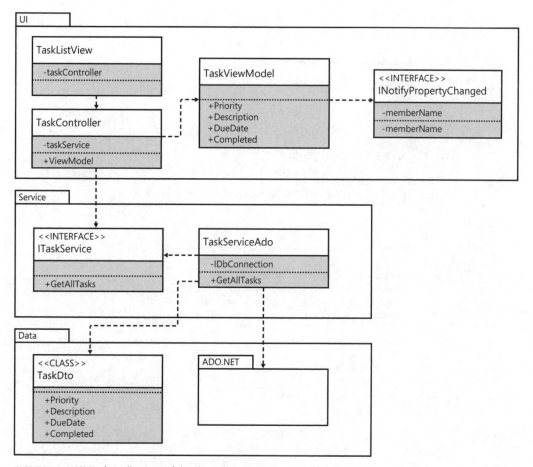

FIGURE 12-2 UML class diagram of the three-layered Task List application, with packages.

The user interface consists of WPF and controller/view model–specific code. The service layer is abstracted from the controllers via an interface, which has an implementation that uses a simple ADO.NET call to retrieve the tasks from persistent storage.

The TaskDto class is returned by the service as an in-memory representation of a task row from storage. This is a Plain Old CLR Object (POCO) and, as such, it is not as feature rich as a WPF view model needs to be. Thus, when TaskController retrieves the TaskDto objects from the ITask-Service, it asks an IObjectMapper to convert them to TaskViewModel objects, which implement INotifyPropertyChanged and can be embellished with other view-specific features.

The ADO.NET implementation of the `ITaskService` interface is shown in Listing 12-3. The constructor is your main concern, but later this chapter will discuss a lingering code smell in this class.

LISTING 12-3 The TaskService is responsible for retrieving the task list data.

```
public class TaskServiceAdo : ITaskService
{
    public TaskServiceAdo(ISettings settings)
    {
        this.settings = settings;
    }

    public IEnumerable<TaskDto> GetAllTasks()
    {
        var allTasks = new List<TaskDto>();

        using(var connection = new
  SqlConnection(settings.GetSetting("TaskDatabaseConnectionString")))
        {
            connection.Open();

            using(var transaction = connection.BeginTransaction())
            {
                var command = connection.CreateCommand();
                command.Transaction = transaction;
                command.CommandType = CommandType.StoredProcedure;
                command.CommandText = "[dbo].[get_all_tasks]";

                using(var reader = command.ExecuteReader(CommandBehavior.CloseConnection))
                {
                    if (reader.HasRows)
                    {
                        while (reader.Read())
                        {
                            allTasks.Add(
                                new TaskDto
                                {
                                    ID = reader.GetInt32(IDIndex),
                                    Description = reader.GetString(DescriptionIndex),
                                    Priority = reader.GetString(PriorityIndex),
                                    DueDate = reader.GetDateTime(DueDateIndex),
                                    Completed = reader.GetBoolean(CompletedIndex)
                                }
                            );
                        }
                    }
                }
            }
        }

        return allTasks;
    }

    private readonly ISettings settings;
```

```
    private const int IDIndex = 0;
    private const int DescriptionIndex = 1;
    private const int PriorityIndex = 2;
    private const int DueDateIndex = 3;
    private const int CompletedIndex = 4;
}
```

The ISettings interface abstracts away from this class the details of retrieving the connection string. An implementation that is an adapter for the Microsoft .NET Framework's Configuration Manager class is provided. It is not hard to imagine that the settings could end up being stored elsewhere at some point, which justifies the use of an interface. Another problem is that the Configuration-Manager class is static and therefore hard to mock. Using it directly would not only limit your options for retrieving application settings such as connection strings, it would also make the TaskServiceAdo class less testable.

Constructing the object graph

Often in this book, it has been an accepted fact that interfaces are injected into constructors. Eventually, of course, interfaces prove to be insufficient, and you must commit to an implementation. There are two main options for accomplishing this: Poor Man's Dependency Injection and using an Inversion of Control container. To exemplify how dependency injection works, this section will first look at Poor Man's DI.

Poor Man's Dependency Injection

This pattern is so named because it does not require any external dependencies in order to function. It involves constructing the necessary object graph for the controller ahead of time. Listing 12-4 shows how to construct the refactored TaskListController and provide it to the TaskListView, which is the application's main window.

LISTING 12-4 Poor Man's DI is verbose but flexible.

```
public partial class App : Application
{
    private void OnApplicationStartup(object sender, StartupEventArgs e)
    {
        CreateMappings();

        var settings = new ApplicationSettings();
        var taskService = new TaskServiceAdo(settings);
        var objectMapper = new MapperAutoMapper();
        controller = new TaskListController(taskService, objectMapper);
        MainWindow = new TaskListView(controller);
        MainWindow.Show();

        controller.OnLoad();
    }
```

```
    private void CreateMappings()
    {
        AutoMapper.Mapper.CreateMap<TaskDto, TaskViewModel>();
    }

    private TaskListController controller;
}
```

This code is the entry point to your application. The OnApplicationStartup method is an event handler that is called by internal WPF code to inform you that you can initialize things. In different types of applications, the entry point varies in style but is always a good place to put your dependency injection code.

The process of bootstrapping the application is very simple. The target is to construct a TaskList-View, because that is the view class that acts as the resolution root of the application. Resolution roots are covered later in this chapter. To construct that class, you need a TaskListController instance. But that class requires both an ITaskService and an IObjectMapper, so you instantiate classes for both—this is where you are committing to the implementations. The TaskServiceAdo, in turn, requires an ISettings implementation, so you commit to the ApplicationSettings, which is an adapter for the ConfigurationManager .NET Framework class. Figure 12-3 clarifies this with a class diagram.

FIGURE 12-3 The interfaces, their implementations, and their dependencies, all of which make up the Task List application.

Each class requires one or more dependencies as sockets that are implemented by other classes that might also require dependencies. It is common for an implementation to be an adapter, such as the MapperAutoMapper and the ApplicationSettings classes. These classes fulfil the interface required of the dependency but delegate the actual work to another class. Even if the class is not an adapter, it is likely to have some dependencies of its own to which it delegates some of the work, like the TaskServiceAdo, which uses ADO.NET for the real retrieval of data. Other implementations of the ITaskService could get the task list from anywhere—a TaskServiceNHibernate class would be an alternative implementation that delegated much of the work to NHibernate. A TaskService-Outlook class could depend on the Microsoft Outlook Add-In framework and read the tasks directly from the built-in task list of Outlook. It is imperative to note that, because the interface does not tie itself to any of these technologies, *anything* could be the source of tasks, assuming that it can fulfil the interface.

Poor Man's DI is verbose. When this application is extended to support adding new tasks, editing tasks, or perhaps notifying of an imminent due date, it is clear that these few lines of construction code will grow significantly, to the point where they are no longer easily understood. However, Poor Man's DI is flexible. Whatever complex object graph you want to construct, the way to construct it is obvious because there is only one way: manually creating instances of everything and passing them to classes that aggregate their functionality, repeating until you reach the resolution root. You can implement any number of decorators for the interfaces that each class depends on; Poor Man's DI allows you to meticulously construct the resulting graph.

Method injection The constructor isn't the only option for providing dependencies to classes. Methods and properties can also be used, and they both have different use cases when compared to constructors.

Listing 12-5 shows part of the TaskListController that has been rewritten to furnish the ITask-Service with its ISettings dependency as a parameter on the GetAllTasks method. This requires the interface for the method to be altered.

LISTING 12-5 The task service now accepts the settings as a method parameter instead of a constructor parameter.

```
public class TaskListController : INotifyPropertyChanged
{
    public TaskListController(ITaskService taskService, IObjectMapper mapper, ISettings
  settings)
    {
        this.taskService = taskService;
        this.mapper = mapper;
        this.settings = settings;
    }

    public void OnLoad()
    {
        var taskDtos = taskService.GetAllTasks(settings);
        AllTasks = new
  ObservableCollection<TaskViewModel>(mapper.Map<IEnumerable<TaskViewModel>>(taskDtos));
    }
}
```

This is useful when the method being called is the only one that requires the dependency. Constructor dependencies indicate that sufficient behavior in the class requires delegation to the dependency, but if only a small percentage of methods truly use the dependency, it might make more sense to pass it in to those methods specifically. The downside of method injection is that it requires the clients who call the method to acquire an instance of the dependency. They can do so either through a constructor parameter or through a method parameter that causes clients to pass the parameter down the call stack until it is used by the target class.

Property injection Similar to method injection, property injection can be used to inject dependencies. Listing 12-6 refactors the prior example to show how the ITaskService could have its ISettings dependencies set by a property. Bear in mind that, again, the interface needs to be changed to support the property, not just the implementation.

LISTING 12-6 Dependency injection can also be accomplished via property injection.

```
public class TaskListController : INotifyPropertyChanged
{
    public TaskListController(ITaskService taskService, IObjectMapper mapper, ISettings
settings)
    {
        this.taskService = taskService;
        this.mapper = mapper;
        this.settings = settings;
    }

    public void OnLoad()
    {
        taskService.Settings = settings;
        var taskDtos = taskService.GetAllTasks();
        AllTasks = new
ObservableCollection<TaskViewModel>(mapper.Map<IEnumerable<TaskViewModel>>(taskDtos));
    }
}
```

The benefit to this approach is that the instance property can be changed at run time. Although a constructor dependency is injected and that instance is used for the lifetime of the class, a property value can be replaced midway through the class's lifetime. However, if a valid instance of the ISettings interface was not provided to the ITaskService before calling GetAllTasks(), this code would fail. Introducing an unenforced requirement like this is a serious code smell.

Inversion of Control

Throughout this book, the examples have focused on developing classes that delegate to abstractions. These abstractions are then implemented by other classes, which delegate some work to more abstractions. Eventually, a class is so small and directed that it need not delegate any further, and the chain of dependency is ended. In order to construct the dependent classes, first their dependencies are constructed and then injected in as dependencies. You have learned how this dependency injection can be implemented by manually constructing classes and passing instances into the constructors. Though this elevates you from a situation in which dependent implementations cannot be swapped or decorated to one in which they can, the object graph is still constructed statically: which part goes where is known at compile time. Inversion of Control (IoC) allows you to defer this construction to run time.

IoC is most well known in the context of IoC *containers*. These systems allow you to link the interfaces of your application to their implementations and retrieve an instance of a class by *resolving* all its dependencies.

The code in Listing 12-7 shows the application entry point rewritten to use the Unity IoC container. The first step is to instantiate a new `UnityContainer` instance. Note that when you are bootstrapping the IoC container like this, there is no alternative but to directly reference the required concrete implementations of infrastructural components.

LISTING 12-7 With an IoC container, instead of using manual construction, you must map interfaces to their implementing types.

```
public partial class App : Application
{
    private IUnityContainer container;

    private void OnApplicationStartup(object sender, StartupEventArgs e)
    {
        CreateMappings();

        container = new UnityContainer();
        container.RegisterType<ISettings, ApplicationSettings>();
        container.RegisterType<IObjectMapper, MapperAutoMapper>();
        container.RegisterType<ITaskService, TaskServiceAdo>();
        container.RegisterType<TaskListController>();
        container.RegisterType<TaskListView>();

        MainWindow = container.Resolve<TaskListView>();
        MainWindow.Show();

        ((TaskListController)MainWindow.DataContext).OnLoad();
    }

    private void CreateMappings()
    {
        AutoMapper.Mapper.CreateMap<TaskDto, TaskViewModel>();
    }
}
```

After the Unity container is created, you need to make it aware of each interface that will need to be resolved at some point during the application's lifetime and map a concrete implementation to each interface. Whenever Unity encounters an interface, it will know which implementation it needs to resolve. If you fail to indicate which class to use for an interface, Unity will loudly remind you that it cannot instantiate interfaces.

After all registration is complete, you need to get an instance of your resolution root: the `TaskListView`. The `Resolve` method of the container will examine the constructor of this class and try to instantiate any dependencies by examining their constructors and trying to instantiate their dependencies, and so on down the chain. Eventually, when there are no more classes to instantiate, the `Resolve` method is able to call the constructors that it found by passing in the instances it has created so far. This is exactly the same process that you follow when using Poor Man's DI, but with that approach you examine the constructors manually and instantiate the classes directly.

The Register, Resolve, Release pattern   All Inversion of Control containers reduce to a simple interface with only three methods, as shown in Listing 12-8. Unity is no exception to this and follows a similar pattern.

LISTING 12-8 Although each implementation will embellish it, this is the general interface for all IoC containers.

```
public interface IContainer : IDisposable
{
    void Register<TInterface, TImplementation>()
        where TImplementation : TInterface;

    TImplementation Resolve<TInterface>();

    void Release();
}
```

The purpose of each of the three methods is explained in the following list:

- **Register**   This method is called first, at application initialization. It will be called many times to register many different interfaces to their implementations. The `where` clause enforces the constraint that the `TImplementation` type must implement the `TInterface` type. Other permutations of this method allow you to register an already-constructed instance of a class and a type without a specific interface. (Such a type will be registered against all the interfaces it implements.)

- **Resolve**   This method is called during the running of the application. It is common for a particular family of classes to be resolved as the top-level object of the graph. For example, this would be the controllers in an ASP.NET Model-View-Controller (MVC) application, the view-models in a ViewModel-first WPF application, and the views in a Windows Forms Model-View-Presenter (MVP) application. The call to this method should be an infrastructural concern. That is, you should not call `Resolve` inside your application's classes for controllers, views, presenters, services, domain, business logic, or data access.

- **Release**   At some point, the classes will no longer be needed and their resources can be released. This might happen at the end of the application, but it also could happen at a more opportune moment during the application's lifetime. In a web scenario, for example, it is common for resources to live only *per-request*. Thus, `Release` could be called at the end of each request. This sort of object lifetime concern is discussed in more detail later.

Dispose

Most IoC containers will implement the IDisposable interface, so it has been included in this reference interface, too. The Dispose method will be called once when the application is shut down. It is distinct from Release in that the Dispose call will clear out the internal dictionaries of the container so that it has no registrations and is unable to resolve anything.

The first IoC example (shown earlier in Listing 12-7) can be rewritten so that all interaction with the container is encapsulated in a class. This moves the verbose registration code away from the code-behind in the WPF application. This is shown in Listing 12-9.

LISTING 12-9 The startup event handler delegates much of its work to a configuration class.

```
public partial class App : Application
{
    private IocConfiguration ioc;

    private void OnApplicationStartup(object sender, StartupEventArgs e)
    {
        CreateMappings();

        ioc = new IocConfiguration();
        ioc.Register();

        MainWindow = ioc.Resolve();
        MainWindow.Show();

        ((TaskListController)MainWindow.DataContext).OnLoad();
    }

    private void OnApplicationExit(object sender, ExitEventArgs e)
    {
        ioc.Release();
    }

    private void CreateMappings()
    {
        AutoMapper.Mapper.CreateMap<TaskDto, TaskViewModel>();
    }
}
```

The entry point is now simpler than it was before, and the IoC registration has been moved to a dedicated class. Listing 12-10 shows this class for the Task List application. When the application exits, it calls the `Release` method, which you can hook into by registering a handler to the appropriate `Application` event.

LISTING 12-10 The configuration class has methods for all three phases of the Register, Resolve, Release pattern.

```
public class IocConfiguration
{

    private readonly IUnityContainer container;
    public IocConfiguration()
    {
        container = new UnityContainer();
    }

    public void Register()
    {
        container.RegisterType<ISettings, ApplicationSettings>();
        container.RegisterType<IObjectMapper, MapperAutoMapper>();
        container.RegisterType<ITaskService, TaskServiceAdo>();
        container.RegisterType<TaskListController>();
        container.RegisterType<TaskListView>();
    }

    public Window Resolve()
    {
        return container.Resolve<TaskListView>();
    }

    public void Release()
    {
        container.Dispose();
    }
}
```

The `Register` method contains exactly the same code as before. As this method grows, however, it can be refactored into multiple methods and generally kept neater than it otherwise might be if it was contained in the application entry point.

The `Resolve` method returns a generic `Window`, which is a common resolution root for a WPF application. Specifically, the `TaskListView` is returned because it is the main window for your application. In other application types, such as ASP.NET MVC, there are often multiple resolution roots—one for each controller. The organization of the composition root for MVC and other applications is discussed later in this chapter.

Imperative vs. declarative registration The registration code to this point has been written imperatively, with procedural calls to methods on a container object. This gives you some advantages: it is easy to read, it is relatively succinct, and it provides a minimum of compile-time checking, such as protection against typographical errors. One disadvantage is that you are tying yourself to an implementation at compile time. If you want to swap out one of your implementations for an alternative, this requires a recompile of the code.

If, instead, you use declarative registration via XML, you can skip the recompile by moving the decision to configuration. Listing 12-11 shows Unity's support for XML registration.

LISTING 12-11 A section in the application configuration file can describe how interfaces should map to implementations.

```
<configuration>
  <configSections>
    <section name="unity"
             type="Microsoft.Practices.Unity.Configuration.UnityConfigurationSection,
  Microsoft.Practices.Unity.Configuration" />
  </configSections>
  <appSettings>
    <add key="TaskDatabaseConnectionString" value="Data Source=(local);Initial
  Catalog=TaskDatabase;Integrated Security=True;Application Name=Task List Editor" />
  </appSettings>
  <unity xmlns="http://schemas.microsoft.com/practices/2010/unity">
    <typeAliases>
      <typeAlias alias="ISettings" type="ServiceInterfaces.ISettings, ServiceInterfaces"
  />
      <typeAlias alias="ApplicationSettings" type="UI.ApplicationSettings, UI" />
      <typeAlias alias="IObjectMapper" type="ServiceInterfaces.IObjectMapper,
  ServiceInterfaces" />
      <typeAlias alias="MapperAutoMapper" type="UI.MapperAutoMapper, UI" />
      <typeAlias alias="ITaskService" type="ServiceInterfaces.ITaskService,
  ServiceInterfaces" />
      <typeAlias alias="TaskServiceAdo" type="ServiceImplementations.TaskServiceAdo,
  ServiceImplementations" />
      <typeAlias alias="TaskListController" type="Controllers.TaskListController,
  Controllers" />
      <typeAlias alias="TaskListView" type="UI.TaskListView, UI" />
    </typeAliases>
    <container>
      <register type="ISettings" mapTo="ApplicationSettings" />
      <register type="IObjectMapper" mapTo="MapperAutoMapper" />
      <register type="ITaskService" mapTo="TaskServiceAdo" />
    </container>
  </unity>
  <startup>
    <supportedRuntime version="v4.0" sku=".NETFramework,Version=v4.5" />
  </startup>
</configuration>
```

This XML is the content of the application configuration file for the WPF Task List. Adding a configuration section for Unity enables the `typeAlias` and `container` elements. The former is used to alias shorter names for longer types, which need to be specified by their assembly-qualified names so that Unity can find them at run time. After the types have been aliased, the latter section performs the same job as the `Register` method: mapping an interface to an implementation.

Some changes need to be made to the application entry point for Unity to read this XML configuration. Listing 12-12 shows that these changes are minimal.

LISTING 12-12 Now the registration phase involves passing the configuration section to the container.

```
public partial class App : Application
{
    private IUnityContainer container;

    private void OnApplicationStartup(object sender, StartupEventArgs e)
    {
        CreateMappings();

        var section = (UnityConfigurationSection)ConfigurationManager.GetSection("unity");
        container = new UnityContainer().LoadConfiguration(section);

        MainWindow = container.Resolve<TaskListView>();
        MainWindow.Show();

        ((TaskListController)MainWindow.DataContext).OnLoad();
    }

    private void CreateMappings()
    {
        AutoMapper.Mapper.CreateMap<TaskDto, TaskViewModel>();
    }
}
```

Just two lines are required. First, you load the `unity` section from the configuration file by using the `ConfigurationManager` class. This is cast to the `UnityConfigurationSection` type so that it can be passed to the `LoadConfiguration` method of a newly instantiated `UnityContainer`. After this, the container can be used, as before, to resolve the main window of the application.

Although declarative registration brings the benefit of configuration-time type mapping, it has significant drawbacks that make it impractical in many situations. The biggest problem is its verbosity. This small example is already a lot more typing than before, but this example is small. In some cases, the registration code could be a few times larger than this, or more. As XML, it would be even larger still. If a typographical error was made in any of the alias or registration sections, it would not be caught until run time, whereas such errors are caught by the compiler in procedural code.

The most compelling reason that declarative registration is suboptimal is that most IoC containers allow for a lot of variation in registration. This can include lambda factories, whereby a lambda method is provided to the registration method, to be called whenever the interface is resolved. Such procedural code is not possible in declarative XML.

Object lifetime It is important to acknowledge that not every object in the application has an equal lifetime. That is, some objects might need to live longer than others. Of course, in the managed languages of .NET, there is no deterministic way to destroy an object, but you can ask it to relinquish its resources by calling the `Dispose()` method, if it implements the `IDispose` interface.

For example, the TaskService from Listing 12-3 earlier in this chapter had a remaining code smell of manually creating a SqlConnection instance. This was left there because the lifetime of that connection could not be matched to that of the TaskService, which is created on application startup and exists for the duration of the application. If the SqlConnection was injected into the TaskService, as shown in Listing 12-13, it would live for the lifetime of the application. This does not mean, however, that the connection would be open for the duration, because opening the connection is a separate operation from its construction.

LISTING 12-13 Some resources have a lifetime that must be carefully managed.

```
private void OnApplicationStartup(object sender, StartupEventArgs e)
{
    CreateMappings();

    container = new UnityContainer();
    container.RegisterType<ISettings, ApplicationSettings>();
    container.RegisterType<IObjectMapper, MapperAutoMapper>();
    container.RegisterType<ITaskService, TaskServiceAdo>(new InjectionFactory(c => new
  TaskServiceAdo(new
  SqlConnection(c.Resolve<ISettings>().GetSetting("TaskDatabaseConnectionString")))));
    container.RegisterType<TaskListController>();
    container.RegisterType<TaskListView>();

    MainWindow = container.Resolve<TaskListView>();
    MainWindow.Show();

    ((TaskListController)MainWindow.DataContext).OnLoad();
}
// . . .
public class TaskServiceAdo : ITaskService
{

    private readonly IDbConnection connection;
    public TaskServiceAdo(IDbConnection connection)
    {
        this.connection = connection;
    }

    public IEnumerable<TaskDto> GetAllTasks()
    {
        var allTasks = new List<TaskDto>();

        using (connection)
        {
            connection.Open();

            using (var transaction = connection.BeginTransaction())
            {
                var command = connection.CreateCommand();
                command.Transaction = transaction;
                command.CommandType = CommandType.StoredProcedure;
                command.CommandText = "[dbo].[get_all_tasks]";
```

```
                using (var reader =
    command.ExecuteReader(CommandBehavior.CloseConnection))
            {
                while (reader.Read())
                {
                    allTasks.Add(
                        new TaskDto
                        {
                            ID = reader.GetInt32(IDIndex),
                            Description = reader.GetString(DescriptionIndex),
                            Priority = reader.GetString(PriorityIndex),
                            DueDate = reader.GetDateTime(DueDateIndex),
                            Completed = reader.GetBoolean(CompletedIndex)
                        }
                    );
                }
            }
        }

        return allTasks;
    }

}
```

The first change is made to the entry point, where an injection factory is used for constructing the service. This is a lambda expression that has access to the container for resolving parameters and returns a new instance of the service. The call to the `ISettings` service's `GetSettings` method has been moved to this injection factory to retrieve the connection string. This is passed to the `SqlConnection` constructor which, in turn, is passed to the service.

In the `GetAllTasks()` method, the presence of the `using(connection)` is problematic. This ensures that `SqlConnection.Dispose()` is called at the end of the using scope. After this call, the connection can no longer be used, yet you could feasibly call this method again.

Instead, what if the `TaskServiceAdo` implemented `IDisposable` and delegated its `Dispose` method to that of the connection? This is explored in Listing 12-14.

LISTING 12-14 The service implements `IDisposable` so that it can dispose of the connection.

```
public class TaskServiceAdo : ITaskService, IDisposable
{
    public TaskServiceAdo(IDbConnection connection)
    {
        this.connection = connection;
    }

    public IEnumerable<TaskDto> GetAllTasks()
```

```
        {
            var allTasks = new List<TaskDto>();

            connection.Open();

            try
            {
                using (var transaction = connection.BeginTransaction())
                {
                    var command = connection.CreateCommand();
                    command.Transaction = transaction;
                    command.CommandType = CommandType.StoredProcedure;
                    command.CommandText = "[dbo].[get_all_tasks]";

                    using (var reader =
            command.ExecuteReader(CommandBehavior.CloseConnection))
                    {
                        while (reader.Read())
                        {
                            allTasks.Add(
                                new TaskDto
                                {
                                    ID = reader.GetInt32(IDIndex),
                                    Description = reader.GetString(DescriptionIndex),
                                    Priority = reader.GetString(PriorityIndex),
                                    DueDate = reader.GetDateTime(DueDateIndex),
                                    Completed = reader.GetBoolean(CompletedIndex)
                                }
                            );
                        }
                    }
                }
            }
            finally
            {
                connection.Close();
            }

            return allTasks;
        }

        public void Dispose()
        {
            connection.Dispose();
        }
}
```

Instead of disposing of the connection in the method, the connection is disposed of only when the service is disposed of. This raises the important question of when the task service should be disposed of. Should all of the task's clients, which will receive ITaskService as a constructor parameter, also implement IDisposable? Who will dispose of these objects? Eventually, you would need to call Dispose() on something.

It is important to note that if a class is handed a dependency via its constructor, *it should not manually dispose of the dependency itself.* The class cannot guarantee that it has been given the one and only instance of the dependency; it might share it with others and therefore cannot dispose of it without potentially having a negative impact on other classes.

The answer to the question of how to manage the lifetime of objects when using dependency injection is much closer to how the service was originally implemented.

The connection factory   The Factory pattern is a way of replacing manual object instantiation with delegation to a class whose purpose is to create objects.

A connection factory could look something like the interface shown in Listing 12-15. This interface has been made slightly more general by returning the `IDbConnection` interface, rather than committing all of its clients to the `SqlConnection` class.

LISTING 12-15 The connection factory interface is very simple.

```
public interface IConnectionFactory
{
    IDbConnection CreateConnection();
}
```

This interface will be injected into the task service so that you have a way of retrieving a connection without manually constructing it, keeping the service testable through mocking. Listing 12-16 shows the refactored service.

LISTING 12-16 Dependency injection can work in tandem with the Factory pattern.

```
public class TaskServiceAdo : ITaskService
{
    private readonly IConnectionFactory connectionFactory;

    public TaskServiceAdo(IConnectionFactory connectionFactory)
    {
        this.connectionFactory = connectionFactory;
    }

    public IEnumerable<TaskDto> GetAllTasks()
    {
        var allTasks = new List<TaskDto>();

        using(var connection = connectionFactory.CreateConnection())
        {
            connection.Open();

            using (var transaction = connection.BeginTransaction())
            {
                var command = connection.CreateCommand();
                command.Transaction = transaction;
                command.CommandType = CommandType.StoredProcedure;
```

```
                    command.CommandText = "[dbo].[get_all_tasks]";

                    using (var reader =
        command.ExecuteReader(CommandBehavior.CloseConnection))
                    {
                        while (reader.Read())
                        {
                            allTasks.Add(
                                new TaskDto
                                {
                                    ID = reader.GetInt32(IDIndex),
                                    Description = reader.GetString(DescriptionIndex),
                                    Priority = reader.GetString(PriorityIndex),
                                    DueDate = reader.GetDateTime(DueDateIndex),
                                    Completed = reader.GetBoolean(CompletedIndex)
                                }
                            );
                        }
                    }
                }

            return allTasks;
        }
}
```

Note that the return value from the CreateConnection method is being disposed of by the using block. This is viable in this instance, because the product from the factory implements IDisposable. Through interface inheritance, it is possible to enforce multiple interfaces on implementers.

However, the question must be asked whether *every* implementation will need every interface. Sometimes they do, but given the wide variety of implementations that an interface can have—long after it was originally written—it is a big assumption to make. When it comes to IDisposable, I'm not sure it always applies.

The Responsible Owner pattern   Instead of artificially forcing the IDisposable interface onto every implementation, you can use it only on those that truly need it. This does cause a problem, though. If the product of the factory—your interface—does not implement IDisposable, you can no longer use a using block to neatly dispose of the product after it falls out of scope. In this case, you must use the Responsible Owner pattern.

Listing 12-17 shows that the using block can be replaced with a try/finally block, and that you can check at run time to find out whether the product implements the IDisposable interface.

LISTING 12-17 The Responsible Owner pattern ensures that resources are disposed of appropriately.

```
public IEnumerable<TaskDto> GetAllTasks()
{
    var allTasks = new List<TaskDto>();
```

```
var connection = connectionFactory.CreateConnection();
try
{
    connection.Open();

    using (var transaction = connection.BeginTransaction())
    {
        var command = connection.CreateCommand();
        command.Transaction = transaction;
        command.CommandType = CommandType.StoredProcedure;
        command.CommandText = "[dbo].[get_all_tasks]";

        using (var reader = command.ExecuteReader(CommandBehavior.CloseConnection))
        {
            while (reader.Read())
            {
                allTasks.Add(
                    new TaskDto
                    {
                        ID = reader.GetInt32(IDIndex),
                        Description = reader.GetString(DescriptionIndex),
                        Priority = reader.GetString(PriorityIndex),
                        DueDate = reader.GetDateTime(DueDateIndex),
                        Completed = reader.GetBoolean(CompletedIndex)
                    }
                );
            }
        }
    }
}
finally
{
    if(connection is IDisposable)
    {
        var disposableConnection = connection as IDisposable;
        disposableConnection.Dispose();
    }
}

return allTasks;
}
```

Only if the connection is of type IDisposable do you then attempt to call the Dispose method on it. This will work regardless of whether the product returned by the factory implements IDisposable or not, but if it does, it will clean up its resources by disposing of it.

The Responsible Owner pattern deterministically disposes of objects if they implement IDisposable. The pattern effectively ignores the objects if they do not implement IDisposable. However, SOLID code often results in multiple decorators that wrap around each other to add extra functionality. In this case, only if the top-layer object implements IDisposable will the Responsible Owner pattern function correctly. When the outer decorator does not implement IDisposable, but subsequent layers do, the Responsible Owner pattern will not correctly dispose of these instances. Instead, you can use the Factory Isolation pattern.

The Factory Isolation pattern   This pattern is able to deterministically dispose of the complex object graphs that often form as a result of SOLID code. It is named after the glove box isolators that are commonly found in laboratories. These are glass or metal boxes with integrated gloves to allow safe, protected access to the contents. In a similar fashion, the Factory Isolation pattern allows safe, protected access to an instance of an object that will be correctly disposed of after use.

The Factory Isolation pattern is only required when the target interface does not implement IDisposable. Extending the IDisposable interface burdens all implementations with the requirement that they implement a Dispose method, even in circumstances where this is unnecessary. Instead, IDisposable should be treated as an implementation detail and assigned only to classes, on an individual basis. This leads to the application of the Responsible Owner pattern and the Factory Isolation pattern.

The examples so far have all targeted the lifetime of the IDbConnection interface. Unfortunately, this interface extends the IDisposable interface. If, instead, the assumption is made that the target interface does not extend IDisposable, the client-side view of the Factory Isolation pattern would look like the code in Listing 12-18.

LISTING 12-18 An example of a client using the Factory Isolation pattern.

```
public IEnumerable<TaskDto> GetAllTasks()
{
    var allTasks = new List<TaskDto>();
    connectionFactory.With(connection =>
    {
        connection.Open();
        using (var transaction = connection.BeginTransaction())
        {
            var command = connection.CreateCommand();
            command.Transaction = transaction;
            command.CommandType = CommandType.StoredProcedure;
            command.CommandText = "[dbo].[get_all_tasks]";
            using (var reader = command.ExecuteReader(CommandBehavior.CloseConnection))
            {
                while (reader.Read())
                {
                    allTasks.Add(
                        new TaskDto
                        {
                            ID = reader.GetInt32(IDIndex),
                            Description = reader.GetString(DescriptionIndex),
                            Priority = reader.GetString(PriorityIndex),
                            DueDate = reader.GetDateTime(DueDateIndex),
                            Completed = reader.GetBoolean(CompletedIndex)
                        }
                    );
                }
            }
        }
    });

    return allTasks;
}
```

The Factory Isolation pattern replaces the common Create method, which returns an instance of a factory product, instead providing a With method, which accepts a lambda method that has the factory product as a parameter.

The advantage here is that the lifetime of the factory product is explicitly linked to the lambda method's scope. This succinctly communicates to the client that it is not in control of the product's lifetime. The factory implementation itself is very simple, as shown in Listing 12-19.

LISTING 12-19 Creating an isolating factory is simple.

```
public class IsolationConnectionFactory : IConnectionIsolationFactory
{
    public void With(Action<IDbConnection> do)
    {
        using(var connection = CreateConnection())
        {
            do(connection);
        }
    }
}
```

The With method can construct a florid object graph of decorators, adapters, and composites—just as SOLID suggests—and manage their lifetimes without the calling client concerning itself with anything but using the final product.

Beyond simple injection

This section covers some more advanced topics of dependency injection.

Dependency injection can be implemented in many different ways, by using a variety of different frameworks. Some patterns out there are benevolent, supporting and enhancing DI while reinforcing what it aims to accomplish. Other patterns do the opposite: they detract from the underlying purpose of DI, actively undermining it and detracting from the whole point.

Two such patterns are particularly insidious. The Service Locator anti-pattern is, unfortunately, all too common. It is used in many frameworks and libraries—sometimes, it is the only way to create a hook to use dependency injection. Worse than the Service Locator is an anti-pattern with an unfortunate moniker that I shall eschew in favor of something a bit more sanitized: *Illegitimate Injection*. This is a middle ground where dependency injection is used "sometimes," allowing the construction of services, controllers, and similar entities without properly providing their dependencies.

When using DI, each type of application requires a different kind of setup. With each, you need to identify the composition root to correctly integrate your registration code. The location of the composition root in a WPF application differs from that of a Windows Forms application. Both will differ from that of an ASP.NET MVC application.

In advanced scenarios, the manual composition of classes through Poor Man's DI and the individual registration of classes through an Inversion of Control container might be too laborious and too verbose. You can eliminate a lot of boilerplate code by deferring registration to one or more conventions. You can also provide some manual registration to handle the edge cases when conventions do not suffice.

The Service Locator anti-pattern

Service locators look very similar to Inversion of Control containers, which is precisely why they are not always thought of as detrimental to the code. Listing 12-20 shows an example of the service locator provided by the Patterns and Practices team at Microsoft.

LISTING 12-20 The `IServiceLocator` interface appears to be just another IoC container.

```
public interface IServiceLocator : IServiceProvider
{
    object GetInstance(Type serviceType);

    object GetInstance(Type serviceType, string key);

    IEnumerable<object> GetAllInstances(Type serviceType);

    TService GetInstance<TService>();

    TService GetInstance<TService>(string key);

    IEnumerable<TService> GetAllInstances<TService>();
}
```

Note that methods such as `TService GetInstance<TService>()` could have been taken directly from the `IUnityContainer` interface—just by swapping the name for `Resolve`. The problem arises from how a service locator is *used*, thanks to the static `ServiceLocator` class, as shown in Listing 12-21.

LISTING 12-21 This static class is the cause of the anti-pattern.

```
/// <summary>
/// This class provides the ambient container for this application. If your
/// framework defines such an ambient container, use ServiceLocator.Current
/// to get it.
/// </summary>
public static class ServiceLocator
{
    private static ServiceLocatorProvider currentProvider;

    public static IServiceLocator Current
    {
        get { return currentProvider(); }
    }
```

```
            public static void SetLocatorProvider(ServiceLocatorProvider newProvider)
            {
                currentProvider = newProvider;
            }
    }
```

The comment hints at the problem. The concept of an *ambient container* implies a leak of knowledge that a container exists. Although there is a laudable decoupling of the specific implementation of the service locator behind an interface, the problem is the acknowledgement—inside any class other than the composition root—of the service locator or container. Listing 12-22 shows how the TaskList-Controller would look if it was rewritten to use the ServiceLocator.

LISTING 12-22 A service locator allows classes to retrieve anything at all, whether appropriate or not.

```
public class TaskListController : INotifyPropertyChanged
{
    public void OnLoad()
    {
        var taskService = ServiceLocator.Current.GetInstance<ITaskService>();
        var taskDtos = taskService.GetAllTasks();
        var mapper = ServiceLocator.Current.GetInstance<IObjectMapper>();
        AllTasks = new
    ObservableCollection<TaskViewModel>(mapper.Map<IEnumerable<TaskViewModel>>(taskDtos));
    }

    public ObservableCollection<TaskViewModel> AllTasks
    {
        get
        {
            return allTasks;
        }
        set
        {
            allTasks = value;
            PropertyChanged(this, new PropertyChangedEventArgs("AllTasks"));
        }
    }

    public event PropertyChangedEventHandler PropertyChanged = delegate { };

    private ObservableCollection<TaskViewModel> allTasks;
}
```

Now there is no constructor, nor is there constructor injection. Instead, when required, the class makes a call to the static ServiceLocator class and returns the service requested. Recall that static classes like this are *skyhooks*—a code smell.

Worse still, the class is able to retrieve anything and everything from the service locator. You are no longer following the "Hollywood Principle" of dependency injection: *Don't call us, we'll call you.* Instead, you are directly asking for the things you need, rather than having them handed to you. How can you tell what dependencies this class needs? With the service locator, you have to examine the code, searching for capricious calls that retrieve a required service. Constructor injection allowed you to view dependencies—all of them—with a glance at the constructor, or at a distance, via IntelliSense.

The problem is not necessarily one of unit testing. The service locator allows you to set an `IServiceLocator` implementation before use, which means that it can be mocked and the classes can be unit tested. At least it does not prevent that. It just seems absurd to register classes and map them to their interfaces—a significant undertaking—only to pollute controllers, services, and other classes with infrastructural code such as this. It is doubly absurd when there is no problem to be solved—constructor injection did not need to be circumvented in this way.

An adapter for the service locator is provided for Unity. Listing 12-23 shows how this is registered after the mappings have been set up.

LISTING 12-23 The service locator will delegate directly to the `UnityContainer` instance to resolve instances.

```
private void OnApplicationStartup(object sender, StartupEventArgs e)
{
    CreateMappings();

    container = new UnityContainer();
    container.RegisterType<ISettings, ApplicationSettings>();
    container.RegisterType<IObjectMapper, MapperAutoMapper>();
    container.RegisterType<ITaskService, TaskServiceAdo>();
    container.RegisterType<TaskListController>();
    container.RegisterType<TaskListView>();

    ServiceLocator.SetLocatorProvider(() => new UnityServiceLocator(container));

    MainWindow = container.Resolve<TaskListView>();
    MainWindow.Show();

    ((TaskListController)MainWindow.DataContext).OnLoad();
}
```

This looks remarkably similar to the prior versions except for setting the locator provider. The call to `Resolve`, though, does not truly "resolve" the object graph; there are no longer any dependencies to inject into the `TaskListView`. They are all fetched individually as and when needed within the methods of the class.

The Service Locator anti-pattern is a good example of literal irony applied to a programming context, in that what is claimed is contrary to the reality. It is claimed that classes do not have dependencies, due to their default constructor, but that is simply not the case: they *do* have dependencies, otherwise you wouldn't be trying to fetch them from a service locator!

Unfortunately, the service locator is sometimes an unavoidable anti-pattern. In some application types—particularly Windows Workflow Foundation—the infrastructure does not lend itself to constructor injection. In these cases, the only alternative is to use a service locator. This is better than not injecting dependencies at all. For all my vitriol against the anti-pattern, it is better than instantiating new classes directly. After all, it still enables those all-important extension points provided by interfaces that allow decorators, adapters, and similar benefits.

Injecting the container

Closely related to the service locator is the concept of injecting the container directly into a class. This, similarly, hands the class the keys to the safe, in that it is then free to retrieve anything that it wants from the container. Imagine such a class that, scattered throughout its many methods, retrieves a dozen services. Now compare it with a class that has a constructor that requires those dozen services and enforces their presence with up-front preconditions that throw exceptions if null references are passed in. Both classes are clearly doing too much—as indicated by the dependencies they require—and should be refactored into smaller classes or their dependencies meaningfully grouped. However, only the latter makes it explicitly obvious at a glance that this smell exists.

Added to this, the class that requires the container as a constructor parameter must also reference the container's assembly. This will proliferate infrastructural code throughout the entire codebase, because each class accepts the container in order to access the services it *truly* needs.

Illegitimate Injection

Illegitimate Injection looks much like normal, correctly implemented, dependency injection. There is a constructor that accepts dependencies, and these are provided either by Poor Man's DI or an Inversion of Control container.

However, the pattern is polluted—indeed, fatally poisoned—by the presence of a second, default constructor. As Listing 12-24 shows, this second constructor proceeds to construct some implementations for the dependencies directly, circumventing DI.

LISTING 12-24 Having a constructor that directly references implementations negates some of the benefits of dependency injection.

```
public class TaskListController : INotifyPropertyChanged
{
    public event PropertyChangedEventHandler PropertyChanged = delegate { };

    private readonly ITaskService taskService;
    private readonly IObjectMapper mapper;
    private ObservableCollection<TaskViewModel> allTasks;

    public TaskListController(ITaskService taskService, IObjectMapper mapper)
    {
        this.taskService = taskService;
        this.mapper = mapper;
    }

    public TaskListController()
    {
        this.taskService = new TaskServiceAdo(new ApplicationSettings());
        this.mapper = new MapperAutoMapper();
    }
```

```
    public void OnLoad()
    {
        var taskDtos = taskService.GetAllTasks();
        AllTasks = new
ObservableCollection<TaskViewModel>(mapper.Map<IEnumerable<TaskViewModel>>(taskDtos));
    }

    public ObservableCollection<TaskViewModel> AllTasks
    {
        get
        {
            return allTasks;
        }
        set
        {
            allTasks = value;
            PropertyChanged(this, new PropertyChangedEventArgs("AllTasks"));
        }
    }
}
```

This means that this class must reference whichever assemblies the implementations are in and, concomitantly, all subsequent dependencies. This is the Entourage anti-pattern all over again. Although the first constructor, which accepts only interfaces, sets the scene for the Stairway pattern and well-mannered DI, the second, default constructor undermines this.

What happens when this "default" implementation is not what you want anymore? This class will be edited to construct the preferred class instead. What about when one default constructor is not enough and, in some scenarios, you want implementation A whereas in others, you want implementation B? That's enough to make a person nauseous.

Sometimes this anti-pattern is used to support unit testing, with the defaults being mock implementations that do not have dependencies and that might reside local to this class. Well, there are much better ways to support unit testing. A common example of this sort of practice is converting `private` methods to `internal` and using the `InternalsVisibleToAttribute` to allow test assemblies to access these methods—rather than testing classes solely through their `public` interface. True, this might appear to be an arbitrarily fine line—after all, DI is much vaunted for its enabling of unit testing. But that is precisely the point: you have already enabled unit testing through the use of interfaces and their injection via the constructor. Mocks can, and should, also be provided through that constructor.

It is worth noting that the classification of Illegitimate Injection as an anti-pattern does not hinge on the visibility of the constructor. Whether the constructor is public, protected, private, or internal, the outcome is the same: you are referencing implementations where you should not be.

The composition root

Only one location in an application should have any knowledge of dependency injection: the composition root. This is where classes are constructed when you are using Poor Man's DI, or where interfaces and class mappings are registered when you are using an Inversion of Control container.

The ideal is for the composition root to be as close to the entry point of the application as possible. This allows you to bootstrap DI as soon as possible, gives you a recognized location to find the DI configuration, and helps you avoid leaking dependencies on the container throughout the application. It also means that for each application type there is a different composition root.

The resolution root

Closely related to the composition root is the resolution root. This is the object type that forms the root of the object graph to be resolved. As in the prior WPF examples, it could be that the resolution root is even a single *instance*, but it is more commonly a family of types unified by a common base.

In some cases, you will manually resolve the resolution root yourself, but some application types that facilitate dependency injection—like MVC—require you to register the mappings while the application resolves the roots itself.

ASP.NET MVC

MVC projects lend themselves very well to dependency injection via an IoC container. They have clearly defined resolution roots and composition roots, and they are extensible enough to support any library that you might need to integrate into the framework for IoC.

The resolution root of an MVC application is the controller. All requests from the browser are made to routes that map directly to methods—called *actions*—on a controller. As the request comes in, the MVC framework maps the URL to a controller name, finds the type to which this name corresponds, instantiates it, and then invokes the action on the instance. Figure 12-4 depicts this interaction in a UML sequence diagram.

When you are using IoC for dependency injection, the instantiation of the controller is, more accurately, the *resolution* of the controller. This means that you can easily follow the Register, Resolve, Release pattern, keeping the Resolve call down to the ideal minimum, which is in one place.

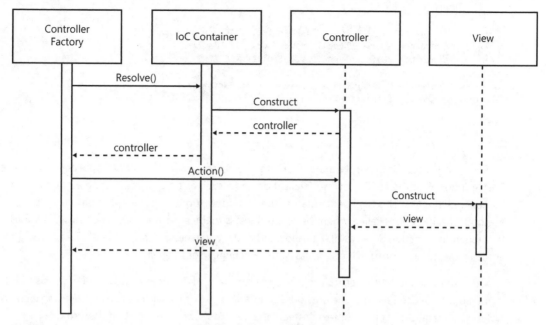

FIGURE 12-4 A UML sequence diagram showing how MVC constructs controllers via a factory.

Listing 12-25 shows the composition root of an ASP.NET MVC user interface for the Task List application.

LISTING 12-25 The Application_Start method of the HttpApplication is a common composition root in web applications.

```
public class MvcApplication : HttpApplication
{
    public static UnityContainer Container;

    protected void Application_Start()
    {
        AreaRegistration.RegisterAllAreas();

        FilterConfig.RegisterGlobalFilters(GlobalFilters.Filters);
        RouteConfig.RegisterRoutes(RouteTable.Routes);
        BundleConfig.RegisterBundles(BundleTable.Bundles);

        AutoMapper.Mapper.CreateMap<TaskDto, TaskViewModel>();

        Container = new UnityContainer();
        Container.RegisterType<ISettings, ApplicationSettings>();
        Container.RegisterType<IObjectMapper, MapperAutoMapper>();
```

```
        Container.RegisterType<ITaskService, TaskServiceAdo>();
        Container.RegisterType<TaskViewModel>();
        Container.RegisterType<TaskController>();

        ControllerBuilder.Current.SetControllerFactory(new
    UnityControllerFactory(Container));
        }
    }
```

Some of this code is boilerplate that is created by default when a new MVC application is created. This includes all of the MVC-specific initialization code, such as that for registering areas, filtering, routes, and bundles. This is all performed at the first opportunity—in the Application_Start method. This method is called when the first request is made after the application has been started in Internet Information Services (IIS). It is located in the code-behind file of the Global.asax and contains the application-specific subclass of the HttpApplication class.

Other than for the MVC-specific TaskController class, the rest of the service interfaces and implementations have been reused. The previous TaskController was centered around WPF, so it could not be reused outside of that context. Instead, the new TaskController does much the same job—retrieving tasks and converting them to a more view-friendly format via the IObjectMapper—but inherits from an MVC base class for controllers. This cements it as a resolution root for the application, because it inherits from the System.Web.Mvc.Controller class. Listing 12-26 shows this new controller.

LISTING 12-26 This TaskController is a resolution root and has a constructor requiring dependencies.

```
public class TaskController : Controller
{
    private readonly ITaskService taskService;
    private readonly IObjectMapper mapper;

    public TaskController(ITaskService taskService, IObjectMapper mapper)
    {
        this.taskService = taskService;
        this.mapper = mapper;
    }

    public ActionResult List()
    {
        var taskDtos = taskService.GetAllTasks();
        var taskViewModels = mapper.Map<IEnumerable<TaskViewModel>>(taskDtos);
        return View(taskViewModels);
    }
}
```

List is the action method that is called by the same view that renders all tasks. Just as in the WPF application, the controller first delegates to the ITaskService to retrieve the tasks, and then delegates to the IObjectMapper to convert the returned data transfer objects into viewmodels for use by the view.

Note The same `ViewModel` that was used for WPF is used here, too. This is okay because the `INotifyPropertyChanged` interface is not strictly WPF-centric (it is located in the `System.ComponentModel` namespace). However, MVC does not care about that interface and will not respond to any events that are fired on the `ViewModel`. Furthermore, MVC allows you to decorate `ViewModels` with validation hints and other such attributes that are part of the MVC assemblies, so it is best to create MVC-specific `ViewModels`.

By default, MVC controllers are required to have public default constructors so that the framework can construct instances of them before calling an action method. But when you are using dependency injection, you need to have constructors that accept the interfaces of your required services. Luckily, MVC uses the Factory pattern for creating the controller and provides an extension point for you to provide your own implementation, as Listing 12-27 shows.

LISTING 12-27 MVC provides many extension points. Providing a custom controller factory facilitates DI.

```
public class UnityControllerFactory : DefaultControllerFactory
{
    private readonly IUnityContainer container;

    public UnityControllerFactory(IUnityContainer container)
    {
        this.container = container;
    }

    protected override IController GetControllerInstance(RequestContext requestContext,
    Type controllerType)
    {
        if (controllerType != null)
        {
            var controller = container.Resolve(controllerType) as IController;
            if (controller == null)
            {
                controller = base.GetControllerInstance(requestContext, controllerType);
            }
            if (controller != null)
                return controller;
        }
        requestContext.HttpContext.Response.StatusCode = 404;
        return null;
    }
}
```

When you constructed the `UnityControllerFactory` in the `Application_Start` method, you passed in the container as a parameter. Here, as emphasized in bold, you can tell that the `Get-ControllerInstance` override uses the container's `Resolve` method to create an instance of the requested controller by type. This is where the controller—the resolution root—is resolved, along with the rest of the object graph that might be required.

It is necessary to bear in mind the different lifetimes involved in this example. The IoC container is created, and mappings are registered, at application startup. The controllers, however, are resolved *per request*. As the request comes in, the controller is resolved, and as the request ends, the controller falls out of scope and is no longer used.

Windows Forms

In a Windows Forms application, bootstrapping dependency injection is more like that of a WPF application than an ASP.NET MVC application. The resolution root of both is the view, with the presenter or controller being passed in as a constructor parameter and the object graph proceeding from there.

Listing 12-28 shows the composition root of the Windows Forms front end for the Task List application. It is located in the `Program` class—in the `Main` method—which is the entry point of the application. As usual, it is important to try to keep the registration code as close to the entry point as possible.

LISTING 12-28 The Program class's Main method is the entry point to the application and makes a good composition root.

```
static class Program
{
    public static UnityContainer Container;

    [STAThread]
    static void Main()
    {
        AutoMapper.Mapper.CreateMap<TaskDto, TaskViewModel>();

        Application.EnableVisualStyles();
        Application.SetCompatibleTextRenderingDefault(false);

        Container = new UnityContainer();
        Container.RegisterType<ISettings, ApplicationSettings>();
        Container.RegisterType<IObjectMapper, MapperAutoMapper>();
        Container.RegisterType<ITaskService, TaskServiceAdo>();
        Container.RegisterType<TaskListController>();
        Container.RegisterType<TaskListView>();

        var mainForm = Container.Resolve<TaskListView>();
        Application.Run(mainForm);
    }
}
```

Note that, in this case, you are able to reuse not only the service implementations, but also the `TaskListViewController` because it doesn't (yet) depend on anything wholly specific to WPF. Of course, in the future, it probably will, so it might be necessary to create a controller or presenter specifically to support the Windows Forms application.

The view in this application is very simple, in that the code-behind accepts the controller as a constructor parameter and initializes the data binding, as shown in Listing 12-29. When you are using the Model-View-Presenter pattern, the view implements an interface to which the presenter can manually delegate calls for setting data.

LISTING 12-29 This view uses data binding to set the retrieved task list to a data grid control.

```
public partial class TaskListView : Form
{
    public TaskListView(TaskListController controller)
    {
        InitializeComponent();

        controller.OnLoad();
        this.taskListControllerBindingSource.DataSource = controller;
    }
}
```

Without a framework to resolve your view for you, you must do it yourself before passing the form in to the Application.Run method, which starts the Windows Forms application. This is only applicable if there is only one main view for the application, which is often the case in desktop applications. Dialog boxes and other child windows would be created via service calls from the controllers or presenters that are implemented by the view.

Convention over configuration

Registering by configuration involves painstakingly mapping interfaces to implementations. Aside from being time consuming, it is also verbose. Instead, you can use conventions to cut down on the amount of code written.

Conventions are instructions to the container that tell it how to automatically map interfaces to implementations. These instructions form the inputs to the container, in place of the registrations. Ideally, the container takes this input and processes it, with the output being exactly the same registrations that you would otherwise have done manually.

Note The "over" here can be read as "instead of." Thus, this topic is about convention *instead of* configuration.

Listing 12-30 shows how the continuing example could use convention over configuration for registering.

LISTING 12-30 The registration phase can be greatly simplified by using conventions.

```
private void OnApplicationStartup(object sender, StartupEventArgs e)
{
    CreateMappings();

    container = new UnityContainer();
    container.RegisterTypes(
        AllClasses.FromAssembliesInBasePath(),
        WithMappings.FromMatchingInterface,
        WithName.Default
    );

    MainWindow = container.Resolve<TaskListView>();
    MainWindow.Show();

    ((TaskListController)MainWindow.DataContext).OnLoad();
}
```

The registrations have been replaced by a call to RegisterTypes, which is the method used to provide the container with instructions on how to find classes and map them to interfaces. The instructions provided in this example tell the container to:

- Register all classes from the assemblies in the bin folder (which is the base path).

- Map those classes to the interface that matches the name of the class. The *convention* here is that the Service implementation class would be registered against the IService interface.

- Use the default to name the mapping when registering each mapping. This default is null, meaning that the mapping is unnamed.

The container will iterate through each public class in each assembly that is in the bin folder, find its implemented interfaces, and map it to the one that matches the class's name (prefixed with an I, for Interface), without providing a name for the mapping. It is not hard to imagine that the resulting registration will be quite greedy, potentially registering more classes to interfaces than you usually would if you were registering manually. However, a more important concern is whether it correctly registers the classes you want to the correct interfaces. This is the new problem introduced by conventions.

The registration is undeniably simpler than its previous incarnation, but only insofar as it is *shorter*: fewer lines of code. With registration by configuration, it was easy to comprehend which implementation was being used for each interface—and that they were definitely registered correctly.

The first parameter to RegisterTypes is a collection of the types to register. The AllClasses static class provides some helper methods for retrieving such a collection by using various common strategies. The second parameter requires a function that accepts a Type passed in from the collection in the first parameter—the implementation type—and returns a collection of Type instances to which it will be mapped—the interface types. The `WithMappings` static helper provides some methods that match this signature and use various strategies for finding appropriate interfaces to map to each type. The third parameter is another function, this time requiring that you return a name for the mapping for each type. The `WithName` static helper class provides two alternatives: `Default`, which always returns `null` (thus the mapping is unnamed), and `TypeName`, whereby the type's name is used for the mapping name. This allows you to call `Resolve<IService>("MyServiceImplementation")` to retrieve the mapped type by its name.

Of course, with the parameters of this method being so general, you can provide whatever methods match the signature so that you can tailor the convention to your needs. As Listing 12-31 shows, the crux of registering by convention is in the conventions that are used to find types, map them, and name them.

LISTING 12-31 Conventions can be tailored to your specifications.

```
public partial class App : Application
{
    private void OnApplicationStartup(object sender, StartupEventArgs e)
    {
        CreateMappings();

        container = new UnityContainer();
        container.RegisterTypes(
            AllClasses.FromAssembliesInBasePath().Where(type =>
    type.Assembly.FullName.StartsWith(MatchingAssemblyPrefix)),
            UserDefinedInterfaces,
            WithName.Default
        );

        MainWindow = container.Resolve<TaskListView>();
        MainWindow.Show();

        ((TaskListController)MainWindow.DataContext).OnLoad();
    }

    private IEnumerable<Type> UserDefinedInterfaces(Type implementingType)
    {
        return WithMappings.FromAllInterfaces(implementingType)
            .Where(iface => iface.Assembly.FullName.StartsWith(MatchingAssemblyPrefix));
    }
}
```

You start by retrieving all of the types from the assemblies in the `bin` folder again. But this time, you limit the acceptable assemblies by returning only those whose full name starts with a specific prefix string. It is common practice to use a "dot notation" for naming assemblies so that they match the top-level namespace that they contain. So `Microsoft.Practices.Unity` is the name of the DLL in which that namespace resides. If that assembly exists in your `bin` folder—and it is certain to if you are using Unity—you might want to omit it from the scan for types to map. A simple way to do this is to retrieve only those types that match the prefix of your own application. Instead of `Microsoft`, you would use something like `MyBusiness` or `OurProject`.

The second parameter has been replaced with a reference to your own local method, which matches the required signature. Given a Type, which is the implementation type, you need to return a collection of other types that represent the interfaces to map to. Rather than write anything particularly complex, you specialize `WithMappings.FromAllInterfaces`, which returns all of the interfaces that the type implements. This list could feasibly include interfaces that you really do not want to map to—`INotifyPropertyChanged` or `IDataErrorInfo`, for example. So again, you only return the interfaces that reside in assemblies that match your assembly prefix. This ensures that you map only your own types to your own interfaces.

Pros and cons

Much like Poor Man's Dependency Injection and vanilla registration with an Inversion of Control container, using conventions involves a tradeoff. You have less code to write, but that code is more algorithmic than the declarative alternatives.

Conventions are initially harder to set up. If you are writing truly SOLID code, not everything will lend itself to a perfect one-to-one mapping of class to interface. In fact, if an interface only has one implementation, that is itself a code smell—and mocks for unit tests do not count toward that total. Whether they are adapters, decorators, or different strategies, it should be common to have more than one implementation per interface, making registration by convention that much more difficult. As it becomes more commonplace to have florid object graphs injected into classes, it becomes harder to devise a general rule by which classes and interfaces can be mapped to each other. Under such circumstances, the conventions cover only a small portion of the required registration code, rather than being the general case.

Mark Seemann, author of the excellent *Dependency Injection in .NET* (Manning Publications, 2011), has explored the three options available for DI and has arrived at the conclusion summarized by Figure 12-5. In brief, the tradeoffs are between two criteria: value and complexity. Value is a utilitarian measure of the worth of the option, ranging from pointless to valuable. Complexity measures the relative difficulty of the option, ranging from simple to sophisticated. As shown in the figure, all three options exist at different points of the curve. Poor Man's DI is simple and valuable, whereas convention over configuration is sophisticated and valuable. The main difference between them, then, is that using conventions is more complex than manually constructing the classes and forming an object graph from those classes.

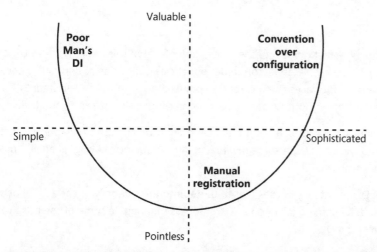

FIGURE 12-5 The tradeoffs between the three options for dependency injection mapped on two axes.

Interestingly, Seemann considers manual registration to sit somewhere between simple and sophisticated on the complexity scale but claims that it is pointless on the utilitarian scale. Why is this? The main reason is because registering types manually with a container is *weakly typed*. If you try to construct a class and pass in an instance for one of its parameters that does not match the type required, the compiler will complain when you try to build. However, no such compile-time error is generated by an IoC container. Instead, you defer the error to run time, which causes you to enter an inefficient loop of write > compile > run > test. Not only that, but you have spent time and energy learning how to register mappings with the container, for little gain and some extra pain.

The choice seems simple: either Poor Man's DI or conventions. If the project is simple and a limited amount of mappings will be required, Poor Man's DI is as simple as can be: just construct the objects manually. If the project is likely to be more complex, requiring many interfaces and classes to be mapped together, target the majority of the registrations with conventions, with the rest of the more specialized mappings being manually registered.

I also highly recommend Mark Seemann's blog, where he explores many topics and is always methodical in his approach[1].

---

[1] *blog.ploeh.dk*

Conclusion

Dependency injection is the glue that holds together every other facet of this book. Without DI, it would not be possible to focus so keenly on factoring dependencies out of classes and hiding their implementation behind general interfaces. Such extension points are key to the development of adaptive code and key to the steady progress of an application as it gains in size and complexity.

There are different options for the implementation of DI, each of which has its own place. Whether you use Poor Man's DI or conventions (with some minimal manual mapping), having DI at all is more important than how it is accomplished.

Some common uses of DI are actually *abuses* that fit better into the category of code smell or anti-pattern. Service Locator and Illegitimate Injection are two abuses that negate some of the positive effects of properly implemented DI.

Each application type has a composition root and a resolution root, the identification of which help you understand how the classes should be organized to facilitate DI. The composition root is always very close to the entry point of the application, assuming that registration is an initialization concern. The resolution root is the only type of object that should be resolved. In some applications, there is only one instance of the resolution root, whereas in others, a family of different subclasses will be resolved.

For all its far-reaching effects, dependency injection is actually a deceptively simple pattern that is nonetheless powerful and misunderstood.

CHAPTER 13

Coupling, cohesion, and connascence

After completing this chapter, you will be able to

- Define coupling and cohesion.

- Identify problematic strong coupling and low cohesion.

- Measure coupling levels through connascence.

The underpinning goal throughout this book has been to improve the adaptability of your code. When code is actively developed and maintained, it is rarely static for long. A single release of a software product or service is a snapshot of code in time, but each new feature added might introduce new complexity. This complexity must be reduced to produce a simple solution, or carefully managed.

The foundations of adaptability, as shown in much of the content covered so far, are the benefits of low coupling and high cohesion throughout a codebase. This chapter walks through the definitions of coupling and cohesion and explains how to measure coupling through connascence.

Coupling and cohesion

There are two qualities that correlate with good code: high cohesion and low coupling. Because there is only a correlation and not a causation, it is not certain that instilling your code with these two qualities will create success. More likely, the inverse correlation has a stronger causal link: low cohesion and high coupling causes software products to fail.

Coupling

Coupling is the strength of the interdependence between software elements. The term "software elements" has been chosen deliberately to cover a multitude of software artifacts—methods, classes, assemblies, components, and even subsystems.

Coupling is measured as low or high, which indicates whether the coupling is weak or strong, respectively. When elements are weakly coupled, they can vary independently.

Coupling determines the effect that changes to software elements have on one another. When coupling between software elements is low—that is, when the strength of their interdependence is weak—a change in one element does not necessitate a change in another element. Low coupling is a situation that programmers strive for. Conversely, high coupling—a strong interdependence of software elements—can cause a change in one part of a system to require a change in another part of the system, with potentially cascading effects. Therefore, high coupling should be avoided.

Cohesion

Cohesion is the strength of the contextual relationship between software elements. As with coupling, cohesion applies to subsystems, components, assemblies, classes, and methods.

Cohesion measures the contextual relationship between variables in a method, methods in a class, classes in a module, modules in a solution, solutions in a system, and subsystems in a system. This fractal relationship is important because a lack of cohesion at any scope is problematic.

Cohesion is measured as low or high, which corresponds to weak or strong contextual relationships between elements. If two classes reside in a module but are unrelated to each other, they are described as having low or weak cohesion. Conversely, when two classes that reside in a module have a valid relationship, they are described as having high or strong cohesion. The former is problematic, the latter is good.

What constitutes a "valid" contextual relationship? Continuing with the scope of classes in modules, a valid relationship between classes occurs when:

- They both belong to the same layer of application architecture.

- They both belong to the same bounded context of the application.

Consider, for example, a class that reads user data from a database and another class that caches this data. These two classes exhibit high cohesion due to the shared context of user data.

Same layer of application architecture

The application architecture might define three layers: user interface, domain model, and data persistence, to use a common three-tiered example. A rule can be applied here:

> *Classes that relate to the same layer can live together in the same module, whereas classes that relate to different layers must be separated by at least a module boundary.*

This rule's use of language is important. When classes relate to the same layer, they only "can" live together. That is: they might not necessarily live in the same module; you might want to separate a large layer into multiple modules. However, those classes that do not relate to the same layer "must" be separated by "at least" a module boundary; that is, they cannot reside in the same module, but they can reside in separate modules, solutions, subsystems, or systems.

Same bounded context of the application

Bounded contexts are officially a construct of domain-driven design (DDD), a software development approach for tackling complexity through an evolving domain model. However, as a concept, the terminology transcends those confines and is generally applicable. Again, a rule can be stated:

> *Classes that relate to the same bounded context can live together in the same module, whereas classes that relate to different bounded contexts must be separated by at least a module boundary.*

The specific use of language applies to this rule as much as to the rule introduced in the previous section.

It is a common code smell to lump code that relates to different modules and different bounded contexts together into the same module. This causes problems in the long term because this monolithic module increases the difficulty of maintenance and future enhancement. Left unchecked, such a module will be very difficult to extend, which increases the time it takes to add new features.

Connascence

Connascence is the complexity of dependencies in an object-oriented software system. It is a metric that helps to determine the quality of code.

Even when your dependencies are explicitly defined with project or service references, that is not enough to determine whether the dependency is good or bad. There are different kinds of *semantic* dependencies, each of which indicates whether the dependency is good or bad on a sliding scale.

This is the connascence of your code's dependencies. Tracking the level of connascence between and within modules is a qualitative measure of its adaptability. Figure 13-1 shows the nine levels of connascence presented in order, from worse at the top to better at the bottom.

FIGURE 13-1 The nine levels of connascence in order, from worse to better.

Each level references a distinct type of dependency. Your code is more adaptive when it contains better levels of connascence, because this limits the number of changes that are required when code is changed. Note that the terms "better" and "worse" are relative, not absolutes like "best" and "worst."

Name

Connascence of name is the first rung on the ladder. It is the bare minimum required in order to have a dependency: code must know the name of a variable in order to use it. In languages where all methods and variables must be attached to a class or interface, like C#, examples that reside only at this connascence level are not common. Static field, property, or method names are really the only examples available, as shown in Listing 13-1.

LISTING 13-1 The Main method requires a name reference to the Utils static class.

```
// Utils.cs
public static class Utils
{
  public static int GetAge()
  {
    return 33;
  }
}
```

```
// Client.cs
public class Program
{
  public static int Main(string args[])
  {
    return Utils.GetAge();
  }
}
```

In a procedural language such as C, which allows for global functions to exist alone, connascence of name occurs whenever a module needs to know just a function's name. Listing 13-2 shows an example of this.

LISTING 13-2 In C, connascence of name is more common due to module references.

```
//module.h
int get_age();

//module.c
#include "module.h"

int get_age() {
  return 33;
}

//client.c
#include "module.h"

int main(int argc, char** argv) {
  return get_age();
}
```

If you change the name of the get_age() method in the module, you would also have to change its name in the client.

Type

This is the most common "lowest" level of connascence in strictly object-oriented languages such as C#. This is because almost every element must exist as part of a class or interface. To interact with an object, you need to know its type. If the type of an object or parameter changes, you must update the code that makes use of the object or passes the parameters. Because C# is a statically typed language, the compiler will catch common type mismatches.

In Listing 13-3, if the Person class or age parameter were to change type, the dependent Program class would also have to be updated.

LISTING 13-3 The Main method has a dependency on the Person type.

```
//Person.cs
public class Person
{
  public void SetAge(int age)
  {
    _age = age;
  }
}

//Client.cs
public static class Program
{
  public static int Main(string[] args)
  {
    var person = new Person();
    person.SetAge(age);
  }
}
```

Meaning

Whenever a special value is used to imply meaning, client code must also infer that this special value has a certain meaning.

In Listing 13-4, retrieving a person's name when the _name field has not been set returns the special value "N/A". The client code must test against this exact string to handle the case when the name is not set. If the special value is changed to, for example, "Not Available", all client code that references the old value must be updated. Note that this change will not cause a compiler warning or error, so this kind of connascence is sneaky.

LISTING 13-4 The Main method has a dependency on the special meaning of "N/A".

```
//Person.cs
public class Person
{
  public string GetName()
  {
    return _name ?? "N/A";
  }
}

//Client.cs
public static class Program
{
  public static int Main(string[] args)
```

```
    {
      var person = new Person();
      if(person.GetName().Equals("N/A"))
      {
        // exceptional case when name not available.
      }
    }
  }
```

Algorithm

Connascence of algorithm requires both the client and the service to agree on the steps used in an algorithm.

This type of connascence can creep into test code when the test replicates the algorithm in the production code. Listing 13-5 shows this kind of connascence of algorithm. Imagine that an extra field is added to the Person class, or a different prime number is chosen by which to multiply the hash. Either of these changes would cause a change to the GetHashCode() method, and the test would fail because it would also have to be updated.

LISTING 13-5 The test method repeats the algorithm for generating a hash code.

```
//Person.cs
public class Person
{
  public int GetHashCode()
  {
    unchecked
    {
      var hash = 17;
      hash = hash * 23 + _name.GetHashCode();
      hash = hash * 23 + _age.GetHashCode();
      return hash;
    }
  }
}

//PersonTests.cs
[TestFixture]
public class PersonTests
{
  [Test]
  public void HashCodeMatchTests()
  {
    var name = "My Name";
    var age = 33;
    var person = new Person(name, age);
```

```
var expectedHashCode = unchecked { (17 * 23 + name.GetHashCode())
  * 23 + age.GetHashCode(); }

Assert.That(person.GetHashCode(), Is.Equal(expectedHashCode));
  }
}
```

Position

Whenever a method that accepts multiple parameters of the same type is called, the order of those parameters is implied by the names of the arguments. Clients could accidentally pass the parameters in the wrong order, and the compiler would not complain. Worse, the parameter order could *change* in the definition, and all clients would be broken without any compile-time errors or warnings.

Listing 13-6 shows this kind of connascence. The client has erroneously set the age of the person to 185 and the weight to 33, which is the wrong way around.

LISTING 13-6 The Person constructor does not differentiate between the types of age and weight.

```
//Person.cs
public class Person
{
  public Person(int age, int weight)
  {
    _age = age;
    _weight = weight;
  }
}

//Client.cs
public static class Program
{
  public static int Main(string[] args)
  {
    var person = new Person(185, 33);
  }
}
```

Execution order

A well-designed class should make it easy for its users to do things right and difficult for its users to do things wrong. Connascence of execution order indicates that a class has been designed badly so that clients could put statements in the wrong order.

Timing

Connascence of timing indicates the presence of a temporal dependency between code. This is likely due to concurrency issues introduced by threading code.

Value

When a special value is depended on by two pieces of code, those two pieces of code have connascence of value.

Identity

If two pieces of code depend on the presence of a specific instance of an entity, they are said to have connascence of identity.

Measuring connascence

Connascence is related to two other measures of code adaptability discussed previously: coupling and cohesion. Connascence is primarily an aspect of the coupling of two components and, as such, the strength of connascence correlates to the strength of coupling.

Locality

Connascence should be assessed in conjunction with the *locality* of the components. If the client and service code are both classes that reside in the same project, maintaining weak connascence is less important. When the components are separated by service boundaries, it is much more important to lower the connascence between them. Take, for example, a call to a WCF service operation. In this case, the position of the operation's arguments is significant irrespective of type: changing the order of the parameters would require remote clients to update.

Unofficial connascence

Assessing the connascence of your code is absolutely a worthwhile activity. However, such a one-dimensional view of your code's dependencies is reductive. There are far more heuristics to evaluating the quality of code dependencies than connascence implies.

For example, there could be a level between name and type: interface.

Interface

Connascence of interface requires knowledge of the name and shape of messages that can be passed to an object. In most languages, these messages take the form of method calls. If you want to call a method on an object, you must know the name of the method and any arguments that must be passed to the method. However, you do not need to know the underlying type of the object. The dependency is only on the *interface* of the type. In some languages, this interface can even be implied—but in C#, interfaces can be explicit.

Listing 13-7 shows a client that does not have a dependency on the AdoNetDataRecord type. Instead, it depends only on the IDataRecord interface, which can be implemented by any number of types.

LISTING 13-7 Connascence of interface, although unofficial, is preferable to connascence of type.

```
//IDataRecord.cs
public interface IDataRecord
{
  void Delete();
  void Save();
}

//AdoNetDataRecord.cs
public class AdoNetDataRecord : IDataRecord
{
  public void Delete()
  {
    // Delete record...
  }

  public void Save()
  {
    // Save record...
  }
}

//Client.cs
public class Client
{
  public void DoSomethingWithRecord(IDataRecord record)
  {
    record.Save();
  }
}
```

Static vs. dynamic connascence

The first five levels of connascence are distinguished as *static connascence*, and the remaining four levels are termed *dynamic connascence*. This distinction indicates that connascence of name, type, meaning, algorithm, and position can be identified by reading the code, whereas connascence of execution order, timing, value, and identity indicate strong runtime coupling of code. All static connascences are weaker than dynamic connascences, because they are easier to identify and easier to remove or improve.

Conclusion

No matter what frameworks for delivery are put in place—whether Agile or waterfall—any problem that is to be solved with software involves the writing and maintenance of source code. Even after the decision of programming paradigm (object-oriented, functional, procedural, or declarative, for instance) is removed, and a specific language and ecosystem have been chosen, there are myriad different ways of implementing features.

By following a test-first approach and writing the simplest code that could possibly suffice for each failing test, you avoid introducing unnecessary complexity. Your solution should never be more complicated than the problem it solves. Only as an extra step—with the safety net of green, passing tests—should you improve the design of your solution through refactoring.

A good design is always one that exhibits low coupling between methods, classes, and modules, and in which the methods, classes, and modules are highly cohesive.

Adaptive tools

This appendix gives you an introduction to source control with Git, which is required to use the code samples for this book. If you have used Git before, you're already aware of its deserved reputation as the foremost source control software. If you have not encountered Git before, this appendix will bring you up to a level at which you can interact with local and remote repositories of code. These skills will translate to working with any codebase that is stored in Git; the content herein is not limited to the code samples for this book. Many popular open-source projects use Git, and it is being adopted by companies to manage their proprietary code, too.

In all contexts, the concept of continuous integration (CI) is an important part of keeping code synchronized between various contributors, so a section of this appendix briefly discusses the concept of CI and introduces a common workflow for its implementation.

Source control with Git

Source control evolved slowly for a long time before being revolutionized with the advent of distributed source control systems such as Mercurial and Git. I would argue that *any* source control is better than no source control, but my preference is certainly for Git.

The purpose of source control in general is to track changes in code over time, making it easy to travel forward and backward in time through the code. It also provides a ready-made backup of the source.

With Git, every developer has their own repository that contains the full source code (see Figure A-1). To make edits to the source, developers should create local branches to which they can commit successive changes. Each branch should have a clearly delineated purpose—to fix a defect, implement a new feature, or make some experimental changes. Whatever their purpose, these changes remain local to the developer's repository until the developer elects to push the branch elsewhere.

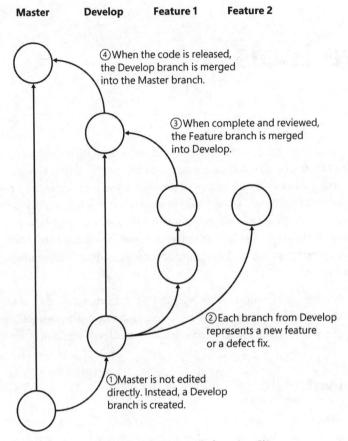

Master **Develop** **Feature 1** **Feature 2**

④ When the code is released, the Develop branch is merged into the Master branch.

③ When complete and reviewed, the Feature branch is merged into Develop.

② Each branch from Develop represents a new feature or a defect fix.

① Master is not edited directly. Instead, a Develop branch is created.

FIGURE A-1 A possible branching strategy for using Git.

Although it is not necessary to have a central repository, it is common to consider one of the repositories the authoritative location for the source. Take a look at Figure A-2. By pushing branches to this repository, developers can subsequently request that their changes be pulled into the main branch of the code. This is called a *pull request* and is often the catalyst for a code review by a developer's peers, which helps to maintain the quality of the code. Each peer who reviews the code can approve or reject the pull request, as appropriate. Each peer can also functionally test the code by pulling the branch to their local repository, compiling it, and testing it locally. If the code is rejected, the original developer can continue to make edits and push the changes back to the central repository until it is accepted. The accepted pull request is then merged into a main development branch, and the other developers will receive those changes when they next update their local repositories with the main branches. They will also need to merge any changes with those of their own in-progress branches.

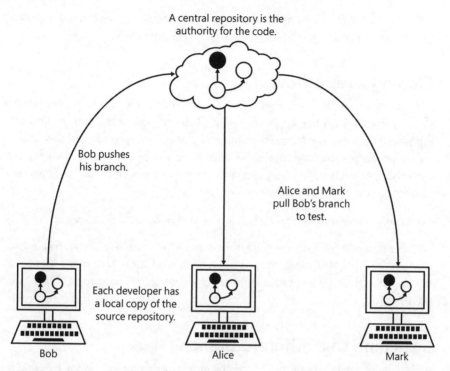

A central repository is the authority for the code.

Bob pushes his branch.

Alice and Mark pull Bob's branch to test.

Each developer has a local copy of the source repository.

Bob

Alice

Mark

FIGURE A-2 Distributed source control is a peer-to-peer system, but it often uses a central repository.

Note The instructions in the readme file inside the repository will be kept up to date with any changes to the structure of the repository. You can use the readme file as the primary source of information for the sample code that accompanies this book.

Git for Windows can be downloaded from *git-scm.com/download/win*.

All of the code listings in this book are available on GitHub, which is a community centered on Git repositories. Go to *https://github.com/AdaptiveCode* to access the code contained in this book.

For those who are new to Git, the following subsections provide a short orientation for navigating code stored in a Git repository. This is far from an extensive introduction to Git, but it should provide you with enough knowledge to follow the code examples and compile them. For more information, the Git Reference[1] is an excellent introduction.

---

[1] *http://gitref.org/*

If you don't like working with the command line, there are several good GUIs available for Git. They are available from *http://git-scm.com/downloads/guis.*

Cloning a repository

The first step is to clone a repository. All Git commands are provided as parameters to the `git` command-line application. The `clone` command requires the address of a repository to clone. The following command clones the repository for this book into a local repository. Remember that Git is distributed source control, so many repositories can exist. You will have full read access to the remote repository but will only be able to write to your own local clone.

```
git clone --recursive https://github.com/AdaptiveCode/AdaptiveCode.git
```

This command creates a new directory called `AdaptiveCode` under the current working directory. By default, the `master` branch is selected. Each of the samples in this book are, however, located on different branches, so you need to be able to switch branches.

Switching to a different branch

After cloning a new repository, change the directory to your local clone by using the change directory command.

```
cd AdaptiveCode
```

The currently selected branch is the default, which for this repository is `master`. As a personal preference, I have prefixed every directory with a `chapter-X`. This indicates the chapter number to which the directory relates. The rest of the directory name is a more free-form description of its content. The github repository's readme file provides a reference of code listings as they correspond to directory names. Move into the directory for one of the chapter's samples.

```
cd ch12-problem-statement
```

If you list the contents of the current directory, as shown in the following code snippet, there is now a new directory called `DependencyInjectionMvc`, which, in turn, contains a Microsoft Visual Studio solution file and some more directories for its constituent projects.

```
C:\dev\AdaptiveCode\ch12-problem-statement> ls


    Directory: C:\dev\AdaptiveCode\ch12\problem-statement\


Mode                LastWriteTime     Length Name
----                -------------     ------ ----
d----        3/16/2017  12:47 PM             DependencyInjectionMvc
-a---        3/16/2017  12:47 PM       1522 .gitignore
-a---        3/16/2017  12:30 PM         84 README.md
```

You can move back to the main directory by using the following command.

```
cd ..
```

From here, you can list all of the sample code of the book.

Continuous integration

Whenever a developer's code is pushed to a central repository, it is common for that code to be compiled on the server. This continuous integration of developers' changes provides invaluable feedback about the state of the code base. If the source fails to compile, it has failed to meet the first prerequisite to the pull request being accepted: without a working build, the request will be summarily denied.

However, compiling the code is often insufficient to confirm that the developer has not broken anything as they were fixing a defect or implementing a new feature. Thus, after compiling the code, the CI server runs all unit tests, and then checks that enough of the code is covered by unit tests. After that, it might even attempt to generate deployment packages from the output of the build.

All of these steps are carried out serially, with the success of each step being a requirement for continuing with the build process. There is no value in running unit tests if the code won't compile; similarly, it makes no sense to check unit test coverage if the unit tests failed, or to generate deployment packages if the unit test coverage was insufficient. A CI server set up to build each pushed branch in this way relieves developers of a great burden. Instead of taking the significant additional time that such checks add to their tasks, they can just compile the code and run the unit tests that they have written, leaving the rest up to the CI. Figure A-3 shows a flowchart for such a continuous integration build process.

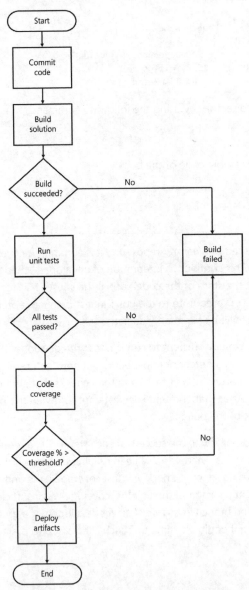

FIGURE A-3 A simplified workflow diagram for a continuous integration service.

Index

A

abstract methods 253–254

abstracting
    capabilities 333–338
    queries 341–342
    sealed code 335

abstractions 38
    design example 328–343
    refactoring for 223–230

acceptance criteria
    product owner responsibility for 9
    user story 15

ACID-compliant database 114

Act phase of unit tests 149, 154, 159

actions, ASP.NET MVC and 376

ActLike<T>() method 137

acyclic digraphs 81

ad hoc Service Discovery 94

Adapter class 130

Adapter pattern
    Class Adapter 130
    Object Adapter 132–133
    Strategy 133–134

affinity estimation 32

aggressive refactoring 203–204

Agile 4
    project management 3
    software development frameworks 1–2
    vs. Scrum 65

Agile Manifesto 4

algorithm, connascence of 393–394

ambient containers 372

Analyze state (Kanban process) 48, 51

anti-patterns 83
    Entourage 324–326, 350, 375
    Interface Soup 308–309
    IsNull property 128–130
    Service Locator 371–374

apocalyptic defects 17

application architecture layers 388

applications, terminating 73

ArgumentNullException 167

arguments, variance rules for 260

Arrange, Act, Assert test phases 148–152, 159

Arrange phase of unit tests 159, 165, 168

arranging preconditions phase 148–149

artifacts, Scrum board 11–23

aspects, applying to layers 111

ASP.NET MVC 376–380

assemblies
    and components 104–105
    and dependencies 70
    referenced, listing of 72
    resolving dependencies 90–93

Assert phase of unit tests 150, 159, 168

asserting expectations phase 150–151

asymmetric layering 112–114

authorization 314–315

avatars 18

X

About the author

GARY MCLEAN HALL lives in Manchester, England, with his wife, daughter, son, and dog.

Gary is an experienced software developer and architect, specializing in patterns and practices. He has worked with numerous Agile teams that have maintained a strong focus on creating code that is adaptive to change. He has worked for companies such as Eidos, Xerox, Nephila Capital Ltd., and The LateRooms Group. In each role, he excelled at balancing the delivery of a software product and the quality of its source code.

Gary is the founder of Igirisu Ltd, a software consultancy, and co-founder and CTO of Dynamic Path Ltd.

Now that you've read the book...

Tell us what you think!

Was it useful?
Did it teach you what you wanted to learn?
Was there room for improvement?

Let us know at https://aka.ms/tellpress

Your feedback goes directly to the staff at Microsoft Press,
and we read every one of your responses. Thanks in advance!